978

D0742797

CP lot 17⁵ᶜ

T. G. MASARYK

Also by H. Gordon Skilling

CHARTER 77 AND HUMAN RIGHTS IN CZECHOSLOVAKIA
CIVIC FREEDOM IN CENTRAL EUROPE
  (*editor with Paul Wilson*)
THE CZECH RENASCENCE OF THE NINETEENTH CENTURY
  (*editor with Peter Brook*)
CZECHOSLOVAKIA, 1918–88 (*editor*)
CZECHOSLOVAKIA'S INTERRUPTED REVOLUTION
SAMIZDAT AND AN INDEPENDENT SOCIETY IN CENTRAL
  AND EASTERN EUROPE

T. G. Masaryk

Against the Current, 1882–1914

H. Gordon Skilling

The Pennsylvania State University Press
University Park, Pennsylvania

Copyright © 1994 H. Gordon Skilling

All rights reserved

First published in the United States and Canada in 1994
by the Pennsylvania State University Press, Barbara Building,
Suite C, University Park, PA 16802–1003

Printed in Hong Kong

Library of Congress Cataloging-in-Publication Data

Skilling, H. Gordon (Harold Gordon), 1912–
    T. G. Masaryk : against the current, 1882–1914 / H. Gordon
Skilling.
        p.   cm.
    Includes bibliographical references and index.
    ISBN 0–271–01042–8
    1. Masaryk, T. G. (Tomáš Garrigue), 1850–1937—Political and
social views.   I. Title.
DB2191.M38S58   1994
943.7'032'092—dc20   93–29636
                                                              CIP

It is the policy of The Pennsylvania State University Press to use
acid-free paper for the first printing of all clothbound books. Publications
on uncoated stock satisfy the minimum requirements of American National
Standard for Information Sciences—Permanence of Paper for Printed Library
Materials, ANSI Z39.48–1984.

To Peter, David and Sally

Masaryk fears neither traditions, nor majorities, nor prejudices. It sometimes happens that he errs, but he never fears to express what he considers to be the truth. He belongs to that sublime class of heretics, and it is just the heretics who bring about progress.

(Ernest Denis, 1910)

Masaryk's entire life was a struggle against the majority opinion, against insidiously imposed moods of society, against fashionable uncritical acceptance of views, traditions and collective myths.

(Emanuel Rádl, 1910)

Not by cringing, adjusting and serving that which forms a momentary wave on the surface, but by thought, radically penetrating into the depths, can we gain insight into what is, and into its meaning, and hence an orientation in the chaos and storms of today and tomorrow.

(Jan Patočka, 1977)

Contents

Introduction:
Re-assessing Masaryk

Few countries have been fortunate enough to have had, in their modern history, a political figure as extraordinary as Tomáš Garrigue Masaryk. Small wonder that during his lifetime, at the peak of his political fortunes, as President, he was almost idolized, by the general public, as a person more than life-size, almost God-like, in his dimensions. Abroad Masaryk was often depicted as 'a philosopher-king', the rare case of a Plato-like scholar holding power and ruling a state. Yet in few countries have later rulers treated a great predecessor with such dishonour, expunging him three times from the historical record and denouncing his life and works. From each of these savage onslaughts he has emerged anew as a source of inspiration and as an example for the future. Each time he has had to be rediscovered, his work re-read and re-evaluated, his achievements re-assessed.

A PERSONAL RETROSPECT

By good fortune I was in Czechoslovakia during the last year of Masaryk's life. As a student of Masaryk's good friend, Professor R. W. Seton-Watson, at the School of Slavonic and East European Studies in London, where Masaryk had delivered the inaugural lecture two decades before, I had learned something of Masaryk's role in the nineteenth century in my study of Czech history. By chance I was present at his last public appearance, in 1937, at the Strahov stadium during the celebration of the battle of Zborov. I watched him as he circled the field in an open limousine, bowing quietly, and with dignity, to the affectionate waving of handkerchiefs by the spectators. Shortly thereafter, following his death in September, I witnessed the outpouring of national grief for the President–Liberator at the time of his funeral.

When I visited Prague well over a decade later, however, Masaryk had been transformed into an 'unperson': his statue removed from the circle of great Czechs and Slovaks in the Hall of Fame in the National Museum, busts and monuments eliminated from countless places throughout the Republic, his name erased from the railway station in Prague and from streets and squares, all cards bearing his name removed from the university catalogues, and his career vilified in historical publications and the mass media. The names and features of Gottwald and Lenin, even of Stalin, had replaced those of Masaryk in public places and memorials. In 1961 it was a surprise to find a bust of Masaryk on a small plinth, inscribed with the historic phrase 'Věrni zůstaneme' (We shall remain faithful) in the little town of Příbor in northern Moravia – one of the few traces left of this great figure in Czechoslovak history. When I visited Masaryk's birthplace in Hodonín in 1967, there had been little change. In the nearby village of Čejc there was a plaque on a cottage where Masaryk had worked a hundred years before as a blacksmith's apprentice. In Hodonín, however, on the Baroque doorway of a school which had been built around the house where he was born, the inscription recording this fact had long since been removed. A friendly parking attendant in the main square told us the location of the birthplace and of statues which had once stood in several squares. He had found an old discarded picture of Masaryk in a dump and had placed flowers around it in the lot as 'our memorial'. His wife, with tears in her eyes, assured us that Masaryk 'still lives in our hearts. ... Whatever is done they cannot destroy memories of him and our love for him.'

In fact within a year Masaryk's statues were back in Hodonín and in other places, and his memory revived everywhere. During the Prague Spring his pictures could be purchased on Václavské náměstí and at the Castle. A book by Milan Machovec, positively appraising his philosophical work, was sold out at once. The book was displayed in a bookstore in Národní trída, in the heart of Prague, with a huge picture of Masaryk and a proclamation signed by prominent Czech personalities appealing for support for a 'Society for establishing a monument to TGM and popularizing his legacy (*odkaz*)'. 'Masaryk must not be allowed to disappear from the memory of the nation,' read the appeal. Several of Masaryk's works were published in 1968 and 1969, and favourable articles appeared in the newspapers and journals. Even party organs praised the democratic features of his life, denounced the earlier condemnation and urged an objective and balanced reappraisal.

Even after the occupation had brought the Prague Spring to an abrupt close the tributes to Masaryk continued. On 28 October, the anniversary of the founding of the Republic, the students struck a medal commemorating this event and the Republic's founder, Masaryk. At Charles University where his bust had once stood at the head of the staircase in the entrance hall of the Philosophical Faculty, a meeting was held at which a speech was given in Masaryk's honour and a resolution was adopted proposing the restoration of the statue. In the cemetery in the village of Lány, Masaryk's grave was piled high with flowers, including a wreath from President Svoboda, and visitors came all day long.

As 'normalization' proceeded during the seventies all such manifestations of love and honour for Masaryk had to cease. Once again his name was stricken from the roster of national heroes and he was officially denigrated as 'a pseudo-democrat' who had prepared the way for the 'counter-revolution' of 1968. A Soviet ideologist, in a book translated into English, condemned 'Masarykism' as a revisionist and anti-communist ideology whose central idea of 'humane socialism' had been exploited in 1968 by the enemies of socialism. But among those who continued to write independently, in *samizdat* form, Masaryk was treated with the respect which he deserved, and his scholarship and his political career re-appraised in positive, if critical, terms by intellectuals such as Václav Černý, distinguished literary historian, and Jan Patočka, eminent philosopher. Abroad, his fellow-countrymen in emigration – for example, the philosopher, Erazim Kohák, and the specialist in comparative literature, René Wellek – published some of Masaryk's works and wrote essays which sought to evaluate objectively his strengths and weaknesses.

THE REDISCOVERY OF MASARYK

These studies, published in the latter half of the seventies, were but the first buds of the blossoming of Masaryk's revival and reached full blossom only in 1980 with the publishing of two symposia, one at home in *samizdat*, the other abroad.[1] The Prague 'publication', *T. G. Masaryk a naše současnost*, over 750 pages long, was edited by Milan Machovec, Petr Pithart and Josef Dubský (*pseud.*), all three former communist intellectuals who had played an important part in the awakening of the sixties and in the Prague Spring. It was dedicated to 'The greatest thinker of modern Czech times and the bearer of the ideal of our national sovereignty.' It was expressly described as a continuation (Vol. VII) of the *Masarykův sborník* (Masaryk Collection), the first six volumes of which had been published in the twenties and thirties.

The symposium, *T. G. Masaryk in Perspective, Comments and Criticism*, published under the auspices of the Czechoslovak Society of Art and Sciences, was edited by Milič Čapek, a philosopher who left Prague in 1939 and after a brief return in 1945, lived and taught in the United States, and Karel Hrubý, a former historian, who, after ten years in prison, took part in the Prague Spring and then went into exile in Switzerland. The 'exile' volume was described in the introduction as 'an appraisal of the works of the noted Czechoslovak philosopher, sociologist and statesman', who 'exerted a decisive influence ... on the thinking and values of a majority of the Czechs and Slovaks'.

The greatness of Masaryk and of his role in Czech history were fully recognized in the two symposia. Jan Patočka called him 'one of the most remarkable and rarest minds which were given to us'. 'Masaryk belongs to the giants of our history, such as are born but once in a century,' wrote Jaroslav Hora. 'His life and work have grown deeply into the very roots of the nation so that they were, and forever remained, an inexhaustible source of nourishment and inspiration.'

Although the contributors to both collections shared an admiration for Masaryk, and praised him in one aspect or another, they were, almost without exception, true to the spirit of Masaryk himself and were highly critical of some features of his thinking or of his deeds. Each essay sought to strike a balance between his strengths and weaknesses, his faults and his achievements. In spite of differences in viewpoints and conclusions, the essays served a common purpose, namely to pay honour to a great historical figure and to inquire into the relevance of his life and work for contemporary Czechs and Slovaks.

Perhaps the problem of rediscovery can best be summed up in the words of Jan Patočka, one of Masaryk's most devoted and most critical followers. 'Masaryk's work, even though conditioned by his time, still represents a certain stage in the process of self-clarification in Czech life and in the effort to recover again amid the turbulence in which we have been enveloped by so many catastrophes in both world wars. We alone, to the extent that we know him and grasp his attempt to create a Czech philosophy, are able to discern his strong and weak points, to perceive wherein he saw correctly Czech and world realities and wherein he was weak.'[2]

CONTINUED RE-ASSESSMENT

After the revolutionary changes of 1989–90 the gates were at least partially opened for a fuller re-examination of Masaryk and his work. There was a renewed interest in him in the newly-liberated media, several books about him were published by the now free publishing houses; the preparation of a complete bibliography of his works was begun at the National Library.[3] At scholarly conferences a number of papers about Masaryk were given.[4] The Masaryk Society, which had existed under the First Republic, and had been restored in 1988, before the democratic revolution developed an active programme of lectures and conferences to promote Masaryk's work and ideas. In January 1990 the T. G. Masaryk Institute (Ústav T. G. Masaryka) was re-established.[5]

Founded in 1932, the Institute was closed down by the Nazi authorities during the war years and its director, Vasil K. Škrach, was imprisoned and later executed. In 1945 the Institute was restored and published a number of Masaryk's books before the communist seizure of power. In 1954 it was liquidated once more; its valuable archives were taken over by the Communist Party of Czechoslovakia and became inaccessible to the public. In 1968, during the Prague Spring, there were plans to re-establish the Institute, under Jan Patočka as curator, but these were interrupted by the Soviet occupation and subsequent 'normalization'.

In January 1990 President Václav Havel authorized the re-establishment of the Masaryk Institute, and appointed as its director the distinguished historian Karel Kučera. In March, after the latter's untimely death, Havel named as his successor Jaroslav Opat, another outstanding historian, who had been deprived of his work during the communist period but had published studies of Masaryk in *samizdat*. The Institute was inaugurated at a ceremonial meeting in September 1991, attended by President Havel. Financial support was afforded by the President and from the Federal Budget, and by the Czech and Slovak premiers. Progress was, however, slow in securing assured financial support and adequate facilities. The Institute was transferred from the President's chancellery to the Ministry of

Culture, and was granted funds which had to be renewed annually, after long and agonizing delays. When I visited in early June 1993, there was no assurance that support for the Institute would continue after the expiry of its present budget at the end of that month. The Institute was therefore threatened with liquidation for the fourth time, and this time at the hands of a democratic regime which avowed loyalty to the traditions of Masaryk. Two weeks later, just prior to my departure and the approaching deadline, reprieve was granted by the extension of support for the balance of 1993. Continued support thereafter was still, however, uncertain.

At the time of my visit the work of the Institute was still quite restricted. After a number of peregrinations it had found refuge in several small rooms rented from the Institute of Sociology of the Academy of Science. For three years it had had no library, and the huge Masaryk archives, regained from the Institute of Party History of the Czechoslovak Communist Party, were scattered in several places in and outside Prague and are now inadequately housed in the Military Archives in Invalidorny, in Prague. They were not yet indexed or fully accessible to researchers. The Institute's staff was small, including only the director, seven other researchers, two archivists and three support staff. Nonetheless work was proceeding; its plan included the gradual publication of Masaryk's major works, and the resumption of the prewar *Masarykův sborník* (Volume VIII appeared in 1993).

The task of re-appraisal of Masaryk is now well under way, at home and abroad, but will not be easy. Masaryk was, and remains, a figure of extraordinary complexity. It is difficult to classify him in customary terms, say, as a liberal, a socialist or radical, or even a conservative, as a man of religious outlook or as a free-thinker, as a loyal Austrian or as an enemy of Austria. He was not only a teacher, but a philosopher, sociologist, historian, political scientist and a politician, public speaker and journalist; his interests spanned countless subjects and his writings on a given topic were often fragmentary and dispersed. His arguments were sometimes obscure and contradictory, and difficult fully to understand and interpret. They were written for a certain historical context and are sometimes outdated and hard to apply to the present day. There was much to admire and to praise in his thought and deeds, but there were also serious weaknesses and inadequacies which were the subject of censure and critical evaluation, before and after 1914, by his contemporaries and by his successors. The task of re-assessment will be a continuing one; the conclusions drawn will vary with the viewpoint of different scholars and with changing circumstances.

The present author is bold enough to add another book to the countless books and articles which have been produced on this theme in the hope that it will offer a distinctive contribution to the interpretation of Masaryk. The book is unique in focusing attention on Masaryk as *a persistent non-conformist* prior to the First World War. For three decades he was an unrelenting critic of conventional wisdom, established institutions, customary practices and habits in Bohemia and in Austria-Hungary as a whole. At every stage of his prewar career he was a radical dissident in all questions of public life as well as in private matters. His criticism was directed at subjects as diverse and manifold as love and the family, and the place of women; education and the university establishment; the interpretation of Czech history and the national question; the government, parliament, and legal system of the Monarchy; Czech politics and the political parties, the position of the Slovaks; religion, the Catholic Church and clericalism; anti-Semitism; labour and the social question; foreign affairs and foreign policy institutions, and the nature and future of the Monarchy itself.

Never afraid to speak his mind and attack the evils of public life and society, Masaryk often found himself alone and suffered the blows of a hostile public and official wrath. In the words of the great French historian of Bohemia, Ernest Denis, Masaryk displayed a rare example of civic courage: 'He feared neither traditions, nor majorities nor prejudices. It sometimes happens that he errs, but he never fears to express what he considers to be the truth. He belongs to that sublime (grand) class of heretics, and it is the heretics who create progress.'[6]

This is not to say that this book will be merely a paean of praise for Masaryk nor make out of him a person of superhuman proportions. I do not consider myself an idolater of Masaryk, although I do regard him as one of the great figures in Czech history. On the other hand the book is not an attempt at historical 'revisionism', designed to depict Masaryk in black or grey tones. Nor do I consider him to be a 'model' for the present and future, but I share the belief of many Czechs and Slovaks, that his work is a source of inspiration and enlightenment and has continued relevance in the contemporary Czech Republic. In each chapter I have recognized his strengths and weaknesses, and noted the criticisms of others, and have tried to present a balanced appraisal of the man and his work. In a final chapter I will attempt a critical reassessment of his importance in the past and his possible influence on the future.

The book is also unusual in not attempting an evaluation of Masaryk's career in its entirety, but in focusing attention on his thinking and actions prior to the First World War. This makes it possible to portray a great person in his contemporary proportions and not in the light of his subsequent career. When, in 1914, at the age of 64, Masaryk went into exile to conduct a struggle for liberation from Austria-Hungary, he embarked on an entirely new phase of his career, a new 'life', so to speak. After the founding of the new Republic, Masaryk began his third 'life,' as President, which ended shortly before his death in 1937.

It would be tempting to write a full biography of the whole Masaryk era which would elaborate the comparisons and contradictions of his three lives. But this task must be left to others. In fact Masaryk's life work has often been treated as a kind of seamless whole and his ideas, for example on democracy or on the Slovak question, have been merged together in spite of the great difference in the contexts in which they were expressed. This undoubtedly has the advantage of making possible a systematic comparison and contrast but it also runs the danger of distorting his prewar career in the light of the course of later events. Had Masaryk died in 1914, or had he not gone abroad, his work and thought would still be well worth study and analysis for its own sake. I have chosen the alternative of concentrating on his 'first' life in the belief that this will give a more correct portrait of the man as he was before 1914 as distinct from the man he was to become in an entirely different context.

The book is distinctive, too, in analyzing Masaryk's life not in mainly chronological terms, as some excellent books have done, but in terms of specific and well-defined themes. This makes possible a coherent and systematic treatment of each in a way which was not possible in the several valuable symposia which have dealt with many facets of his life. Although I have not used archival sources, I have exhaustively combed all other materials, especially the writings of Masaryk himself before 1914. I have frequently presented his thoughts in his own words and reserved my evaluations for the concluding paragraphs of each chapter and of the book as a whole.

I would like to express my deep appreciation to Tim Farmiloe of the Macmillan Press in England for his continuing interest in publishing works by or about T. G. Masaryk and Czechoslovakia and for his warm support of this publication, and to Sanford C. Thatcher, Director of the Penn State Press, who published several other books of mine when he was at Princeton University Press and showed keen interest in publishing this present one. I am also grateful to several persons who have been extraordinarily helpful, notably Dr Vilém Prečan, Director of the Documentation Centre for the Support of Independent Czechoslovak Literature, in Scheinfeld, Germany, and of the *Ústav pro soudobé dějiny* (The Institute for Contemporary History) in Prague, Czechoslovakia, for his unflagging personal support; George Kovtun, of the Library of Congress, who helped me with advice and by providing certain important materials; and Professor Ladislav Matejka, editor of *Cross Currents*, who encouraged me by publishing several chapters in that journal. I have profited greatly from discussions of Masaryk over many years with Professor Jan Havránek, of the Archives of Charles University, and I am indebted to him for finding me the picture which appears on the cover. I have also enjoyed frequent valuable talks with Dr Jaroslav Opat, the Director of the Masaryk Institute.

Thanks should go to Jane Lynch and her colleagues in the Inter-Library Loan Department of the Robarts Library of the University of Toronto for borrowing countless books for me and to Dana Kalinová, of the *Národní knihovna*, in Prague, Czechoslovakia for searching out needed materials, as well as to other librarians elsewhere, including those at the libraries of Harvard University, Yale University, Columbia University, and Indiana University, the National Library in Prague, the Staatsbibliothek in Vienna and the British Library in London, England. For the preparation of the jacket design, I want to express my appreciation to Jane Francis, of Victoria, BC and to Tony Hooper at Macmillan.

I would also like to acknowledge permission to publish chapters which appeared in journals or books, i.e. to Professor Matejka, just mentioned (Chapters 5, 8 and 9), Professor E Możejko, Managing Editor, *Canadian Slavonic Papers* (Chapter 1), Michaela Harnick, Managing Editor, *Czechoslovak and Central European Journal* (Chapter 6) and Professor John Morison, editor, *The Czech and Slovak Experience*, selected papers from the Fourth World Congress for Soviet and East European Studies, Harrogate (Macmillan and St Martin's Press, 1990) (Chapter 7).

I wish also to express gratitude for financial support to the Social Science and Humanities Research Council of Canada, the Humanities and Social Sciences Committee of the Research Board of the University of Toronto, and the Centre for Russian and East European Studies at the University of Toronto.

Toronto, Canada   H. Gordon Skilling

1 Academic Iconoclast

The arrival of Tomáš Garrigue Masaryk in Prague in 1882 was charged with significance for modern Czech history and was to cause an upheaval in the history of the nation. Jan Herben, his devoted admirer and one of his biographers, wrote in 1898 that the decade of the 1880s was a time of a 'revolution in ideas in Czech life; new strivings and new yearnings were born; new fractions and tendencies were formed'. This ferment developed in and from the Czech university, which had been created by the partition of the Charles-Ferdinand University into Czech and German parts.[1] Professor Masaryk, newly arrived at the Czech university in its first year as a separate institution, stirred up controversy almost immediately by his teaching and by his day-to-day actions. He soon made the university a platform for an effort to influence the Czech intelligentsia and to reform Czech life in all its aspects, educationally , culturally and politically.

Tomáš Masaryk was highly critical of the prevailing intellectual standards in the university and in Bohemia in general. He had a wider intellectual outlook than the existing academic community and sought to broaden the horizon of the university and its students. His lectures and his writings pointed towards a very different orientation of Czech intellectual and cultural life and brought him into conflict with the old guard. His assault on the literary manuscripts, sacred to the national cause, caused a storm of controversy, not only within the university, but among the broader public, and submerged him beneath a wave of abusive condemnation. His impact on the students was immense. His whole approach to scholarship and his methods of teaching were radically different from prevailing patterns; his personal relationship with students outside the classroom was unusual. As a result he soon acquired devoted followers or disciples who adopted his approach as their own. There were, however, others who were strongly opposed to his ideas. Masaryk also had very definite opinions as to how students should behave, both in their scholarly studies and in life generally, including politics. He showed a keen interest in the student movement and sought to influence its attitude toward political life. As an educationalist he advanced radical plans for the reform of Czech schooling at all levels. In all these respects Masaryk assailed cherished beliefs and challenged the conventional wisdom, and inevitably became an object of admiration and the target for attack.

MASARYK AND THE UNIVERSITY

Masaryk had mixed feelings about going to Prague. He was aware of his lack of friends, of his lack of knowledge of the Czech scene and of his imperfect command of Czech. He considered other possibilities, such as appointment to another

Austrian university or even emigration to America. But by 1879 he was keen about going to the centre of Czech life and actively sought a post at the new university. In the end he accepted an offer as an extraordinary professor, at a salary of 1600 crowns, plus supplements per student and for the conduct of a seminar. He was promised promotion to the rank of ordinary professor in three years.[2]

Once in Prague he discovered that he liked the city very much, but his various fears were confirmed.[3] As he later recalled, he disliked the 'petty conditions' of the university where there was no criticism, and no exchange of opinions.[4] The institution was old-fashioned and conservative and was dominated by older patriotic 'authorities' such as Martin Hattala and W. W. Tomek, whose conservative academic attitudes produced a 'lack of freedom of thinking, feeling and acting'. There were, it was true, some younger professors, such as Jan Gebauer, who represented newer, modern currents of thought and with whom Masaryk established good relations. But it was almost inevitable that Masaryk, as an outsider who had previously been untouched by the Prague atmosphere, would clash with it.[5]

Although the Vienna authorities had expected that he would be a moderating influence,[6] he soon became a disturbing factor in the placid life of the university. Masaryk did not seek conflict but almost immediately, in his public lectures on Hume and Pascal, he challenged the previous monopoly of German philosophy and stirred up controversy. He was criticized privately by old-guard professors, denounced to Vienna by outsiders as a traitor to the nation and a nihilist, and reported by the police as a cosmopolitan. In academic circles, according to his colleague, Albín Bráf, Masaryk met with criticism, open or veiled. Although Bráf himself admired Masaryk's talent and courage, he criticized his lack of tact, his autocratic tendencies, his excessive criticalness and his intervention in disciplines far from his own competence.[7]

From the beginning Masaryk made it a point to associate as much as possible with his colleagues, both in Prague at the Hotel de Saxe, a favourite meeting place, and during the summer in the village of Potštyn. He earned sympathy and respect, but at the same time awakened distrust. Even though a junior member, he took an active part in council meetings and intervened, sometimes negatively, in questions of promotion and habilitation.[8] His central role in the manuscript controversy caused trouble when the time came in 1886 for his promised promotion. A tied vote in secret balloting in the professorial council led to the rejection of his proposed appointment. Only a year or two later, in 1887–88, fourteen members of the council raised a complaint to the Academic Senate against Masaryk and the Athenaeum; Jan Kvíčala presented an even stronger complaint, which sought to remove Masaryk from the university entirely. When the hearings took place, Masaryk put up a a strong defence and made a counter-complaint. The matter was closed in February 1888, with a strict warning that if he continued in his behaviour, his removal from the university would be considered. On appeal to the Ministry of Culture and Education, the complaint and the decision were confirmed, and Masaryk's charges were rejected.[9] Masaryk again ran into conflict with the establishment, and even with many students, during the Hilsner case at the turn of the century and he once more considered leaving Prague and going to America. In the event he had to wait until January 1897, i.e. fifteen years, for promotion, and his salary increased at a slow pace.

MASARYK AND CZECH SCHOLARSHIP

In his work as a scholar, Masaryk was, according to Nejedlý, a reformer, indeed a revolutionary, who sought to 'clear a path to new tendencies in scholarship' in his lectures, and in his writings, he 'gave a new direction of thinking' not only for students but also for professors. In Machovec's words, Masaryk was 'a reformer of scholarship' who sought to 'regenerate society through science, hence at the same time, of course, to regenerate science within itself'. Masaryk did this not as a specialist in any particular field, but as a 'philosopher, searching for the mission of science as a whole for man'.[10]

In a memorable article, 'How to raise the level of our scientific literature', written not long after his arrival in Prague in 1885, Masaryk analyzed the inadequacies of scholarship in Bohemia and set out 'a programme of work, a veritable Magna Carta of all his strivings'. Whereas other nations had developed their culture over centuries, 'we had slept: we must catch up and create as soon as possible the conditions for further scientific development'. Among his specific proposals were the writing of specialized articles and monographs; the preparation of translations from world scientific literature; the establishment of a Czech Academy of Sciences; the publication of a new Czech scientific encyclopedia, of specialized journals, and of a popular journal for spreading knowledge of what was going on in the world; and the study of foreign languages.[11]

Masaryk had already taken a concrete step in this direction in 1894 by founding the *Athenaeum*, a 'journal for scientific literature and criticism', as its subtitle stated. It was to be 'a critical register of contemporary scientific and scholarly literature'. In justifying this step, Masaryk had said: 'We need a paper through which we would become familiar with scholarly life at home and abroad.' As promised, the *Athenaeum* carried reports on books and scholarly work throughout the world, and served as a forum of scholarly criticism and debate. There followed shortly thereafter, in 1885, the completion of the arrangements for the publication of a Czech scientific encyclopedia, to be edited by Masaryk. Unfortunately the manuscript controversy prevented him from implementing his detailed plans for this work, although an encyclopedia was launched in 1887, ironically without Masaryk as its editor. The controversy also prevented the implementation of his proposal of a Czech Academy; but some three years later such an Academy was founded, again without Masaryk.[12]

He set a high example in his own scholarship. Before coming to Prague he had published a number of articles in Czech magazines and had completed two larger studies; his doctoral thesis on Plato and his habilitation study of suicide (which was published in German and was well received). During his first few years in Prague, Masaryk showed himself to be a prolific and original scholar. In rapid succession he published short works on Hume and Pascal (1883 and 1884), a study of T. H. Buckle's theory of history, an essay on the study of poetical works (1884) and *Základové konkretnélogiky* (The Foundation of Concrete Logic) (1885). The latter work, which appeared later in German, contained a systematic analysis of all branches of knowledge, and cited, wherever possible, the works of Czechs. Masaryk managed to combine this prodigious output with his editorship of the *Athenaeum* and his lectures at the University and with the publication of innumerable articles and reviews.[13]

For lack of space and competence the present author must refrain from dealing with the immense body of work by Masaryk on literature, and on linguistics, of which the little essay on the study of poetical works (1884) was but a foretaste. Between then and the close of the century Masaryk published many critical studies of both Czech and foreign literature, demonstrating a profound knowledge and great originality. His primary interest was not in the aesthetic merit of a work, but in its content; he viewed literature as a reflection of a country's society and as a means of raising the moral and cultural level of a nation. His *chef d'oeuvre* in this field was his monumental study of Russian literature in his book on Russia and Europe published in 1913. His literary work was subject to praise and to criticism by his contemporaries and by later scholars.[14]

Among Masaryk's most innovative and influential works were his lectures on 'practical philosophy on the basis of sociology' which were unpublished but circulated in lithograph form.[15] These dealt with problems such as man and nature, man as an individual, sexual life, including prostitution and the family (matters rarely discussed openly), and society and the social order (state, religion, property, race and nation). They were in effect studies in sociology, a subject not hitherto taught. These lectures introduced students to new ideas and approaches, and in an unusually open manner, and had a great impact on their thinking. They also shook university scholarship to its foundations and implicitly challenged the wisdom of older authorities. In broader circles the lectures were disturbing to conventional ideas and led to charges that Masaryk was 'corrupting the students'. As early as 1884 Masaryk, already aware of the unpopularity of his ideas, once again considered the possibility of emigrating to America.[16]

THE MANUSCRIPT CONTROVERSY

This was but a prelude to the controversy over the genuineness or falsity of ancient Czech manuscripts, supposedly discovered in 1817 and 1820, but in fact forged at a later date. Masaryk did not himself initiate the dispute, but he at once became 'the organizer and publicistic spokesman of the critics'. Although the philologist, Jan Gebauer, was the principal scholarly critic, Masaryk was 'the dynamic spirit of the whole struggle, its methodological coordinator and organizer'; he built up at the university 'the general staff for the manuscript struggle' and was himself 'the general, who directed the struggle'. The university became a battlefield; there was a polarization between conservative professors, such as Martin Hattala, and later Jan Kvíčala, who defended the manuscripts, and more progressive members, such as Jan Gebauer and Jaroslav Goll, who criticized them as false. Although Masaryk was primarily the organizer of the struggle, he also made significant scholarly contributions to the debate.[17] For the critics the chief issues at stake were scientific truth and the freedom of research and learning. Masaryk had expressed this idea in moral and national terms at the very outset in an article in the *Athenaeum*: 'I have no doubt that the honour of the nation demands the defence and the recognition of truth – nothing more; it is much more moral and courageous to acknowledge error, rather than to defend it, even though the whole nation shares in it.'[18]

What began as a scholarly debate became almost at once a violent political struggle in which Czech journalism played an important part. The critics tried to maintain an objective scientific stance throughout the controversy, but the defenders made it a public issue and a test of patriotism. Julius Grégr used his newspaper, *Národní listy*, as a forum and made himself the judge and executioner in the court of public opinion. The campaign took the debate from a high scholarly level to the lowest level of vituperation and personal denigration; the critics were denounced as traitors to the nation, German *Kulturträger*, cosmopolitans, national nihilists and advocates of 'national suicide'. The main target of abuse was Masaryk who was rightly regarded as the leading spirit in the campaign. The attacks against him mounted with the publication in the weekly, *Čas*, edited by Jan Herben, of an article on the Czech question wrongly believed to have been written by Masaryk. *Národní listy* condemned Masaryk as 'a loathsome traitor' and called on him to leave 'this sacred land of ours'. A few months later, the conservative clerical journal, *Čech*, published a vicious attack on Masaryk, as one of 'the enemies within our gates' who must be 'utterly extirpated' if they were not 'to fill the whole Czech atmosphere with the poison of a grossly unpatriotic spirit and to destroy the moral foundations of our young people'.[19]

Masaryk showed himself to be a man of extraordinary courage in taking on himself the burden of responsibility in this struggle. Although he won considerable support for his stand among students and a part of the intelligentsia, he made many enemies among his university colleagues and was condemned by a broader public, inflamed by journalistic agitation. The manuscript campaign consumed invaluable time needed for scholarly work, interrupted many of his projects and, as noted, led to an effort to remove him from the university.[20]

Nonetheless Masaryk rejoiced that the university had proved itself to be a real centre of enlightenment and the embodiment of moral and humanistic ideals and that the controversy had led 'to a revision of the entire spiritual life of the nation, including even the political'. Roland Hoffmann described the victory of the critics as a remarkable landmark in modern Czech cultural development. Theodore Syllaba believed that the Czech University gradually became the most significant base of Czech scholarship and one of the recognized centres of European scholarship. Milan Machovec believed that Masaryk had forced scholarship to recognize that it was possible 'to serve the nation only through truth, the exacting demands of science, and maximum self-criticalness'.[21] Two scholars, writing in *samizdat*, drew similar conclusions. The criticism of the manuscripts, wrote Jaroslav Opat, was '*de facto* a blow at the very foundations of Czech spiritual life of that time'; the critics 'counterpoised acknowledged scientific truth against a deeply rooted national myth'. In Milan Otáhal's words, the victors in the struggle succeeded in their aim of 'winning the right of scholarship to freedom of research, and to the acknowledgment of truth.'[22]

THE MEANING OF CZECH HISTORY

Hardly had this controversy subsided when Masaryk became involved in another intellectual conflict which pitted him against major historians as well as some of his political colleagues. From 1894, in a series of studies of the Czech question (later published in book form under that title) he set forth his ideas of the meaning of Czech history, defining it in terms of the concepts of '*humanita*' and of nationality.[23] 'The idea of humanity is the whole meaning of our national life. The programme of humanity gives sense to all our national striving and legitimizes it. Humanity is our final national and historical objective; it is our Czech programme'.[24] Humanism was, however, derived, not only from the French Revolution, but from the Czech Reformation, as represented by Jan Hus, Jan Amos Komenský and the Bohemian Brethren. Stressing the religious essence of the Czech question, Masaryk declared that 'the ideal of humanity, the fundamental and cardinal idea which guides all our efforts at revival and reawakening, is the idea of our Reformation; humanity is but another word for the Brethren'.[25]

Developing this theme further, Masaryk repeatedly stressed the importance of the twin themes of humanity and of nationality in the writings of the so-called Czech and Slovak enlighteners. First and foremost, Jan Kollár believed that humanity was, both in terms of ethics, culture and reason, the national ideal (*Č. o.* p. 15) Kollár, he said, 'conceived the nation and nationality as the natural organ of mankind (*človečenstvo*), and 'demanded in the name of humanity freedom of the nation and of the Slavs generally' (p. 23). All the national awakeners – Šafařik, Dobrovský, and Jungman, and later Palacký and Havlíček, and the philosopher Augustin Smetana – had followed Kollár in invoking humanity as the basis of the national struggle (e.g. pp. 142, 218, 236, 385).[26]

Masaryk interpreted the concept of humanism to justify many other elements of the Czech national programme. Humanity meant that we should everywhere resist evil, both our own inhumanity and that of others, and the inhumanity of society and all its organs – cultural, political and national, as well as the Church (*Č.o.* p. 208). For him humanity was a highly ethical approach, based on the principle of 'love thy neighbour'; this in turn required the broadening of the Czech question to include the social question and socialism (ibid., pp. 163, 218–19, 249, 270). Humanity also rejected revolution and the use of violence and offered instead a peaceful, non-violent tactic in seeking social change (ibid., pp. 144–5, 337–9, 342–5). This tactic was particularly suitable and practical for a small nation which could not maintain itself or make progress by the use of violence (ibid., 43, 247–8, 420). At the same time humanity accepted the idea of natural right and implied that all nations had an equal right to strive for their national rights; this justified an independent Czech development within Austria-Hungary and eventually the claim for complete political independence. Yet humanity was not a narrowly Czech ideal, but a universal one, nor was it identical with chauvinistic nationalism; humanity encouraged love, not hatred of other nations, a fraternity of nations in Havlíček's words, and suggested an international organization embracing all mankind.[27]

Masaryk's idea of *humanita* as the guiding idea of Czech history was not received with enthusiasm by contemporary scholars and politicians. In fact, as he himself admitted, it was a highly ambiguous concept. The French historian Ernest Denis confessed he did not fully understand it. The Czech scholar, Jaroslav Goll, who had collaborated with him in the manuscript struggle, expressed a similar opinion. Another historian, Josef Pekař, rejected the entire concept as a falsehood, 'a mythical and mystical ideology', which was in conflict with the facts and was romantic rather than realist. He denied there was any evidence of continuity between the Czech Reformation and the national awakening, and argued that national consciousness, not religion, was the central feature of Czech history.[28]

Masaryk's political colleague in the Realist movement, Josef Kaizl, while praising the book for its innovative ideas, rejected completely Masaryk's central idea that humanism was derived from the Czech national awakeners, and ascribed it rather to Western liberal enlightenment, notably Rousseau and Herder. Humanism was not primarily religious, as Masaryk would have it, but liberal and national, as Palacký and Havlíček had understood. He also severely criticized Masaryk for failing to recognize that the state was 'organized and legalized violence', although, it was true, violence played a lesser role as the state acquired authority and respect. He also argued that Masaryk's idea of socializing the state, far from reducing its power, would augment it.[29]

MASARYK AS A TEACHER

It was in this academic atmosphere that Masaryk began to teach and to exercise his influence on students at the university. One of his 'disciples', Edvard Beneš, in a *Festschrift* for Masaryk's sixtieth birthday in 1910, wrote: 'he taught them to understand ever new sides of life, broadened their horizons immensely, and taught them to learn unknown worlds'. Most of all, he did not speak as 'an authority, delivering unquestionable opinions and indisputable facts, but as a highly critical, sometimes self-critical, speaker, who sought to encourage students to think for themselves'. He admitted the possibility of error and called on them not to accept unthinkingly what he told them, but to think the matter through themselves and come to their own conclusions, perhaps different than his'.[30]

Masaryk considered lectures an obsolete form of instruction and, as he admitted, lectured reluctantly and with difficulty; his lectures were not particularly systematic and sometimes not well attended.[31] He delivered his lectures in a quiet, unhistrionic style, but they were accompanied by effective gestures and had an enormous impact on his listeners. Jan Herben, writing in 1898, stated that his lectures (and articles) were 'difficult, incendiary and did not claim to be infallible'. In 1910, František Drtina spoke of his impressive appearance, and of his 'critical spirit and wide horizon'; '[he presented us with] 'something new, interesting, vital and independent, and frequently stirred up our scientific and our patriotic conscience'. Otakar Fischer wrote that Masaryk's seminars differed from others. 'One could not speak of teachers and pupils'; Masaryk 'spoke to people completely equal to himself, he debated with colleagues'. 'He was not a pedagogue, but an inspirer, not a historian, but a creative artist, not a superficial dabbler (*vědator*), but a great man.'[32] In 1930, in retrospect, a number of women remembered the remarkable impact of his lectures, including those outside the universities, in the 1890s and the 1900s.[33]

Another source of Masaryk's influence was his personality and the way he dealt with his students outside the classroom. He drew people to him, not only by his scientific knowledge but by the 'magic' of his personality – 'by his frankness, happy spirit, compassion, and moral purity'. He was always in good humour and often smiled. He was glad to continue discussion after his lectures, often during walks on the way home, and was ready to loan them books from his private library. Unlike most of the professors of the time he invited students to his home for dinner and an evening devoted to discussion. His wife, Charlotte, usually participated in these Friday evenings and exerted her own influence. Students came to feel that he was ready to see them at almost any time of day or night, and turned to him for personal as well as academic advice. This close relationship with a professor astonished his students and increased their respect for him as a person as well as a scholar. He became an 'embodiment of the scientific spirit' and a kind of model for students, who repeated his ideas and terms, and even aped his speech, tone of voice and gestures.[34]

Masaryk's approach, according to Beneš, had some negative results. His whole manner of speaking and instruction 'repelled some of his listeners and made them confirmed opponents'. Others, not fully prepared for his methods, became so enamoured of his critical approach that they used this weapon against Masaryk himself, and developed 'the not very nice, non-democratic, aristocratic type of

Czech Realist, who criticized everything and turned the masses of people away from them'. Moreover, although Masaryk did capture the younger generation and almost the whole of the intelligentsia, the youth did not really understand an essential feature of Masaryk's character, 'his idealism and optimism', 'the motive force which threw him into his struggles'; hence the intelligentsia did not influence Czech political life as much as it ought to have done.[35]

STUDENT CONDUCT AND BEHAVIOUR

Masaryk was deeply concerned about the way students conducted their lives outside the classroom and gave them strict injunctions as to how they should behave in sexual matters and in drinking. 'The single state', he urged, must 'in every respect, physical, spiritual and moral, be a preparation for married life.' This required purity and chastity, and a single standard for men and women. Masaryk condemned prostitution which later, in 1912, he called a sad chapter of Czech student life. He urged students to avoid brothels and warned of the danger of syphilis. Masaryk also strongly opposed alcoholism, and indeed drinking in general. 'A sensible student will become an abstainer,'as he himself had done at a certain time in his life.[36]

Masaryk had no hesitation in laying down rules as to what young people should and should not do in other spheres of personal life. In an article published in 1889, Masaryk declared that the youth had 'a right to be really young' and should be concerned with recreation and health. Students should engage in physical training, join the Sokol gymnastic organization and take part in sports, such as fencing and sculling. Students should also join the student clubs, in spite of their failings, and should form new ones. During the holidays, in the countryside, students should take a rest but also use the opportunity to spread their ideas about university life or art.[37]

Years later, in 1912, in a lecture in which he gave advice to incoming students, Masaryk added strict new norms of behaviour. Students should seek to have a 'healthy mind and a healthy body'. They needed fresh air, but not merely by loafing or strolling (*bumlování*) on Ferdinand Avenue. They needed other forms of recreation, including dancing, but these should be 'proper' and 'decent'. They should not waste their time drinking beer in a tavern or sitting around in a café taking notes or carelessly reading. In his digs (flat) the man student should not become indebted and 'fall into a trap' with the daughter of his landlady. And all of these rules, Masaryk warned, applied equally to girls as well as to lads – there were no differences, except for natural ones. Girls should not fall into lax behaviour and merely imitate boys.[38]

Masaryk invoked the legacy of Jan Hus, as a former teacher and twice rector at Charles University, to support his call for purity of life. He cited Hus's message to a pupil in 1414 in which he warned against a disorderly life, wasting one's fortune on feasts and fine clothes, and called on him to concern himself with the poor and the humble. He also quoted Hus's testament to the teachers and students of the university at the end of his life (27 June 1415), in which he appealed to them to love each other and to avoid discord, but on the basis of 'standing by the recognized truth'. Hus was persecuted as a heretic, said Masaryk, because 'he defended the truth to his death and stood up against external authority'. Others were accustomed to accept the authority of Pope and Emperor and of learned doctors, but Hus chose 'the liberation of the individual religious and moral conscience'. Czech students, and intellectuals generally, he said, must continue the work of the Reformation and of the national and moral awakening. Hus gave us an example, as a teacher and philosopher, and as a professor, of 'how to combine scholarship, reason, and the defence of truth, with religion – i.e. to seek out, with all our reason, moral and religious truth, a more intimate and higher religion – a new religion not based on revealed truth'.[39]

In lectures given in 1898, published under the title *How to Work*, Masaryk also gave advice to students about their studies, providing hints as to how to read and how to take notes. Students need not attend all lectures, but should do so only to supplement their reading. Students should go to the library, read a specialized journal and attend seminars; they should seek to have direct contact with professors. Especially important was the learning of foreign languages since a general education was impossible with only a knowledge of Czech. Students should consider learning a Slavonic tongue, such as Russian or Polish, and even Hungarian, and of the world languages, especially English. German was widely known but the aim should be to end our dependence on it. We should aim not at cosmopolitanism, but at 'an understanding of the world from our Czech view-point'. Young people should study art, literature, theatre and music. They should educate themselves in social and political matters and study politics as a science. This did not necessarily mean that students should join political parties; they should be active outside parties, e.g. in social service work.[40]

STUDENTS AND POLITICS

Masaryk gave a full exposition of his views on the role students should take in politics in his article 'On the Tasks of Czech Students' in 1889 (cited above). In counselling against direct political participation, he expressed views unpopular in the emerging progressive student movement but did not budge from this position in later years. The main tasks of student youth, he asserted, were education and preparation for life. It was, he admitted, impossible to forbid students to concern themselves with politics, but this should be done, as befits intellectuals, in a concrete manner (*věcně*). 'If you wish today to be a political person (*politik*) acquire the appropriate education by the study of those fields and writings which are necessary.' Read Aristotle, Mill, Spencer, Maine, de Tocqueville, Palacký and Havlíček. 'Feelings and ideas were the moving forces of history and should be the subject of a student's attention; study national economy and statistics, literature, philosophy and history'. Political activity was not the most fruitful activity for the nation and for mankind. 'The student works best for the nation if he prepares conscientiously for his future profession.'[41]

Later Masaryk included his 1889 article in his book, *The Czech Question*, and reiterated the idea that political activity did not mean 'activity in the service of a certain political party'. Newspaper work, making speeches at meetings, electoral agitation, etc. could not be combined with full-time academic study. More important, in any case, was 'activity that was not directly political', e.g. pursuing professional academic work, and studying politics in a scientific manner. Students will inevitably be partisan but should devote their efforts to perfecting student parties rather than engaging in 'blind struggles and inflammatory party agitation', especially in view of the state of decline of the old political parties.[42]

In the programme of the Realist party (1900) Masaryk's views were restated without significant change. As a result of the broadening of the suffrage and the political organization of the workers, the political significance of the students had declined and they must seek their function in other fields, especially social. They must, however, prepare for future political activity and develop themselves culturally. 'The Czech student benefits the nation most if he educates himself generally and philosophically, if he diligently studies his own field, if he concerns himself with his own deeper political and social cultivation, if he remains young and preserves his masculine (*sic*) strength and freshness by a pure life.' This did not mean that the student should remain a bookworm but he should 'not waste money, health and his youth'. Nevertheless he should enter upon social and civic–political duties and be active in non-student associations.[43]

Masaryk gave a good example of the kind of political education which students should seek in his lecture in 1909, 'The Student and Politics'.[44] He restated his view that students should acquire political self-education, since formal education was not adequate, for instance, in the law faculty. The student might become a kind of Intern (*hospitant*) in a party, which would in turn offer him political training. In his lecture Masaryk sketched out in outline what the student needed to know about politics, including the state, constitutionalism, aristocracy and demo-cracy, monarchy and republicanism, internationalism and independence, church and state, nationality and cosmopolitanism, economic and social organization, and history and politics; he devoted a special section to the struggle for political independence, the concepts of historical and natural rights, and the Czech idea of *humanita*. He suggested three rules for politics: not to step forward publicly unless absolutely necessary, to conduct a 'reasonable and honest politics,' and, finally, 'not to lie'.

In 1912 Masaryk discussed the problems which democracy presented to 'the thinking person', especially to Czech students, in a lecture on 'Democratism in Politics'. He set forth his understanding of democracy as a system which involved universal suffrage, the democratization of the legislative power, of military and foreign policy, and of the educational system, and constitutional monarchy. The modern democratic movement stood in opposition to aristocracy, whether in religion, language and nationality, or in the economy. Democracy was not something natural but had to be achieved by effort. The democratic intellectual must strive to be 'a conscious democrat, not only on the speaking rostrum, but in all his behaviour'.[45]

Although the democratic movement was opposed to the use of violence, Masaryk acknowledged that revolution could not be excluded from politics. 'For me an intellectual and philosophical revolution is an inevitable condition of modern democracy.' The revolutionary was 'a critic of everything old, not only in politics but in literature, philosophy, etc. – the ideal is to place society on a completely different basis'. Modern man, however, 'rejects catastrophalism, and admits that progress is made by steps, not by a great leap; it is accomplished by almost infinitesimal changes'. The thinking democrat was distinct from the blind radical, either on the right or the left extreme, but did not seek merely a golden middle way; he must base his political programme on conviction.[46]

MASARYK AND THE STUDENT MOVEMENT

At the time of the founding of the university, the student movement and its leaders were in the tow first of the Old Czechs, and then increasingly of the Young Czechs, and did not have a concrete political programme of their own. At the time the main student organization, *Academický čtenářský spolek* (Academic Reading Club),was, in Jan Herben's view, 'a student association without student life' and indulged mainly in nationalistic sloganeering and ostentatious celebrations.[47] The younger professors, and notably Masaryk, introduced the students to new philosophical tendencies and ideas. The *Athenaeum* and *Čas* were also influential in freeing students, even those in middle school, from the thrall of the nationalistic newspapers. Although the AČS at first defended the authenticity of the manuscripts, Masaryk's strong stand awakened great sympathy among students. Toward the end of the eighties, however, the student movement became increasingly radical, sometimes supporting the nationalist position of the Young Czechs, but they often embarked on independent actions, espousing what they called progressive views and engaging in massive student demonstrations in 1890.[48]

Masaryk, right from the start, took a special interest in student groups, attending their meetings as a lecturer or as a listener. His important article on the tasks of students, published in the second issue of the journal, *Časopis českého studentstva*, had a marked influence on the attitude of the AČS. However, contrary to Masaryk's injunctions, leading students soon moved toward a more openly political stance. As a result of a message of greetings to French students, in 1889, the AČS was dissolved by the authorities; its place was taken by *Slavia* which was, however, also dissolved a few years later (1894). In a bitter controversy over a plaque in honour of Jan Hus on the National Museum, Masaryk, in the face of noisy conservative opposition, sided with the students and linked Hus and Christ together as embodying integrity and purity.

By 1890 Masaryk had joined the Young Czech party but he still enjoyed the respect of the more progressive students and more than once was given an ovation in the classroom. In 1891 he received strong support from them in his successful campaign for a parliamentary seat. In the same year, at the first conference of the Progressive Slavic Youth, Masaryk expressed his approval of many student demands, and praised their rapprochement with the workers, but there were signs of emerging differences. In his address Masaryk once again sought to direct students away from direct political participation and toward cultural work. The congress, however, agreed on a radical political programme which stressed the social question, combined national and social objectives and urged Slavic solidarity.[49] These ideas were reasserted at a second Slavic congress in 1892, and were espoused in the progressive student organ, *Časopis pokrokové studentstva*, which also strongly defended freedom of instruction and scholarship.

Although Masaryk's views were still praised, he began to lose support among the increasingly radical-minded progressive students. In 1893 the streets of Prague were disturbed by a series of nationalist, anti-dynastic and anti-Austrian demonstrations. The government explained these events as the work of a secret conspiratorial organization, the Omladina, and responded by declaring a state of siege in Prague, arresting many students and putting on trial alleged leaders of the Omladina. The judicial proceedings offered no serious evidence that such a group existed, but severe prison sentences were meted out to the accused, who included several former leading figures of the progressive students, such as Ant. Hajn, A. Rašín, J. Škaba and K. Sokol.[50]

Masaryk disapproved of the demonstrations but was severely critical of the official treatment of the radical youth. He showed his sympathy with the victims by visiting them in prison, in sharp contrast to other Czech political leaders, who disowned and condemned the *Omladináři*. After the trial Masaryk admitted uncertainty as to whether a secret society existed or not, but in general deplored tactics of secrecy and conspiracy, and condemned radical or revolutionary strategy and the use of violence.[51]

MASARYK AND THE PROGRESSIVE STUDENTS

After 1893 there was a widening gap between Masaryk and the former progressive students who were themselves deeply divided after the Omladina affair. Masaryk's resignation from the Young Czech party and the growing estrangement of progressives from that party brought them closer to Masaryk, but did not overcome the deep differences between them. According to Karen Freeze, Masaryk was opposed to the radicalism of the progressives, and their unwillingness to work within the existing system, and assumed, unjustly, that they were ready to use violence. He called for 'quiet cultural work'. The progressives did not accept Masaryk's realism or his philosophy of 'absolute humanity'; he disagreed with their advocacy of historical right as the foundation of a reformed Austria. There were also differences as to the proper relations with the Young Czechs and the Social Democrats.[52] Opposing the Progressives were the so-called Independents, represented by the journal, *Časopis studentstva Českoslovanské*, who were closer to Masaryk's moral approach to politics but parted company with him on other issues, such as their open anti-Semitism.

Masaryk set forth his perception of the differences between realism and progressivism, in a highly polemical controversy with Antonín Hajn in 1893–94, republished in *Our Present Crisis*.[53] He charged the progressives with lacking an independent and unified philosophy and defended his doctrine of humanity and reform, not violent revolution. He did not oppose revolution in the sense of 'a fundamental transformation of an old unjust social order' and called for 'a revolution of the human spirit' but was absolutely opposed to the use of violence, except for defence when no other means was available. He defended a policy of 'small-scale, ordinary daily work', of 'peaceful cultural work, not the sword'. Hajn, in spite of his earlier respect for Masaryk, disagreed and replied with strong criticism.[54]

In *The Czech Question*, Masaryk expressed an exalted view of the role historically played by Czech students as the heralds of progress and new ideas. He recognized that the student movement was going through a crisis, that only a minority were progressive and that others were strongly opposed. He welcomed the interest of the progressives in social questions, including the problem of student poverty, their linking of national and social questions, and their cooperation with young workers and with Social Democrats. He also was pleased that the university had become an important influence on student thinking and had thus weakened the previous dominance of the newspapers. He still believed 'that political activity should not be the main thing and that the Czech student should learn to understand the humanist ideals of the (Czech) enlightenment and renaissance and seek to fulfil them'.[55]

It is impossible to describe here the intricate evolution of the progressive student movement during the next two decades. There were conflicting tendencies, some favouring realism, others a more radical national and social politics, and still others sharing social democratic views. The various groups formed and reformed, and their publications came and went. There were bitter struggles for control of the newly formed *Slavia* by students of opposing orientations. This period was described by one of the historians of the student movement as a time of chaos and crisis in the progressive student movement and of its gradual decline and eventual extinction.[56]

In these confusing times Masaryk remained an influential but controversial figure. He was praised for his exceptional relations with students (1901 and 1910), and for his insistence that they should form their own opinions independently (1908, 1912, 1913),[57] but he was also often criticized. During the Hilsner case, for instance, at the turn of the century, he became the target of abusive student demonstrations for his stand against anti-Semitism, but he was also strongly defended by other students for his defence of freedom of thought.[58] At that time he asserted that the issue of scholarly freedom was a common concern of students and professors, but strongly defended the right of students to demonstrate against him. In 1907 and 1908 he was a strong advocate of freedom of scholarship against Catholic clericalism and censorship in the schools and supported student strikes on this issue.[59]

Masaryk's controversial position may be illustrated by two events. In 1906 he was made an honorary member of the *Svaz českého studentstva*, and was praised for his defence of 'the right of the human spirit to think things through', and to 'work and create freely', and for his Czechism (*češtví*), for teaching his students to work for a distinctive Czech culture. Yet a year later, Masaryk was reproached in a student newspaper, *Přehled*, for his mistakes in Czech politics, his narrow-minded moralism, his incorrect opinions on the Czech renaissance, the untenability of his religious standpoint and of his humanist theory, his introduction of doctrine into politics, the sterility of his ideology, etc.[60]

MASARYK AS EDUCATIONAL REFORMER

Masaryk was severely critical of the deficiencies of the Czech school system as a whole and repeatedly advocated reform. In one of his earliest speeches in the Austrian parliament, in 1891, he called for a thorough reform of the entire school system; he returned to this theme again and again in later speeches and articles. His concern extended to all levels, from elementary schools to institutions of higher education, and ranged widely over many themes. He regarded education as having great economic and social, and also national, significance. He invoked great figures of Czech history – Hus, Palacký, and Komenský – on the importance of education, and argued that a small nation could compete effectively in all fields only through training and developing itself.[61]

Masaryk outlined his general theory of education and instruction in a series of lectures at the end of the century.[62] He believed that education began in the home and continued permanently through living in society. As for the schools, Masaryk's far-ranging discussion touched on matters such as discipline and punishment (the teacher, as a role-model, must be democratic, not despotic), and methods of instruction best suited to develop the child's capacity to think precisely and independently. Instruction should not be dominated by intellectualism and a scholastic approach, but should aim at the cultivation of spontaneity and imagination. There should be less emphasis on facts and words and more on general conceptions. Teachers should not be obsessed with matters of method; the main thing was that they should know the subject matter. They should acquire a knowledge of literature, history, biography, art, culture, and aesthetics, foreign languages, sociology, psychology, economics and politics. Education often caused physical and mental harm by overburdening the student and overemphasizing reason; schools should teach crafts and encourage physical labour and promote greater care of the body, less through gymnastics than by walking, running and other outdoor activities.

Masaryk also advanced certain more general aims of education. Schools were becoming more democratic and more practical, but at the same time more scientific. Their aim should be 'a full life, both individual and social'. Schools at all levels should develop among pupils and students an awakened national consciousness; they should imbue students with an understanding of the past and present of the Czech nation, and with love and devotion to their own nation and toleration of other nations. This required extensive instruction in the Czech language and literature and in Czech history, Czech textbooks and translations from the languages of the world. Schools should teach ethics, including sexual morality. Instruction should be imbued with religion, but not in a dogmatic sense; they should inculcate real devoutness and morality, and encourage tolerance. Schools should be assured complete freedom so that teachers and students alike would be able to teach and learn, free of bureaucratic controls from above.

Pupils at all levels should be encouraged and taught how to continue their education on their own outside the classroom. In particular, workers' education should be promoted through a Workers' Academy which would provide industrial workers with two to three years of schooling; the emphasis should be on general and theoretical, not practical training. There should be extension lecture courses for popular education, at high schools and at the university. Self-education should be encouraged. Women should have equal facilities for education in high schools and universities; as one-half of the nation, they could exert a beneficial influence on society.[63]

The most systematic exposition of Masaryk's views on all aspects of education, including the universities, was given in the successive programmes of the political parties which he led, notably the Realist party, in 1890, and the Progressive party, in 1912.[64] Both documents described the aim of all education to be 'the development of a harmonious and all-sided (physical, rational and moral) Czech man'. Schools should be free of charge; they should be co-educational, lay and non-confessional; they should be free of bureaucracy and clericalism. This required a reform of school administration, reducing church and state influence and replacing alien centralism by establishing national sections at every level of administration so as to assure each nation an influence on its own school system. All students should be instructed in their own language; in mixed districts minority schools should be established.

The middle schools should move towards a unified system, which would reduce old distinctions between Gymnasium and Realschule. The curriculum should include the study of Greek culture, compulsory learning of Latin and German, and the teaching of other languages, including English and a Slavonic language, especially Russian and Polish. There was no place for militarism in the schools, and there should be no compulsory religious exercise or service.

University studies should be reorganized in accordance with contemporary conditions. The legal faculty was too one-sidedly historical and did not have close contact with modern life and society.[65] Law students should be required to study the social sciences, especially national economy and political science, and have easier access to general education at the philosophical faculty. The philosophical faculty should be reorganized so as to offer theoretical studies of the disciplines taught at other faculties. The theological faculty did not enjoy freedom of research and did not teach religious matters objectively. There should be equality of all religions, either by establishing faculties for all confessions or by separating the Catholic faculty from the university. A higher school of politics and journalism should be established. A veterinary faculty was also needed.

At all faculties, freedom of research should be established by law, and appointments of professors should be made on the basis solely of scientific qualification, not for political or nationality reasons. There should be a freer disciplinary code as demanded by the students, and improvement in the salaries of professors, especially for docents. Both party programmes urged the further development of the Czech University and the technical colleges in Prague and called for a second university in Brno, a demand first raised by Masaryk in 1883 and pressed repeatedly , but in vain, down to the fall of the monarchy.[66]

CONCLUSION

In 1910, speaking at a celebration of his sixtieth birthday, Masaryk reminisced about his earlier lack of plans for a career. As the son of a coachman, and later as a blacksmith, he had had no clear idea of his future, and became a school teacher more or less by chance. In Vienna he had wanted to become a diplomat but had no thought of being a professor. Rightly or wrongly, he became a university teacher; he wondered aloud whether he had been very successful. His only plan, at sixty, was to live until he was eighty and to write what he really thought.[67]

Perhaps this was a bit of false modesty. The picture we have sketched above portrays a man of high academic attainments, both as teacher and scholar; a man who dedicated his life to scholarship and education and sought unceasingly to elevate the standards of both. As a professor he was devoted to his students and strove to inspire them to lead a good life and to seek the truth both in their scholarly and in their personal life. Whether deliberately or not, Masaryk, in 1882, embarked on a career which was designed to educate the nation as a whole, in accordance with precepts enunciated in one of his earliest writings, in 1877: 'Each individual has the right to education as he has the right to live'; 'it is the first requirement of humanity. ... that everyone should be educated'.[68]

In carrying out his educational objectives Masaryk was, as a recent biographer put it, a national iconoclast.[69] Some of his students likened him to Socrates for the moral foundation of his thinking, his cold faith and reason, and his lack of faith in authority.[70] Like Socrates, and like his Czech predecessor, Jan Hus, Masaryk stood his ground and suffered for his beliefs. Although his fate was not as serious as theirs, he paid a high penalty in condemnation by large sections of the nation whose interests he was attempting to serve. Although his educational work was not directly or explicitly political and was carried out in accordance with his favourite 'watchword' of 'non-political politics', it left a lasting legacy for Czech cultural and political independence in an unforeseen future.[71]

2 Champion of Democracy

During more than three decades prior to 1914, Tomáš Garrigue Masaryk was a tireless defender of democracy within the Austro-Hungarian monarchy. His views on democracy can only be understood in the context of his attitudes towards politics in general, both in theory and practice. For Masaryk, politics was an integral part of philosophy and closely related to morality and religion, as well as to science. In fact it was both a science and an art. For him democracy developed as the antithesis of aristocracy, or as he termed it, theocracy. In contrast to the latter, democracy embodied rule by the people, self-government at all levels, and respect for the individual. In a comparative analysis of contemporary political systems Masaryk manifested his profound respect for the constitutional systems of Great Britain and America and his deep hostility to the absolute monarchies of Germany, Russia and his own Austria-Hungary. The state and politics, in his view, had to have a national content, reflecting the Czech struggle for state rights and independence, but should also reflect a humanist approach to the world and to life. Masaryk was a keen student of the social question and urged that all politics, both the state and parties, be given social content, or 'socialized'. He put his faith in democracy, progressive populism and moderate socialism and was critical of liberalism, Marxist and clerical socialism, communism and anarchism, as well as conservatism, whether in feudal or clerical form. He was a decided opponent of violent revolution and a warm advocate of small-scale work, and of gradual reform. He also believed in the importance of what he called 'non-political politics', i.e. work in the cultural, social and economic fields, as well as in personal relations.

As in other aspects of his thinking, Masaryk did not present a detailed and coherent exposition of his political theory. Major works, such as *The Czech Question* and *The Social Question*, touched only briefly on politics and democracy. More systematic treatment is given in his study of Havlíček, in *Russia and Europe*, and in several lesser works.[1] His thoughts in these writings and elsewhere are usually embedded in discussions of a host of other subjects from which they have to be gleaned and reduced to some degree of order. His practical activity in Czech and Austrian politics will be treated elsewhere.[2]

DEMOCRACY AND POPULISM

It has been pointed out that, in the earlier years of his political activity, Masaryk paid little attention to the concept of democracy, and even, it is argued, condemned it. Cited in favour of this argument was his statement in 1895, in *The*

Czech Question, repeated in 1900, in a commentary on the programme of the People's Party: 'We are no longer democrats; we are populists (*lidovci*).' We shared, he wrote, Havlíček's view of democracy as opposed to aristocracy, but we thought this concept was too narrow and concerned itself too much with governmental forms. Their 'populist' approach was broader and cared more about the inner content of these forms and extended the term to include 'the people', especially those who were politically and economically weaker.[3]

Masaryk's view of democracy at that time reflected an increasingly negative attitude to liberalism, with its concept of bourgeois democracy, as represented by the Young Czech party, and his growing sympathy for the socialists, and their idea of social democracy. In *The Czech Question* he explained his statement that 'we are not democrats, but populists', as meaning that bourgeois democratism had in fact degenerated into non-democratism, into a bourgeois and plutocratic aristocracy, and was being superseded by a more social (or socialist) democracy. *Lidovost* rejected the old idea that the politically active classes were the nation, and instead supported the political demands of the classes hitherto without rights, i.e. of the people. It was the '*lidova*' character of Havlíček which marked him off from Palacký and from contemporary party liberals. Havlíček expressly rejected the idea of a republic in Austria but called for a monarchy which would be democratic, but in the populist sense.[4]

By the end of the century, however, Masaryk began to use the terms democratic and populist more or less synonymously. In his study of the social question, in 1898, Masaryk wrote that democracy was 'a consistent and integral view of life and the world' which led to a 'a really vital and universal politics'.[5] In Parliament, in July 1907, he offered the struggle for universal suffrage as an example of their democratic politics which sought to democratize all the public institutions of Austria.[6] In 1908, Masaryk declared: 'Our political aim and programme must be democracy, literally government of the people, the many; all have to govern'. Democracy involved not just political institutions; but required that all inequalities, economic, social, cultural, linguistic and religious, be replaced by equality. To be a democrat meant not to die for the nation, but to work for it, in all spheres. And that meant not just to vote, but 'to think, to have a plan, a programme, to study, and most of all to think'.[7] In its 1912 programme the Progressive party declared its goal to be democracy, which included parliamentarism and universal suffrage so that every citizen could say that he was the state.[8] And in a lecture, 'Democracy in Politics', in May 1912, Masaryk talked of democracy in terms of universal suffrage, parliamentarism, human rights, local self-government and autonomous corporate bodies (such as the trade unions) – in short, 'management by the people' (*lidovláda*).[9] Clearly Masaryk had by that time fully integrated the concept of liberal democracy into his thinking and it became central to his campaign for universal suffrage and for his struggle for reform of the Austrian monarchy.[10]

DEMOCRACY DEFINED

Masaryk did not formulate a systematic theory of democracy. Although he often defined democracy in negative terms, as an alternative to authoritarian systems, and especially as opposed to the Austro-Hungarian monarchy, and as a reaction to the inadequacy of liberalism, it was also interpreted in more positive terms. Antonie van den Beld has set forth Masaryk's four main criteria of democracy.[11] The first fundamental characteristic of modern democracy, since direct self-government in the Athenian sense was impossible, was control by the people through popular representation based on regular elections.[12] The second essential was political equality, which meant universal adult suffrage, proportional representation, and one man one vote. Universal suffrage, it went without saying, must include women, and must also be applied to the provincial diets, and to city and local governments.[13] A third requirement was freedom of speech, freedom of the press, and freedom of assembly; criticism and openness were conditions of democracy. This involved, too, the right to put oneself up for election, the right to criticize, and the right to take initiatives in policy.[14] The fourth feature was the principle that the majority prevailed, both in elections and in Parliament. At the same time the minority must be represented, and its rights and its views respected.[15]

Not mentioned in the above scheme was Masaryk's belief in individualism as a crucial element of democracy. At the turn of the century, in lectures on 'How to Work', Masaryk asserted that the chief political problem was to comprehend the relation of the individual to society, the problem of individualism and collectivism. Although he admitted the difficulty of solving this problem, he expressed disagreement with the older view that individual action was 'a manifestation of the whole, ...of the divine', and with the contemporary idea, exemplified by Marxist socialism and political liberalism, which emphasized the whole to the detriment of the individual; he also rejected anarchism as an extreme form of individualism. Even though, at that time, he seemed somewhat uncertain, he concluded that individualism was 'far more warranted than collectivism, which would completely destroy individual opinion and conscience'.[16]

A year or two later, in his *Ideals of Humanity*, Masaryk defined individualism as 'an expression of humanistic strivings', but rejected any form of extreme individualism, which failed to relate the individual to others and placed the individual on the level of God. Once again rejecting the extremes of anarchism and Marxist socialism, he approved 'a moderate individualism, a really philosophical and ethical individualism, which sought to elaborate certain characters and personalities on the basis of love'.[17]

In his book *Russia and Europe*, in 1912, Masaryk, once again curiously discussing individualism in the context of anarchism, charged that in its extreme form it often neglected the social whole, or even superimposed itself over society. Yet liberal individualism, in the earlier progressive phase of liberalism, was justified as a struggle for freedom in all spheres – freedom of faith and conscience, of thought and speech, of science, scholarship, and education, of schools and the press, and of commerce and labour contracts. 'Freedom was conceived as the greatest possible development of individuality in the sense of an ethical personality'.[18]

DEMOCRACY CONTRA THEOCRACY

In his thinking on democracy Masaryk counterposed it to theocracy, aristocracy, or oligarchy, in both Church and State, and to absolute monarchy, using all of these terms almost interchangeably. The Russian revolution of 1905 was, it seems, the turning-point in his thinking and led him to set forth his views in his book on Russia in 1912.[19] The term theocracy referred to the intimate relationship of Church and State, which traditionally 'formed in fact a single whole'. 'The throne rests on the altar; the altar on the throne'. This was true of the Catholic and Orthodox, but also in some degree the Protestant countries, too. 'Monarchs rest their power and their right on religion.' The essence of aristocracy, as of oligarchy, was 'a hierarchical organization, as is best seen in the army and in the Roman hierarchy'. In Austria aristocratism was first of all religious, but it was also political; against this Masaryk posed democracy or *lidovost*.[20]

Masaryk considered Russia the prototype of theocracy, and fully analyzed the concept in a chapter entitled 'Democracy Versus Theocracy'.[21] There theocratic aristocratism had developed as Caesaropapism and democracy was only in its beginnings. Russian theocracy was based on Catholic Orthodoxy, taken over from Byzantium, and its stress on orthodoxy constituted the spiritual absolutism from which the Russian people suffered. Autocracy received theocratic sanction which also guaranteed to the aristocracy their position by the grace of God. It maintained its absolutism by violence, but also by the general recognition of the people. Theocratic absolutism had so long trained the Russians that the constitutional beginnings of democracy seemed without significance. Even the revolutionaries sought democratic equality rather than freedom (*R.e.*, II, pp. 653–8).

The aristocratic organization of society consisted in a relationship of superiority and the subordination of the individual and individual organizations. It involved a completely different evaluation of man, and proclaimed inequality as necessary. 'People were classified into a minority of lords and a majority of subjects. Aristocratism was not only political and military, economic and social, but also prevailed in the sphere of morality and religion. In the Middle Ages the aristocratic Catholic Church was inwardly linked with political aristocratism; this culminated in absolute monarchy in both Church and State (II, pp. 633–4).

In contrast, the essence of democracy was defined in the Great Revolution by the slogan of freedom, equality and fraternity. Democracy was 'a free and fraternal coexistence in which each person stood beside the other'. Democracy wished to remove political and social domination (*panováni*) and the relationship of servitude (*poddantsvî*). Literally it meant government of the people, but not just government: it meant administration 'of the people by the people and for the people': since the people could not directly govern themselves (as Rousseau himself understood) democracy in practice developed inevitably into an oligarchy; the problem was to make sure that this did not degenerate into aristocratic hierarchism and took 'concrete form as a federation of social organizations and their individual members' (II, pp. 633–5).

Democracy, Masaryk observed, developed only gradually and could not be guaranteed by programmes and institutions alone. Even universal suffrage did not assure democratic thinking. 'The real democrat will everywhere feel and act democratically, not only in parliament, but also in the community, in the party, in the circle of his friends, in the family.' Democracy was 'a new world view and a new way of life' (II, p. 642).

In Masaryk's view the Protestant countries and peoples were more favourable to the development of democracy than the Catholic. He cited as examples America and England, the Scandinavian countries and Finland. In countries of mixed religion, such as Germany, the Netherlands and Hungary, the Protestants were the bearers of parliamentarism. Wrestling with the fact that Catholic France was a parliamentary country, even a republic, Masaryk argued that parliamentarism had developed there through a series of bloody revolutions, whereas in the Protestant countries political progress was more stable and gradual. The political revolution had taken place at the same time as a religious reformation which had encouraged individualism; the individual conscience became the authority, not a single Pope or the priest. In the spirit of the Reformation the philosophical ideals of humanity provided the basis of freedom, equality and fraternity, civil and human rights, and of social legislation. In France the revolutions were mainly political and had only indirectly had an influence on religion. France developed a civilized culture, a progressive economy and the ideas of freedom, liberty, equality and fraternity, but achieved this against its own Catholicism and in spite of it. France was radical and revolutionary, and not really democratic (II, pp. 646–53).[22]

Another crucial difference between democracy and aristocracy was the attitude towards work. As early as 1898, in lectures later published as *How to Work*, Masaryk emphasized the moral and metaphysical significance of work. 'We become people; we become characters; we become independent only as we work. The idle man is not free, nor is the idle nation'. Although he assigned great importance to mental, especially scientific work, he also stressed the value of ordinary or physical work, which also had mental aspects and should not be despised. 'The workman sometimes has to think much more than the professor.'[23] In 1912 he repeated this: 'Aristocracy does not work; it does not do small-scale, "black" work"; for this there were slaves.' And in his book on Russia, he wrote that aristocratism was a government of non-workers over the working people; democracy demanded work from each and every individual. This work would not be great deeds of heroic lords and leaders, but hard, small-scale work by all.[24]

STATE AND SOCIETY

In *The Czech Question* Masaryk noted that the concept of state had not received much attention among Czechs and had undergone change in the course of historical development. In the old view the state was a kind of independent being, outside and above society, and was regarded mythically as a kind of semi-God or God. Nowadays some still looked on the state in this way, as 'an enormously great being, wise and all-knowing, to some good but to others evil'.[25] The more modern concept, however, viewed the state, not only democratically, but also in a populist manner (*lidové*), rejecting its omnipotence, and 'socializing' it, i.e. extending political rights to the broadest classes, and taking account of the needs of all classes, and of course, 'the greatest class, the people'. 'The state is all of us; we are the state.'[26]

Masaryk did not offer a precise definition of the state. He argued in fact that the state must not be looked upon abstractly, but concretely and in real terms, i.e. as so and so many people, with certain spiritual and physical characteristics, so many officials, administrative and judicial, so many ministers, so many soldiers, and a defined ruler. While he did not deny the power of the state, he regarded it as only one of many cultural and social factors, and not by any means the highest one; it was not the 'personification of omnipotence'. 'State power and influence stood beside social powers and other influences, each of them intersecting and mutually influencing the other.' The state tried to gather to itself control of these activities, and still exercised great administering, centralizing and controlling power. But it was not as powerful as the religious, educational, scientific, moral, and cultural strivings and yearnings in general and must respond to other opinions. 'For society this cultural life and its foundations were more important than political activity, which is only one of its parts....' This strikingly pluralistic view of the state was confirmed by his positive attitude toward the role of political parties, to be discussed below.

The concept of the state had also to distinguish between the organized central state power and the autonomous or self-governing (*samosprávný*) powers of the territorially subordinate powers, of which the state consisted – i.e. the lands, provinces, regions, and individual communes (*obci*).[27] Under the Austrian constitution, the executive or administrative power, at each level of jurisdiction, was dual in character, with the lion's share exercised by the so-called 'imperial and royal' (*kaiserliche und königliche*) organs and a very restricted share enjoyed by self-government (*Selbstbestimmung* or *samospráva*).[28]

Although in *The Czech Question* Masaryk made no mention whatever of the concept of autonomy or self-government, it later became one of his central concerns. The People's Party programme of 1900, in a brief reference, demanded 'the 'broadest *samospráva* of all communes and political entities' and an autonomy which would be not only political, but also economic, social, national and cultural, especially in the sphere of education.[29] The theme was developed at length in the 1912 Progressive Party programme. The *obec* was described as closer to the citizens than the state, since they lived and made their living there and it cared for their health, streets, water, parks, theatre, etc. *Samospráva* was a support and defence against an unfavourable state system, a kind of self-help (*svépomocný*) force in reserve for cultural and social progress. It offered the best school where Czechs could train to be citizens and where they could show that the nation was ripe for political independence. Unfortunately the *obec* (used here to represent all local and regional entities) had become an organ of the state; under the dual system of local administration the autonomous element was subordinated to the bureaucratic element. The need for a reform of the administrative system was all the more pressing in view of the growth of economic, social and cultural tasks of the local government. Through administrative and electoral reforms the *obec* must be made into a real *obec*, i.e. a community of all citizenry.[30]

SCIENCE, RELIGION AND MORALITY

In one of his earliest writings, when he was only 26 years old, Masaryk wrote extensively on the relationship of state and politics to science and morality.[31] In a series of articles entitled 'Theory and Practice', he quoted Bacon that 'knowledge is power', and Plato that philosophers should rule, and argued strongly that politics should be based on 'political science', which included sociology, law, geography, and especially history. He who wished to govern his country must know and study it, and act on the basis of scientific rules. Again quoting Plato, he urged that politics and morality must not be separate and that 'right and justice were above power'; he rejected Machiavelli's view that 'power was above right'.

In 1897, Masaryk again touched on the relationship of state and politics to science, religion and morality. In an essay on politics as a science and art, Masaryk referred to the modern state as one based on 'expertness' and outlined the relevant social sciences which were needed for an understanding of politics. He also wrote of the modern state as being the product of a historical process of 'unchurching' (*odcírkevnění*) by which it acquired functions hitherto exercised by the Church. Political actions ought to be subordinated also to moral judgement and political practice justified by humanist ethics; he railed against the Machiavellian idea that the end justified the means.[32]

In 1899, in a lecture series on the progress of European society, Masaryk returned to these themes, speaking of the importance of science and knowledge for developing the power of a nation, and in particular that of a small nation, such as the Czechs. There was need for general education and for continuing education so as make science accessible to the general population.[33] In the same year, in *The Social Question*, Masaryk dilated on the problem of assuring the enduring influence of political experts. Modern politics had to be made a practical art based on science. 'The masses – the majority – the minority – the individual – neither one nor the other could stand up creditably without the power which knowledge grants.'[34]

In 1912 and 1913 Masaryk again touched on these matters. Politics, he wrote, is 'not only an empirical art, but first and foremost, a science'. The task of democratic politics was to observe the given social facts, to recognize the needs of society and to propose and to use 'correct methods'. But it also required judgement, not only in pragmatic but also in moral terms, even though this might be condemned as moralizing and preaching. Politics was based on morality, and thus necessarily had a religious character.[35]

In his study of Russia, Masaryk developed these ideas more fully. Democracy, he said, counterposed science and philosophy against theology and scholasticism. The theocratic priest was 'the guardian of divine revelation', whereas the modern scientific worker based his knowledge on observation and thought. Science itself must be democratic in its methods, and must seek to win general agreement. Thus there must be popularization of science so that all people would be able to think and perceive. A new democratic politics and administration involved knowledge based on criticism.

Democracy was not against religion, as many thought, but was only against the Church hierarchy and theology. There was required a new religion with a new evaluation of the human personality and the acceptance of the supreme moral commandment – love of one's neighbour. Authority must not be based on God's authority, represented by emperor, kings and the state, the church and the Pope, but on 'the recognition of an inner authority by the critically thinking man'.[36]

CONSTITUTIONALISM AND PARLIAMENTARISM

In his essay on politics as a science and an art,[37] Masaryk counterposed absolutism, under which everything was administered according to the slogan ascribed by legend to Louis XIV, 'I am the state', with constitutionalism and parliamentarism where the democratic slogan was upheld – 'the state is all of us, i.e. the ruler, the officialdom and the people'. The modern state was characterized, however, not only by greater democratism, but also by 'the growing practicality and precision of administration – by bureaucracy and militarism'. The old state was a political organization of the aristocracy; the new state separated ruling and administering, and developed 'a special, great administrative and military body'. In Austria constitutionalism had developed from a completely absolutist state and still signified that the supreme power in the state was held by the monarch, but shared in part with representatives of the state, the parliament and diets.

Examining the supposed difference between a monarchy and a republic, Masaryk cited, and presumably approved, Havlíček's reasoning that the two systems were not so different from each other as was usually supposed and that it could not just be assumed that a republic was based on democratic principles and that a monarchy was a despotism. For instance, in England and Belgium monarchical forms had developed so as to guarantee the greatest degree of personal freedom and the sovereignty of the nation. France, on the other hand, had wavered, after the Revolution, between monarchy and a republic. Other republics were not without faults, as was demonstrated by Sparta, Rome, or Venice, in the past; and in the present, Switzerland, France and America.[38] Even in the latter, the republic was not necessarily democratic but was permeated with elements of plutocratic aristocracy, and of militarism and imperialism.[39]

The decisive criterion in distinguishing constitutional state forms, in his view, was not whether a country was a monarchy or a republic, but whether the monarchy was based on the old conception of the absolute rule of the dynasty, or whether this power had been limited by the development of parliamentary institutions. The institution of parliament was important, he thought, both as a representative of the people, as an agency of control over the government, and as a tribune for discussion of legislation and public issues. The English and French models of parliamentarism signified that the parliamentary majority decided and ruled. As he explained to an American audience, the English government was a government of the majority and if it was defeated in a vote, it resigned.[40] In another lecture in America he asserted that Austria had a constitution but did not have parliamentarism; the Emperor enjoyed the full powers of an absolute sovereign; he exercised constitutional rule, but not parliamentary rule. The government of his country was not responsible to Parliament, but only to the emperor, and only to a very small degree to Parliament as well. Moreover from a democratic point of view, Austrian parliamentarism was weakened because of the great influence exercised by the nobility, the bureaucracy and the Catholic Church.[41]

Masaryk was well aware of the weaknesses of parliamentarism and even spoke of a general crisis of parliamentarism and democracy.[42] His first impression, as a newly-elected deputy in the Austrian Parliament, was that it resembled a mill, with its clatter, a stock exchange, or even a theatre or church, where politics was, however, made. More seriously, he wrote, Parliament often became 'a playground of demagogues, a theatre of political actors' and expert knowledge was often brought to bear only indirectly, in committees. Government ministers and ministries were often miserably weak, and deputies did not exercise their right of initiative. He realized, too, that government by majority was not necessarily the best (although better than an aristocracy), and urged that minorities be represented through a system of proportional representation. He feared, too, the exaggeration of parliamentary work, especially work in the central Parliament, and constantly urged that there be decentralization and autonomy, at the lower levels of government, and that attention be paid to non-political cultural activities outside Parliament. Above all, there was a need for a broadening of the suffrage so that Parliament would really speak for the majority of citizens.

Shifting the meaning of the term 'constitutional' somewhat, Masaryk inquired into what would be the perfect form of a legal or constitutional government. Citing verbatim Havlíček's 1909 essay, 'What exactly is a constitution?' he argued that such a government would conduct itself according to the will of the nation and would assure citizens security of person and property; order and freedom of movement; and progress, cultivation and social bliss.[43] To achieve this, it should consist of three independent powers. The legislative power, which determines rules, laws and rights, is exercised by the parliament, together with the Emperor and government. The Parliament, elected by the people, expresses its will. Parliament deliberates on all laws; no law can have validity, nor can taxes be raised, without its approval. The executive power is exercised by the government but only according to the will of Parliament. The judicial power is independent of the government. The administration must be conducted publicly; this would be guaranteed by freedom of the press and of association. A constitutional government must assure freedom of belief, and self-rule of the local communities.

POLITICAL PARTIES AND PARTISANSHIP

Masaryk shared Havlíček's view that political parties were part of the constitutional system; in fact, they were an essential part of democracy. They fulfilled certain necessary functions in society, such as representing the interests of citizens, expressing these views in public discussion and in Parliament, and providing the leadership not only of the parties themselves but also of governments. They must be judged, however, not according to their names or slogans, but according to what they did for people and what they stood for and against.[44]

In an excellent essay on political parties written in 1899 Masaryk was very positive toward the existence of different parties; this was the natural product of differences of opinions, tendencies and interests and showed that society was alive.[45] New parties arose when society felt the need of new principles or methods, and were usually born from criticism of the old parties. Differences between parties were based on convictions and interests, notably religious and philosophical beliefs, economic interests, and interests of nationality. There were usually two main political parties, conservative and progressive (liberal), the former dogmatic, seeking to preserve the old; the latter critical, seeking the new. Between these two, there might also be moderates, and on the extremes of each, reactionaries or radicals. Within each party there were usually factions and different tendencies and shadings, which sometimes had much in common with similar factions in the other main party. Parties might also be based on the personal influence of individuals although that was less common and less desirable.

Masaryk was conscious of universal weaknesses of parties. Even the most democratic parties had oligarchical and bureaucratic elements; they suffered sometimes from too strict discipline of members and excessive partisanship.

There were party leaders who thirsted for power, and there were people who often wished to be ruled. The object must be to make parties as democratic as possible and to strive for informed and responsible leadership.

As we shall note in the two succeeding chapters, Masaryk was, however, highly critical of all of the existing parties and disagreed with their objectives. He censured them for lack of adequate programmes, for poor leadership, and for faulty tactics (opportunism or obstruction). He was convinced that only his own small Realist or Progressive party offered the optimal course.

THE SOCIAL QUESTION

A crucial element of Masaryk's thinking about politics and democracy was 'the social question'. In his book written under this title in 1898, he defined the social question as 'the fact of economic and social poverty, poverty both material and moral, which we have before our eyes, whether among the rich or the proletarians, in the cities or in the country, in the street or in the home'. The social question meant 'unrest and discontent, yearning and fear, hope and despair, of thousands and millions'. It also meant in practice the question of socialism, and chiefly Marxism, and was therefore not merely an economic but also a philosophical question. 'Socialism is today the crux of our knowledge, our conscience and consciousness.'[46]

Masaryk's interest in the social question was manifested as early as 1890, in the draft of a people's programme in which he laid stress on the moral aspect of the social question and urged social reforms to improve the conditions of those who were suffering. He supported the efforts of the workers for non-violent change, the removal of glaring inequality and the reform of the social order.[47]

In one of his earliest parliamentary speeches, in 1891, Masaryk criticized the Austrian government's handling of the workers' question, using repression instead of adopting a positive approach through compulsory old age and disability insurance, and universal suffrage. He criticized both the main Czech political camps, conservative and liberal, and called for a solution of the workers question by the implementation of the Christian principle of 'love thy neighbour'. 'The workers' and social question was first and foremost a spiritual and moral question'. In his view only legal measures would avert the serious danger of revolution.[48]

In *The Czech Question*, in 1895, Masaryk urged moving forward from a one-sided national interpretation of humanism to a broader humanism with a greater social emphasis. The social question, he argued, was part and parcel of the Czech national question; it was 'a central one, in all areas of our thought and struggle – in politics, in literature and art, in science and philosophy'. If we did not find 'a just solution to social demands, in the spirit of our historical ideals, we will return to our grave never to be resurrected again'. 'The task was primarily a moral one, not just one of winning labour over to the national cause but of developing a sense of justice throughout our society'. He personally felt a moral duty to support the justified demands of the workers, although he rejected the Marxist doctrine of social democracy.[49]

Masaryk's concern with the social question is often ascribed to his humble origins and his early manual labour in Moravia, to his early acquaintanceship with Christian socialism there, and to his study of socialism, including both *Katedra* socialism and Marxism, in Vienna. As early as 1873, he read *Das Kapital* and in the following decades he read widely in the field of Marxism and socialism. In his early writings, for instance, on suicide, in his lectures, both at the university and at workers' meetings, and in articles in *Čas* and *Naše doba* during 1889 and the early 1900s, he discussed social problems and expressed sympathy for social democracy and the workers' movement. He was personally acquainted with a number of socialist leaders and helped them in founding their newspaper, *Právo lidu*. Masaryk also had a substantial influence on the socialist ideas of the student movement.[50] He was an ardent advocate of equal and universal suffrage, including women; he urged the eight-hour working day, to be guaranteed by state regulation and international agreement, and supported strikes to attain this end. He favoured the founding of a Workers' Academy in the interests of the education of the working man. He also urged the popularization of science and art, through university extension courses and through self-education by reading and social work.[51]

He also believed that although socialism was anchored in humanism, it also had its roots in Czech history. He cited Jan Hus and the Taborites for their strong accent on social problems, in the latter case the adoption of communism, and found further support for this approach in the writings of the Czech philosopher Augustin Smetana. Socialism required democracy in all fields, not just the material; it required equality and fraternity everywhere. Politics should become social; the state should socialize itself.[52]

Masaryk also saw a close relationship between socialism and religion. He often compared socialism with the teaching of Jesus – especially his commandment to love one's neighbour – and noted that early socialism was often religious in character. Marx, however, advocated a non-religious and a non-moral socialism with a scientific basis. Although he admired the clerical movement for raising the social question and advocating social measures, he condemned it for failing to act according to these principles and becoming itself an economic and capitalist power and a system of theocracy. He preferred the socialist approach because it sought to be scientific and saw the solution not in mere philanthropy, but in social legislation.[53]

PROPOSED SOLUTIONS

Masaryk's specific views on solutions to the social question were reflected in the programmes of the political parties with which he was associated. For instance, the People's party, in 1900, in its economic and social programme, called for the development of the nation as a whole, not only of certain of its classes.[54] The division of the national income should guard against the exploitation of the weaker classes, especially the working class, through social and political legislation. Agrarian policy should protect the small and middle peasant classes, not the great farmers, and agricultural workers should enjoy the same benefits as the industrial proletariat. Small business should be assured cheap credit and assisted through self-help cooperatives. The workers should be protected by law against the economic predominance of capital by the guarantee of freedom of association, by shortening the working day, and by supplementing existing accident and sickness insurance, to include coverage of the aged, widows, and orphans, and vacation time. There should be special care for the very poor both by public and private action. Taxation policy should also seek to even out property differences and should avoid indirect taxes on culture and existential needs. There should also be either state ownership or state regulation of important enterprises, such as mining, banking and transport. These measures should be carried through not by sudden and violent interruption of historical development, but systematically and according to a general plan based on the real means available.

In 1912, the Progressive party adopted an even more comprehensive economic and social programme. For instance, it laid stress on the need for a progressive system of taxation, which would shift the emphasis from consumers' goods to income, property and inheritance. It proposed the establishment of compulsory conciliation and arbitration courts, and a Ministry of Labour. It also urged that work by children under 14 years of age be forbidden and that special protection be given to youth and women at work. It urged reform of housing and measures to reduce poverty, including charitable funds and institutions for the disabled or handicapped.[55]

SOCIALISM AND MARXISM

Masaryk's great book *The Social Question* did not provide a systematic study of social reform, as he had intended.[56] Instead it offered a remarkable critique of Marxism and its attempt to achieve 'an all-embracing view of the world'. In the words of a reform Marxist, Milan Machovec, Masaryk was the first European non-Marxist who, as early as the 1890s, understood the significance of Marxism as 'a comprehensive theoretical system of thought' and the first to subject it to rigorous yet positive criticism.[57]

Masaryk believed that Marxism was going through a deep and far-reaching crisis (*Otázka sociální*, II, pp. 353–60). This was evident not only in the contradictions and revisions found in the writings of Marx and Engels themselves (Marxism was itself 'an unsuccessful synthesis of different views') but also in the significant changes in its very principles introduced by revisionist Marxists such as Bernstein and Kautsky. Nonetheless socialism would remain a significant force, rooted as it was in the imperfections and immoralities of the social order, and in the material and spiritual poverty of the great masses of all nations. Moreover it was not possible to overestimate the contribution of Marx and Engels to the understanding of the social question of the working class and in leading the masses to a theoretical and practical solution of these questions (II, pp. 264–5). Although he did not share the Marxist striving for absolute equality, he did support efforts to reduce inequality to a minimum. It was necessary to introduce social reforms, including (these were the only specific examples given in this volume) a progressive income tax, the assurance of an existential minimum, the abolition of usury and parasitism, the strengthening of social insurance, and the abolition of unemployment. Although Masaryk rejected state socialism, he did not hesitate to demand strict state supervision of the economy. Economic reform was, however, not enough; there was also need of 'a reform of morals and opinions' (II, pp. 20–4).

Much has been written on Masaryk's comprehensive critique of Marxism; only a few brief comments are possible here.[58] In the first place Masaryk did not accept the fundamental principles of dialectical and historical materialism which was, he believed, a one-sided interpretation of the complexities of historical development. Although Masaryk acknowledged that economic factors were influential, he believed that Marx did not recognize the many other elements of human reality, such as religion, morality, art, science and philosophy, state and nationality, etc. (I, pp. 200–1, 230, 241). Similarly, while admitting the existence of classes and of class conflict in history, Masaryk did not accept the stark confrontation of but two classes, and denied that revolutionism belonged only to the proletariat; it was found in all classes, and originated in dissatisfaction with the old regime in all aspects – religion, the Church, philosophy, politics, and the social and economic system (I, p. 236). He did not agree with Marx's belief in revolution and argued that it should be used only in extreme cases.

In the second place Masaryk rejected Marx's amoralism which led him to minimize the importance of individual consciousness and responsibility and subordinated them to the masses and the collective. 'Justice and morality', he wrote, 'are real social factors, justified not only by their usefulness for society and the individual, but rooted in the feeling of humanity given to man.' He was also convinced that there could be 'no adequate humanitarian ideal or socialism without a religious foundation' and without a recognition of the importance of love.[59] Real love, he said, means constantly to work against poverty, and to resist evil, and without violence (II, pp. 231–4). As Masaryk put it in *Russia and Europe*, 'democratic love of one's neighbour requires the legal establishment of equality, it demands justice; this is the essential meaning of socialism'.[60]

REVOLUTION OR REFORM

Masaryk also parted company with Marxism on the question of violence and revolution, a problem with which he wrestled throughout his life. His attitude shifted according to time and changes in circumstances and was often marked by ambivalence.[61] Although he was in principle opposed to the use of violence in politics and to revolution as a means to achieve social objectives, he acknowledged from the outset the necessity of the use of force in self-defence, and especially after the Russian revolution, placed more emphasis on its admissibility in certain circumstances. In Austria he chose social reform, rather than revolution, but in the course of time he became increasingly doubtful that the Monarchy could be reformed peacefully. The question of Masaryk and revolution has often been discussed but requires extended consideration, even at the cost of some repetition; it illustrates both the consistency and the inconsistency of his thinking on this crucial issue.

In his early university lectures Masaryk expressed sympathy for the pacifism of Christ, the Bohemian Brethren, Chelčický and Tolstoi, who spoke out for consistent non-violence, embodied in the ideas of 'love for thy neighbour' and 'non-resistance to evil'. Masaryk eventually criticized the latter concept and argued in favour of resistance, if necessary, to evil.[62] Again in *The Czech Question*, he stated his basic opposition to the use of violence and his belief in peaceful measures of reform.[63] In *Our Present Crisis*, in a polemic with Antonín Hajn, he developed the theme in greater detail in the fourth chapter, Reform or Revolution?[64] He was against any kind of revolution by violence, and stood for constitutional reform. Violence was not, however, equivalent to revolution, which meant, in his view, 'a basic transformation of an old unjust social order'. Violent revolution, however, was at present nonsense, especially for a small nation such as the Czech. In a constitutional state there was no reason for violence. A more realistic tactic was humanism, which, however, did permit self-defence by arms (*železo* – iron), but only in self-defence. It involved revolution, but 'a revolution of opinions and morals', a revolution of the human spirit, a revolution in the hearts and minds'. He appealed to František Palacký and especially to Karel Havlíček, who advocated, in place of violence, legal and peaceful means, and the exercise of free speech.[65]

In his critique of Marxism (1898) and in his study of Russia (1913) Masaryk shifted his ground somewhat in favour of revolution, but continued to balance this with a conviction of the preferability of peaceful reform. In the former book he rejected the Marxist belief in the necessity and desirability of revolution as an inevitable outcome of historical development. He asserted that in 1848 Palacký and Havlíček had better judged the situation than Marx, who had condemned the Czech leaders for failing to support revolution. Revolution, thought Masaryk, was utopian and mystical, a political superstition, and political primitivism. It was usually the work of a minority and secretive and was seldom successful or creative.[66]

Once again, in this study, Masaryk showed his ambivalence on the question. Resort to revolution had to be judged morally. According to his ethical convictions, 'we must consistently renounce any kind of violence. We can, indeed we have to, defend ourselves, and in extreme circumstances with iron. But in doing so we must avoid any new act of violence.' Ethically it was impossible to renounce every revolution; one had to accept it as an inevitable defence. But 'Revolution cannot be an aim..., it is but a means, to be used only in the most extreme case.' The better alternative was love, *drobná práce*, everyday work, 'reform, not revolution'. Without a real reform of heart and mind, without a reform of thinking and of morals, we can remove the devil, only to put Satan in its place. Even Marx and Engels, Masaryk noted, had wavered in their advocacy of revolution and in later years recognized the futility of a struggle on the barricades and the possibility of a parliamentary road to socialism.[67]

In his study of revolution in Russia, Masaryk grappled again with the problem but was unable to resolve the dilemma.[68] He noted that the very word revolution had many meanings, some involving blood and violence, and others not; for example, religious, moral, literary or scientific revolution, or the industrial revolution. Like Marx, the Russian social democrats used the term in its several meanings and confronted the same dilemma as to the merit or necessity of a political revolution. Some, such as Lenin, favoured revolution, others, such as Plekhanov, rejected it. Other parties, such as the Populists, the Anarchists, and the Social Revolutionaries, favoured the use of violence and even terrorism.[69]

Again, later in the book, Masaryk tried, with little success, to escape from the contradictory tendencies in his thinking. A violent revolution required one to lay down one's own life, but also to kill. May we kill? The humanist ethic stipulated that no man had the right to kill another, yet also acknowledged that every man must resist a threat to his physical and spiritual life. 'Every one has the right to defend himself against violence.'[70] However, every revolution had to be judged ethically from the standpoint of motive. 'Social and political self-defence, the defence of one's own life, or that of others, and of the general weal, in particular, moral and spiritual interests, is permitted against the violence of rulers; it is in fact a duty'. In the struggle against aristocracy and theocracy, which were in essence violent, revolution could be morally justified. Even a bloody revolution might be required in face of a state which had many failings and itself used violence to preserve itself. But there was danger of a revolution springing out of rage and revenge.[71]

'The true revolution was a reforming revolution.' 'It must be spiritually prepared, and could only have success if it were well-thought out and conducted according to plan.' The motivation was crucial. A revolution must really correspond to the genuine interests of the people, and must mean real progress in democratic evolution. 'Ethically a revolution is in every case permitted only as a last resort. Not until all other available means are exhausted, can we have recourse to the final extreme measure of revolution, and then only when the decision is made with scrupulous conscientiousness'. Even if revolution were deemed necessary, this did not mean that every phase of a revolution could be justified or that the end justified the use of any means.

In a third volume of *Russia and Europe* which remained unpublished until 1967, in a chapter devoted to Tolstoi, Masaryk expressed his most positive attitude toward violence and revolution and even condoned the resort to war.[72] In his opinion, Tolstoi misinterpreted the precept of Jesus to love mankind, by failing to recognize that this not only permitted but actually demanded resistance to evil. 'Indeed, we have to defend ourselves against evil by arms where necessary if we are to become really human.' Although he tended to agree with Tolstoi that we must not counter force with force, he did not agree that to defend oneself is the same as the mere use of force. It was the motive which determined the nature of an act; the act of killing was very different in different circumstances. It was 'difficult to abide by the precept to defend oneself without committing an act of violence, even while meeting violence', but then adherence to Tolstoi's precept was just as difficult.

Masaryk sympathized with Tolstoi's condemnation of revolutionaries, especially anarchists and terrorists, who were 'attempting to achieve a noble goal by entirely wrong means'. But Tolstoi was wrong to believe that progress had only been achieved through a growth in moral stature and ignored the fact that most revolutions were in fact successful.[73] Tolstoi rejected revolution *in toto* and did not see 'various justifications of and motivations for revolutionary action at different times in different countries'. History taught, he argued, that armed resistance, wars and revolutions had sometimes brought about rather good results, e.g. the Russian revolution of 1905. Even war might not be the worst fate that could befall mankind.[74]

CONCLUSIONS

In conversations with Karel Č apek, Masaryk reminisced that he was 'born to politics; everything which he did was aimed, even if indirectly, toward politics'. But, he said, politics was but an instrument; the goal was religious and moral.[75] His thinking on this subject, as we have already noted, was sometimes contradictory and ambiguous – for instance, in defining the relationship of humanity and nationality, the influence of morality and religion on politics, the choice between revolution and reform, the role of science and the relative importance of the experts and the people. This confusion was in part the product of the inherent difficulty, if not actual impossibility, of reconciling these opposites, but it was compounded by his own uncertainty as to how to resolve these hard questions.

Another example of this was Masaryk's view of the importance of a kind of non-political form of politics which was dictated by the lack of independence of the Czech nation and the limitations of the Austrian political system. He first used the term 'non-political politics' in his work on Havlíček, where he described the latter's advocacy, in the 1850s, in the absence of politics in the real sense under the conditions of absolutism, of a non-political organization to raise the level of the education and consciousness of the nation, and especially of the intelligentsia. In this way a nation which was not independent could replace a government which was not its own by its own moral government.[76]

In the vastly different conditions of the nineties and after, although he was deeply involved in politics, Masaryk continued to believe that parliamentary politics was not the only kind of political work, and was often not the most effective. In urging non-political politics, he laid great emphasis on non-political organizations of the workers, such as consumers' and economic cooperatives, and cultural associations. All of this would raise the political level of the people and give vitality to democracy.[77]

A further illustration was the question of the role of the expert and of the people in politics. Roman Szporluk pointed out that, in his earlier writings, Masaryk accepted Plato's idea that society should be led by philosophers and that outstanding individuals, and the experts, should play a decisive role. Szporluk argued that in later life Masaryk remained faithful to the Platonic idea. He had a low estimate of the 'masses' and thought that democracy was something other than merely the rule of the majority. Democratic administration required management by technicians and professionals. Yet Szporluk acknowledged that Masaryk was firmly committed to democracy and rule by the people and that its foundation was the inner authority of the individual.[78]

Eva Schmidt-Hartmann, in her article cited above (n.10), used somewhat similar arguments, but drew a different conclusion. Masaryk, according to her, wavered between a commitment to liberal democracy, which placed the emphasis on popular participation and procedural safeguards, and the concept of a people's democracy, in which government articulates the will of society as a whole. His belief in science and the experts, and in a new religion, represented a kind of utopianism in which political power guaranteed the public 'Good' and imposed it on a society that was basically 'evil'.[79]

In her later book Schmidt-Hartmann presented her position in a more sophisticated but equally destructive manner. Although her thought was not always clear and was often self-contradictory, the thrust of her argument was that Masaryk's system of thought sought a kind of social consensus (p. 177) or an ideal society to which man should be moulded (p. 193); it minimized the role of the autonomous individual and of institutions and disregarded the conflict of autonomous social forces. This system which 'denied legitimacy to the coexistence of autonomous intellectual approaches' was closer to Rousseau's concept of the general will and 'invoked comparison with modern totalitarian systems' (pp. 193–4).[80]

The evidence presented in this and the two following chapters, suggests a very different picture. There were elements of utopia in Masaryk's vision of the ideal society, but he fully recognized the value of the play of different social forces, opposed viewpoints and conflicting parties, and the significance of democratic institutions and procedures, as well as non-political organizations, which would guarantee popular participation in politics and protect and expand the individual's human rights. True, Masaryk did not succeed in resolving the unresolvable problem of how to achieve both popular rule and rule by leaders and experts. Perhaps naively, he thought it could be achieved by education or cultivation, not just of the leaders but also of the masses, a theme which he stressed over and over in *The Czech Question* and in other writings.[81] This was not a simple matter, he admitted. But democracy was still in its infancy and would develop only slowly and gradually; it still faced many difficulties which it was not easy to overcome. Especially difficult was 'education and self-education for democracy'. But he was convinced that democracy represented the dominant trend of history and would eventually triumph.[82]

3 Political Dissenter

When Tomáš Garrigue Masaryk arrived in Prague in 1882 he knew little about the political situation but soon resolved that he must direct his efforts to the promotion of a new style of politics, which would break with the traditions and habits of the past and espouse new ideas and programmes. What was the proper course to attain this end? In spite of their conservatism, Masaryk at first considered the possibility of joining the Old Czechs, as the long-ascendant National party was called, but when this failed, he turned to the National Liberal party, or Young Czechs, his opponents in earlier literary struggles. After successful negotiations he joined that party and represented it in the Vienna Parliament for three years. But the partnership was marred by discord and was short-lived. With Kaizl and Kramář, he had already formed his own grouping, the Realists, but the young trio soon parted company and went their own separate ways.

In the two decades which followed, Masaryk continued to criticize not only the two main parties, but also the other parties which were eventually formed. Although he was inclined toward socialism, and even called himself a socialist, he was critical of the Social Democratic party and did not join it. Although he was a strong exponent of Czech national interests, he was critical of the National Socialist party which tried to combine nationalist and socialist aims. Although he believed in Czech 'political independence', he was even more critical of the hyper-nationalism of the extreme state right parties. Although he was a proponent of farmers' interests, he also had little sympathy for the Agrarian party.

Convinced of the inadequacy of existing parties, Masaryk founded two parties of his own, the People's, and later the Progressive party, but neither was able to win widespread support, having at first only two representatives, and later only one, Masaryk himself, in the Vienna Parliament. Down to the end of the Monarchy his was often a lone voice calling for his own programme of change in all the institutions of the Monarchy and in all aspects of public life. Nonetheless, independent and rebel that he was, he exercised a significant influence on the political scene.[1]

MASARYK'S ENTRY INTO POLITICS

When Masaryk moved to Prague from Vienna in 1882, Czech politics had just emerged from a crisis, resulting from a long period of abstinence, by the return of their representatives to the Reichsrat in 1879. Within a decade the new beginning had ended in fiasco. Under Rieger's leadership during the eighties, Old Czech leaders had sought to win small favours from the regime by participating in the

Austrian government of Count Taaffe. By the end of the decade a new crisis arose as a result of general disaffection with this policy of 'crumbs' and by the concessions made to the Germans in the Compromise (Punktace) of 1890. This was expressed in the overwhelming victory of the Young Czechs in the elections of 1889 and 1890. Having themselves criticized the policy of opportunism, the Young Czechs, after an initial period of radical opposition, soon embarked on a similar policy which they called 'positive'. Some thought that both the main political tendencies had served useful purposes but others felt that Old and Young Czechs suffered from the same disease of authoritarianism, personal polemics and demagogy, and were equally incapable of providing the political leadership needed.[2] The decade of the nineties was another turning point in Czech politics, which brought into play a new generation and introduced 'a period of history marked by a penetrating change in everything, in politics, literature, art, science and social life'.[3]

Masaryk's first ten years at the University coincided with this continuing Czech political crisis. During his early life in Moravia and his years in Vienna, he had not been in close touch with Prague and Czech affairs. In 1878 he professed to know nothing about Czech politics. Two years earlier, however, he had been critical of the policy of abstention, and had urged a return to Vienna, 'a neutral ground', where Czech leaders could get to know each other and also their opponents. After the Czech return to Parliament, he was able to observe at close hand the activities of the newly-elected Czech representatives and was not too well satisfied; he thought that Czechs were bad politicians; better deputies were needed.[4]

In 1882, when Masaryk entered the scene, he was an outsider and was new to everything that was happening. At first he was not directly involved in politics and concentrated his attention on literary and cultural activities, such as the founding of the *Athenaeum*, in 1886, the manuscript controversy in 1886–87, and the establishment of *Čas* in 1889. Later, looking back, he said that he had been immersed in literary work and in his teaching, and that politics came second. He acknowledged that the manuscript controversy in particular was not merely a literary struggle, but 'a struggle for our whole national life'. These apparently non-political activities, were indeed freighted with political significance and were later interpreted as the beginning of 'realism'.[5]

At that time, as Masaryk later admitted, he did not feel either Old Czech or Young Czech; as a professor he moved in Old Czech circles but mentally he was somewhat closer to the latter. His first political efforts were designed not to form a new political party, but rather to try to improve the general atmosphere of politics, and to do so, if possible, by regenerating either one or both of the two main parties. He was in fact ready to join either of the two parties to accomplish his aim.[6] The first step was to develop a 'realist' programme which would set forth the appropriate objectives and values to be sought in Czech political life.

THE BIRTH OF REALISM

The publication of the weekly, Čas, under the editorship of Jan Herben, in 1886, marked the beginning of the expansion of realism from culture to politics. The paper, to be devoted to 'public affairs', began at once to apply the same standards to the political sphere which had been applied to the cultural realm – open criticism of the deficiencies of national life, and the pursuit of truth.[7]

The school of political realism proper was launched by three young men of quite different backgrounds: Josef Kaizl, an economist and professor at the Czech University, an Old Czech who in 1887 resigned in disagreement with the party's policy; Karel Kramář, a freelance historian living in Vienna and associated with the Young Czechs; and Masaryk, also a professor, who was non-party. What they had in common was a deep dissatisfaction with the character of Czech politics, and with the courses pursued by both Old and Young Czechs, and a desire to raise the level of Czech politics. They were also convinced of the need for a new political newspaper, and sought at first to associate themselves and Herben's Čas with the Young Czech party. When this failed they themselves assumed the management and direction of the paper and made it the spearhead of their effort to change the entire atmosphere and style of Czech politics; the first issue under their direction, on 1 January 1889, has been termed 'the birth of political realism.'[8]

In this number Čas outlined its intention to discuss freely all public questions and thus to work out a positive programme of political and national activity. In a later issue, it was argued, the great fault of the present political leaders was that they did not lead the nation to a realistic understanding of political conditions and did not instruct them how, through tireless political work, to acquire position after position. Although they did not constitute themselves as a new party, they believed that a party must be found which would speak clearly to the people and prepare the way for a rebirth of Czech national life.

In later issues the new weekly defined the purpose of the Realists as being to seek 'an honest and reasonable politics' which was possible only if 'the national organism was healthy'. They were in favour of what they called 'an active policy', which sought to acquire political weight and then to build a majority in the Reichsrat with other parliamentary factions, and to use this majority to attain benefits for the nation and thus to prepare for an eventual struggle for Bohemian state right.[9]

The ideas of the Realists received a systematic formulation in the draft 'People's Programme' in 1890.[10] This document broke new ground in Czech politics by declaring that the goal was to bring 'our state right aspirations into harmony with the needs of today's state'. The immediate task was to achieve 'the moral, intellectual and material elevation (of the nation)' and, in particular, its 'inner strengthening'. There followed an exposition of needed improvements in the educational system; proposals for the support of Czech industry and for social reform to meet the needs of the workers; and demands for freedom of speech and of thought and for universal suffrage. The programme went on to call for close cooperation with Moravia and Silesia, and on the basis of a mutual agreement, with the nobility, and with the other Slavs of the Monarchy, seeking the common goal of national equality. Finally, the programme urged, as an ultimate goal, the establishment of a federal system of individual provincial groupings, each with its own independent legislation and administration.

REALISM AND THE OLD PARTIES

In an essay on political parties written a decade later, Masaryk expressed his belief that the existence of parties was the product of differences of opinions, of religious and philosophical beliefs, economic interests and nationality concerns. There were usually two main political parties, conservative and progressive (liberal) and, between them, moderates, and on the extremes, reactionaries or radicals.[11]

This essay was couched in generalities and made no mention of specific parties in Bohemia, but certainly reflected Masaryk's views of the existing parties, and of the role of the Realists. He was highly critical of both parties but thought that each was performing a necessary function. At first the Realists did not aspire to create a new party, although the idea was broached by Dr E. Albert as early as 1888, and was revived in various forms from time to time thereafter.[12]

The Realists were divided as to which of the main parties to turn to first, Kaizl and Masaryk tending towards the Old Czechs, Kramář towards the Young Czechs, but each shifting his position as time went on. The first approach was made to the Old Czechs, before the publication of the draft People's Programme, in negotiations in January 1889 between Masaryk and Rieger.[13] There were many past differences between the two men, especially in connection with university politics and the manuscript controversy. Rieger, however, had considerable respect for Masaryk's talents and wished to strengthen the Old Czech position in face of competition from the Young Czechs and to counteract the agitation of their main organ, *Národní listy*. There was also fear that the Realists might gravitate towards the Young Czechs or form their own party. The Realists, for their part, wished to gain a new status and greater influence over Old Czech politics and newspapers.

The talks provided an opportunity for little more than getting acquainted with each other, and exchanging opinions. Masaryk also met with his university colleagues, Professors Albín Bráf and Josef Kalousek, both Old Czechs. Further talks, in November 1889, between Masaryk and Kaizl, and the veteran Old Czech, Karel Mattuš, and Bráf, indicated in more specific terms what the Realists wanted: seats in the Reichsrat and in the Diet, membership in the club's trustees, and influence on the Old Czech newspaper, *Politik*. *Čas* would continue to concern itself with cultural life and deal with politics from a theoretical viewpoint and in a popular way. In the end the talks came to naught, largely due to wide differences of opinions and the opposition of other Old Czechs, especially Masaryk's colleague, Jan Kvičala, and, in the end, Professor Bráf.

By 1890 the Old Czechs, the architects of a compromise with the Germans on the national question in Bohemia, who were bitterly criticized for concessions made, were in full decline, and the Young Czechs, its foes, were in the ascendancy. The Realists, who had supported the Compromise at first, now turned against it. In spite of past conflicts with Julius Grégr, editor of *Národní listy*, both sides realized that they had the same common interests which had led to Old Czech–Realist negotiations.[14]

In early 1890 Kramář, who was more anxious to deal with the Young Czech party than were his two colleagues, wrote several long letters to Julius Grégr, which paved the way for meetings between the two old enemies, Masaryk and Grégr.[15] In these letters Kramář urged the need for a new programme for the Young Czechs and proposed the use of the People's Programme as the basis of discussions. Final agreement was reached in talks between Kaizl, Kramář and Masaryk in Prague in December 1890. The party was not to change its name, as originally proposed by Kramář but, with the Realists, would constitute a single political formation. The three Realists were to join the Young Czech party, Kaizl was to become a member of the Czech parliamentary club, and Masaryk, a member of the executive committee. The Young Czechs saw in this a strengthening of their party by acquiring new talents. The Realists rejoiced that full agreement had been reached on the main points of a programme. A new stage in Realist activity had begun in which, they hoped, they would be able to play a significant part in Czech politics and steer it in a new direction.

MASARYK AS A YOUNG CZECH

Young Czech–Realist cooperation, although it lasted only from 1891 to 1893, was an interlude of great importance in Masaryk's political life, in which he for the first time moved from theory and study to political action.[16] The election of the three Realists on the Young Czech ticket in the general election of 1891, and their entry into the Czech club in the Vienna Parliament, afforded them the opportunity to play a substantial role in Czech politics. The party's electoral declaration had been drafted in part by Kaizl and Masaryk and resembled the People's Programme in many respects. Masaryk was elected to represent a constituency in southwest Bohemia and in December he won a seat in the Bohemian Diet. In the Reichsrat he made a number of substantive and well-prepared, but sometimes polemical, speeches in which he forthrightly set forth his views on major issues such as legal studies, the social question, educational reform, clericalism, nationality problems, the Czech question and Bohemian state right, the latter bringing upon him a charge of treason by a German nationalist deputy. In the Delegations he spoke forcibly on Austrian foreign policy and in particular on the question of Bosnia-Hercegovina, thus acquiring a reputation as a courageous and knowledgable statesman throughout the Monarchy and Europe. Although in many respects Masaryk pursued a moderate course in Czech politics, in his parliamentary addresses he increasingly showed himself to be an uncompromising, even radical, exponent of Czech interests.[17]

The Young Czech party was divided into many schools and factions, and was under constant pressure from extremists within its ranks, such as Jan Vašatý, and from Julius Grégr and his newspaper. Within the party the three Realists formed a distinct grouping which sought to correct the party's deficiencies, but caused friction by their independent actions.[18] Meetings of the club and the party's executive committee were often occasions for polemics and personal denunciation over substantive issues. The Realists frequently voiced criticism of the radicals, both the Grégrs and Vašatý, and were themselves the target of attack. The Realist organ, *Čas*, constantly engaged in polemics with *Národní listy*. Masaryk in particular became a kind of *enfant terrible* within the party and was criticized for breach of party discipline.[19]

The Realists had differed as to the place they would take in the Young Czech party.[20] Although more or less agreed on policy in general, the Realists were divided on tactics. Kaizl was more sympathetic toward Young Czech policies, but became increasingly critical. Kramář was moderate and also came to deplore the actions of Julius Grégr and the radicals. Masaryk adopted an even more critical stance and insisted on complete freedom of discussion. Although his colleagues often agreed with his criticisms, they were embarrassed by his behaviour and felt that as long as they were members of the party, they should remain loyal and confine their criticisms to inner party circles.

Although Masaryk professed a liking and respect for Grégr, the old personal antagonisms were soon revived. As early as September 1891, in a major speech to his constituents in Strakonice, he expressed his approval of the party's programme in general, and its 'forceful but proper' behaviour as an opposition party; but he condemned those who, without having a radical programme, called for more radical action. He considered the state right programme and the demand for universal suffrage as progressive and indeed radical, but categorically rejected passive opposition, i.e. abstention from Parliament. The Reichsrat was a public forum where they could set forth their rights and demands before the whole world. As for Austria, he stressed the need for agreement with the Austrian Germans, and declared that, like Palacký; 'we sincerely want Austria'. In conclusion, he endorsed 'the policy of a free hand'; the deputies should not go begging, but should demand what the electors wanted. He also urged the need for a new daily newspaper.[21]

Although Masaryk spoke relatively moderately and criticized official party policy more by implication, his speech was regarded by some as contrary to party policy and as being too conservative and 'Austrian'. Grégr sought to have the executive committee deliver a public reprimand of Masaryk but failed. There followed other quarrels between Grégr and Masaryk; the climax came with the so-called Šramota affair. The controversy was unleashed by a report by an Old Czech journalist, František Šramota, of an alleged private apology by Julius Grégr in a letter to the Lord Lieutenant, Count Thun. Masaryk was said to have been implicated in revealing Grégr's letter, although he denied having anything to do with the matter. The affair was finally concluded when the Young Czech executive committee absolved Grégr of all guilt and reprimanded Masaryk for harming the party's interests, but refrained from expelling him from the party.[22]

Not having had a chance to defend himself at the meeting, Masaryk submitted to the executive committee an extensive memorandum which was in effect his swan song as a Young Czech. He censured the unclear and ambiguous programme of the party and its shifting tactics, sometimes demonstrative but in reality passive and negative, and lambasted the party organ, *Národní listy*, for its arrogation of power and its untruthful attacks on himself and the Realists.[23]

The decision of the executive committee was in fact the last straw for Masaryk, who had for some time been considering resigning his seat in Parliament so as to be with his family in Prague, as well as to be in a position to influence students and the general public and counteract the influence of *Národní listy*. Although Kaizl and Kramář were very dissatisfied with the state of affairs in the party, and even despaired of changing it, they tried to persuade Masaryk not to resign, and were not willing to do so themselves. They were both highly critical of Masaryk's behaviour, Kramář implying that he was a Napoleon, and Kaizl referring to him as a troublemaker (*povážlivý rváč*). Thus Masaryk found himself isolated, and finally, in 1893, resigned his parliamentary seat as well as his seat in the Diet, thus terminating his first parliamentary career. Although he remained a member of the party and of its executive committee he did not take an active part in political life and confined himself to the politics of the pen.[24]

CRITIQUE OF OLD AND YOUNG CZECHS

During the next five years Masaryk devoted himself to study and writing, seeking to promote, through 'non-political politics', what he considered more important than politics, namely the cultural development and inner strengthening of the nation. He took the first steps in this direction by establishing in 1893 a new journal, *Naše doba*, which was to be the forum for his ideas until 1914. In rapid succession he produced *The Czech Question* (1895), *Our Present Crisis* (1895), *Jan Hus* (1898), *Karel Havlíček* (1898) and *The Social Question* (1900). Apart from the last named, these books, as we have seen, sought to set forth a national ideology on the basis of the central idea of 'humanity' and thus to provide the basis for a political programme more suited to the needs of the time and to prepare the nation for more effective political action in the future.[25]

Masaryk's important book *The Czech Question* was devoted largely to a discussion of the Czech past and dealt with contemporary politics only in Part IV. *Our Present Crisis*, based on previously published articles, from 1889, 1893 and 1894, continued this discussion but was largely devoted to a critique of the embryonic Progressive movement.[26] Here attention will be directed largely to Masaryk's views on contemporary politics, as set forth in his severe critique of the two main parties, the Old and Young Czechs, in his criticism of the Progressive movement, the Social Democratic party, and anarchist, syndicalist and clerical tendencies, and in his exposition of the meaning of Realism.

The central thesis was repeatedly stated, in somewhat different versions, namely that Czech politics was in a state of extreme crisis resulting from the decline of both the two main parties. The symptom of the crisis was the decline of what he called the whole Old Czech system, but equally the decline of Young Czechism, which was no more than a continuation of the former. The problem was not one of persons, but of principles. Its essence was the failure of Czech politics to elaborate the programmes of Palacký and Havlíček so as to reflect the needs of the time and the increased capacity of the nation. Although Masaryk had serious reservations about both Palacký and Havlíček, and he did not make clear the essence of the revised programme which was required, Masaryk hammered away at the need for such a new national programme and held that Realism provided an approach to one.[27]

For Masaryk, the Old Czech party was the first national party, and formulated the first national programme, based on the thought of the awakeners, especially Palacký, but had not brought it up to date. The Old Czechs were too much under the influence of their allies, the Bohemian nobility, and the latter's clerical and anti-national views. In economics they were socially and financially reactionary and paid no attention to urgent social problems. They overrated the importance of politics, especially politics in Vienna, and neglected the need for cultural work and 'inward politics'. The leadership was traditional and authoritarian; its policies were conservative and openly reactionary.[28]

The Young Czechs, on the other hand, embodied the worst aspects of contemporary liberalism. They did represent some progress in comparison with the Old Czechs; in keeping with the thought of Havlíček, they were more popular (*lidový*), more democratic, and more progressive. But they had failed to revise the programme of Havlíček so that it was in essence the same as the Old Czech programme. They were justified in their opposition to Old Czech tactics, but they were negative rather than really critical. Their approach was characterized by a narrow-minded economic liberalism, which neglected the social question, by religious indifference, and by a one-sided nationalism. The Realists had been disappointed in their hopes of engendering change by working within the party after 1891.[29]

PROGRESSIVES AND SOCIALISTS

Masaryk had been close to the student movement during the late eighties and had sympathized with the progressive wing in its criticism of Young Czech policies and its emphasis on the social question. He had, however, urged students to refrain from direct political activity and thought that the progressives had moved too soon from literary to political activity and had shown a tendency toward radicalism.[30]

In *Our Present Crisis* Masaryk launched a full-fledged attack on the progressive movement and on Antonín Hajn, one of its chief spokesmen. In a highly polemical fashion he charged Hajn with misunderstanding and distorting Masaryk's programme of humanism. In particular he condemned Hajn's conception of 'relative humanism', and his alleged belief in the necessity of violence. He acknowledged that the progressives held views in common with his own, especially on the social question. However, he randomly labelled them as materialistic, 'liberal' and even reactionary, and treated them as a mere radical wing of Young Czechism. Masaryk recognized, however, that the progressives were divided, and made a great point of distinguishing the emerging Progressive party, the *'pokrokáři'* (extreme progressivists) as he pejoratively called them, from the progressive movement as a whole, and argued that the party's programme was not in harmony with the principles of the latter.[31]

Masaryk's attitude toward social democracy was given in detail only several years later, in *The Social Question*, and has been analyzed by this author elsewhere.[32] It combined deep respect for its striving for social justice and complete rejection of its Marxist philosophy. He rejected the Marxist view of the role of violence in social change, but noted that socialists themselves were coming to see that in a constitutional state, especially with universal suffrage, there were other more effective means to attain their ends. Although he recognized that social democracy, following Marx and Engels, was international in its outlook, it was no more so than the capitalists, and had, in Germany, France, and Austria, gradually taken up a more national position. [33]

CRITIQUE BY KAIZL AND HAJN

Not surprisingly, the main targets of Masaryk's assault – the Young Czechs and the Progressives – reacted strongly to his criticism. Josef Kaizl, his fellow-Realist, could not accept Masaryk's wholesale condemnation of liberalism, whose task – to defend freedom – had already been accomplished in Western Europe, but remained to be fulfilled in Austria-Hungary. Liberalism also sought to reduce the power of the state through decentralizing its functions, and was opposed to the aggrandizement of the state through socialism. Kaizl was as critical as Masaryk of the Old Czechs and admitted that the Young Czechs had been influenced by Old Czech ideas. He admitted the party's weaknesses and the differences within it, but he believed that its programme represented great progress compared with that of Palacký and Havlíček. It endorsed the ideas of social reform, human rights and freedoms and universal suffrage, and offered a 'real code of humanity', a combination of liberty and social progress as well as of national and humanist ideas. [34]

Antonín Hajn, also an ally of Masaryk's, agreed with many of Masaryk's ideas, including the need for democratization and social reform, and accepted the importance of the concept of humanity. However, he wrote, all political parties, including the social democrats, accepted the goal of humanity. What he objected to was Masaryk's insistence on his own version of humanity as an 'entire world outlook', which gave priority to spirit above matter and emphasized the spiritual side of life as against physical existence (p. 401).[35] Hajn also parted company with Masaryk on the use of violence. Absolutely humanist methods were impossible in view of the inhumanity of opposing forces. We must strive for humane tactics, yes, but as Masaryk himself admitted, there was a place for violence in case of extreme need.

The differences of view were equally subtle in respect to politics. Hajn agreed with Masaryk's stress on cultural work, but believed that politics was more necessary than Masaryk admitted. He agreed as to the progressive character of the Young Czech programme (largely due to the influence of the Realists); in practice, however, the party, and its organ, *Národní listy*, acted quite differently and were characterized (as were the Realists) by authoritarianism and intolerance.

POLITICAL REALISM DEFINED

In criticizing the old parties, Masaryk had written that salvation was not to be found in any one party, but only in what he termed 'an invisible party of serious and thoughtful people' within all the parties. This presumably referred to the Realists who had already set forth a programme, although only in fragmentary form, in 1890. In *The Czech Question* Masaryk elaborated his own personal thoughts on the meaning of Realism. Over and over again, in a manner hard to reconcile with his own use of historical arguments, he stressed that Realism sought to avoid historicism, or at least 'exaggerated historicism' (as illustrated in the manuscript question), i.e. 'to subordinate the past to the present, and to elucidate the present by the past'. This meant, he argued, always 'to get to know the core of things'; to emphasize 'real learning' – to 'cultivate the nation' through the 'real sciences' (natural and social).[36]

Realism did not want to be a political party; or only a political party; it was a 'direction and a method'. Its political programme was first and foremost 'substantial social reform, cultural work and inward politics'. This meant to 'nationalize our culture and philosophy' and to 'socialize Czech politics', by working for the good of those previously excluded from cultural work. Only the Realists offered a definite programme; this marked them off from the old parties, especially from the clericals, and from the progressives and the socialists, with whom they shared some similar views. They could be regarded, it was said, as standing midway between conservatives and radicals, seeking progress, not through great leaps, but step by step, and not through revolution but through small-scale work.[37]

4 Leader of an Independent Party

Up to the end of the century Tomáš Garrigue Masaryk had stood for a non-political politics and opposed making Realism into a political party. In spite of his criticisms of other parties for not offering a satisfactory political programme, he had not set forth a clearcut and substantial programme of his own. The reaction to his writings, however, indicated that the time had come for open political action. Especially after the adoption of the Nymburk programme in 1897, Masaryk was increasingly hostile to the Young Czechs. *Čas*, soon to become a daily newspaper, provided a vehicle for vehement criticism of that party. Meanwhile differences between Masaryk and his two Realist colleagues, Kaizl and Kramář, had mounted and led to the breakup of the movement. Realism came to be represented by the person of Masaryk and a small band of devoted younger followers, such as Jan Herben, Josef Gruber and František Drtina. It was this group which drafted the first 'framework' programme of the People's (Realist) party, which was adopted at a founding conference in March and April 1900.[1] This programme, revised somewhat in 1906, and then elaborated in 1912, as the programme of the Progressive party, remained the basis of Masaryk's political actions down to the end of the Monarchy.

THE PROGRAMME OF THE PEOPLE'S (REALIST) PARTY

The programme was an open and bold challenge to all other parties, old and new. In Masaryk's words, it was a Czech national and populist (*lidová*) programme which continued the tradition of humanism of the awakeners of the early nineteenth century, especially Palacký and Havlíček. However, in breaking with long-held and cherished habits and slogans of Czech politics, it reflected Masaryk's iconoclastic and somewhat unrealistic approach to politics. This showed itself particularly in its treatment of the idea of the historic rights (*státní právo*) of the Bohemian lands which was espoused by all other parties except the Social Democrats.

The programme vigorously asserted that 'every nation strives to be politically independent and free (*samostatný* and *nezávislý*); to be its own master'. But it frankly acknowledged that complete independence of the Czech lands at that time was impossible, due to their small numbers, their inner state position, and the German (and Polish) population of these lands. This forced them to associate with other nations and lands. It also recognized that there was a worldwide trend toward greater states, and that the freedom of independent states was relative. The problem was how to guarantee cultural and national independence through political independence and to what degree such political independence was possible.

The ancient state right of the Bohemian kingdom had to be judged within this context. The Czech national movement should appeal, not to such historic rights, which had been largely invalidated by the constitutional centralization of Austria, but to the natural right of every nation to be free and independent. This did not mean the rejection of the historic state right, said Masaryk, but it did mean the rejection of state-right utopianism which characterized the other parties. Realism required the recognition of realities and the search for the means to vindicate state right (pp. 118–20). Specifically this could be attained through the far-reaching autonomy of all nations of the Monarchy, including Governors responsible to the Diets. In Bohemia autonomy could not be achieved without reconciliation with the Bohemian Germans, including the acceptance of their demand for territorial partition of Bohemia on a national basis.

It is not surprising that such a programme, which struck at many of the most sacred idols of Czech politics, was rejected by all Czech parties except the Social Democrats and did not gain widespread national support. The programme expressed profound dissatisfaction with all other parties and concluded that this was precisely the reason why the Realists had decided, contrary to their earlier disposition, to form their own separate political party.[2] It charged that the Old Czechs were under the influence of the feudal and clerical ideas of the landed aristocracy, and had merged historic right with complete or partial recognition of the existing constitution. The clericals misused religion in order to attain political domination, and served the wealthy and the mighty. Christian Socialism was clerical and hierarchical and only occasionally manifested more democratic and populist tendencies. The Agrarian movement showed inclinations towards clericalism and feudalism and had given up its support of universal suffrage.

The Young Czechs advocated the theory of historic right in words but in fact were carrying out a policy of radical nationalism. Among the Progressives, the State Right Radical (Progressive) party was nothing but a left wing of the Young Czechs and used extreme state-right radicalism as a catchword. The Radical Progressive party vacillated between socialism and nationalism, and between historic right and nationalism. The Social Democratic party could be regarded as a legitimate representative of the working class, but was rejected for its materialism and class approach. National Socialism (and Christian socialism) had some justification as opposed to Marxist socialism, but the former were not able to formulate a really Czech socialist programme and had succumbed to anti-Semitism, which the programme condemned.

Only the Realists offered an alternative programme, a positive policy which emphasized inward cultural action and small-scale work and which represented a new kind of political work based on careful study of the national needs. The new party was a Czech party; consciously linking up with the glorious past of reform, but also continuing it in the spirit of modern knowledge, and a progressive party, which rejected both opportunism and radicalism. It would be a party above parties, not organized against other parties. It would not oppose anything which other parties did that was good; it recognized the need for criticism in its own ranks. They did not merely seek seats in Parliament or follow only partisan interests; they did not strive for power but for influence.

PROGRESSIVE PARTIES IN BOHEMIA

The Czech Progressive party came into existence in October 1905, as a result of the decline in the fortunes of the Realist party and the splitting-up of the former progressive movement. The Realists, a party of the intelligentsia, had not been successful in winning mass, and especially rural support, and in 1905 fell into serious crisis, as a result of the so-called Herben affair. Jan Herben, owner, publisher and editor-in-chief of the party organ, *Čas*, found himself the target of sharp criticism by some Realists for mishandling the financial affairs of the paper and for the weaknesses of his editorial work. Some called for him to be removed from his editorship and expelled from the party. Masaryk, Herben's long-time sponsor and ally, was charged by some with betraying the party's programme and with exercising the strict authoritarianism of a 'Dalai-lama', or 'Pope'. A number of prominent Realists left the party, some joining the Young Czechs. The affair was terminated by an ambiguous compromise, only part of which was published, which exonerated Herben from the charge of fraud and cancelled an earlier decision to exclude him from the party. As a result of these events, the party had been seriously shaken and its influence weakened.[3]

A crisis had also erupted within the progressive movement, which was divided into several conflicting tendencies, differing as to the proper relations with the Young Czechs and with the Social Democrats, and as to the relative emphasis to be placed on state right and social reform. Alois Hajn became increasingly critical of the state right priority and, in 1897, with his brother Antonín, he broke with the progressive movement to form a separate Radical Progressive party. Its programme referred to the 'restoration of Czech state right on a popular and progressive basis as a means to the attainment of the independence of our nation'. It paid more attention, however, to the need for political freedom and universal suffrage and for social reform and expressed a willingness to cooperate with the Social Democrats in spite of differences over state right.[4]

In 1904 Alois Hajn, who had developed a strong sympathy for Masaryk and the Realists, broke with the Radical Progressive party, and with his brother, Antonín, to form a Progressive Club in Pardubice which strongly defended the imperative of social policy. In 1905, at Hajn's initiative, the Pardubice progressives and the Realists agreed to merge to form the Czech Progressive party. At its first congress in 1906, the party approved a brief programme which had none of the detail of the 1900 People's programme and did not contain an elaborate discussion of Czech traditions and of state right.[5] In a single sentence it referred to 'a political independence, which would be within the framework of a free and progressive Austria'. Alois Hajn, in his introductory speech, admitted that the question of state right was not acute. The main task was to work to attain universal suffrage and the democratization of Austria, and to seek 'an appropriate share in government and power'. Masaryk, who had remained in the background, made only a few impromptu remarks, including an admission that, in the years since 1848, centralism had strengthened itself, and that they had not really moved toward political independence.

It seemed therefore that both Realists and Progressives had embarked together on a promising road of unity. In 1912 a revised programme gave a more detailed exposition of party aims, laying great stress on the attainment of democracy, but giving more positive treatment to the state-right idea. Surprisingly it reverted to the People's programme of 1900 for its formulations on independence and state right and on the problem of a small nation. Although it restated the idea that state right was not at present possible, it observed that they had no right to decide the issue for future generations. It declared that they sought political independence within the framework of the Austro-Hungarian empire.[6]

In the meantime, the other wing of the progressive movement formed the State Right (Radical) party in 1899 which reasserted the objective of state independence of the Czech lands and refused to recognize as legal the existing Austrian constitution or the Parliament. It struck a strongly national note and justified anti-Semitism. In 1908 it united with the remainder of the Radical Progressives to form the State Right Progressive party and issued a militant statement declaring war on Austrian centralism on the basis of Czech state right; the Czech nation must have its own state made up of Bohemia, Moravia and Silesia. In 1912 the party adopted a detailed programme, proposed by Antonín Hajn, which forthrightly demanded Czech state independence on the basis of Czech state right and of its people's and progressive demands and restated its refusal to recognize the legality of the Austrian constitution or the Reichsrat. It declared that the Czech question had become an international question; this required international action by Czech leaders to gain the sympathy of all European nations.[7]

PROGRESSIVE PARTIES IN MORAVIA

Meanwhile a Moravian People's party had come into existence gradually from 1891 on and was formally established in March 1893.[8] Its programme was couched mainly in terms of state right and nationalist interests. Headed by Adolf Stranský, editor of the *Lidové noviny*, it was originally a branch of the Young Czech party and was not directly associated with Masaryk's People's party in Bohemia. However, Masaryk, himself a Moravian, spoke at the founding conference and called upon the party to oppose Germanizing influences, which were much stronger in Moravia than in Bohemia; he also urged it to work toward improvement of the Czech national position, including more schools and a second university in Moravia, and a social policy to meet the needs of farmers and workers.[9] By 1896–97 the Moravian People's party, cooperating even with the Old Czechs in elections, had become the strongest party in the Moravian Diet and was well represented in the Reichsrat. It moved gradually away from the Young Czech party and broke entirely with it in 1907.

Meanwhile a younger progressive left wing emerged within the People's party under the name Young Moravia, and broke away from it in 1896. In 1897, in the presence of Alois Hajn, this wing formed a Moravian Radical Progressive party. Other progressive clubs were established in several regions and cooperated for some years in opposition to the main Moravian parties and to clericalism. In the Diet elections of 1906, they achieved the modest result of winning five seats. Only in 1907, after successfully helping to elect Masaryk to the Reichsrat (six Realists were elected) did they form a separate Progressive party on the model of the Czech Progressives.[10]

Within two years, however, in 1909 this group rejoined the People's party to form the Moravian Peoples' Progressive party, again headed by A. Stranský. Its 1910 programme perhaps lacked the strongly progressive accent of its Czech counterpart. But it spoke of attaining the independence of the lands of the Czech crown, within the framework of the Monarchy, and described state right as having historic and natural-right roots. It demanded the expansion of the sphere of legislative activity of the Diets, an independent provincial executive power, and the appointment of Czech officials in accordance with the number of the Czech population. It placed great emphasis on resisting clericalism and German predominance, and seeking the development of the Czech nation, especially in the school system.[11] At a second congress in 1912, to which Masaryk and Hajn sent greetings, the tone of the speeches and resolutions adopted was more radical. Meeting at a time of international crisis, the congress censured Austrian foreign policy and declared solidarity with the Balkan Slavs. 'It was necessary to revive the Czech question and to resurrect the old state right ideal', declared parliamentary deputy, Richard Fischer.[12]

In the parliamentary elections of 1911 the new party, in association with the Social Democrats and the Agrarians, elected only four deputies as well as supporting the successful independent candidacy of Professor Masaryk.

MASARYK'S RETURN TO POLITICS

Masaryk's election to parliament in 1907, and again in 1911, may be said to mark his return to active political life after a break of fourteen years. In a sense, however, he had never left politics. Even during the years devoted to scholarly study in the nineties Masaryk had been preparing the ground for the development of a new politics by his critique of existing political movements and his advocacy of what he called political realism. The first step towards resuming an active political career was taken with the founding of the Realist party in 1900 and the drafting of its long programme, a major work of over 100 pages. The second and third steps were the founding of the Czech Progressive party in 1905 and of the Moravian Progressive parties in 1905 and 1909. Masaryk became the leading figure in Czech Progressive politics during the subsequent decade. The final step came with his two elections to parliament when he became the party's chief spokesman between 1907 and 1914.

The fifteen years from 1900 to 1914 were years of intense activity in which it is not easy to separate the political and scholarly aspects of Masaryk's career. Throughout all this time Masaryk carried on his teaching at Prague University and was actively engaged in editing and publishing, and contributing to Čas and Naše doba. He found time also to write books and articles, dealing with a wide diversity of subjects, which were often highly political in content; to speak and write directly about politics; to travel – to the U.S.A. in 1902 and 1907, to the Balkans in 1908–9, and to Russia in 1910, and in the latter years to serve and speak in Parliament. He was also involved in a number of serious and time-consuming controversies on the Jewish question, clericalism and state right, as well as in Parliament on questions of foreign policy. It is difficult to know how Masaryk found the time, in the midst of all his other work, to prepare over many years his profound study of Russia, which was published in German in 1913. As a result of this frenzy of activity Masaryk stood out as a figure of extraordinary importance in Czech life, and his sixtieth birthday in 1910 was marked by the appearance of two Festschrifts in which his work was assessed and praised. At the same time he suffered much public obloquy for what was regarded as his radical stance on many issues.[13]

The People's party had not been successful in electoral forays into the Bohemian Diet in 1901 and 1908, in the latter of which only one candidate was elected and Masaryk, in a campaign in which he suffered personal abuse, was soundly defeated. With the introduction of universal suffrage, which Masaryk had strongly supported, in 1907, the time seemed ripe for new efforts, this time with ten candidates, of which only two, František Drtina and Masaryk, won seats in the Reichsrat.

Masaryk had responded with pleasure to the proposal of a group of progressives that he run in a Moravian constituency, Valašské Meziříčí, since a victory in Bohemia would have been difficult.[14] The outlook for election was not, however, very bright, as this was a stronghold of clericalism, and clerical forces were determined to defeat this 'atheist' from outside. Masaryk faced two opponents, V. Povondra, candidate of the Moravian small traders, an Old Czech at heart, it was said, who enjoyed the full support of the clericals, and A. Smetana, a strong Social Democratic candidate, who declined to withdraw in favour of Masaryk but promised support on the second ballot. The clericals waged a bitter campaign, one of their leaflets calling Masaryk a candidate of the Jews, a German by birth, and an enemy of religion, Christ and God.

Masaryk conducted a strenuous campaign in the entire region, and impressed voters with his well-informed speeches. In his main address he made only brief mention of Czech independence and devoted most of his time to a detailed exposition of the causes and the solutions of the problems of small business and the peasants. He also advocated social reform, denying that he was a Marxist but acknowledging that he was socialistic in outlook. In Zlin he noted that he had been a worker himself, had experienced poverty, and still felt keen sympathy for the working class. He openly declared that he favoured the separation of Church and State and the 'unchurching' of education. In Valašské Meziříčí, he advocated the legalization of divorce in preference to the alternative, favoured by the Church, of legal separation which would bring with it the social ills of 'wild marriage'.

On the first ballot Masaryk, although having the support of some Social Democrats, ranked second; in the second round, in which he had the full support of the Social Democrats and even the National Socialists, he won a decisive victory. Once more Masaryk had secured a foothold in the parliamentary system, this time as an independent deputy, beholden to no party. In 1911, Masaryk was re-elected in the same Moravian constituency, this time as a Progressive, again with the support of the Social Democratic party, which did not put up a candidate. His colleague, Drtina, after a campaign of vilification in which Young Czechs and the National Socialists joined forces, was defeated. Masaryk therefore returned to Vienna alone.[15]

It is hardly necessary to say much about Masaryk's parliamentary performance after 1907 and 1911, since his speeches have been thoroughly discussed elsewhere in this book. He took his parliamentary duties seriously, prepared his speeches carefully, and delivered them effectively, even if at times they were highly polemical and not always models of organization.[16]

MASARYK AND THE YOUNG CZECHS

The Young Czechs were a powerful force in Czech politics for forty years, and after 1891, the dominant factor. Even after the erosion of their strength in 1901, and still more in 1907, they remained important down to 1914. After the death of Kaizl in 1901, Karel Kramář was their most prominent spokesman. Masaryk's relations with the Young Czechs and with Kramář passed through many shifts over these years, ranging from his early membership in the party (along with Kaizl and Kramář), his growing estrangement and ultimate break in 1893, and his ever sharper criticism of its policies and its leaders, especially Kramář.[17]

Masaryk's most cogent critique of the Young Czech party was given in a speech in Hradec Králové in 1903 in which he declared that the party was in a state of profound crisis, citing *Národní listy* in support of this claim.[18] Reviewing its entire history from its birth within the Old Czech party, he argued that it had suffered 'a chronic crisis', wavering between opportunism and radicalism, and was not adequate to the progressive needs of the time. On the fundamental question of

Bohemian state right, it had constantly wavered between this and natural right, and had on different occasions, strongly upheld, or roundly condemned, the former. Similarly it had moved away from its earlier democratic standpoint, weakening in its support for universal suffrage, and had shifted from its earlier liberalism toward reactionary intolerance, including anti-Semitism and chauvinism.

Kramář was ready to acknowledge the serious crisis of the party, and did so frankly in a brochure published in 1906.[19] From the first the party had been composed of mixed elements and was divided as between its parliamentary representatives in Vienna and its leaders and newspaper in Prague. The attempt to pursue 'positive parliamentary work', as adopted at Nymburk, was, according to Kramář, frustrated by the radicalism of some of its members and the public, a radicalism promoted not only by Vienna's policy toward the Czechs, but also by Masaryk's bitter personal attacks on the party after leaving it (pp. 12–13). The willingness of Count Badeni in 1897 to meet Czech language demands made possible a positive policy of support of his government but his fall led to another wave of radicalism in the form of renewed parliamentary obstruction. He did not believe that an empty state-right radicalism would succeed in destroying the Monarchy; Bohemian state right could only be eventually achieved by the progressive fulfilment of Czech national needs. This required a 'policy of the free hand' (pp. 43–4) which would allow the party to decide on obstruction or on positive action according to need. The ultimate objective was the achievement of state right in the form of the autonomy of the lands of the Bohemian crown, with a Governor responsible to the Diet. Austria should be preserved but it must be a new and different Austria, based on the equal rights of all nations; only if this failed would Czechs have to seek independence outside Austria (pp. 52–8, 65, 75).

Although in important respects this was somewhat similar to Masaryk's position, the latter launched a counter-attack, in which he did not acknowledge this and made no attempt to analyze Kramář's views. He devoted most of his attention to the events of the early nineties, rejecting the charge that he had been responsible for the rise of radicalism, and placing the blame on Jan Vašatý and *Národní listy*, and on the party's policy of support for Badeni. He waxed vituperative in his condemnation of Gustav Eim, Vienna editor of the newspaper, who had promoted radicalism by his avid support of the Viennese authorities. He also criticized Josef Kaizl, who completely rejected state right. His earlier hopes of a reform of the party had proved vain, he lamented.[20]

MASARYK AND THE NATIONAL SOCIALISTS

The National Socialist party was founded in 1898 as an immediate reaction to the anti-state-right declaration of the Czech Social Democratic party made on their entry into the Vienna Parliament in the preceding year.[21] In a declaration in 1897 the embryonic party declared its firm attachment to Czech state right and condemned the Social Democratic standpoint. The foundation of the welfare of the Czech worker lay in the independence of the Czech nation. Social Democracy was condemned as an instrument of large-scale capital, and as a pioneer of Jewish-German culture. In the programme adopted in 1898, the new party called for self-determination and independence for the Czech nation and the realization of Czech state right through the federalization of Cisleithania. The Czech state should be based on the widest democracy, including universal suffrage and freedom of the press, association and assembly. The programme proposed reforms within the existing social order; it rejected class struggle and called for the unity of work and capital and the cooperation of all parts of the nation. Although the programme itself contained no open attack on Social Democracy and no anti-Semitic comments, Klofáč, in a long introduction, condemned Social Democracy and bitterly attacked the Jewish role in that movement. The revised programme of 1911 placed priority on national interests, democratization and social reforms, but reiterated the demand for state right and the restoration of a sovereign and independent state for the Bohemian lands. Noticeable this time was the absence of any criticism of Social Democracy or the Jews, and religious anti-Semitism was expressly repudiated.[22]

In the elections in 1901, the National Socialists opposed the Young Czechs, as well as the Social Democrats and the Masaryk Realists, and won five seats (in comparison with three for the Social Democrats). The party entered Parliament with a strong declaration in favour of state right. In the elections of 1907, allied with the Radical Progressives and the State Right Radicals, they obtained only three of the nine seats won by the group (the Social Democrats won 24); in 1911, in alliance with the Young and Old Czechs, their number rose to 14 (Social Democrats, 26).[23]

Václav Klofáč, the leading spirit of the new party, gradually moved away from Julius Grégr toward Masaryk. As a student he had admired Masaryk's independent attitude on the manuscripts and on other questions, and was favourably impressed by Masaryk's performance in Parliament after 1891 and by his books. He shared Masaryk's admiration for Havlíček, his advocacy of social justice and universal suffrage, his support of workers' strikes, and his rejection of clericalism. Differences, however, were already apparent in the party's programme of 1898, which differed from the Realist viewpoint in its stress on state right and its hostility towards social democracy. Masaryk condemned it as a programme of anarchy and its leader, Klofáč, as a demagogue. Nor was Klofáč enamoured of the Realist party; in 1901 he criticized Masaryk for his Austrianism (*Rakušanství*). Other conflicts of view emerged in ensuing years. The new party was radical, conducting constant demonstrations and obstruction in Parliament. Although denying he was racially anti-Semitic, Klofáč defended anti-Semitism for economic and national reasons. In these and other respects he parted company with Masaryk's more moderate approach to politics, and his condemnation of radicalism and anti-Semitism.[24]

In spite of differences, the National Socialists and Realists maintained relatively good relations until 1911, when the electoral coalition of the former with the Young Czechs drove them apart. In the United Czech Club in the newly-elected Parliament the National Socialists joined forces with the Agrarians, the Young and Old Czechs, and the National Catholics. On the other hand the Moravian People's and State Right parties, the Progressives and Realists formed the Association of Independent Progressives, which was headed by Masaryk and represented by him in the Czech Club. The coalition of National Socialists and Young Czechs was brief, however, and broke up when the former parted company with the Czech Club in voting against military credits.[25]

By 1912 Masaryk and Klofáč were drawing closer to each other, as a result of a certain congruence of views in their common campaign against Austrian foreign and military policy. Unlike Masaryk, however, Klofáč took part, with some reservations, in the Neo-Slavist movement, although he was critical of its leader, Kramář. He supported Russia in the Russo-Japanese war in 1904 and urged that Austria draw closer to Russia as against Germany. Like Masaryk (but unlike Kramář), he condemned the occupation of Bosnia-Hercegovina in 1908, and made many speeches in Parliament and in the Delegations, censuring Austria's Balkan policy.[26] He was a more militant critic of Austrian militarism, illustrated by his early advocacy of the use of the word 'zde' (here) instead of the German 'hier' in the Austrian army, and by his later crusade against other aspects of military policy. 'Not a soldier nor a penny for the army', was his slogan.[27]

During the Balkan wars, Klofáč waxed ever more radical, predicting war and the collapse of Austria, and sought to mediate between Serbia and Bulgaria. He became increasingly conspiratorial in his actions and engaged in secret conversations with the Russian Foreign Minister, Sazonov, in January 1914. Klofáč was much more open in his condemnation of the entire Austrian system and in his call for Czech independence, whereas Masaryk continued to calculate upon the Monarchy's existence and hoped for peaceful reform. As war grew more likely, however, the latter had begun inwardly to lose faith in the possibility of reform and, in theory, to recognize the admissibility of revolution.[28] As a result of this and Masaryk's friendly intervention in the case of Šviha within the National Socialist party, Klofáč and Masaryk met together to contemplate the possibility of closer cooperation.[29]

The Šviha affair arose from the charges made in *Národní listy*, in March 1914, that Karel Šviha, parliamentary leader of the National Socialist party, was a police spy. The ensuing violent controversy rocked the party to its foundations and became a divisive issue of Czech politics. A 'trial' by selected prominent Czech politicians showed that Šviha had indeed received money from the Prague police, and led to his resignation from Parliament. Masaryk believed him to be the victim of injustice, in this case of Young Czech political manipulation, and appeared as a witness on his behalf. Masaryk was not convinced of his innocence but believed that Šviha's main fault was even more heinous; he had engaged in secret negotiations with Archduke Ferdinand during which he provided the heir to the throne with a long memorandum on the rebuilding of the Monarchy on a trialist basis. Masaryk's intervention was welcomed by Klofáč, who had been personally shaken by the affair, but he was bitterly condemned as supporting a traitor by the Young Czechs and by the Social Democrats. The subsequent election of a National Socialist (supported by the National Socialists and a part of the Progressives) over a Social Democrat (supported surprisingly by the Young Czechs) worsened further Masaryk's relations with both the Young Czechs and the Social Democrats. As a result, his relations with both Kramář and Bohumír Šmeral, the Social Democratic leader, were shattered and Masaryk was more than ever isolated in Czech politics in the months preceding the outbreak of war.[30]

MASARYK AND SOCIAL DEMOCRACY

Masaryk's positive attitude to socialism and to the Czech Social Democratic movement has been fully explored elsewhere in this book.[31] He shared similar views with the Social Democrats on many issues – support of women's rights, opposition to clericalism and anti-Semitism, rejection of narrow nationalism and appreciation of the international aspects of the Czech question, and the struggle for universal suffrage. He was almost alone in expressing sympathy for their declaration in 1897 rejecting the goal of state rights.[32] However, Masaryk openly put the national question and the attainment of democracy to the forefront, whereas the Social Democrats placed the priority on social questions and were affiliated with the all-Austrian Social Democratic party. However, the autonomous position of the Czech socialists within that party, after 1899, their growing emphasis on Czech national interests, and the development of reformist or revisionist views within the entire Marxist movement, brought their views closer to Masaryk's. Even the more orthodox and international Bohumír Šmeral found some sympathy with Masaryk's views.[33]

Masaryk actively threw his support behind the Social Democrats in their campaign for universal suffrage in 1905 and after. This movement, he believed, reflected not only the Russian revolution against Tsarist autocracy in that year but also the national feelings stirred up by the Austrian government and Parliament, and especially the monarchy and aristocracy, which, like their Russian counterparts, failed to carry through necessary reforms. On 10 October 1905, Masaryk participated in a peaceful demonstration of 100 000 people outside the Bohemian Diet, calling for universal suffrage for that body, as well as for the Vienna Parliament. In a subsequent much smaller demonstration of 12 000 on 5 November, one young man was killed and many injured. Masaryk laid the blame for this bloodshed squarely on the government and the police. This event, and the funeral of the victim, Jan Hubáč, brought together representatives of all Czech parties, including not only the Social Democrats, National Socialists, and the People's party, but also the Young and Old Czechs, the Agrarians and others, in an uncommon display of unity. A common declaration gave support for universal suffrage and condemned the use of violence.[34]

In a number of speeches in 1905 and 1906 Masaryk openly acknowledged his sympathy for socialism and social democracy, and proposed cooperation with the latter in the forthcoming elections.[35] At a meeting in Prague, in 1905, for instance, he supported the demands of the workers, and declared that far from being traitors, they were saviours of the Czech nation. At Písek, in 1906, he acknowledged that although not a Marxist nor a social democrat, he felt that he was a socialist. His credo was: '1. always for the worker and the working people; 2. very frequently with socialism; and 3. seldom with Marxism'. His Progressive party was 'bourgeois', he acknowledged, but it must be democratic and radical in advocating social reforms.

In 1907, in a series of six lectures on socialism in Europe, he linked socialism with the world movement for democracy, which opposed absolutism and sought freedom and equality. It was based on a new concept of humanism, based on religion and morality, and embracing not only political and national, but also economic and social equality. Czech socialism was not something 'foreign' or 'unpatriotic', but was 'purely Czech', having deep Czech roots in Hussitism and in the 1848 revolution. The Czech nation was itself 'proletarian', with a majority of 'the small man'; our whole life, including our literature, was 'socialistic'. 'The Czech national question problem must be solved in a worker's fashion.'[36]

On the eve of the war Masaryk's relations with the Social Democrats cooled as a result of the Šviha affair (just noted) and the differing attitudes toward Austria-Hungary and the Czech national movement.[37]

MASARYK AND INTER-PARTY COOPERATION

The proliferation of political parties led to repeated efforts to coordinate them in the interest of common goals, sometimes in the form of a Czech National Council, as in 1900, or in electoral agreements, or in a common parliamentary club, as in 1907 and again in 1911. These cooperative actions had seldom embraced all parties, and had never included the Social Democrats; they were usually *ad hoc* groupings of conservatives or progressives, or of those favouring cooperation with the government or those preferring opposition, or even obstruction. These efforts to achieve unity invariably foundered on continuing disagreements, which were often expressed in voting in Parliament on the budget or specific legislation.[38]

From 1906 the idea of a 'concentration' of Czech political parties was often raised from all sides, although the actual content of such a coalition varied with the source. Masaryk favoured such a concentration, provided it was an organic one, based on the real differences within as well as between the parties, and reflected the dynamic development of each party. His ideal was a system of two basic parties, one conservative and undemocratic, the other progressive and democratic, but he had difficulty giving content to this scheme. The conservatives, he thought, would include the Old Czechs, the Young Czechs, the State Right Radicals, and the National Socialists. On the progressive side he could find only the Progressives, a certain left wing of the Young Czechs and even of the Old Czechs, the Social Democrats, and possibly the Agrarians. The organic fusion of parties was unlikely, but cooperation could nonetheless be achieved, especially on the all-important question of universal suffrage and in the struggle against clericalism.[39]

Whatever his disagreements with the other parties, and especially the Young Czechs, in practice Masaryk was ready to put aside differences in the interests of a common struggle for democracy. During 1906 and 1907, prior to the elections, he sought an even broader alliance of democratic parties in what he called a 'division of national work'. He actively put out feelers for cooperation with the Young Czechs, and also with the Social Democrats, but without success, except to some degree in Moravia. After the elections, in which three more or less equally strong parties were represented in the Reichsrat – the Agrarians, the Social Democrats and the Young Czechs – and his own party had only two representatives, Masaryk was ready to join a common parliamentary club which included even the Catholics, but excluded the Social Democrats. This broke down in the following year when a Young Czech and an Agrarian joined the government as ministers, and Masaryk and other parties persisted in opposition and remained outside the club.[40]

As we noted in Chapter 2, Masaryk was basically pluralist in his attitude toward politics. In a series of lectures in 1908, he restated the view, already voiced in 1899, that the formation of new parties and tendencies was a natural process, sometimes due to personal factors, or differences over tactics, but mainly due to differences of ideas and of social composition. He welcomed rather than feared the formation of new parties, often as a result of a breakaway from the Young Czechs, which would defend the interests of certain groups or classes, such as the workers, farmers and small traders.[41]

As of 1908, Masaryk's basic attitude toward the other parties had not changed. Although he recognized their legitimacy, he distinguished sharply between what he called the conservative and radical groups, and a vaguely defined centre. He was basically opposed to the conservative parties, including the Old Czechs, the Feudals[42] and the Clericals.[43] Having lost the leadership of the nation to the Young Czechs, the Old Czechs still represented narrow circles and was primarily a 'town hall' party, which dominated municipal bodies and economic institutions. Masaryk also ranked among the conservatives the Young Czechs, who had remained in a common club with the Old Czechs. Originally democratic and liberal and attracting many farmers, even some workers, and the progressive intelligentsia, it had become a party of 'notables', including in its ranks parliamentary deputies, ministers, high officials and mayors.

Also in the conservative camp were the Agrarians and the Clericals. The Agrarian party, founded in 1899, had by 1907–8 become the strongest Czech party in both the Reichsrat and the Diet, but had not shown itself to be capable of leading the nation. It was a party of the rural bourgeoisie and had views similar to those of the urban bourgeoisie.[44] The Christian Social party was, Masaryk said, a party of the priesthood, which was guided by the hierarchy, and thus linked with the aristocracy.

On the radical or left side, and in the democratic camp, there stood only the Social Democrats. Organized initially as a Marxist party, it had, as a result of the attainment of universal suffrage, adopted parliamentary practices, and this had led to revisionism in its programme. The National Socialist party, although it represented a part of the working class, was led by the petty bourgeoisie. Its anti-Semitism inclined it toward clericalism, and its extreme nationalism toward non-progressive elements. In elections it still tended to go with the governing party and even with the Old Czechs.

Toward the progressives, Masaryk had mixed feelings. He felt close to the Radical Progressive Party, and had united with a part of it, under Alois Hajn; similarly he had good relations with the Moravian Progressive party. But he did not approve the abstract state right programme or the extreme nationalism of Antonín Hajn and the State Right Progressive party. It was not enough nowadays to organize a party on a national basis, since all Czechs were 'nationalist'. Nor was the programme of state right a good divider between the parties.

For Masaryk the crucial question still remained whether a more united centre could be organized as a kind of loose coalition, including Young Czechs, Agrarians and his own Progressives as a kind of left wing. This was hindered, he believed, by the conservative character of the Young Czechs and their close link with the Old Czechs, and by the fact that they, as well as the Agrarians, were government parties and were still allied with the Clericals. Yet Masaryk, as we have seen, was not always certain as to how to classify individual parties and recognized potentialities for change in some cases. For instance, he even welcomed the Old Czech party's attempts to organize itself anew and believed that, if this were based on principle, it might have a good influence. Similarly, although Masaryk could not support Young Czech political practice, he admitted that he felt closer to them in programme. He also hoped that the Agrarian party would enlist the entire agricultural class and become democratic and progressive, a party of economic reform.

His own small party, the Progressive party, was described (in 1908) as being in essence a non-workers, bourgeois party, and having no aspirations to become a mass party. It would remain a party of inward politics, democratic and progressive in outlook, and would act as a kind of leaven or ferment, like the British Fabians, influencing all other parties.

In Parliament the party's tactics were usually those of opposition to the government of the day, but it did on occasion support a motion which served national interests.[45] Although Masaryk tried hard to achieve cooperation with other parties, he succeeded in attaining this only on an *ad hoc* basic, e.g. with the Social Democrats during the elections of 1907 and 1911; with the National Socialists in opposition to the Austro-Hungarian customs agreement in 1907, and with them, the State Right Progressives and the Social Democrats in 1908 in opposition to the Bosnian annexation; with the State Right Progressives, the National Socialists, and to some degree the Agrarians, in opposition to militarism, also in 1908; with the State Right Progressives and National Socialists against the war budget and war measures act in 1912; and with the Agrarians, the National Socialists, the State Right Progressives and the Moravian Progressives in opposing (by obstruction) the proroguing of the Bohemian Diet in 1913.[46]

In spite of repeated efforts Masaryk failed to establish any permanent alliance with other parties, even those on the same side of the political spectrum. His greatest achievement, in 1911, was the Association of Independent Progressives of which he was the spokesman. Down to the outbreak of war, his tiny party, of which he was the sole parliamentary representative and in which he had invested so much effort and hope, was an independent force which could not be ignored but remained more or less isolated from the main stream of Czech politics.[47]

5 Friend of the Slovaks

Tomáš Garrigue Masaryk was unusual among Czech politicians for his deep interest in the Slovaks of northern Hungary and for his persistent striving to assist them in their struggle for national rights. Most other Czech political leaders felt constrained by the Dualist System not to interfere in the affairs of the Hungarian Kingdom and bent their efforts almost exclusively to the attainment of Bohemian state right for the Czechs in Austria. Masaryk, however, was a bitter critic of the Dualist system and of the oppressive policies of the ruling Magyars with regard to their national minorities, especially the Slovaks. He also severely criticized the attitudes of the dominant Slovak Nationalist movement, and inspired the development of a new Slovak tactics for attaining national rights. He exerted a great influence on younger Slovaks, both those who were studying in Prague, and those at home in Slovakia. As on so many other issues, however, Masaryk was a somewhat isolated figure, supported by a relatively small fraction of Slovak nationalists and bitterly attacked by the Slovak leaders of the old school. Although a number of other Bohemian Czechs were concerned about the fate of the Slovaks, they were interested mainly in giving them a helping hand in literary and cultural fields and did not usually share Masaryk's more political approach.[1]

MASARYK'S SLOVAK ROOTS

Masaryk was born in 1850, in Hodonín, a Moravian village in what was known as Slovacko, or Moravian Slovakia, situated on the border of Slovakia proper and having a mixed population of Slovaks, Moravian Czechs, and Germans, and a medley of Czech and Slovak dialects. His father was a Slovak peasant, who spoke only Slovak; his mother was a Germanized Moravian Czech who spoke primarily German and had some difficulty with Slovak. Tomáš grew up as 'a real *Slovácký* lad', according to Nejedlý. As a boy and youth his language was Moravian or Slovak, and as an adult he could still speak Slovak. His name was spelt in different ways in the several dialects of the region (Masárik, Masařik, etc.) but as early as 1868 his own preference was Masaryk, a form more Slovak than Czech. He knew German well as a result of the influence of his mother and his early schooling, of wide reading of German literature, and of study and teaching in Vienna. He gradually developed a knowledge of literary Czech but did not at first write it perfectly. During his years in Vienna, as a student, Masaryk maintained his interest in his homeland by frequent visits and was active in Czech and Slovak student groups. When he went to Prague as university professor in 1882, he had consciously to make himself a Czech by acquiring a greater proficiency in the language. Thus it is not easy to identify Masaryk's real national origin or even his national consciousness. Although in his earlier years he sometimes called himself a Czech or a Moravian, in later life he claimed that he was Czech and Slovak, or 'half-Slovak' or, sometimes, that he was of pure Slovak origin.[2]

THE SLOVAK SITUATION

In 1900 Slovaks numbered approximately two million, about 10–12 per cent of the population of the Hungarian Kingdom. Largely agrarian in occupation, they were poor and socially disadvantaged, and had only a weakly-developed petty and middle bourgeoisie. The Magyars were the big landowners and dominated industry. The social misery of the Slovaks led to an enormous emigration – some 300 000 between 1899 and 1913. It also produced a strong tendency towards assimilation to the ruling nation, due in part to a striving for social advancement, but also to strict official policies of Magyarization in education and other spheres of life.[3]

For decades Slovaks had been uncertain as to their linguistic identity, some favouring the use of Czech, others, such as the Catholic priest Father Bernolák, a distinct Slovak language, based on the Western Slovak dialect, and others, such as the poet Jan Kollár, and the scholar, Pavel Josef Šafařík, advocating a unified language, alternately called Czechoslovak or Czechoslav. In the 1840's, under the influence of L'udovít Štúr, Slovaks opted for a separate Slovak language, based on the Central Slovak dialect, thus separating themselves from the Czechs linguistically.[4]

With the establishment of the Dualist system in 1867 Slovaks were also cut off from the Czechs by a political frontier and enjoyed no political autonomy in the regions of northern Hungary which they inhabited. In the revolution of 1848 they sided with Austria against Hungary and again in 1861, in a memorandum presented to the Emperor, they sought support from Vienna. After 1867 their only recourse was to appeal to Budapest, requesting legal recognition of the Slovaks and their language, and the establishment of an Upper Hungary Slovak Region, as set forth in the memorandum of 1861. Hungarian centralized absolutism had no sympathy for these claims and adopted, in breach of the Nationality Law of 1868, a policy of ruthless Magyarization of schools, offices and cultural institutions. A very limited suffrage, and Magyar manipulation of elections, as well as an initial policy of non-participation, blocked significant Slovak political participation. In four elections between 1869 and 1881 they had no seats in the Hungarian parliament; in a fifth, in 1872, only two. In the next five polls, between 1901 and 1907, Slovaks were able to elect a total of 15 representatives, with a high point of seven in 1906; this representation fell to three in 1910 and 1912.[5]

By 1900 the demands of the 1861 programme fell into desuetude and and the national movement recognized the integrity of the Hungarian kingdom. They focused their demands on the implementation of the 1868 nationality law and concentrated on cultural activities such as establishing Slovak schools. The memorandum of 1910, for instance, set forth language claims only. No help was forthcoming from Vienna or from the Czechs in Bohemia and Moravia, and Slovaks had to face the Budapest regime alone and almost unaided. Efforts to achieve cooperation with other national minorities met with some success in 1905 with the formation of a nationality party, grouping together in the Hungarian parliament eight Romanians, one Serb and one Slovak, Milan Hodža. In the elections of 1906 their number was increased to 25, including seven Slovaks.

THE SLOVAK POLITICAL SCENE

The Slovak political scene in the eighties and nineties was dominated by the conservative and nationalistic attitudes of an old guard of leaders, of whom the most influential figure was the poet, Svetozar Hurban-Vajanský. An impassioned defender of Slovak national interests, he enjoyed widespread respect and was several times imprisoned for his polemical articles. The base of the movement was the small town of Turčiansky Svätý Martin, where its newspaper, *Narodnie noviny*, was published and the cultural organization, Matica Slovenska (1863), was located. During these years, the Martin centre, in the tradition of Štúr, stood for the distinctiveness of the Slovak language and nation but offered no concrete proposals for the attainment of national goals. Pessimistic about achieving any improvement by its own efforts, the Martin centre was driven into a kind of fatalism and political passivity including, for some years, non-participation in elections. After 1900 it became more politically active and scored some modest electoral successes. The leaders, all intellectuals, had no close relations with the people, and were anti-Western and anti-modern in their thinking. Vajanský travelled often in Russia, admired Russian literature and was acquainted with Russian Pan-Slavists. Fascinated by the great Slav country, he believed that the only escape for Slovaks from a hopeless situation was some future catastrophic turn of events in which salvation would come from the East.

Vajanský, however, also associated himself with Slav solidarity among journalists, and even with the idea of Austro-Slavism, and was personally acquainted with a number of Czech cultural figures; he was at first on friendly terms with Masaryk and his family. Later, however, he came to distrust him and the Czech national movement, fearful of what he thought was their objective of a linguistic merging of the two nations. Convinced of their own rightness and fearful of national disunity, the Martin leadership condemned any criticism of their policies. They were characterized, according to Vavro Šrobár, by a 'tyrannical authoritarianism', and their paper became a kind of 'court of inquisition' which condemned alternative views as treasonable and a threat to national unity.

Slovak politics was inchoate and confusing.[6] The only political party before 1900 was the National Party, founded in 1872, which remained the main Slovak party down to the war. Although it enjoyed a kind of monopoly position, there were increasing signs of dissatisfaction with its policy, even among ardent supporters. Within the party there were other groups which did not at first form their own political parties, such as an agrarian wing, headed by Milan Hodža, the Catholics, and the Hlasists, who favoured cooperation between Czechs and Slovaks.

The Catholics for some years supported the aims of the Martin centre and did not seek to be an open opposition to it but they were highly critical of its Pan-Slavism and of its tactics. They were deeply interested in the social question and were much closer to the village people through their local parishes. Under Father Hlinka and others, and with their organ, *Katolické noviny*, they acquired considerable influence among the common people.

After 1900 the Slovak working class and the workers' movement represented another challenge to the National movement but also to the Catholics. Slovak workers in Budapest and Vienna, and later in Bratislava and Hodonín, turned towards socialism, mainly within the Hungarian Social Democratic party, which, however, often refused to support their national claims.

In 1905, two new parties were formed – the Social Democratic party, and the Slovak People's party. The latter was founded by some Catholics and leading Hlasists, to challenge both the National Party and the Catholic movement. In 1906 the party won six of the seven seats in parliament – two were Hlasists and four Catholics. The National Party obtained only one seat.[7] In 1913, after controversies with the National party, a new (Catholic) People's party was formed, under the leadership of Andrei Hlinka. Only in the final hours of the Monarchy, in May 1914, did the National party, the Hlasists and the Social Democrats (but not the Catholics) agree to establish a common Slovak National Council.[8]

A greater challenge to Martin was offered, in the late nineties, by a new generation, 'a new type of Slovak intelligentsia'who began to criticize the conservatism, provincialism and romantic Russophilism of the Martin centre and to look to the Czechs for guidance and support. In Vienna, Slovaks met with progressive, democratic, free-thinking and even socialist ideas. Masaryk introduced them to the Anglo-Saxon world and to an alternative conception of politics, involving morality, small-scale work, realism, and a critical attitude towards leadership and the established wisdom. Under his influence, they increasingly looked to the West for inspiration and sought salvation in their own efforts. As Šrobár put it, 'In politics we shall go to the people and together with the people we shall acquire power and rights for the nation. We freed ourselves from passivity; we ceased to wait for salvation from abroad; we shall awaken the people with newspapers, meetings and books.'[9]

The Hlasists[10], as they came to be called, followed their 'leader and teacher', Masaryk, advocating activism, 'small scale work of ordinary people', and democracy. This was, for Šrobár, the 'justified demand of the times', and involved personal freedom and freedom of expression, freedom of the press, association and assembly, and religious and national tolerance. Alliance with the Czechs was the only way to realize their goal of the moral, political, economic and cultural revival of Slovak life. There was, however, some difference among them on the language question. Some favoured a fusion of Czech and Slovak into one language. Šrobár, on the other hand, emphatically rejected a single literary language or any fusion of the two nations in a political sense. There were other sharp differences of opinion, which led to the forming of several factions, all of which, however, continued to pursue a Czechoslovak policy.

CZECH INTEREST IN THE SLOVAKS

From the eighties on, there gradually developed, among Czech cultural and professional persons, a substantial concern for the Slovaks and a desire to promote Czech and Slovak cooperation. Their aim was to aid the Slovaks in cultural, and later in economic, fields, and did not involve political cooperation. The most important manifestation of this attitude was the founding, in 1895, of *Českoslovanská Jednota* (Czechoslav Association), which sought to spread knowledge of the Slovaks among Czechs by lectures and a journal, and to support the former in their cultural strivings by sending books and periodicals, by supporting Slovak publications, by assisting the study of Slovaks in Czech schools in Moravia, and by aiding Slovak banking institutions. This organization was limited in numbers, having, in 1912, 2361 members, of whom 140 were Slovaks. After a meeting of Czechs and Slovaks in the Slovak spa, Luháčovice, in 1905, there followed annual meetings down to 1913 designed to promote better understanding of the two national groups. According to the historian, Bokes, the Luháčovice meetings denied the goal of Czechizing Slovaks and recognized a dual literary language. From 1905 Jednota was more active in spreading knowledge about Slovakia, organizing, in that year, a conference of friends of Slovakia in Hodonín, sponsoring in 1907 a new periodical, *Naše Slovensko*, in Prague, and organizing lecture tours by Slovak leaders. The bloody police repression of a Slovak gathering in Černová in 1907 stirred up great indignation among Czechs and led to many protests against Hungarian policy. This tragedy also awakened interest abroad, in Norway (the writer, B. Bjørnson), in England (R. W. Seton-Watson), in France (E. Denis), in Russia (Lamansky) and in other parts of the Monarchy (in Austria, Karl Renner; in Hungary, O. Jaszi; and among Austrian Slavs) and also among American Slovaks.[11]

There were other efforts to bring Czechs and Slovaks together, e.g. among Catholics, especially in Moravia, and among industrial workers. In the Social Democratic movement there was frequent interaction and cooperation, and Czech Social Democratic leaders, such as F. Soukup and F. Němec, and the party itself, expressed sympathy for their Slovak comrades and gave support to their publications. Masaryk and the Hlasist Šrobár, as well as Milan Hodža, were not unsympathetic to the Slovak socialists. Masaryk's critical view of Marxism influenced their conception of socialism along evolutionary or reformist lines.[12] Hodža also established contacts with the Czech agrarians.

CZECH POLITICAL PARTIES AND THE SLOVAKS

Leading Czech politicians were on the whole indifferent to the Slovak question. Ladislav Rieger, the 'grand old man' of Czech politics, blamed the Slovaks for separating linguistically from the Czechs and believed that they should Czechize their language use. He accepted the reality of the Dualist system and concentrated on Bohemian state-right objectives within Austria. Young Czechs, such as Josef Kaizl and Karel Kramář, were also at first indifferent. The latter, in spite of his Neo-Slav approach to politics and foreign affairs, did not sympathize with the Russophilism and Pan-Slavism which were prevalent among Slovaks at the time.[13]

Most Czech political parties did not even touch on the Slovak question in their programmes and were consumed with their goal of achieving Bohemian state right. The tragic events in Černová in 1907, however, aroused greater interest, expressed by Czech deputies in parliament, and also in the programmes of the Social Democratic and the National Socialist Parties.

The parties with which Masaryk was associated endorsed his view that the case for Czech independence within Austria should be based rather on natural than on historic state right but did not openly argue for Czechoslovak unity in an Austrian federation. In fact the programmes paid meagre attention to the Slovaks and the Slovak question. The People's party programme of 1900, for instance, recognized the rights of the lands of the Hungarian Crown, and merely noted that Slovaks, like other Hungarian nationalities, were suppressed in their linguistic, national, economic and cultural relations (p. 14). There was a brief mention of Palacký's idea in 1848 of joining Slovak and Bohemian land (p. 71). After the adoption of the programme, Jan Herben read a letter from Slovakia, which begged the congress not to forget the Czech nation under the Tatras. The task of the 'Czechoslav' realists was to solve the practical results of the unity of the Czech nation for the Slovaks, too, and should not forget a programme, if not at present political – then at least cultural and economic – for Slovakia. Although the Slovaks would have to carry it out themselves, there should be a single programme (p. 194).[14]

Progressive Party programmes in 1900 and 1906 were a little more emphatic. In both reference was made to the fact that a quarter of 'our nation' lives in Hungary, and while recognizing the political position of the Hungarians, 'we demand full nationality protection for the Slovaks and for all non-Magyar nations, especially the Slavic'.[15] In 1912 the Progressive Party, repeating the reference to Slovak oppression from the 1900 Realist programme, went on to declare:

We consider the Hungarian Slovaks a part of the Czech nation, but we recognize their special position, given by political conditions, and do not deny them the right to speak of a 'Slovak nation'. We accept the literary Slovak language as a fact but we deem it more suitable for Slovaks to use Czech for scholarly writings and Slovak for other literature and for journalism.[16]

MASARYK ON THE SLOVAKS

As early as 1895, in *The Czech Question*, Masaryk described the Slovak question as 'of the greatest importance' for Czechs. From his days as a student in Vienna, he had developed a deep interest in Jan Kollár, the apostle of Slavic reciprocity, whose thinking had had a deep impact on the Czech awakening as well as on Slovak thought. In *The Czech Question*, Masaryk ascribed great significance to the fact that Kollár was himself a Slovak and that his idea of Slavic reciprocity was born among Slovaks. He shared Kollár's admiration of the virtues of devoutness, hard work, innocent cheerfulness, love of language, and peace-loving tolerance which he attributed to all Slavs, and which, thought Masaryk, were possessed by the Slovaks. He recognized that they had faults, as did other nations, but this did not prevent a 'natural love for one's own people, language and nation'. Both Czechs and Slovaks, he felt, could find a an escape from their tribal smallness by uniting with all Slavs.[17]

A year later, in his book on Havlíček, Masaryk summarized the latter's views on the need to awaken the national consciousness not only of Bohemia, but also of Moravia, Silesia and Slovakia. Havlíček condemned the linguistic, national and cultural independence of what he called the individual 'Czechoslav' (*Československský*) tribes and lands. He ascribed to the Slovaks a purer national consciousness and believed that they would become 'the leader of the whole Czechoslav nation in political, literary and public affairs generally'. The Moravian Slovaks, occupying a transitional position between Czechs and Slovaks, should be considered the real centre of the Czechoslav nation. Havlíček recognized the right of the Slovaks to their own culture, but was opposed to the establishment of a separate Slovak language which, in view of the struggle for life and death in which the Bohemians, Moravians and Slovaks were engaged, would be suicidal. Although Masaryk did not explicitly identify himself with Havlíček's views, he did not criticize them and, except for Havlíček's condemnation of a separate Slovak language, presumably agreed with them.[18]

In discussing the events of 1848 in this book, Masaryk referred to Palacký's plan of an Austrian federation based on natural rights, a principle which would have grouped the Czech parts of Bohemia, Moravia and Silesia, together with the Hungarian Slovaks, in what he called the 'Czechoslav' group. He noted that Palacký had wavered as between this and a federation based on the historic rights of the kingdoms and lands (which would have left Slovaks in the Hungarian kingdom), and had ultimately given up the former plan. Havlíček had also wavered, according to Masaryk, but favoured an ethnic federation, a position which seemed more to Masaryk's liking.[19]

Masaryk was not himself a passionate defender of the Bohemian state-right concept, which other parties regarded as central to their goal of freeing the Czech nation. In his essay on natural and historical rights, written in 1900, Masaryk severely criticized dependence on ancient historic rights and argued that the natural right of a nation was a better basis for the goal of national self-determination, and for an Austrian federation. Masaryk made no direct reference to the Slovaks in this essay, and did not explicitly use the two concepts as a basis for including Czechs and Slovaks together in a federated Austria.[20]

In a later lecture on the problem of a small nation, in 1905, Masaryk made explicit what was clearly implied in his earlier writings, namely that he regarded the Slovaks as part of the Czech nation.[21] In a parliamentary speech, in 1907, in which he condemned the inhuman treatment of the Slovaks by the Magyars, he also referred to the two million Slovaks as 'belonging to our nationality', as 'co-nationals'. In a speech in Budapest in 1911 he again asserted that the existence of a separate Slovak language did not stand in the way of Czech–Slovak reciprocity. Recognizing the reality of the Hungarian state in which the Hungarian minority ruled, he urged that the best way to resist Magyarization was for the Slovaks to make themselves independent politically, culturally, nationally and socially.[22]

Unlike Havlíček, however, Masaryk did not seek to eliminate the separate Slovak language which had developed, and did not regard its existence as an obstacle to the the conception of a single Czechoslovak nation. There were other active Slovakophiles, such as Karel Kálal and František Pastrnek, who urged the Slovaks to abandon a separate language and adopt Czech. So also did the Slovak scholar, Jaroslav Vlček, K. Salva, editor of *Slovenskélisty,* and the young Slovak doctor, Johann Szmetanay. Masaryk, however, held to the view that the Czech and Slovak languages should continue to exist separately – a view which was shared by the poet, Pavel Orszagh-Hviezdoslav and other Slovaks, and that this linguistic difference was subordinate to common values and traditions.[23]

MASARYK'S INFLUENCE ON THE SLOVAKS

Masaryk was apparently not associated with the Jednota, but exerted his influence as an individual, and especially through his friendship with Slovak students at the University. The latter formed an organization, Detvan, as early as 1882, a tiny group which had only 268 active members during its thirty years of existence. For the first ten years it was supportive of the views of the National party in Slovakia. Gradually, however, Slovak students who attended his lectures and visited his home came under Masaryk's influence. Discussions with Masaryk in 1889 or 1890 did not lead to the publishing of a journal, as he had recommended. It had a longer-term effect on some of them, such as Vavro Šrobár, president of Detvan, who began to visit Masaryk often and to read *Čas* regularly. Other Slovak students studied Masaryk's works, such as *The Czech Question, The Social Question,* and *How to Work.* They were attracted by his critical attitude and and were thus gradually weaned away from their devotion to the National party and from its Russophilism. After Šrobár's departure from Prague, Detvan was often divided in its views and tended to revert to a pro-Martin orientation; later, under the influence of Milan Štefánik, an active member, and later its president, it swung back to a Czech orientation.[24]

Among other students who fell under the influence of Masaryk was Anton Štefánek, who has described his visits to the Masaryk household and the impact of Masaryk's ideas and of his methods of teaching. Štefánek, and others, were led, he said, to criticize the Martin leadership and to accept the idea of Czech and Slovak cooperation. Masaryk also gave them a new view on nationalism, religion, socialism and the social question, and morality, and led them to fight against Russophile messianism, anti-Czech separatism, and political passivity. At the same time Štefánek was of the belief that the two literary languages could coexist within a single nation.[25]

Another Slovak, who was befriended by Masaryk during his fifteen years as a poor student and who became a close personal friend, was Milan Štefánik. He was a bitter foe of the Martin leadership and an ardent Hlasist and Realist, passionately supporting Masaryk's ideas of Czechoslovak unity and cooperation. He contributed many articles to *Čas* and during 1902–3 was its Slovak correspondent. He was also active in *Českoslovanská Jednota* and strove to promote closer relations between Czechs and Slovaks.[26]

Another convert to Masaryk's point of view was Milan Hodža, who had studied in Budapest but had been influenced by Masaryk. He was strongly favourable to his progressive and democratic approach, to his ideas of *drobná práce,* and to Realism and, like him, tried to subordinate the question of language to broader social and democratic objectives. Later, as editor of *Slovenský týždeník,* his was a strong voice for unity of action by Czechs and Slovaks, especially in the economic field. As a member of the Hungarian Parliament from 1906 to 1910, he spoke up for Slovak interests and, as a leading figure of the Nationality party, developed close relations with the Romanians, Serbs and other national minorities. Hodža was a bitter critic of Hungarian feudal society and the policy of Magyarization, and was in close touch with left-oriented Magyars, including the Social Democrats and agrarian spokesmen. In spite of these leanings, Hodža cooperated closely with Archduke Franz Ferdinand, heir to the throne, in an effort to achieve a revision of the Dualist system which would destroy Magyar hegemony and enlarge the position of the non-Magyar nationalities. By 1914, according to Gogolák, Hodža foresaw the collapse of the Monarchy and envisaged a political union of Czechs and Slovaks.[27]

Among Catholics, the parish priest, Father Andrei Hlinka, was a harsh critic of Magyarism and of the Jews, and a fervent advocate of Slovak national interests. Initially he favoured unity of Czechs and Slovaks and was well-known to the former through lectures in Bohemia and Moravia. His role in the Černová events and his imprisonment made him a popular hero among Slovaks and also among Czechs. After his return from prison, however, Hlinka began increasingly to oppose Czech influences, and rejected any cooperation with Masaryk and the Hlasists.[28]

Masaryk's ideas also stirred up interest in other Slovak communities, e.g. in Vienna and in Budapest. In Vienna at the end of the century, it was reported by Anton Stefánek, there were sharp quarrels between the supporters of Vajanský and Masaryk and the latter remained in the minority. Many students were strongly critical of Czechs in general, expressing what he called Czechophobia. In Budapest Czechs and Slovaks had few contacts and seemed (in retrospect) to Štefánek to belong to two cultural worlds. Their organizations were dominated by conservative Slovak nationalism, and Masaryk's ideas were known to only a few individuals. In America Masaryk gave his views during his visits and they were also presented by visiting Slovaks and by Czech organizations. In the years before the war, according to Štefánek, the idea of Czech and Slovak cooperation and unity prevailed over the views of the Slovak League.[29]

MASARYK AND THE HLASISTS

Masaryk had his first direct contact with Slovaks in their homeland during summer holidays spent in the village of Bystřička in western Slovakia, a practice which he began in 1887 and continued, with only a brief interruption during his three years in Parliament, down to 1902. This enabled him to deepen his knowledge of Slovak conditions and to become acquainted with many young Slovaks, including Hurban-Vajanský and his family. Masaryk was made aware of the reality of the Slovak situation in 1893, when, with his family, he went to Kollár's birthplace but was barred by the police from attending the ceremony in honour of Kollár's 100th birthday.[30]

A decisive event was a meeting with several young Slovaks, including Šrobár, in Bystřička in 1897, to discuss the publication of a journal, eventually founded later that year as *Hlas*. Agreement was reached on the main points of a wide-ranging political programme which Šrobár filled out in greater detail and which remained the basis of action by the Hlasists in ensuing years.[31] As the most extensive summary of Masaryk's thinking on the Slovak question and as the expression of a consensus between Masaryk and young Slovaks, this deserves to be summarized in some detail.

The sketch included a severe criticism of Hungary as 'a medieval feudal state'. and described its Magyarization policy as 'moral violence'. The Slovak people were 'overwhelmingly agrarian and were living almost in serfdom'. The Jews were instruments of the government and were usurers, so that anti-Semitism was justified. The Church was a bureaucratic institution, but was struggling against Hungarian liberalism and the Hungarian state. The clergy must become nationally-minded, understand the suffering of the people and seek to raise them morally.[32]

The programme also attacked the attitudes of the national leaders in Martin, arguing that polemics should not be avoided in the interest of unity and that criticism would strengthen the nation. Pan-Russianism and Slavic cosmopolitanism must be replaced by the idea of Slavic reciprocity in the cultural sense of Kollár and Šafařík. Relations with the Czechs must also be based on common ideas; language was not an obstacle to Czechoslovak reciprocity. The language question was not the supreme goal of the nation, although it was 'a beloved and precious medium in the family, in literature, and in communications'. But it was impossible at present, or even in the distant future, to use Slovak in scholarship and science. Kollár had called for 'reciprocity of ideas and of people, not of language'. Language was not 'an obstacle to Czechoslovak reciprocity'. Nor was it anti-state to cultivate Czechoslovak reciprocity.[33]

The political points in the programme called for the recognition of dualism and the integrity of Hungary, and of Magyar as the state language and as a common medium of communications. But Slovak should be used in office, church and school in the nationality areas. Slovaks must seek parliamentary representation and develop a national programme. Its aims should be universal suffrage, local autonomy, a progressive tax, reform of the judiciary and administration, free instruction, including Slovak high schools and a university, and freedom of the press and of assembly.

The publication of *Hlas,* a 'monthly for literature, politics and the social question', which began in 1898, and lasted until 1904, was a turning-point away from the Martin leadership and toward Masaryk and Czechophilism. Edited at first by Pavol Blaho, it grouped together a small group of young Slovaks, perhaps no more than 30, including Šrobár, Hodža, Štefánek, and Štefánik. Among its collaborators were Catholic priests, including at first Father Andrei Hlinka, and some Protestant clergy. Although the majority of the Slovak intelligentsia remained pro-Martin, the paper served to awaken Slovak youth to a new attitude toward Hungary and the Czechs; according to Štefánek, 'it revolutionized the hearts and minds of the young generation in particular'. Although it perished for financial reasons in 1904, it was succeeded by other publications written in the same spirit.[34]

The first issue contained an editorial by Šrobár which was written entirely in the spirit of the Bystrička programme and of Masaryk's thinking on politics. 'We want first and foremost that the Slovak people should be reborn morally'. He bitterly attacked the Slovak intelligentsia, who were shut off from the people and cared little for their interests. They 'stood isolated among two and a half million people, bound by the power of the state, caught in the Jewish spider net, lacking civic consciousness and spiritually and materially uncultured'. Openly declaring war on Martin and Russophilism, Šrobár called for realism, criticism, work among the people, and economic policies. Above all he stood firm for Czechoslovak reciprocity, for 'the cultural and national unity of the Czechoslovak nation'. As he wrote elsewhere, this did not mean the formation of a single literary and written language. The political and linguistic unity in which Czechs and Slovaks had once lived had been dissolved; 'now we speak of two nations which ought, however, to cultivate the closest mutuality between themselves'.[35]

Even after *Hlas* ceased to publish, in 1904, other Slovak newspapers appeared, for instance *Slovenský týždeník* (M. Hodža) and *Prúdy* (A. Štefánek, Pavol Blaho, and Vavro Šrobár) which, in spite of some changes, stuck in large measure to the original *Hlas* programme and continued to work in the spirit of Masaryk. B. Pavlů, for instance, in an article in *Prúdy*, in 1910, thanked Masaryk as 'a teacher of young Slovaks who led them toward inner strength, culture and an eternal struggle for truth and justice'. Hodža and Štefánek cooperated with Masaryk in the struggle for universal suffrage.[36]

MASARYK'S CRITICS AND DEFENDERS

Masaryk's 'interference' in Slovak affairs earned him bitter abuse in some Slovak circles and few accolades among Czechs. As the target of Masaryk's sharp criticism, the Martin nationalists felt their position of leadership threatened and in the early nineties turned against Masaryk and his ideas. Vajanský came to regard Masaryk as the 'poisoner' of the minds of young Slovaks and as 'an evil spirit of foreign origin.' In 1901 he wrote a novel, *Kotlín*, which was a polemic against realism, Hlasism, and Masaryk. In another vitriolic diatribe against Masaryk, Vajanský wrote of him as 'arid in spirit', 'a half-comic, half-tragic figure', 'a moderate radical', 'a non-Czech Czech', 'a humanist with a rapacious and revengeful inhumanity', 'a man without past or present. ...who wished to destroy everything and to spit on himself'.[37]

Masaryk was regarded with suspicion as a symbol of 'Pan-Czechism' or 'Czechization'. His condemnation was also motivated by fear and dislike of his ideas in general – in particular his Westernism, progressivism, philo-Semitism, as it was called, and above all his religious views. His strong criticism of the Catholic Church and his devotion to Hussitism earned him the reputation of being anti-religious, even an atheist, which particularly turned Hlinka against him. The clerical press mounted a vicious campaign against him as an 'apostate' and 'a religious renegade' (*odroň*) and as 'a spiritual poisoner of Slovak youth'. His critique of Russophilism was regarded as anti-Slav, and his views on Czechoslovak unity were interpreted as anti-Slovak.

Hungarian circles, while remaining strongly opposed to Slovak nationalism, were afraid of Masaryk as representing the even greater danger of Czech and Slovak unity and as typifying Western progressive thought, anathema to the Magyar ruling class. The Magyar government gave its full support to a book, originally written in Magyar, by a Samuel Czambel, a 'patriotic Slovak', who warned against Czech influence and Czech–Slovak solidarity, and defended a separate Slovak language. Another Slovak, František Jehlička, originally a

Hlasist, later a professor at the University of Budapest, attacked Masaryk as 'a materialist, a non-believer, a fornicator and liar, and a destructive element' and warned Slovak Catholics and Protestants against supporting him.

There were others who protested against the conservative views of the Martin leaders and were sympathetic to Masaryk's ideas.[38] This was notably the case of the poet, Pavel Országh-Hviezdoslav, whose work Masaryk had made known in the Slavic world. Although he was of noble origin, Hviezdoslav developed a close friendship with Masaryk by correspondence and by exchange of visits. A strong believer in the value of a separate Slovak language, he also accepted the idea of the necessity of Czech help for the benighted Slovaks. Under pressure from Vajanský, however, he wavered in his support of the Hlasists but did not fully approve Vajanský's course.[39]

An anonymous author, writing under the pseudonym *Mea kulpinský*, published in 1901 a brochure which expressed the belief that Slovak misery was due not only to Magyar repression but also to negative features of the Slovaks themselves. The only hope could come from Czechoslovak political and cultural unity; together Czechs and Slovaks formed a single nation of seven-and-a-half million. The two peoples spoke different dialects of the same language, and the latter should adopt the Czech language, culture and literature.[40]

ČAS AND NAŠE DOBA ON SLOVAKIA

Masaryk's lively interest in the Slovaks was expressed in his journals, *Čas* and *Naše doba*. From its founding in 1894, *Naše doba* published occasional articles and reports, some of them by Masaryk himself. For example, in 1901 he severely condemned Vajanský's novel, *Kotlín*, as a tendentious polemic against new currents of Slovak thought. In 1904, in a brief note, he lamented the fact that the Czechs had no programme touching on 'two millions of our own people' living under foreign rule. His articles on more general themes, such as Kollár, Czech history, Marxism, and religion, undoubtedly also influenced Slovak thinking.[41]

An important series of anonymous articles in 1901 were thought to have been written by Masaryk himself but were in fact the work of a close friend of his, a Moravian schoolteacher, Karel Kálal, a tireless protagonist of Slovakophilism. The articles ruthlessly dissected the weaknesses of the Slovaks themselves, especially the intelligentsia, who were lazy and pleasure-seeking, and remote from the ordinary people. The author denounced the Martin leadership, including Vajanský personally, and its newspaper, *Narodnie Noviny*. The latter offered no programme for national work or for the moral rebirth of the nation, writing, for instance, nothing about the disease of alcoholism. The newspaper cultivated political and Slavic romanticism, especially Russophilism; it neglected Czech affairs and made no mention of Czechoslovak reciprocity. According to the author, the paper descended to the lowest level of abuse, describing, for instance, an article in *Čás* as filled with 'filthy passion, incessant poison, and devilish and sinister attacks', which were said to be far worse than anything written by Magyarones, Jews or paid informers. The Hlasists were attacked as 'hooligans, fools and traitors'.

The author offered a working programme for the future, which stressed moral regeneration (a fight against alcoholism, prostitution, etc.), cultural training of the people through books and lectures, economic associations, and electoral activity. He proposed a meeting of Slovaks and Czechs for discussion of a working Slovak programme and a programme of Czechoslovak cultural reciprocity (which led to the Luhácovice meeting mentioned above).[42]

POLITICAL UNION OF CZECHS AND SLOVAKS

Even among those most wedded to the idea of Czech–Slovak reciprocity, the idea of a political union of the two nations was not regarded with favour. For instance, in 1902, Šrobár wrote: 'There cannot be any question of a fusion in the political sense; we are citizens of the Crown of St Stephen and have recognized this publicly; we are obliged to defend the integrity of our homeland (*krajina*) against anyone.' Such romanticism and utopianism could only bring about persecution from powerful enemies and make the struggle for the rights of the Slovak people more difficult. 'Therefore we expressly reject *a priori* all debates on our fusion with the Czech nation in the political sense.'[43]

On the Czech side there was almost no open discussion of Czech–Slovak political unification. Masaryk, for instance, although a strong protagonist of an Austrian federation, did not openly advocate the Palacký and Havlíček idea of a Czech–Slovak entity. But in 1906, in reviewing a book by Aurel Popovici, Masaryk complained that his proposal for a federation of the Monarchy neglected the Bohemian state right and on the other hand, proposed the unacceptable idea that Czechs and Slovaks, as 'members of one and the same nationality, would form two separate states'.[44] On the initiative of Jednota, a meeting of representatives of all Czech political parties in Prague in April 1914, organized by the Czech banker Rudolf Pilat, protested against the persecution of Slovaks and Romanians in Hungary and spoke in favour of a federation of the entire monarchy, with common state citizenship, on the basis of the equality of all nations in Hungary.[45]

As war drew nigh, Slovaks began to turn their thoughts towards a unified Czech and Slovak state. In 1913 leaders of the National Party, in a meeting with the Archduke Franz Ferdinand, reached an agreement which was incorporated in the party programme.[46] In a questionnaire conducted by *Prúdy* in 1914 a number of prominent Slovaks declared themselves in favour of national unity, even at the eventual price of abdicating written Slovak, and pledged themselves to work for Czechoslovak unification.[47] One year before the outbreak of war, Rudolf Pilat, a strong advocate of Czech–Slovak solidarity, in a letter of September 1913 to a leading American Slovak, Milan Getting, wrote: 'Confidentially we can inform you that on the Czech side there have been preparations that in the event of the defeat of Austria, Bohemia, Moravia and Silesia would be joined with Slovakia in one state.'[48] In another letter in May 1914, Pilat admitted that, although the Slovaks could not publicly demand more than a so-called Slovak region within the framework of Hungary, Hodža and Štefanek, he reported, thought it would be better if the Czechs themselves publicly proclaimed the programme of Havlíček for a union of Bohemia, Moravia, Silesia and Slovakia in one organic part of the empire'.[49]

The same idea was broached by A. Štefánek in a letter to Getting, on 19 May 1914: 'Slovaks are striving for cultural, economic, social and political independence, in the sense of a Czechoslovak agreement; they are striving to unite the territories of the Bohemian crown, Moravia, Silesia and Slovakia in one autonomous entity.' This was the ideal, he said, which might be realized after the death of the Monarch and the succession of Franz Ferdinand. In what would appear to be another part of the letter Štefánek advocated cooperation with the Czechs, not only in the cultural and economic, but also in the political field. A number of Czech politicians, including Kramář, he said, had broken off relations with Magyar politicians during the meeting of the Delegations in that year. On the other hand, Slovaks and Czechs were meeting daily, he reported; only the latter were defending us in the Delegations and in Parliament. 'They are our deputies.'[50]

The shift in Slovak thinking was indicated in the revised programme of the Slovak National party in 1914. Although it did not openly urge Czech and Slovak political union, it spoke of the centuries of a common literary language and common culture, and cooperation of Slovaks with 'our brother Czechs', including half a million Slovaks in Moravia. 'We demand the closest cultural and economic union with them so that we would each have an irreversible conviction that what is Czech is also Slovak, and vice versa. Culturally we are one, we have one literature, written in two literary languages – that is our credo.' 'The closest Czech–Slovak reciprocity is our programme'.[51]

A climax·was reached, on the eve of war, at a meeting of Czech and Slovak leaders in Vienna during the Delegation meetings in May 1914. Slovaks agreed among themselves on the formation of a Slovak national council (as above, p. 67) and also held talks with Czech leaders, at which they agreed to act jointly against Hungary and to coordinate their policies with the Serbs, Croats and Romanians.[52]

CONCLUSIONS

Before 1914 one could distinguish at least four tendencies among Slovak political activists. There was, first, the declining but still influential conservative Nationalist group, representing the traditions of Štúr and typified by Vajanský, with his passionate faith in the Slovak nation. In his view the Slovaks were 'an ethnical group....endowed with all the qualifications, all the criteria of an autochthonous nation, with its own territory, personality, language, customs, ethnographical boundaries, history, merits, and sacrifices, its loyalty tried and tested in war and peace'. The second was the powerful Catholic tendency, representing in some degree the tradition of Father Bernolák, and personified by Hlinka, which supported Slovak national rights but within a clerical framework and had a widespread influence among ordinary people. Third was the group which favoured a Czechoslovak orientation, in the tradition of Kollár, Havlíček and Šafařík, as typified by Šrobár and Hodža, which, by their own admission, enjoyed more limited support among Slovaks, even among the younger intelligentsia. Finally, there was the relatively marginal social democratic tendency which favoured Czech and Slovak cooperation but within the framework of Marxist internationalism. Within each of these groups there were, of course, nuances of difference, and often sharp conflicts. The relative strength of the several tendencies is difficult to estimate in the absence of evidence of public opinion polls or even of electoral strength. Of the three deputies in the Hungarian parliament after 1910, for instance, two represented the Catholic tendency (Hlinka and F. Styčak) and one the Czechoslovak orientation (P. Blaho).[53]

The role of Masaryk in Czech–Slovak relations before 1914 has been variously interpreted in accordance with party or ideological standpoints. Some extreme Slovak nationalists ignored Masaryk altogether or downgraded his influence. Marxists in the 1950s treated him as a mere exponent of Czech bourgeois interests, but in the 1960s and 1970s, some of them dealt with his role with more objectivity. Slovakophiles among Czechs, or Czechophiles among Slovaks, emphasized Masaryk's impact; those writing after the establishment of a Czechoslovak state often tended to glorify his role. Scholars without party or ideological affiliation argued that Masaryk exerted a powerful influence on some Slovaks, but acknowledged that his Slovak followers remained a minority.

Differences of opinion as to Masaryk's views on the Slovak question are due in part to a certain ambiguity in his utterances and also to some changes in his attitude over time. There is no doubt that he was a strong advocate of Czech and Slovak cooperation, both to buttress the position of the Czechs in Austria-Hungary and to assist the Slovaks in their plight in Hungary. Yet, while recognizing a distinct Slovak identity, he believed that the Slovaks and Czechs formed a single nation, separated only by differences in language, history and culture. On the language question he acknowledged that the two languages were different, and believed that no fusion was likely or desirable. But he also stressed the desirability, at least for the immediate future, of the use of the Czech literary language by the Slovaks. Nor did Masaryk advocate before 1914 the political unification of Czechs and Slovaks in an independent state or even within Austria-Hungary.

Masaryk enlarged on his view of the language question in 1917 when, in retrospect, he wrote that at the Bystrička meeting in 1897, he had 'laid great stress that the language question should not be exalted. Let the Slovaks write as they wish. The main thing is that we are in fact one, for the Slovak understands the Czech, and the Czech understands the Slovak. From the nineteenth century Slovaks were cut off from us and did not have their own independent political growth, so that they held on to older forms of their language and their dialects. Now that their language has been accepted as a literary language, let it remain so, as far as they recognize it as necessary. I know that Kollár and Šafařík were against separation and even Hurban-Vajanský was at one time in favour of linking them together. This linkage, however, can and must be achieved politically. Let us leave language development to future generations. Let us reckon with facts as they are and bring them into organic harmony. Slovak exists and may not and must not stand in our way'.[54]

As one of his supporters, Karel Kálal, wrote in 1930, Masaryk was several decades ahead of the nation, the greater part of which did not understand him. But there can be no doubt that he awakened many Czechs to the importance of the Slovak question. Similarly among Slovaks, although again his appeal was limited to a part of the nation, his influence on younger Slovaks was great and he guided them away from national separatism towards Czechoslovak cooperation. As Šrobár wrote in 1910, as a result of his influence, the younger generation freed itself from the influence of the old guard and began to think and act in the spirit of his views. He was 'the father of a movement which had a beneficial influence on the vitalization of the Slovak people'; his disciples regarded him as 'their teacher', and 'loved him as the best friend of the Slovak people'.[55]

Viewed in historical perspective, it is undoubtedly true that Masaryk unwittingly prepared the ground for the unification of Czechs and Slovaks in a single state in 1919. Another of his disciples, Anton Štefánek, writing in 1931, stated that the 'Masaryk school performed a significant historic task'; 'without the direct intervention of T. G. Masaryk, events in Slovakia before the war and during the war would hardly have moved in the direction in which they did'. Writing elsewhere in the same year, he expressed the view that although the Slovak Hlasists did not identify themselves entirely with Czech realism, and in many things worked differently, they did constitute a movement which was 'purely Masarykian and prepared the ground, frequently unconsciously, for a fateful time'.[56]

6 Foe of Anti-Semitism

A classic example of Tomáš Garrigue Masaryk's courage and non-conformity was his defence of Leopold Hilsner, a poor Jew, who was condemned to death for murder in 1899.[1] In performing this deed Masaryk stood almost alone in the face of overwhelming public hostility and became the target of hatred and vicious abuse throughout the Austrian half of the Monarchy. In what he and others called 'a Czech and Austrian Dreyfusiad', Masaryk assumed the unrewarding role of an Émile Zola, who, but a few years before, in France, had protested the injustice committed against the Jew, Captain Alfred Dreyfus, sentenced, without cause, in 1896, to a life in exile, amnestied in 1900 and rehabilitated in 1906. Although, like Zola, he suffered public calumny and abuse, Masaryk scored only a partial success in the case itself but, with his French counterpart, exerted a continuing positive influence in the struggle against the plague of anti-Semitism. As a recent biographer has written, Masaryk, in conduct 'certainly unusual for Czech scholar and k.k. (Imperial and Royal) Professor', displayed a rare combination of qualities as 'a theoretician, a scholar and publicist' and an 'energetic and active practical man'.[2] In the words of an admirer, his action in the Hilsner case was 'the brave and undaunted intervention of a great thinker and defender of the truth against human stupidity and dark, medieval and false ideas'.[3]

The Hilsner case has been the subject of innumerable accounts by contemporaries and by scholars and others and need not, and cannot, be here described in detail.[4] Leopold Hilsner, an itinerant cobbler and pedlar, of doubtful reputation, was charged with the murder of a young Christian girl, Anežka Hrůzová, in Polná, a village in northwest Bohemia on the Moravian border; and, after a five-day trial, was sentenced to death on 16 September 1899. The verdict was soon annulled and a new trial called. This took place in Písek, in October and November 1900, and lasted eleven days. Hilsner was once again condemned to death, this time for the alleged murder, not only of Anežka Hrůzová, but also of another young woman, Marie Klímová, killed under similar circumstances several months before the Polná tragedy. Six months later the sentence was commuted to life imprisonment by the Emperor, Francis Joseph. Year after year thereafter attempts were made to secure a revision of the Písek verdict, but in vain. Hilsner's own appeal for pardon in 1906 was denied. He was released only in 1918 by order of the new Emperor, Charles, and died ten years later without exoneration. In 1961 the brother of Anežka was reported in the press to have confessed, on his deathbed, that he had himself killed his sister for personal gain, but no evidence has been found to confirm this.[5]

Although Masaryk later admitted that at first he had no special interest in the case and denied that he had entered the fray for the sake of Hilsner, he had at once perceived what he considered a miscarriage of justice. Hilsner was, he wrote, 'a good-for-nothing who long ago belonged in a reformatory', and deserved little sympathy as a person. The case against him was weak, however, 'a monstrous non-legality', based mainly on his reputation as a lazy idler and woman-chaser and without any direct evidence that he was involved. The ritual murder myth was not explicitly the basis of the charges against him, but it was openly referred to in the speeches of the prosecutor and of Dr Karel Basa, who acted on behalf of the Hrůza family, and refuted at length by the defence counsel, Dr Zdeněk Auředníček. The witnesses and the jury, made up of local people, acted under the influence of a kind of 'crowd psychosis' in an atmosphere of widespread anti-Semitism and general acceptance of the myth of ritual murder. This doctrine, Masaryk argued, was completely without foundation, was not backed by any historical evidence and rested solely on prejudice against Jews. There was nothing in the Old Testament or in the Talmud which justified ritual murder nor were there any known secret sects which practised it.[6]

Masaryk took up the case on his own initiative and acted throughout as a private person, without any official involvement in the two trials. Although warned by a friend that it was 'political suicide,' he threw himself into a campaign to secure a review of the Polná trial and did not realize the high price which he would have to pay personally – both in the expenditure of time, energy and money, and in the strain and tension of constant assaults on himself and his reputation. His strategy was to mobilize public opinion against the verdict with the hope of achieving its reassessment and the refutation of the ritual murder theory.[7] He did this by consulting medical and legal experts all over Europe, studying the relevant literature on ritual murder and bringing this knowledge to bear in detailed and careful examinations of the conduct of the trial in two brochures and in article after article in his own newspaper, *Čas*, the Vienna *Die Zeit*, and the *Berliner Tageblatt*. In these writings he argued his case and defended himself against the barrage of attacks on him in Czech, Austrian and German newspapers. He made two journeys *incognito* to Polná, and at least one visit to Vienna to seek information and to exert pressure.

The two brochures, a brief one published right after the Polná trial, and a longer one just before Písek, examined in great detail every aspect of the trial, including such matters as the time and place of death, the location and position of the victim's body, the nature of the wound inflicted, the amount of blood left in the corpse, the evidence of the witnesses and the content of the preliminary inquiry and the indictment. He also presented possible alternative motives for the murder (adultery, necrophilia, robbery, suicide, etc.) and discussed relations within the Hrůza family which suggested the possibility that Anežka's brother may have been guilty of the murder. Masaryk severely condemned the unobjective and prejudiced treatment of the case by the prosecution and by the Hrůza counsel and criticized the autopsy by local medical examiners. He particularly opposed the assumption that this was a ritual murder. He concluded his second booklet by deploring the trial and the press discussion as 'a sad sign of the decay of our Bohemian and Austrian culture' and 'an outrage against the healthy mind of humanity'.[8]

Masaryk was convinced that the facts which he set forth contradicted all the presuppositions of ritual murder and that his analysis was at least partially vindicated by the annulling of the verdict and the ordering of a new trial. Masaryk found welcome support in the works of foreign legal and medical experts and in a booklet by J. A. Bulova, a practising doctor in Karlín, a suburb of Prague, and an energetic campaign which the latter waged.

The medical faculty of the Czech University in Prague delivered an expert opinion which, although it did not mention Masaryk's arguments explicitly, confirmed his position on many essential points and seemed to put an end to the myth of ritual murder.[9] In the second trial the superstition disappeared from the formal proceedings but remained a powerful undercurrent both in the legal arguments and in public discussion. Although the judgement was even more negative than the first, Masaryk drew comfort from what he considered a victory of 'the scientific struggle against crude superstition'.[10]

Masaryk repeatedly stated that he was led to assume this heavy burden for purely ethical considerations and out of a sense of law and justice. The trial, he declared, was 'an assault on healthy reason and humanity'. In view of the 'unbelievable carelessness and superficiality of the entire procedural process', he was forced to 'act for the honour and the life of the people'.[11] 'It was his duty', he felt, 'to throw a clear light ... on this sad matter' and thereby to 'help the completely obvious truth to victory.' In 1914, in retrospect, he declared that it was not enough 'to speak out for truth, to salute before its majesty, and to wish that it would be victorious; one must act for truth; most of those who are devotees of truth do not show themselves capable of doing this'.[12]

What disturbed Masaryk most of all was that the ritual-murder myth had been widely accepted by the Czech people, and especially its intelligentsia – this was 'a terrible indictment of the Czech nation'. 'The more one thinks about the myth, the more absurd and the more dangerous it appears for our people'. 'Who believes [in this myth]', he said, 'is not a Czech but a man who does not think.' The trial, in his view, offered 'a painful and oppressive picture of our Czechoslovak–Austrian conditions, of the morality and culture of the population, the lawyers, judges, doctors and especially of our journalism' – of the 'political wretchedness of our narrower and broader homeland'. He wrote bitterly of 'the lack of judiciousness and of thoughtfulness, the passionate hot-headedness, and the lack of humanity, even cruelty', all of which testified to 'the nervous tension and abnormality of our Czech and Austrian life'. 'The Polná trial is a bloody memento for us.'[13]

As the campaign against him in the press and at the University mounted, a new consideration entered the picture – the threat to freedom which was involved. During a student demonstration which prevented him from speaking in his own classroom by shouting and booing, Masaryk wrote on the blackboard that he had 'defended the right of freedom of thought and feeling, and would always defend it, without regard for diplomacy'.[14] On 27 November, when he was again able to speak, he declared that what was at issue was 'whether freedom of conscience and feeling will be preserved, whether I shall enjoy freedom in this chair of Bohemian learning, whether or not I may say what I consider correct ... . I stand behind my opinion and will defend it with all my powers; I expect that you, too, will defend my freedom, for in my freedom lies your freedom, in your freedom mine.'[15]

Although Masaryk sometimes condemned his own nation for its attitude to the Jews and the ritual-murder myth, he also asserted on occasion that one could not 'blame the nation or people, but rather its leaders, lawyers, clergy, its journalism'.[16] In his often strongly polemical statements, Masaryk spared no person or institution in his indictment. His chief targets were the newspapers of the political parties, especially the Young Czech *Národní listy* which had adopted an anti-Semitic stance in both the Dreyfus and the Hilsner cases. Masaryk criticized the majority of Czech intellectuals who either shared these false beliefs and anti-Jewish prejudices, or remained silent in the face of injustice. Especially at fault were the doctors and lawyers who became 'helpers in this loathsome and ravaging superstition' and who should have explained to people the meaning of 'science and Christianity'. He was disheartened by the attitude of the University and of his own colleagues who did not take a public stand on the issue and gave him little or no support, and some of whom even shunned him. The Rector, Jan Gebauer, old friend and ally during the manuscript controversy, Dean V. E. Mourek, and two of his colleagues, Jaroslav Goll and Jaroslav Drtina, deplored the student demonstrations but only the latter spoke out openly in favour of Masaryk's position. He was deeply hurt that many students joined the hunt against Hilsner and himself, thus taking a stand, he said, against freedom of conscience.[17] Masaryk also condemned the weaknesses of the judicial system as shown by the conduct of the prosecutor and the judge, and the procedures employed in the two trials. His critique represented a severe judgement on Austrian justice and emphasized the need for a reform of the criminal code.[18]

Masaryk aimed his sharpest arrows at what he called 'clerical anti-Semitism', expressed by Church dignitaries, by many priests, and particularly by the Catholic newspaper, *Katolické noviny*, which he regarded as the chief purveyors of the ritual-murder myth. Although several papal bulls and encyclicals in the past had condemned anti-Semitism and the ritual myth, the Church, in spite of appeals to it, remained silent. One of the main sources of anti-Jewish prejudice and of ritual doctrine was the writings of a German Catholic theologian, Professor August Rohling, of the German University in Prague.[19] For Masaryk this was an intolerable abuse of Christian faith. In 1907, in the Vienna Parliament, he asserted that he had written his first brochure not to defend Hilsner, but to defend Christians against superstition. 'I am certain', he declared, 'that no one who believes in Jesus can be an anti-Semite ... . One can be either one or the other, either Christian or anti-Semite.'[20]

As in the controversy over the manuscripts Masaryk stood almost alone in facing the 'wave of hatred' against him and became, in the words of his close friend and ally, Jan Herben, 'the most isolated man among the Czech public'. Most deplorable was the campaign against him in the press, where he was accused of splitting the nation, of philosemitism and of taking financial aid from the Jews.[21] Student demonstrations occurred on four occasions, including the one mentioned in his classroom, and another outside his home on the Malá strana, when the crowd was dispersed only by the words of his courageous wife. For a time his lectures were suspended by the Dean, and later he himself refused to lecture as a protest against the University's failure to support him. For some years Masaryk's addresses in various towns in Bohemia were interrupted or disturbed by angry audiences and he was personally abused on the street. (The defence lawyer, Zdeněk Auředníček, was booed outside the courtroom and his practice fell off so badly that he had to move to Vienna. Baxa in contrast was hailed as a hero by the crowds.) Masaryk also had considerable difficulty in getting his booklets published, both in German and Czech. The first one was at first confiscated officially and was permitted only after an interpellation in the Austrian Parliament. In February and March 1901 Masaryk was three times charged with offences under the law for the first brochure and for later articles, and was fined each time. He received many poison-pen letters and had to engage in an expensive and time-consuming correspondence with persons who sought aid for victimization in connection with the trial. The affair also severely hampered Masaryk's political work at a critical time when he was seeking to make *Čas* a daily newspaper and to organize the Realist party. As a result of the campaign against him he gave up the idea of running for a parliamentary seat in an election in January 1901.[22]

Masaryk was not entirely without support, however. Apart from his own Realist papers, *Čas* and *Naše doba*, a number of newspapers wrote in favour of his actions and against anti-Semitism – this was especially true of the social-democratic press. Several student newspapers, including *Studentský sborník*, edited by the social democrat, Bohumír Šmeral, rallied to his cause. Other students showed their sympathy. One statement, signed by 604 persons, published in *Studentský sborník*, expressed regret at the unbecoming behaviour of other students who should have presented their disagreement quietly and with dignity. Another group of students called for the reinstatement of his lectures, saying that his enforced leave represented 'the yielding of scientific authority to the unthinking behaviour of one part of the student population'. Among Progressive circles, too, there was support for Masaryk. Jewish organizations held meetings in protest against the trials and defended Masaryk. There were some signs of sympathy among the workers.[23]

These events, which interrupted his scholarly work, hindered his political activity and made life at the University distasteful, plunged Masaryk into depression. In retrospect, in 1914, he admitted that this was a time of great personal suffering and grief, not only because of its effect on him but even more because of what it revealed about the Czech nation, and especially its intelligentsia. His despair was at times so great that he seriously contemplated emigrating from Bohemia, a step from which only his devoted wife dissuaded him,[24] arguing that he could do more at home than abroad.

Nonetheless Jan Pǎtocka later considered that what Masaryk had experienced 'was an unusual and burdensome test of his intellect, his ability to work and his character', which showed him to be capable of 'great achievement'. Although at home his position was weakened and shaken, abroad Masaryk gained a reputation and stature as 'a fighter for truth and humanity'. His activity, especially when he was himself on trial, was reported in the newspapers throughout Europe; glowing tributes were sometimes paid to him; for instance, as 'one of the brightest personalities who ever adorned a European university,' or as 'a man of scholarly significance such as few exist in the Czech nation at the present time, whose name acquired a good sound far beyond the borders of his land'. Little did he then realize, although he acknowledged it later, that this reputation, especially among Jews throughout the world, was to stand him in good stead during his struggle for independence during the First World War.[25]

ANTI-SEMITISM IN AUSTRIA AND BOHEMIA

The full dimension of Masaryk's heretical stand in the Hilsner case can be measured and explained only against the background of Austrian and Bohemian anti-Semitism. Hostility toward Jews was a general European phenomenon during the last quarter of the nineteenth century, taking the most extreme form in Russia, but present also in Germany, France and other countries. Anti-Jewish attitudes developed in Austria after the stock-market crash in 1873 and became a major force in Austrian and Czech life and politics during the nineties. Street demonstrations and riots occurred in 1892, directed against Germans and Jews alike, and rumours of ritual murder spread widely. Similar actions against Jews and Jewish property (as well as German) occurred between 1897 and 1899 in connection with the government's language policies. The Polná case therefore took place at a high point in this anti-Semitic wave and stimulated a new surge of popular manifestations against Germans and Jews and of extreme anti-Jewish opinions in the press and in public life.

It is beyond the scope of this chapter to go deeply into the causes and the nature of anti-Semitism among Germans and Czechs of the Monarchy.[26] Although Czech anti-Semitism was influenced by worldwide tendencies and events (e.g. the Zola case in France) and developed parallel to German anti-Semitism in Austria, it had distinctive features. The Jews in Bohemia occupied a special and rather uncomfortable position in the middle, between Czechs and Germans, and lived largely in the Czech areas of the region. As long as nationalism did not develop on both sides, the Jews could adopt a kind of neutral stance, reflecting the tradition of a utraquist (bi-lingual) Bohemia as defended by the aristocracy and by the dominant Old Czech party. Many Jews were loyal to Vienna and to the Monarch, Francis Joseph, and to his wife, Elisabeth, who was openly favourable to Jews. With the rise of industry in the Bohemian lands, which was mainly in the hands of Germans and Jews, Jews tended to lean towards Germanism, speaking German and absorbing the predominant Austro-German culture. During the long period of dominance of the German liberals in Austrian politics, among whom Jews played an important role, the Jews in the Bohemian land favoured this tendency and looked to the *Neue Freie Presse*, the Vienna liberal organ, for their ideas and inspiration.

As nationalism mounted on both Czech and German sides during the eighties and nineties the Jews found themselves in an increasingly difficult position. The collapse of German liberalism during the Taaffe period and the rise of radical nationalism, in which anti-Semitism was often an integral part, among Austrian and Bohemian Germans, made it harder and harder for Jews to remain pro-German or to consider themselves Germans. The rise of clerical anti-Semitism among the Germans of Lower Austria, promoted by the People's party of Karl Lueger, an extreme racial anti-Semite, caused Jews to fear German conservatives as well. Nonetheless although the majority of Jews regarded Czech as their *Umgangssprache* (language of daily life), most attended German schools (including the German University and Technical College in Prague) and remained attached to German culture and ways of life. For Czech nationalists this pro-German inclination seemed to buttress the predominant position of Germans in politics, culture and business, especially in Prague and other urban centres. German-language Jewish private schools were seen as instruments of Germanization. The rise of a Czech business class, especially in small industry and trade, caused Czechs to see the Jews as rivals, and to make the petty bourgeoisie an easy prey to anti-Semitism. This led to the movement for economic boycott, directed partly against Germans, partly against Jews, and to the explosion of demonstrations and riots against the Jews. Even some workers were infected with anti-Jewish prejudice as they saw the Jews, along with Czechs and Germans, as capitalist exploiters.[27] In 1904 and 1905 there were more demonstrations which were directed indiscriminately against Germans and Jews and their property. This rise of Czech anti-Semitism complicated the position of the Jews still further and discouraged tendencies toward assimilation with the Czech nation.

Anti-Semitism began to pervade Czech political and public life. Ironically this was fed by German sources in Vienna: e.g. the pan-German Georg von Schönerer, the Christian Socialist, Karl Lueger, the German nationalist parties and their press.[28] The main purveyors of anti-Jewish attitudes were, however, the Czech political parties themselves. Although their programmes paid lip-service to principles such as tolerance and racial equality their adherents often displayed extreme intolerance and prejudice. Jewish hopes were at first raised by the ascendancy of the Young Czechs, who professed liberalism and democracy, but were dashed when extreme nationalism, including anti-Semitism, took precedence over more progressive ideas. Open and extreme anti-Semitism was proclaimed by Young Czech extremists, Jan Vašatý and Václav Březnovský, and the latter scored a resounding victory in the elections to the elections to the Reichsrat in 1897. The Young Czech establishment was not free of the virus, as was shown by the views expressed by Eduard Grégr and his newspaper, *Národní listy*, especially during the Zola and Hilsner affairs. The burgeoning of progressive tendencies seemed at first comforting, but the movement soon divided, with one wing, under Antonín Hajn and Karel Baxa (who founded the Radical State Right party in 1899), expressing anti-Semitic ideas. The same was true of the new National Socialist party, headed by Václav Klofáč. The Old Czech veteran, F. L. Rieger, a member of the House of Lords, gave expression to anti-Semitic views, e.g. during an interview in October 1901 when he was reported to have described the Jews as a 'disintegrating (foreign) influence' and condemned Masaryk as 'a sworn enemy of God'.[29] Counteracting political forces such as Czech social democracy and a Progresssive wing under Alois Hajn, as well as the Realists under Masaryk, were relatively weak and unable to dam the spread of anti-Semitism. The statement, often quoted, by Jan Herben, that 'the whole Czech nation was with some exceptions anti-Semitic' may have been overdrawn but pointed to certain features of Czech political culture of the time.[30]

MASARYK AND ANTI-SEMITISM

Although Masaryk often discounted the importance of anti-Semitism and the Jewish question as motives for entering on the Hilsner case, there is no doubt that long before 1899 he was deeply interested in this phenomenon. As early as 1883 he described it as 'a hateful disease which has put our organism in a fever' and called for 'non-Semites and Semites to get to know each other better' and 'to clear everything out of the way which mutually alienated each other'. As he himself was ready to admit, he had personally gone through a gradual evolution of thinking on this subject and had to overcome earlier prejudices. As a child, under the influence of the Moravian village environment, and of his mother and a certain parish priest, he had shared the prevalent anti-Semitism of the time and the region and had even accepted the ritual murder thesis. Only slowly was he weaned away from these biases by his personal experiences with Jewish schoolmates and later with students and scholars in Vienna and Prague, and through his studies. As a result he developed a positive attitude toward the Jewish people and their faith and a revulsion against anti-Semitism.[31]

Although Masaryk read widely and exhaustively on Jewish history and anti-Semitism, he did not elaborate his views in any systematic work, but expressed them peripherally in studies of other broader issues. In his earliest scholarly book, on suicide, published in 1881, for instance, Masaryk praised the Jews for their belief in God, for holding fast to their religion in adversity and for their joy of living and practical optimism which 'did not permit the development of a pathological tendency toward suicide'.[32]

In 1883, in a brief review of a book by Ernest Renan on Jewishness (*Judentum*), Masaryk defended the view, years before it was expresssed by Theodor Herzl, the founder of Zionism, that the Jews constituted a special nation, 'quite different from ourselves', not merely a religious community, as argued by Renan, and should be recognized as such in Austria.[33]

In 1896, in his study of Karel Havlíček, the mid-century Czech journalist, Masaryk noted that Havlíček in 1846 took a similar view that the Jews in Bohemia and Moravia were 'a special Semitic nation' which 'only accidentally lived among us' and were tied together by a bond which was 'much more powerful than that which links them to their own land (where they live)'. 'Anyone who wished to be a Czech must cease to be a Jew,' Havlíček concluded. If they were to assimilate at all, it should be with the Germans whose language they had already accepted. According to Masaryk, this 'rejection of the Jews' by Havlíček was modified later into 'a more moderate anti-Semitism'. In 1850 he wrote positively of the emancipation of the Jews. While he recognized that most Czechs were opposed to equal rights for Jews and were alienated by the behaviour of Jews, especially in commerce, Havlíček argued that these bad qualities were in large part produced by the way in which they were treated by the non-Jews and would gradually disappear if they were granted equal rights and if they were treated as equals by others.[34]

Masaryk refrained from defining his own views in his book on Havlíček, but elaborated them in his study of Marxism, *The Social Question*, in 1899.[35] Karl Marx's interpretation of the Jewish question was 'brilliant', but not convincing. Marx adopted a too-exclusively economic analysis of the Jewish people, whom he characterized as 'wheeler-dealers' (*čachráři*) who, in bourgeois society, were characterized by egotism, and had, as their wordly God, Money. Egotism was, however, common to both Jews and Christians, the latter having become Jews and the Jews Christians, wrote Marx. Under these conditions the Jews 'had no nationality other than that of the merchant, the banker'. The emancipation of the Jews would come only when socialism freed them from their egotism, and at the same time emancipated Christians and society as a whole.

In contrast Masaryk re-stated his view that the Jews were a separate nation, on the basis not of language, but of their religious faith. The Jews were not just 'wheeler-dealers', but had their Jeremiah, Spinoza and Christ, and like other nations, had good as well as bad features. Christians must recognize these good sides and try to work out a synthesis of Jews and Christians. The solution did not lie in contemporary anti-Semitism nor in Marx's anti-Semitism. But the Jews, too, must admit their own defects and strive to overcome them; they tended to be self-satisfied and to blame everything on the Christians. They must seek their own emancipation through the reform of their moral character. Zionism, he believed, could contribute something to this revival of Jewry, although not necessarily through emigration to Palestine, but through moral regeneration wherever Jews lived.

Shortly thereafter, in 1900, in a contribution to a book edited by a German scholar, Masaryk acknowledged in even stronger terms that Zionism appealed to him because it showed that the oppressed Jew was not ashamed of his nationality. He also saw the desire to colonize Palestine as eminently justified as a goal and an idea, but reiterated his view that Zionism was for him a moral question. It expressed the realization of the thinking Jew that there were imperfections in his character and philosophy and that he must be 'born new again'. 'For this a change in milieu is not enough; it is a question of a rebirth from within in which the Christians must also cooperate since they, too are, responsible.'[36]

Masaryk further developed his ideas on the Jews and the Jewish question in a brief section of the programme of his People's party in 1900.[37] Although Masaryk re-stated his earlier criticisms of the Jews, he also emphasized their good sides and expressed a stronger condemnation of anti-Semitism than in previous writings. The programme pointed out the weaknesses of the Jews: their 'ambiguity' and 'lack of unity'; tendencies' towards clericalism and scholasticism; their striving for revenge after long persecution; their social and economic one-sidedness. Yet admittedly they were not worse than Christians whose Jesuitism mirrored Jewish Talmudism. On the good side was the high morality of the Old Testament and their high culture; their yearning for knowledge; their enterprise and temperance; and their strong family feeling.

The programme condemned anti-Semitism of all kinds: both Catholic (and Orthodox) with its ritual-murder superstition and violent tendencies, and Protestant, based more on philosophical, national or racial and economic considerations. Anti-Semitism, it argued, exaggerated the significance and influence of the Jews in the social and economic field.

As in previous writings, Masaryk, in the programme, emphasized the responsibility on both sides, Jewish and Chritian, to overcome old prejudices and thus to diminish mutual tension. There must be a genuine cultural and philosophical synthesis and a reform of the moral and religious life of both Jews and Christians. As before, Masaryk stressed that the Jews must themselves recognize the need for reform and should seek it at home rather than in emigration. 'We demand tolerance towards the Jews and decisively reject the ritual myth proclaimed and exploited for their own ends by clericalism – and now by the radicals. With all tolerance, however, we demand on both sides openness and honesty; only in this way can we overcome our mutual prejudices.'

As can be seen from the above, Masaryk's attitude toward the Jews was balanced and objective, and his hostility to anti-Semitism unambiguous. His analysis of the causes of anti-Semitism, which was expressed briefly from time to time but was not given systematic exposition, was somewhat more ambivalent and not free of contradictions.[38] Anti-Semitism in Slovakia, for instance, he explained, and even justified, in terms of Jewish 'usury' and capital. In Moravia the national element, engendered by the tendency of Jews towards Germandom, was important, and in Bohemia both economic and national factors were present. His most extensive explanation of anti-Semitism, in an article written in 1899, recognized the complexity of the problem, but laid stress on the social and economic elements, especially the financial straits and embitteredness of the broad working masses in the countryside. But he noted more specific causes: the disorientation of the Czech bourgeois camp; the arousing of the public by the Dreyfus and Polná affairs; the national element in Moravia; and the influence of foreign anti-Semitism, especially from Vienna.

Masaryk's views were more definite but still equivocal on the vexing question as to whether Czech Jews should seek assimilation with the Czech nation or turn to Zionism as a way out of their situation.[39] The Jews in Bohemia and Moravia were themselves undecided and divided on the solution. As noted above, although most of them spoke Czech, they tended to identify themselves with the Germans, owing to the overwhelming attraction of German culture and economic superiority. Only a small minority, the so-called Czech–Jewish movement, took up the idea of assimilating to the Czech nation, in many cases attracted by Masaryk's humanism, but rising Czech anti-Semitism discouraged this. A few turned to Zionism as an alternative, but this tendency was weak even among German Jews and still weaker among Czech Jews. Some turned to socialism but this served the German and Czech nationalists as a further argument against the Jews. In literature there was a flowering of both Czech and German Jewish writing, and some of these writers (Franz Kafka, Max Brod *et al.*) played an extraordinary mediating role between the three worlds of Prague.[40]

Masaryk, imbued with his sense of the mission of the Czech nation, really saw little advantage in the assimilation of Jews, most of whom were more or less Germanized, to the national community, and he was strongly opposed to any organized effort at assimilation. As time went on Masaryk pronounced even stronger views on assimilation. In an interview with a Lvov newspaper in 1909, he expressed his opinion that assimilation was 'completely impossible and even laughable', in view of the failure to achieve this goal in spite of efforts made during the past decade. Once again he expressed his sympathy for Zionism as a movement which sought to organize the Jews and thus to achieve their 'rebirth'.[41]

Not surprisingly, this interview was extremely disappointing to those Czech Jews who were striving for assimilation (many of whom were Masaryk's supporters), and was regarded as discouraging their efforts and encouraging their Zionist rivals. In an effort to placate Jews of this orientation, Masaryk gave another interview, this time to the Czech Jewish paper, *Rozvoj* (9 April 1909), in which he explained that his sympathy was for 'the general idea of Zionism' in that it had awakened the conscience of the Jewish masses. He considered the colonization of Palestine as 'utopian'. The Jewish question will not be solved by a policy of immigration which would not diminish the number of Jews and would not attract many American Jews, such as the 600 000 Galicians in New York. On the other hand 'assimilation of blood' was impossible, but cultural assimilation was 'justified and natural'. The Jews could become 'cultural Czechs' but would remain different in 'origin and race' and in religion and tradition. Moreover it would be 'no misfortune if the Jews form an element in a people different from others for a time'.

During the fifteen years after Polná, Masaryk continued to concern himself with the Jewish question and anti-Semitism, following the course of events in all countries and reading widely in the Jewish press and scholarly works. Although his positions on assimilation and Zionism, as seen above, were not always clear or certain, he left no doubt of his genuine concern with the fate of Bohemian Jews and continued to urge full rights for them and to oppose anti-Semitism. In 1907, for instance, in his speech in the Vienna Parliament already referred to, he responded to anti-Semitic statements by Karl Lueger who had personally attacked Masaryk for his role in the Hilsner case. Reviewing the ethical reasons for his involvement which have been referred to earlier, Masaryk declared that he felt he had done the right thing and if ever he felt satisfied with anything in his life, it was in this case. In response to another Christian Socialist deputy, Masaryk described anti-Semitism as 'immoral, crude and vulgar' (*unsittlich, grob* and *roh*) and went on to make his celebrated statement (quoted above) that a Christian could not be an anti-Semite; 'Jesus himself was a Jew, the apostles were Jews, and the old Christianity, especially Catholicism, contained very much Jewish in itself.'[42]

On the eve of the Great War Masaryk once more entered the fray when a ritual murder trial was held in Kiev on 6 October 1913 and lasted three weeks.[43] A Jewish brick-worker, Mendl Bejlis, was accused of the murder of a Russian boy and was held in prison from April 1911 until the trial. In this case the authorities officially described the case as one of ritual murder and sought to manipulate the trial so as to secure a verdict of guilty. The trial was a fiasco, with some of the witnesses, including an *agent provocateur*, withdrawing their pre-trial statements, and several expert witnesses denying the truth of the myth. The case was based in large part on the evidence of a Catholic priest, Pranaitis, an 'expert', for whom Professor Rohling was the chief authority in his 'proof' of ritual murder. The jury, most of whom were poor and illiterate peasants, nonetheless found Bejlis innocent.

The trial produced a sensation throughout Europe, and led to protests from many countries and meetings in Vienna and Prague. This time, in contrast to Polná, many Czechs publicly condemned the trial in resolutions signed by leading intellectuals, newspaper editors, and political leaders. In early October, after a meeting in the Corn Exchange in Prague, a resolution was drafted by Dr Teitz, editor of *Rozvoj*, and edited by Masaryk.

Another meeting on 23 November, right after the conclusion of the trial, welcomed the outcome of the trial and noted with satisfaction that Czech press and leaders had come out against it. On this occasion Masaryk gave a major speech, in which he subjected to critical analysis the testimony of the 'expert' witnesses and the writings of Russian newspapers. He exposed the evidence of Pranaitis as 'a hodge-podge and a plagiarism from Rohling'. He again denied that, among eleven million Jews throughout the world, there was any evidence of the existence of ritual murder.

Masaryk used the occasion to call for a re-examination of the Hilsner case and justice for the victim. The resolution adopted gave support to this demand. The movement for revision spread after the trial, and meetings were held in Prague and Vienna in this cause. In the fall of 1913 Dr Auředníček directly urged the Emperor to grant a pardon, but in vain – Hilsner was to remain in prison for another five years, a sad contrast of official Austrian justice to the Russian!

In spite of this, and continuing evidence of anti-Semitism in Austria, the Bejlis case demonstrated an extraordinary change in Czech opinion since Polná, due in large part, as *Čas* with justice claimed, to the work of Masaryk and of *Čas* itself. B. Šmeral, Social Democrat, who had supported Masaryk in 1899 and 1900, noted that what was then 'a small band' had become a 'powerful ferment in society', whose opinion had completely changed. As Patočka wrote, this must have given Masaryk great satisfaction and helped to dispel the 'hidden bitterness' he had felt after Polná. The battle had not been entirely won, as was indicated by charges by *Národní listy* in early 1914 that Masaryk had been strongly supported financially by German Jews in the Hilsner case. Masaryk admitted that he had had to seek support, not among Czech Jews, but among Jews in Vienna and even in Germany, but with little success. *Čas* and he firmly denied the authenticity of the 'proof' submitted by the newspaper.[44]

Nonetheless the situation had changed decisively since 1900. The ritual-murder myth was no longer widely accepted, and the tide of anti-Semitism seemed to be ebbing. Masaryk was no longer an outcast in his own nation and among Czech intellectuals and abroad he had acquired a reputation as a hero and a fighter for justice. When war came, Masaryk was at first estranged from Czech Jews (including even his own Realists) by his strongly anti-Austrian stance. Many Jews throughout the world, however, rallied to Masaryk's struggle for liberation and backed it with money.

As Roland Hoffmann has written, Masaryk in his struggle against Czech anti-Semitism had placed in question the credibility of his postulate of humanity as the sense of Czech history. He had literally to fight *for* his nation *against* the nation and to win over the conscience of the Czech intelligentsia. Masaryk never relinquished his belief in his programme of humanity and waged a hard battle against the actual reality of Czech prejudice and intolerance. In the end he can be said to have carried through 'an ethical catharsis of Czech thinking' and abroad had changed the image of his nation. Polná had become an affair of the distant past, and Masaryk, once the most-hated man in his nation, had become the most-beloved.[45]

7 Religious Heretic

Religion runs like a red thread through all of Tomáš Garrigue Masaryk's thinking and writing and affected, at least indirectly, many of his public actions. In his opinion, life without religion was unthinkable; it provided a secure basis for national existence and for an ethical personal life. Yet in spite of the importance he assigned to religion, wrote R. R. Betts, 'he never tells us what religion is. An admiration of Jesus and a somewhat vague belief in Providence seem to be the substance of his theology. To him religion is primarily ethical and practical.'[1]

His own personal evolution from Catholicism to Protestantism left unclear the exact nature of his faith. His views on religion were set forth in his scholarly work from 1879 on and in particular in lectures on the struggle for religion in 1904. His discussion was highly abstract and although often concrete in his criticism of Catholicism and of Protestantism, he did not really make clear what he meant by the 'new religion' which he professed. His attitude to Protestantism was defined largely by his highly positive attitude toward Jan Hus and the Czech Reformation, and by the close link which he made between the latter and the national revival of the nineteenth century. His attitude to Catholicism was made clear in his discussion of the *Los von Rom* movement in the early years of the century and in the struggle for non-confessional schools and freedom of thought later in the decade.

As was usual in Masaryk's intellectual life, all of these writings involved him in bitter controversies and often resulted in personal obloquy. The main onslaught came from the clerical Catholic side, but he was condemned also by Czech nationalists and progressives for his accent on religion, by Czech historians for his religious interpretation of Czech history, and by Protestants and even his fellow Realists. Through all these battles Masaryk stood his ground courageously, and defended his views with fervour and often in highly polemical fashion. For the objective observer there could be little doubt of Masaryk's religious faith (although he was sometimes denounced for his lack of it). As Jaroslav Opat observed, however, Masaryk remained a heretic to both Catholic and Protestant churches, although not an enemy of either.[2]

MASARYK'S PERSONAL FAITH

Masaryk's personal religious evolution has been often described. Born in strongly Catholic Moravia and brought up in a Catholic family, Masaryk, as a boy, was an ardent Catholic and took part in local religious pilgrimages with his devout mother. He was greatly influenced by her and by the local priest whom he assisted in services. Masaryk was impressed by the religious life of the village community and, as some have said, remained inwardly Catholic for the rest of his life.[3] Even as a high-school student, he was assailed by doubts, and these were intensified by his studies in Vienna, notably by his work with the philosopher, Brentano. Like the latter, Masaryk broke, at least mentally, with the Church after the enunciation of the doctrine of papal infallibility in 1870. For a decade or more he remained in a kind of limbo, at first describing himself as a Uniate Catholic and not becoming a Protestant until later.[4] A turning-point came during his stay in Leipzig, as a result of his studies of Protestant theology under Protestant professors, but above all, under the influence of his future wife, Charlotte Garrigue, an American of Huguenot origin and Unitarian faith. According to his own testimony he acquired from her 'the best elements of Protestantism: the unity of religion and life, religious practicality and religion for everyday life'.[5] It was not until 1880, however, that Masaryk formally joined a Protestant church, the Evangelical Church of the Helvetian confession. Pastor Císař, who conducted the ceremony, had tried to discourage him, partly because of the damage this break with Catholicism might do to his career. He was also not fully convinced that Masaryk was really a Protestant; and thought that he was acting merely out of a negation of Catholicism and a desire to create a family based on Protestantism for the sake of their children. Even after his conversion, according to Nejedlý, he did not become a 'normal' Evangelical church member and was not a genuine Evangelical.[6] In an interview with the Catholic newspaper, *Katolické listy*, in 1902, Masaryk was reported to have said that he had chosen Protestantism for family reasons but did not find Protestantism sympathetic, nor did he attend Protestant services. As a result of his early experiences, and especially the influence of his mother, 'I feel myself above all to be a Catholic. I am a decided theist.'[7] Whatever the authenticity of these statements, his Protestantism, according to Jaroslav Opat, was 'his own distinctive Masarykite Protestantism'.[8] As he himself said, in 1907, he was by then 'a dead member of the Church'. He was not interested in collective worship in church; prayer and the reading of the Bible were his principal religious activities.[9]

SCHOLARLY VIEWS

Whatever his views were about the two main branches of the Christian religion, Masaryk, in his scholarly writings from 1879 on, expressed a profound belief in the importance of religion and Christianity for modern life. In his first major work, on suicide, he set forth the view that this central problem of civilization was in large part due to the crisis of the modern world which had resulted from the decline of religious faith and the spread of irreligion.[10] The remedy for this universal evil was the revival of religion, not necessarily in Catholic or Protestant form, but as a new religion, the form of which, however, he did not define.

In this early work Masaryk expressed his belief in the high value of religion, a belief which was to dominate his thinking in ensuing decades. 'The morality of man, all his actions and strivings, acquires in religion that special dedication which stamps man with the mark of the divine'. 'Religion, through faith in God and in immortality, gives man comfort and hope in all circumstances and amid the adversities of life and strengthens his love for humanity. ...The religious man is therefore joyful in all situations; his faith, his conviction and his certitude bind him not only to heaven but at the same time to earth and to life.'[11]

Examining the causes of suicide at different stages of history and in the contemporary world, he analyzed the effect of different religions in different countries, sometimes based on statistics, more often on his own intuitive judgements. Masaryk had no doubt that Christianity as a whole, with its belief in God and in immortality, embodied in the example of Jesus Christ, gave man support and hope and discouraged suicide. He shows, however, a continued ambivalence toward both his original Catholic faith and his emerging Protestantism. In the medieval world the Catholic Church had provided an all-embracing faith or *Weltanschauung*, which gave people guidance, assured them happiness and peace and inspired obedience, and thus discouraged suicide. The Church achieved this harmony of outlook, however, by imposing external authority on believers, e.g. in the modern dogma of infallibility. The spread of scepticism, in France, for instance, and of religious indifference, in Austria, produced a greater tendency toward suicide.

Protestantism, on the other hand, encouraged freedom of inquiry and of the individual, 'the infallibility of all', and a belief in the power of reason, but it also created doubt and despair. In the case of Lutheran Germany, bureaucracy and German philosophy destroyed Christianity and imbued people with pessimism and a weariness with life, and hence a greater propensity towards suicide. However, in Britain and especially in the USA, a true religious freedom and unity of outlook was achieved among many independent sects, including the Catholic. People were truly religious in both countries and morbid suicide was not present. In the Orthodox world, with its enforced conformity and faith, and the deep religiosity of the ordinary people, suicide was a lesser problem. Masaryk gave scant consideration to other faiths than the Christian, but praised the Jews who, in spite of their troubles, found hope and faith in their God and did not show a tendency to suicide.

In the face of this confusing and contradictory picture Masaryk did not have a clear view as to the solution of the problem of suicide. He was convinced, however, that it did not lie in political and economic reforms, but in the cultivation of ideas and feelings on an ethical basis. 'Man needs religion to live as much as he needs air to breathe' (p. 223, English; p. 250, Czech). What was needed was the restoration of something akin to the universal harmony of the Middle Ages but not through the restoration of Catholicism, or even a reformed Protestantism. It could be reached through a 'new religion' based on the example of Jesus, which would contribute to a spontaneous unity based on internal authority. This would give man assurance and confidence and reduce the tendency to suicide. In these earlier works Masaryk only touched on the Czechs, who were in a special situation because of their enforced Catholicization during the Counter-Reformation and the continuance of a kind of internal Hussitism (p. 83, English; p. 205, Czech).

Masaryk made mention of religion, at least briefly, in all his subsequent studies.[12] He presented a fuller exposition of his views as of that time in a series of articles in *Naše doba* in 1896–8, published much later in book form, and in English under the title *Modern Man and Religion*.[13] Masaryk regarded this work as a continuation of his study of suicide and, as he clearly hinted, it was written while he was passing through a crisis of belief and disbelief (English, p. 45). According to Milan Machovec, Masaryk was most successful in defining his position on religion in this book; this was 'the core of all his other writings and of his practical public activity'.[14] In characteristic style he conducted his search for the meaning of human life through an immanent critique of the thought of other scholars, using each one to criticize the others, without stating his own position. He examined in turn the thought of Hume (scepticism), Kant (morality), Comte (positivism) and Spencer (historicism) and a little-known Czech philosopher, Augustin Smetana (creative love). He drew the conclusion that 'science and philosophy (by this I mean the modern, the most modern, philosophy and science) are not anti-religious'. He also held to his belief in the importance of religion. 'Religion is the basic content of the spiritual life of man; it is as necessary for life as air.' He was not satisfied by any of the philosophies examined and concluded that philosophy should seek to achieve 'a creative synthesis' of these doctrines, but he did not himself attempt to provide it (pp. 55, 211). A Czech philosopher, J. B. Kozák, later wrote that, although Masaryk was able to state what religion was not, he seemed unable to define what religion really *was* and kept silence on his own opinion.[15]

At the cost of breaking chronological sequence, it seems appropriate to refer here to a later presentation of his views on religion in lectures in 1904 which were published as a book, *On the Struggle for Religion*.[16] In a chapter entitled 'What religion is and is not', Masaryk argued that religion was not a philosophy or a science, nor a theology; it was not blind faith or even morality alone; it was not a church, a ritual or religious affiliation. He came closer than ever before to defining what religion was. 'As to content religion was a solution of the problem of eternity. It is not merely a theoretical but also a practical solution. Man may not merely think about the meaning of his life, but must actually live that life in his very being. Religion is life *sub specie aeternitatis*; it is the consciousness of our relationship to the world and of the true meaning of life. Religion is life's central and leading spiritual force; it is a striving for a new life, for new and higher values of life' (p. 22). Jesus was 'the best example of pure religion' and of a higher morality which 'taught men, through the love of God, to concentrate on our fellow-man' (pp. 23, 27).

These articles were written, as Masaryk said, at a time of general crisis for which neither of the two main Christian churches and religions was capable of providing a solution. The Roman Catholic Church was based on the absolutism of its papal hierarchy and demanded of its adherents a blind faith in its commands. Protestantism, having freed itself from papal theocracy, exchanged papal authority for the authority of the Bible; it smashed the authority of the Roman theocracy, but built up its own authoritative theological system; it took over from Rome, not only the Bible, but also the Credo and other Catholic traditions. Especially under Luther it was nothing but a negation of Catholicism and had shown itself incapable of carrying through the permanent reformation which was necessary. Only here and there it had developed into Unitarianism or other free churches, but these were weak in ideas and practice. 'Today Catholicism – and that is true also of Eastern Orthodoxy – and orthodox Protestantism are out-dated, theoretically and practically, morally and socially; the official Christian churches no longer exercise cultural leadership in anything' (pp. 37–40).

The only solution was a new religion 'more perfect, higher, and more noble' (pp. 23–36, 42–4) This must be based on conviction, not blind faith; it must be spiritual and personal, not materialistic; it must be social, supporting economic and social reforms. The 'honest Czech' could not be satisfied with anti-reformist Catholicism nor with orthodox Protestantism but must strive for a religious renaissance based on the ideas of our Czech reformation, of Jan Hus and the Bohemian Brethren (pp. 29–30, 44).

RELIGION AND NATIONALISM

Until the mid-nineties Masaryk's writings on religion were universal in scope and did not discuss in any detail its national aspects. Before going to Prague, he did not devote himself to the study of the Czech question as such. With the launching of the journal *Naše doba*, he began to publish a series of articles which marked a new nationalist phase in his thought and the beginning of an attempt to elaborate a Czech national ideology. For the first time, in a series of books produced in rapid succession, Masaryk examined the relationship of religion to the Czech question and linked these two inextricably together.[17]

In his famous book on the Czech question Masaryk developed at length his views on Czech history and his belief that humanity was the central idea of the Czech national renaissance of the nineteenth century. His study was, however, primarily a study of 'the awakeners' of that time, and the relationship of modern Czech politics to these traditions. He made only passing reference to the religious aspect of these questions.[18] In his study of Palacký, however, he declared that the religious idea was the leading idea of Czech history, and the 'main content' of Czech development from the times of Charles IV until the end of the eighteenth century, and that 'our so-called revival [*obrození*]' was 'a natural and logical continuation' linked with the idea and the ideals of our Reformation. Palacký viewed the Bohemian Brethren in particular as the 'peak of our national development'.[19]

Masaryk gave a fuller exposition of these ideas in his lectures in 1895, published as *Jan Hus, Our Revival and our Reformation*.[20] The awakeners of the nineteenth century, from Dobrovský to Smetana, 'consciously strove to link up with the spiritual heritage of their forefathers, and to continue in their spirit'. Contrary to the views of liberalism, the origin of the Czech ideal of humanity was to be found, not in the French Revolution, but in the Czech Reformation. 'The idea of humanity, the basic and pivotal idea which guided all the strivings of the awakeners, is the idea of our reformation; *humanita* is only another word for Brotherhood; Palacký in particular based our national programme on this thought' (pp. 8, 9).

For Masaryk the heroes of the Czech Reformation were Jan Hus, Petr Chelčický and Amos Komenský. Hus, who suffered a martyr's death for his ideas, stood against church and papal authority – and state authority, too – in defence of freedom of conscience and freedom of religion (pp. 17–19). Hus must be seen, not mainly in national terms, but as a religious reformer, pointing up by his example the need for firm religious convictions (pp. 103, 105–6). Hus was not a theologian, but a reformer, who sought a 'regeneration of the conduct and practice of life'; the final goal of man and the meaning of life was ethical (p. 17).

The followers of Hus organized a Czech national church, the Bohemian Brethren, which used the Czech language, and pursued the same ethical and religious goals – 'the revitalization of morals and of life generally' (p. 16–17). 'Brotherhood sought to make Christ's "Love thy neighbour, as thou wouldst love thyself", become a social reality' (p. 21). Petr Chelčický rejected the violence used by the Counter-Reformation but also by the Hussites and advanced his radical doctrine of non-violence as the leading idea of the Brethren (pp. 29, 149). Amos Komenský based his whole pedagogy on the moral and religious ideas of Hus and his followers (p. 20). What mattered most for him in religion was not dogma but devotion and morality; what would benefit the Czech nation most was quiet work and and cultivation based on knowledge and morality.[21]

WAGING WAR ON CLERICALISM

In his lectures on Hus, Masaryk was writing less as a historian than as a person seeking ideas and inspiration for contemporary life and setting forth his views as to how the Czechs should behave in the light of their traditions. As noted, Masaryk was highly critical of what he called the 'foreign idea' of liberalism, not only for its failure to understand the religious significance of the Czech national question but also for its economic materialism, its egotistic nationalism, its religious indifferentism, and in spite of its liberal and constitutional politics, its advocacy of mere improvement, not fundamental reform (*Jan Hus*, pp. 11–14, 43–4, 81–3).

Masaryk directed his sharpest censure at Catholic Church authority, which had moved further towards absolutism with the doctrine of papal infallibility. The Church was still an authoritarian hierarchy which subordinated Christ's preaching of love of God and one's neighbour to dogmatic doctrine (pp. 57–9). The Catholic zealots today condemned the Czech Reformation and defended the Counter-Reformation which followed the Czech defeat (pp. 49–50).

In a lecture in 1910, Masaryk's criticism of Rome and clericalism became even more extreme. He described the history of the Czech struggle against the enormous spiritual power of church and state during the Reformation and the horrors suffered by the Czechs during the Counter-Reformation. He depicted as anti-clerical both Hus and his successors, who demanded that the Church practice what it preached. The task today, Masaryk declared, was to continue this struggle against clericalism (were priests necessary to mediate between man and God?) and against Rome, 'overcoming the Rome within ourselves'.[22]

In a more popular lecture to Slovak youth in Hodonín in 1911, Masaryk called for a continued struggle against clericalism; again including the 'clericalism within ourselves'. Indifference and tolerance were not enough; criticism of Church religion from the scientific point of view was necessary. The real religion of Christ required not religious rites and ceremony but love of God and of one's neighbour. He was ready to cooperate with the clericals but they showed no sign of wanting to do so. The authentic Christian religion to which he belonged was 'the religion of Christ and not a religion of a Pope, a Church, a chaplain, or a *hejtman*' (local governor).[23]

PROTESTANTISM AND A HIGHER RELIGION

Masaryk's criticism of Protestantism was only a little less severe. Protestantism offered a higher form of religion, based, not on authority, but on the free exercise of reason, but it had shown itself unable to complete its development and to avoid some of the same failings as Catholicism (*Jan Hus*, pp. 56–62). The Czech Reformation, and especially the Church of the Bohemian Brethren, was, as Palacký believed, 'the best Church, the peak and centre of the Czech historical nation, ...the purest national manifestation of Czech humanity and of divinity' (pp. 62, 64–5). He shared with Kollár, whom he repeatedly quoted, an enthusiasm for the Bohemian Brethren as a Church proclaiming 'freedom of thought (*rozum*) bounded only by the Gospel'. The Evangelical Church, however, had suffered from its absorption in German Protestantism and by the Catholicization of the Czech nation during the Counter-Reformation. (pp. 52–3, 55) Thus Protestantism, he concluded, like Catholicism and also Orthodoxy, was a hindrance to a solution of today's religious question ; 'it is not a solution of our Czech religious problem' (p. 71).

As we see, Masaryk's attitude toward religion was ambivalent, and indeed confusing. No clearer was his recommendation as to what a 'thinking Czech

person' (p. 48) should believe in contemporary circumstances. He seemed to hold
the view that an imperfect Catholicism and an imperfect Protestantism should
overcome their polarity and should seek to supplement and penetrate each other
as much as possible, and that mutual toleration, not war, should be their slogan
(pp. 56–61). He offered, however, no concrete idea of what kind of synthesis of
the two might be achieved; nor did he indicate in what way the tradition of the
Brethren could contribute to a solution of the religious problem. The task was
'not to seek an ideal visible church, but rather inwardly to experience and live
through the entire development of ideas begun by our Reformation and revival,
and then with others to continue further along this line' (p. 71).

THE CULT OF HUS AND *LOS VON ROM*

From 1890 on Masaryk engaged in highly polemical debates on the interpretation
of Czech historical tradition. This controversy focused on a number of closely
intertwined issues – the practical one of erecting a monument to Hus in the Old
Town Square in Prague, and the more theoretical questions of the meaning of
Hus and Hussitism, the Los von Rom (Away from Rome) movement among
Germans, and a comparable one among Czechs, and the relationship of Hus to the
Orthodox church (the Cyril–Methodius tradition). This brought him into sharp
conflict not only with the Young Czech nationalists, and the distinguished
historian, Josef Pekař, but also with Catholic and some Protestant spokesmen,
and even members of his own Realist party. Only a highly simplified summary of
this complicated struggle between rival conceptions of Czech national traditions
can be attempted here.[24]

Let us begin with the 'cult of Hus' by the Young Czechs, who interpreted Hus
in largely national terms and used this tradition for contemporary political purposes. The controversy focused on the proposal to erect a monument to Jan Hus
in Prague. First advanced in 1889, this was not carried out until 1915. Masaryk
was a leading protagonist of the project and, in an effort to disarm both German
and conservative Catholic opposition, at first emphasized the moral aspect of the
Hussite tradition.[25] Masaryk would have preferred to have the statue erected on
Bethlehem Square, outside the chapel in which Hus had preached for ten years.
The Young Czechs, however, sought to give it a maximum of national emphasis
by having it in the Old Town Square where the Bohemian nobles had been
executed in 1620. As a compromise Masaryk accepted the idea of locating the
memorial in the Small Old Town Square, but the town council, in 1900, in
approving the proposal, decided on Old Town Square as the site.

By the time of the laying of the foundation-stone in 1903 Masaryk had adopted
what was to be his fundamental position: that Hus was to be interpreted, not in
national terms, but in religious terms. This aroused substantial criticism from the
Young Czechs, who charged that, by placing priority on religious rather than

national factors in Czech tradition, he was playing into the hands of the Germans at home and 'working for the king of Prussia'. Masaryk retorted by condemning the Hus cult in its nationalist form as an abuse of religion for political purposes.[26]

With the Catholics, and in particular Josef Pekař, the historian, the conflict was even more fundamental. Although the differences were often razor-thin and difficult to define precisely, the polemics were sharp on both sides. Pekař, a Catholic, was himself a great admirer of Hus and the Hussite tradition, and was equally opposed to the Hus cult in the Czech press. He acknowledged the moral and religious aspects of Hus, but believed that Masaryk was profoundly in error in ascribing to the Hussite tradition a primarily or exclusively religious character, and in linking it directly with the enlightenment of the nineteenth century. In contrast, Pekař stressed the national idea as the great motive of Czech history from Cyril and Methodius on. Pekař also drew attention to the fact that Hus, as a reformer, recognized the Papacy and did not try to establish a new Church.[27]

Masaryk's position was also ambiguous since he, too, recognized the national significance of Hus and the Hussite tradition. However, he always came back to the argument that the Czech question was primarily a religious one and that religion was the dominant theme of Czech history. He was also angered by Pekař's attempt to reconcile the Catholic and the Reform phases of Czech history, represented, in the latter's mind, by the presence of the Marian Column in the Old Town Square where the statue of Hus was to stand.

The controversy between the two men flared up again and again between 1900 and 1912. It was a highly personal quarrel and reflected deep differences over contemporary issues as much as historical questions. Further evidence of this was the way in which the argument was inextricably, and confusingly, linked with the discord over the question of the so-called 'Los von Rom movement, in both its German and Czech variants.[28]

The Los von Rom movement was launched at the end of the century by extreme nationalists and pan-Germans, who called on their fellow Germans in Austria to leave the Catholic Church. For the Young Czechs this was a treasonable movement, designed to prepare for the annexation of Austria by Protestant Prussia. Masaryk, on the contrary, saw no such danger. By 1902 only 30 000 people had left the Catholic Church, one-third converting to Old Catholicism and the rest to Protestantism. By 1913, 73 629 had converted, in Bohemia some 40 000 joining the Protestants and 15 000 the Old Catholics. Masaryk believed, moreover, that this was primarily a religious, and not a nationalist or political movement, and reflected a religious crisis throughout Europe and the world and the widespread demands for the reform of the Catholic Church. It had counterparts among Protestants, many of whom were seeking to get rid of ecclesiasticism and the old confession and also within other religions such as the Russian Orthodox Church and among the Jews.

In Bohemia, too, there was a Czech variant of Away from Rome in the form of Reform Catholicism and the Protestant churches. Masaryk's own conversion to

Protestantism was, of course, an example, as was his unrelenting campaign for the Hus tradition and for a new Czech religion. Although this aroused the opposition of the higher nobility, the high Catholic clergy, and other Catholics, especially in Moravia, and even of the 'Modern' Catholics, Masaryk's appeal to the Hus tradition had national overtones which contributed to a certain consensus among widely-separated tendencies, such as the Young Czechs, National Socialists and Social Democrats, and even Catholic nationalists such as Pekař; but his emphasis on religion and on the Reformation alienated some of these circles. Some Protestants believed that their church represented a kind of Czech Los von Rom movement. However, Masaryk's hostility to Evangelical clericalism produced disquiet among Protestants, including some in his own Realist party. The latter was sharply divided on these issues, and its attempt to forge a kind of compromise position, including neutrality toward all Churches, was not fully satisfactory to all its members and further upset Protestants outside the party.

A specific form of the movement away from Rome among Czechs was the revival of the tradition of Cyril and Methodius, the two monks of the Eastern Catholic Church who had brought Christianity to Moravia in the ninth century. This was propagated in particular by Young Czechs, who called for a revival of the Cyril–Methodian tradition and the use of a Slavic language in church ritual. An extreme form was the advocacy of conversion to the Orthodox Church, as exemplified by the Young Czech, Karel Sladkovský, in the sixties. For Masaryk this approach ignored the immense differences between Orthodox dogma and Hussite doctrine and overemphasized the national aspect of religion. He admitted that some of the Bohemian Brethren, and some of the awakeners, had perceived a link between Hussitism and the Eastern church, but argued that Hus had always been associated with the development of the Western church, and had sought to reform it rather than to break away from it. He stated categorically that Hus and the Bohemian Brethren had nothing in common with Orthodoxy other than what every Christian confession had in common. Nor did Hus and his successors have anything in common with the theology of the modern liberal Cyril–Methodians. Sladkovský's conversion to the Eastern Church was merely a part of a political programme and illustrated the confusion of the Young Czech party on the religious issue. On the other hand, the invocation of the Cyril–Methodian tradition by Catholics was, in Masaryk's view, not unjustified since Cyril and Methodius were Catholics and their church, although using the Slavic language and the Eastern ritual, was Catholic and Roman, not Eastern.[29]

FREEDOM OF CONSCIENCE AND INSTRUCTION – THE CATECHISTS CASE

As early as 1893, in a major speech on education in the Austrian Parliament, Masaryk had spoken out vigorously against the proposal for confessional schools advanced by Prince Liechtenstein. He noted that in the Catholic state of Austria, as in most other states, whatever their religious domination, control of the schools had passed out of the hands of the Church into those of the state. The Catholic Church, however, did not wish to recognize the validity of free scholarship and sought to overcome this through confessional education in school. He 'stood on the side of science and scholarship', declared Masaryk; 'Our party wants nothing else than freedom in our schools'.[30]

Ten years later, in a speech on 'Religious Liberty and Freedom of Conviction,' Masaryk reiterated his demand that the schools be emancipated fully from the Church and that confessional requirements for public employment be removed. He strongly condemned 'blind faith' and even more so, the imposing of faith by political power or by spiritual and physical violence, as practised by the Jesuits. What science and the Church proclaimed could not be reconciled; these were 'two different worlds'. Scientific truth was verified and well-grounded; 'in order to believe something or someone there is no other authority than science and the knowing man'. The Church relied on established doctrine, and was aristocratic, serving the powerful and the rich, and neglecting the poor. In Austria it was worse than churches elsewhere; 'the ruling state church is as ever an anti-Reformation church, whose essence is still the spirit of violence of the Inquisition'.[31]

These were strong words but even stronger were yet to come. In early 1906 a meeting was held at Helm's, in Prague, to protest the denunciation of a middle-school teacher by a Catholic priest and his transfer to another school as punishment. Masaryk's speech on that occasion was interrupted by the government representative who dissolved the meeting. Masaryk denied the authenticity of the published report of his speech, as well as of the notes of the single witness at the subsequent trial. Soon after, at a student meeting in Prague, Masaryk gave much the same speech, which was published in full by a student journal.[32] There followed judicial charges against Masaryk and others; in the case of Masaryk, a criminal charge that he had 'insulted religion', and separate civil complaints by 308 catechists that he had slandered their honour by accusing them of denunciation. Conviction would have led to Masaryk's removal from his university post, and the loss of his pension, and in the latter case, the payment of costs in over three hundred cases. In the end the courts dismissed all the charges against Masaryk. The clerical campaign against this profoundly religious man thus suffered a resounding defeat.[33]

In his speech at Helm's Masaryk had denied that, because he opposed religion in the schools, he was against religion. He was not against a 'positive religion, whether Catholic, Protestant or Jewish', but demanded religious freedom 'in the interest of science, the school and religion' (p. 30). 'What I am opposed to is a degenerate religion which needs politics for its defence. What sort of God would it be which needed politics, executive committees and police for the exercise of His power?' This was the passage at which Masaryk's speech had been interrupted and which was used in the indictment: Masaryk was also reported to have stated categorically that 'the catechist in today's schools is nothing but a government-paid informer,' but there was no such reference in his later published speech.[34]

The speech was a wide-ranging analysis of the relationship of science and Church religion. Citing extensively from scholars and theologians, Masaryk argued that science and philosophy, as taught at the University, were incompatible with Church religion. For the Church everything which he taught was 'anathema'. He listed the names of philosophers, writers, historians and even reform theologians, who were on the Catholic Index, which included, for example, Comte, Darwin, Descartes and Pascal. Science and scholarship were based on empirical fact and assumed that nature, history and society were law-ordered. Theology and Church religion were based on authority, and on revelation and miracles; in science 2×2 equals 4, but in theology, sometimes 5.

In the schools the conflict of science and theology was mirrored in a similar conflict between catechists and teachers, and, in turn, in the community at large between the 'freedom camp' and the 'Church camp'. It produced a crisis among the pupils, who, as early as the fifth grade, did not believe in what they were taught in catechism, and a crisis among teachers, who did not believe in what they were teaching. Both were afraid to draw attention publicly to the conflict because of the 'terrorism' exercised by the catechists in informing school and public authorities on teachers and schoolchildren. Yet neither the catechists nor the authorities had a right under the law to control and punish someone who did not recognize Church doctrine or did not live according to its provisions.

The only solution was *Divorçons*. Church and state should be separated. Only this would guarantee freedom of conscience. Religious instruction must be removed from the schools; religion should be taught only outside the schools.

Masaryk presented his ideas again at a meeting organized by the Progressive Club in Hradec Králové on 23 October, 1906. This took the form of a debate which lasted more than six hours. Other participants were two bishops, a Jesuit father, and two members of the Free Thought movement.[35] After Masaryk had spoken, the Jesuit Father sought to prevent further discussion by calling on people to leave, but only a small minority did so.

Masaryk sought to explain why the intelligentsia had fallen away from the Church. He drew on his personal experience in describing his own attitude to religion and the Church. Although he had left the Church, he was, he said, a Catholic in his very bones, and knew Catholicism better than his Catholic opponents. He was not prejudiced against religion and was certainly not an atheist. From his first years in Prague he had criticized liberal intellectuals who did not recognize the seriousness of the religious question (pp. 139–42).

In his long and sharply-worded speech Masaryk went so far as to call the Church 'a spiritual corpse which destroyed religious life'. Quoting many Catholic theological sources, Masaryk condemned the doctrine of papal infallibility, the enforcement of conformity through the Index and the Syllabus, the dogma of the Immaculate Conception, the worship of relics, the granting of indulgences, and the support of superstitions such as the evil power of the freemasons, and the ritual-murder myth.

His objections to Catholicism were, however, largely of an ethical character. The Church placed more emphasis on ritual than on moral principle. Devout Catholics, including priests, were often morally worse even than atheists (p. 102). The official Church did not lead the struggle for moral progress, so that it was left to lay persons to fight against alcoholism and prostitution, and for social and political progress. The Church was more concerned with political power and constituted a theocratic and absolutist system (p. 117); its fundamental reform was impossible (p. 133).

FREEDOM OF CONSCIENCE AND SCHOLARSHIP – PARLIAMENTARY DEBATE

Masaryk was re-elected to Parliament in the 1907 elections, defeating a candidate representing the small traders' movement in a Moravian district where clerical influence was strong. The tone of the campaign may be seen in an electoral leaflet supporting his opponent, which called on citizens to vote against Masaryk as a candidate of the Jews, who wished to fling religion out of the schools. Once a German, he now pretended to be a Czech. He sided with Hilsner the Jew and brought disgrace on the whole Czech nation. 'Masaryk speaks about Christ in blasphemous words, denies His divinity, ridicules the forgiveness of sins, rejects miracles, rejects the grace of God – in short, he is no Christian.' In spite of active efforts by the Catholic clergy, Masaryk, with social democratic support, won handily on the second ballot.[36]

In Parliament Masaryk soon launched a new campaign against clericalism and for freedom of conscience. In late 1907 Masaryk introduced an urgent motion in Parliament calling on the government to give guarantees that it would protect the freedom of scholarship and of teachers recognized by state laws, and freedom of scholarship, belief and conscience. This was provoked by a speech at a Catholic conference in November by the Mayor of Vienna, Dr Lueger, whose Christian Socialist party had two seats in the cabinet and the chairmanship of the House. He had proclaimed that the clericals must gain control of the universities which were described as 'hot-beds of subversive ideas, revolution, anti-patriotism and godlessness'. After Masaryk's first speech, the Minister of Education declared in the name of the government that freedom of higher education and of scholarship would be protected. After three days of fiery debate and an amendment which diverted the attack from the Christian Socialist party to 'every kind of party political attack' (which Masaryk accepted), the motion was adopted with the support of all parties, including the Christian Socialists.[37]

In three speeches Masaryk reiterated his long-held conviction that there was an absolute conflict between the science and scholarship pursued at the universities, based on reason and experience, and requiring freedom and criticism, and the spiritual work of theology and the Church, based on authority and revelation and enforced by the Index of forbidden authors and the official Syllabus for teaching (pp. 12–13, 39–42). The universities were not subversive or revolutionary, although scholars did seek to 'revolutionize the spirit' and to 'subvert the medieval world view'. In social and political matters, however, Austrian universities were conservative, not revolutionary (pp. 11, 24–5). He cited his own personal experience – the long delay in his promotion due to denunciations by high-ranking Catholics, and cited other cases of persecution of professors. He complained that university teachers in general were poorly-paid, thus explaining the decline of Austrian universities. He denied once again that he was against religion, and responded to slanders on his personal life. He was not even opposed to Catholicism as such, but noted that the Church was divided into two camps. He sympathized with those Catholics who sought a reform of Church and Church doctrine and a reconciliation between science and religion. He defended his role in the Hilsner case and condemned anti-Semitism as contrary to Christ's teaching (pp. 44, 47–9). As always, Masaryk called for an end to the teaching of religion in the schools and urged the separation of Church and state. He condemned Czech priests who, in slandering him, had acted 'like hyenas'. The Czechs, he asserted, the nation of Hus, Chelčický, and Komenský, were not, and could not be, clerical.

FREEDOM OF CONSCIENCE AND SCHOLARSHIP – THE WAHRMUND CASE

A new battle with Catholicism ensued in 1908 when Ludwig Wahrmund, professor of ecclesiastical law at the University of Innsbruck, published a book entitled *The Catholic World Outlook and Free Learning*, in which he argued that there was an unbridgeable conflict between the Church outlook and that prevailing in the world of scholarship. As a result of a question raised in Parliament by Dr Lueger, Wahrmund was dismissed from his post and later transferred to the German University in Prague. A brochure based on his speech was officially confiscated.

Masaryk intervened with a provocative speech in the Reichsrat on 4 June, 1908 in which he attacked the government for its legally unjustified action, the Catholic Church for its campaign against Wahrmund, and Christian Socialists, such as Prince Liechtenstein and Lueger, for their attempt to 'conquer the schools'.[38] He did not hesitate to use words such as scholasticism, Jesuitism and mysticism to characterize Catholic attitudes and, citing many German and Austrian theologians, pointed out the errors of the arguments used by his opponents. Constantly interrupted by heckling, he showed himself a skilled and aggressive debater.

In his long address Masaryk endorsed the view that there was a fundamental incompatibility between the official Church religion and scholars, and summed up the differences between the 'two separate worlds' as follows:

We in the world of learning have accustomed ourselves to recognize the existence of universal laws at work, not only in nature, but also in history and society. We eliminate every miracle; while the theologians desire miracles. ...Our methods are different. On the one side the idea of revelation, on the other, the custom of using experience and generalization; there, authority, here, the individual, subjective understanding and conscious criticism; there, tradition, the past, the ancient, if possible the oldest, here criticism of tradition, progress, the present and the future, the freeing of the modern working man; on the one hand absolute infallibility, on the other, relativity, criticism; there, exclusiveness and orthodoxy, here, tolerance; there, belief, trust, obedience, here, conviction and criticism (without criticism we cannot believe) (pp. 23–4)

The only solution was the separation of Church and state, the separation of the school from the Church, 'Our whole modern world and life outlook, our science and art, our morality and politics, are freeing themselves from the Church. At last our religion is being 'unchurched' (*entkirchlicht*) (p. 48).

Another conflict with Catholics occurred in 1912 as a result of the confiscation of certain passages of a reader by the Czech poet, J. S. Machar, which was attacked by the Catholics as wounding their religious feelings and blaspheming Christ and the Virgin Mary. Masaryk introduced an interpellation in the Abgeordnetenhaus which had the effect of cancelling the ban and was viciously attacked in Parliament and in public meetings.[39]

MOVEMENT FOR FREE THOUGHT

In the summer of 1907 Masaryk was invited to speak at the Fourth International Congress of Religious Liberals in Boston, and gave a lecture on the religious situation in Bohemia which was published in English in the proceedings. He also gave five lectures at a congress in Chicago of the *Svaz svobodomyslných* which published the whole series. Although the Czech word, *svobodomyslný*, literally 'free thinking', simply meant liberal, the majority of its members *were* Free Thinkers, associated with a world movement for Free Thought (*Volnámyšlenka*) which was holding a conference in Prague at the same time.[40]

Although Masaryk was one of the founders of the Free Thought movement in Prague, he was highly critical of some of its positions. For him 'free thinking' had a broad meaning, embracing all forms of freedom, both political and religious, which rejected authority and dogma. For example, Jan Hus and the Czech Reformation, and the Czech enlightenment, stood for truth as opposed to dogma and church authority. Protestantism, too, was a struggle for free thought against the dogma and mysticism of the Catholic Church; science and modern philosophy were also characterized by freedom of thought. In modern Czech history, Havlíček, although a Catholic,was a leader of liberalism (*svobodomyslnost*) who resisted both political and religious absolutism and demanded, in the spirit of Jan Hus, a reform of the Church of his time.

It was the desire of the Free Thought Movement for complete freedom of thinking which attracted Masaryk but he could not accept their position fully. Within the movement there were those who believed that religion was 'finished', as well as those who sought a new and higher religion, based on conviction. Outside the movement there were also 'free thinkers' who were religious. There were also agnostics within the movement. Masaryk declared more than once that he was not an agnostic, still less an atheist, and he strongly disagreed that religion was 'finished'. Nor did he believe that religion could be replaced by science, philosophy or even by ethics. Science was opposed only to Church religion, whether Catholic or Protestant, and was not at all incompatible with a religion based on reason and freedom of thought. Religion was 'an inner life'; not a science or philosophy.

Even morality or ethics, without belief in God or immortality, could not replace religion. Masaryk was opposed to pantheism and declared himself to be a theist, accepting as a hypothesis that there was a personal God and that there was personal immortality. To be without confession, as in his own case, was not the same as being without religion. Some people did live without religion, and even lived better lives than religious persons, but man needed religion. 'A man who lives religiously is more in harmony with himself' (p. 70).

SOCIALISM AND RELIGION

In his American lectures Masaryk noted that there was a direct relationship between free thought and socialism, especially in their early common hostility to official Christianity and the Church. Later 'scientific socialism' was organically linked with freedom of thought, and believed that the Church and religion had been superseded by scientific thinking. Although Marx rejected both Church and religion, he did concede that the latter was a private matter. In Bohemia, Masaryk argued, socialism had developed on the basis of free thought, and rejected theology and Church thinking.

In these lectures Masaryk expressed the view that, although Jesus was not a socialist, his doctrine of 'love for one's neighbour was not unlike the modern socialist's belief in social justice'.[41] He had already developed this theme in greater detail in a speech in early 1907 on 'Clericalism and Socialism'.[42] In the latter he observed that for some socialists, socialism, based on Jesus's concept of love, was genuine Christianity. Citing the New Testament, Masaryk noted that Jesus had 'felt with the people', with the poor, and was against the rich and the powerful, and could be considered a social reformer, although not a socialist. Modern socialism, however, was different, had raised new demands and stood on legal, not moral and religious grounds. The Church, which in its early period enunciated doctrines that implied the desirability of a 'communist order', had become a political power, a theocracy, a government of priests; it had amassed great wealth and become 'a large-scale capitalist institution'.

The Reformation had, however, been the 'mother of religious socialism', as for instance in the communism of the Czech Taborites in the fifteenth century. In the nineteenth century early socialists had been religious, and only later had Marx placed socialism on a non-religious basis. Although Church religion professed Jesus's doctrine of love for one's neighbour, it applied it mainly in the form of philanthropy. Socialism, on the other hand, sought to apply it by seeking justice and the removal of poverty by social legislation. Moreover, in contrast to the Church's 'aristocratic' spirit, based on faith, authority and obedience, socialism demanded democracy and equality, not only economic, social and political, but also moral, religious and spiritual. This approach to social questions was particularly needed by the Czechs, a nation of 'the small man', relatively weak in comparison with other nations. For the Czechs, with their Taborite tradition, socialism was 'purely Czech' and not something foreign. We must not merely love our neighbour but should realize this through social legislation. 'This should be the Czech ideal.'

In spite of Masaryk's emphasis on the importance of social reform in religion, he totally rejected the views advanced by Marx and Engels that religion was primarily a 'costume' or 'disguise' covering its essentially economic basis and that religion in the modern world was an illusion or an opium of the people. In his book *The Social Question*, he presented a systematic refutation of dialectical and historical materialism and rejected its interpretation of religion.[43] Religion, he argued, was not a mere reflection of economic factors; its ethical element should not be ignored, as Engels had done. The Reformation could only be understood as a religious and moral movement which liberated consciousness and promoted science, and gave birth to the ideas of equality and democracy.

Religion exerted a powerful influence of its own on all aspects of life. For instance, the dualism of Catholicism and Protestantism, one authoritarian, the other democratic, had an impact on the state (authoritarianism vs democracy), on the economy, and on nationality, and even on socialism itself. The character of the latter in different countries was influenced by the relative influence of Catholicism or Protestantism, e.g. socialism was radical or revolutionary in France, reformist and democratic in Britain. Marxism itself was closer to Protestantism in its content and direction. None of this was to deny that socialism and religion were often closely linked, as for instance, among the Czech workers who thought of socialism in religious terms and even sometimes identified socialism as a religion. Marxism was itself a faith and awakened hope and confidence in the future among its adherents. Even some of its leaders, such as Bebel, in their fanatical atheism, were acting as believers.[44]

RELIGION IN RUSSIA

Masaryk's great work, *Russia and Europe* (The Spirit of Russia), published in 1913, was devoted, as the sub-title indicated, to the Russian philosophy of history and religion.[45] On a vast canvas Masaryk presented an analysis of Russian history, philosophy, literature and socialism in each of which the role of religion and the Church was an underlying theme. A central argument was that, although Russia was in many ways unique, it had been greatly influenced in modern times by Europe which, for the old Russia, amounted to a spiritual and political revolution. The result was a complex synthesis of its own independent development, sometimes paralleling European development, and the absorption of European ideas and practices – for instance, the Renaissance, the Reformation and the new philosophy (pp. 604, 611, Russian; 481–7, English). As far as religion was concerned, Russian Orthodox Christianity had evolved independently, but had been subject to the influences of the two great Church systems of the West, Roman Catholicism and Protestantism. While it shared many of the features of Roman Catholicism, it had also been greatly affected by Protestant influences and by German philosophy (pp. 627–31, 687–9, Russian; 500–5, 553–5, English).

For Masaryk the defects of the Western Church were present in even more exaggerated form in the Eastern Church. The Russian Church was based on the same ideas of orthodoxy and absolute authority; it was an aristocratic organization in which the priests, and particularly monks, played a more important role than in the West. It had, however, a special relationship to the state which involved, unlike the West, not the separation of church and state, but the close union of both, with the church enjoying primacy of spiritual power but recognizing the state as the supreme leader in secular affairs. This constituted, in Masaryk's view, a theocracy, or Caesaropapism. In the absence of Protestant churches, the Eastern Church exercised undivided influence over state and society (pp. 614–23, Russian; 489–96, English).

Masaryk was also critical of official Church religion in Russia, not only for characteristics which it held in common with Catholicism and Protestantism, but for its distinctive features. Like its Western counterpart, Orthodoxy was based on absolute faith and the belief in revelation, as opposed to science. It was characterized by a greater degree of mysticism, and laid less stress on ethical questions than in the West (Russian, pp. 600–6). Asceticism, especially of the monks, played an important role. Like the Western Church it tended to subordinate 'love of one's neighbour' to faith in God and in the priests. In politics, whereas in the West Protestantism promoted democratic ideas, Orthodoxy, even more than Catholicism, buttressed autocratic rule. It also contributed to the revolutionary and atheistic character of Russian socialism (Christian socialism did not manifest itself) and to tendencies toward anarchism, nihilism and terrorism (pp. 624–7, 646–58, 680–7, Russian; 497–500, 517–27, 546–52, English).

CONCLUSION

Masaryk's understanding of religion, it is clear from the above, is complicated and defies easy summary. Although Masaryk made many attempts to expound his views on the subject, he was not able, as he admitted later (1927) 'to get the problem straight in his mind and to create a systematic whole of his thoughts'.[46] Perhaps one might, however, modify the severe judgements of Kozák and Betts cited earlier (pp. 1, 6) and admit that Masaryk was trying to define something which by its very nature was undefinable.

Although his views underwent change over the years, and were sometimes characterized by contradictions and ambiguities, there was also a remarkable consistency in his thinking. For Masaryk religion was an extremely personal matter, to be resolved by each person on his own. It was also a practical matter, which expressed itself in real life. Retrospectively, in his conversations with Karel Čapek, he summarized his views as follows. 'Religion is a practical matter, a question of life in the deepest sense of the word. It is not adequately defined by dogmas, by ritual, or even by its history, but only by an understanding of its essence, i.e. the consciousness of the dependence of man on divinity, on God. This means the consciousness, but at the same time the overcoming, of human weakness, physical, spiritual and moral. For religion is confidence and hope; hopefulness is the essence of religion'.[47]

Masaryk, as we have noted, was a bitter critic of the contemporary Catholic Church, of its theology, its practices and its priesthood. Although he had a positive attitude toward Protestantism as a challenge to Catholic authoritarianism, he was also highly critical of contemporary Protestant ecclesiasticism. Yet he did not attempt a systematic analysis of Protestantism, or make the same sustained assault on it as he did on Catholicism.[48] Masaryk was also highly critical of the Orthodox Church. Although he did not conduct a systematic study of other religions of the world (except to a limited degree, the Jewish), he urged the need for toleration of other beliefs.

His ideals were found in the Hussite Reformation and the Bohemian Brethren which derived from it. The legacy of Hus, for him, was 'not to believe what he believed, but like him, to reform, and reshape, always inwardly to renew, our surroundings'.[49] Yet even Hussitism and the Brethren, while offering inspiration and guidance for the present, had their weaknesses and inadequacies and had to be adapted to modern conditions. Perhaps the only one to escape his criticism was Komenský, who represented in Masaryk's mind a synthesis of Chelčický and Hus and who expressed the purest conception of religion.[50]

Religion was closely intertwined with morality but their exact relationship was left unclear. Religion was certainly not only morality but the latter was one of its decisive elements. Morality, on the other hand, was not an alternative to religion nor was it sufficient by itself. Both seemed to support each other mutually, but one without the other was not sufficient. Masaryk asserted that religion was a higher morality but sometimes he suggested that morality took priority over religion.[51]

For Masaryk the model of religion and morality was Jesus, who, he said, regarded devoutness and morality as the main elements of religion. My own faith, he confided to Čapek, rested in 'Jesus, the love for one's neighbour, effective love, and reverence before God'.[52] Concretely the love for one's neighbour meant that religion must concern itself with social questions. It could not be satisfied with mere philanthropy but must strive for concrete political and economic legislation to deal with social problems. In this respect he found liberalism wanting for its lack of a radical social programme as well as for its religious indifference. Socialism was more attractive because it accepted the need for social reform but the Marxist economic interpretation of religion was unacceptable.

Masaryk found no incompatibility between religion and science as long as religion was based not on faith and on authority, but on reason and conviction. Yet his own theism, his belief in God and immortality, which he called a hypothesis, and his trust in a Providence which guided mankind, were not susceptible to empirical proof.[53] In general, however, religion should recognize and accept freedom of scholarship and should not have the right to control instruction in schools or in universities.

It is not surprising that Masaryk's views met with misunderstanding and with outright hostility, and that he suffered persecution for them. Yet, as a German philosopher, W. Schmidt, wrote in 1910, this martyrdom did not destroy Masaryk but on the contrary gave him added strength. And the great secret of this strength, according to Schmidt, lay 'in religion'.[54]

8 Defender of Women's Rights

Tomáš Garrigue Masaryk was preeminent among men in Bohemia in the late nineteenth century as an advocate of women's rights.'[1] Masaryk spoke out boldly and in radical tones against the enslavement of women in all spheres of life, including the home and family. In speeches and articles, and in his journal, *Naše doba*, he hammered away at what he considered false beliefs about the inequality of women and criticized unjust limitations on women's place in society. In a manner which endorsed the major claims of the contemporary women's movement and anticipated many of the demands of the feminist movement of the future, he called for absolute equality for women in all spheres – equal responsibility of men and women within the family, equal access to education and the professions, equal pay for equal work, the enfranchisement of women, and full participation of women in public affairs. He condemned prostitution and what he called 'polygyny' (*mnohoženství*), i.e. sexual relations with more than one wife or with several women. He was severely critical of prevalent views about the nature of love and of sex expounded both by official Catholic doctrine and by socialist theory, which, he felt, demeaned women and distorted love and marriage. He also condemned ideas expressed in modern literature, which encouraged sexual laxity. Alois Hajn, active in contemporary Czech progressive politics, later described him as 'a pioneer of the ideas on the women's question' whose words created 'a veritable revolution among Czech youth' at the time.[2]

INFLUENCES ON MASARYK'S THINKING

In the forming of Masaryk's viewpoint on the women's question a number of influences were at work. The first was the position of women in Bohemian society during the latter part of the nineteenth century. Women suffered many liabilities, such as an inferior place in the family, discrimination in the economic sphere, limitations on educational opportunities, denial of the franchise, and discouragement from participation in public affairs, not to mention prevailing opinions that women were inferior to men and should rightly suffer inequality. Nonetheless, from the 1870s on, women's associations were formed, and a strong women's movement came into existence. By 1900 women were able to secure education at all levels, to enter the professions, and to participate to a limited degree in public life. By 1914 women had already begun to advance toward emancipation to a greater degree than in other parts of the Austrian empire.[3] At the turn of the century, when Masaryk concerned himself with the question, there was, however, still much to be done to achieve genuine equality of men and women.

More direct and personal was the influence exerted by his wife, Charlotte Garrigue Masaryk.[4] Masaryk himself spoke of the impact on his own life of his mother and of his wife. He told Karel Čapek of the great influence of his mother, a 'wise' and 'devout' woman; he also said of Charlotte that 'our whole marriage was cooperation.'[5] During their courtship in Leipzig, where she was studying music, the couple had often read together and had been greatly attracted by the ideas expressed by John Stuart Mill in *The Subjection of Women* (London, 1869). Charlotte later translated this book into Czech. After their marriage Masaryk adopted Charlotte's maiden name as his middle name and later gave it to each of his children.

Charlotte was a woman of marked intellectual capacity and a highly developed social conscience. Brought up as a Unitarian she was devout and deistic; like Masaryk, her religion was highly personal and free of any respect for Church dogmas or practices. After coming to Prague, she learned Czech well, studied Czech literature and history, and became an ardent patriot. She had a wide knowledge of literature, but her great love was music. She played the piano and wrote several articles on Smetana, her favourite composer, then not held in high repute. She was a strong advocate of women's rights and became active in the Czech women's movement, and in other social work. She was deeply concerned with social problems, and, unlike her husband, joined the Social Democratic party and took part in its activities.

During their married life Charlotte and Tomáš continued to pursue their common intellectual pursuits, often reading or playing music together, and attending concerts. Charlotte worked in close cooperation with Masaryk in his social and intellectual activities and is said to have left many 'traces of her spirit' in his writings and in his plans. Hajn later wrote that Charlotte had been not only 'a wife but a helper and collaborator in all his life's work, a close friend and comrade'.[6] Masaryk himself later declared that his views on women had been 'determined by the living model of my wife'; 'she had been the most decisive influence on the maturing of all my views and on my character'. One of his major statements on the women's question, *Polygyny and Monogyny*, he said, was 'as a matter of fact my wife's work.' He was once quoted as saying that in the women's question 'I am only a peddler of my wife's opinions.'[7]

Inseparable from this was the influence on Masaryk of his strong personal beliefs on marriage and the family. In one of his earliest writings he stated that the family was 'a real school of love for one's fellow-man' and of 'altruism and of work.' He laid special stress on the role of the mother; 'mother love is actually the basis of all human society'.[8] Many witnesses testified that Masaryk's married life was a model of a happy and harmonious marriage. One of his closest friends and admirers, Jan Herben, wrote of their marriage as 'rare and beautiful', undisturbed by serious conflict.[9]

Their style of living was simple and modest. They usually had household help, especially after the beginning of Charlotte's illness in the late eighties. Food was simple and without luxuries. Masaryk himself did not drink or smoke after 1888. He imposed strict rules of dress and behaviour on the children but was attentive to them, playing with them in the early years, and enjoying social games and singing in the evening at home. Masaryk worked every morning in his study, and spent the afternoons walking, reading newspapers in cafés, and visiting his editorial offices. Charlotte looked after the household and devoted much time to the children but also assisted her husband in his work.[10]

Masaryk's family life thus seemed to be an embodiment of his own ideas of love, marriage and the family, to be discussed below. It is impossible to be sure how far the reality conformed to Masaryk's personal memories and the nostalgic reminiscences of their friends and children. There is no evidence of serious conflict between Tomáš and Charlotte. But in 1916, when she was already afflicted by the illness which was to bring about her death a few years later, Charlotte, in a letter to her daughter, Alice, then in prison, expressed dissatisfaction with her life in Prague. She had enjoyed a 'nice traditional life' but had missed 'the ability to think religiously'.[11]

With the children the relationship did not entirely conform to Masaryk's precepts. Alice, who had studied at the first women's gymnasium in Prague and had been the only woman medical student, took her degree in philosophy and became a high-school teacher. She remained single, perhaps as the result of an action by her mother in an earlier relationship. On her death bed, she admitted that she had had a love affair early in life and regretted that she had not married.[12] Olga, whose marriages ended in divorce, spoke later of the 'rare friendship' she enjoyed with her father, and of the feeling of 'complete freedom and openness' in her life in the family.[13] Herbert, an artist, married the widow of his former teacher and the couple added two children to her three. Masaryk's relations with his son, Jan, were perhaps less than happy since the latter left home and family in his late twenties and made a life for himself in America and Britain until his return home just before the war.[14]

Masaryk's trip to America in 1893 had a profound effect on his thinking about the place of women in society and in the home. During a visit to the small college town of Oberlin, Ohio, he was greatly impressed by the position of women, who had free access to all schools and studied at all faculties of the university, including even theology. They could act as preachers, could serve on school boards and in some states had voting rights. He was affected by the general deportment of women, who were 'freer, and hence men were freer there'. No one would kiss a woman's hand as was the Czech custom at home, and she in return would not address a man with the greeting 'my respects' (*Máúcta*). Young women could talk with young men about matters of common interest, including politics. 'All this is a new world,' he said. This freedom 'signified a higher cultural development, a higher moral level, a purer relationship between man and woman.' He believed that in Bohemia there should be 'greater freedom of thought'; 'the woman would cease to be a slave (cook, housekeeper, wet-nurse and concubine), and the man would cease to be the lord over the woman'.[15]

THE 'WOMEN'S QUESTION'

Masaryk did not attempt a systematic scholarly study of the women's question. Apart from a few brief references in his works on suicide, the social question, and the Czech question, he expressed his views in several major speeches and articles which reflected not so much empirical research as his own beliefs in strict morality in personal and public life, and in social justice, national equality and democracy.[16]

The question of the place of women in society was, for Masaryk, first and foremost a moral one and involved new attitudes on the part of both men and women. In reporting on the first women's congress in Prague in 1897, Masaryk asserted that 'it is not enough merely to proclaim oneself a friend of women's emancipation....it was necessary to give practical expression of this opinion in every aspect of life and in the most mundane affairs'. This meant 'a turning of one's whole life, a completely new way of looking at one's own "I" and at human society. It meant a real inward revolution by which a person becomes a new person. Emancipation of women is the emancipation of men.' It was thus necessary 'to correct ideas previously rooted in our education and social atmosphere, both in men and women', and 'to struggle inwardly, to learn to be just and thus less egoistical'.[17]

Masaryk also expressed his belief that 'the women's problem and the social problem went hand in hand.' If one 'admits the principle of justice to woman, one certainly wishes justice in all of human life'. In his essay on 'The Modern View of Women', he stated even more emphatically: 'I have not spoken and do not like to speak of a woman's question. Since there is not a woman's question, so there is not a merely man's question. It is a question of society.' 'It is incorrect to pose men and women against each other – society, the nation, are millions of men and women, millions of individuals mutually linked in a single whole; there must be a common concern of man and woman that this should be an organic whole'.[18]

In the same essay Masaryk argued that the women's question was a part of the national question. He observed: 'this modern effort of men and women is a necessary continuation in the work of national revival. Our revival will not be a reality as long as the Czech man, along with the Czech woman, does not undergo a revival, a spiritual, moral and social revival.' 'The modern Czech woman signifies for our small nation a doubling of our strength' (*Masaryk a ženy*, pp. 67, 69).

Masaryk's views on women were intimately related to his belief in 'democratism'. In an appeal to youth in 1906, Masaryk declared that 'Democratism is first and foremost the equality of woman and man, mother with father, sister with brother.'[19] In an undated statement quoted by Alois Hajn, Masaryk observed: 'The women's movement is a product of democratism; women wish to be equal. The woman and the man form an intimate unity; there cannot be any talk of a women's question, just as there cannot be talk of a man's question. The woman's question is not only a woman's question, but it is also a man's question, a children's question, in a word, it is a cultural and a human question.'[20]

THEORIES OF INEQUALITY REJECTED

Masaryk's intention, as he expressed it, was 'to formulate in positive terms what seems to me a really modern progressive view of woman' and to express the essence of 'this new opinion, this new life, this new world'. This required the refutation of old views and prejudices and the destruction of myths about men and women, held equally by both sexes as to the 'enormous difference' between them, especially concerning the inferiority of women to men (*Masaryk a ženy*, pp. 61, 85).

In the first place, women were not 'weaker in intellect (intelligence)': 'our mothers and wives, as to capacity, profundity and perceptiveness, do not think less nor worse than we men do. The proper care of a poorer household and everything connected therewith demands greater intellectual strain than activity in any office, university chair or pulpit' (p. 62). 'Do you really think that a woman worker or peasant, professor or official, who brings up perhaps five children by the sweat of her brow, in performing this work, thinks less than her husband, some boring – or perhaps not so boring – scholar. A scholar who knows much, and knows how to make a living with his head, does not think as much as his plain wife, toiling away from morning to night, unseen by anyone' (pp. 85–6). Women, he noted, 'did better than men at the university, and everywhere else' (pp. 72–3).

Women were not physically weaker than men. There *was* a 'physiological difference'; by virtue of certain sexual functions (pregnancy, nursing, etc.) a woman was excluded for a time from a man's employment. Perhaps women were 'muscularly' weaker but even this should not be exaggerated. But it was doubtful that she was weaker as far as 'nerves' go. 'Bringing up several children, especially in poorer, or even straitened circumstances, demands much more nervous strength than a man's work in public service, instruction in schools, or anything else'(pp. 87, 62).

Nor did women have more 'feeling' than men, who, it is said, were more devoted to 'cold reason,' were 'rougher' and less 'delicate'. 'We must especially get used to differentiating over-sentimentality in novels from real feeling.' (p. 86), even though such 'old wives' tales' were repeated in scientific books. 'Just as in the case of men, there are women with deeper feeling and women without feeling. It is not true that a woman has in particular some kind of special feeling' (p. 73).[21]

Women were also not morally superior. 'A woman is not better, nor is she worse than a man; it all depends on the individual. Men and women develop together from the beginning; they mutually influence each other everywhere and constantly, so that is not possible that the moral or the generally spiritual state of one or the other is lower or higher' (p. 62). 'Woman and men are always together; there is such intimate contact among them that there cannot be such a difference' (pp. 86–7).

Nor were women more religious or more devout than men, who are supposed to be more rational. True, more women than men go to church, but this is because the woman is excluded from social life, not because she is more devout. 'While the man sits in the tavern, there is nothing else left for the poor soul.' If she is more devout than man, 'she, and not the godless man, ought to be a priest or a pastor' (pp. 73–4).

Masaryk also felt obliged to dispose of a number of myths concerning women and their role in society and the family, especially that of domesticity (p. 63), which assumed that the woman in the household was 'cook and servant'. Women were therefore discouraged, or prevented, from seeking or taking work outside the home. In Masaryk's view, the household would not suffer if the woman had outside employment. Many tasks, such as washing, ironing and sewing, did not need to be performed in the household, just as baking bread was no longer a necessity. There was even the possibility of having domestic cooperative or large family houses with common heating and kitchens. The household was indeed 'sacred' but that did not require the woman to be a 'domestic slave' or be deprived of a career. There should be equality within the household, as outside it. This would make the woman 'spiritually independent' and would require her husband to respect her and treat her as an equal (pp. 71, 64, 163).

The opposite side of the coin was the escape of the man from home. Although the father should share the task of caring for their children, the man usually shifts the family responsibilities on to the wife'. 'Hardly has he come home than he goes out again into non-family life – let us say it openly – to the tavern'. 'O, these horrible Czech taverns, which steal the husband and the father and destroy the sacredness of the family' (pp. 70–1, 66).

Another myth was that women were not able to compete equally in economic life. Masaryk regarded as totally false the ideas that women should not be forced to compete in the marketplace since, as 'delicate creatures', they were not able to compete, and that work would destroy family life. If women were to earn a living themselves, men would to that extent be relieved of responsibility and would have an easier position. Moreover, among peasants, men and women work equally both in the field and at home; and among workers, too, the problem had been to a considerable degree solved. Only in the middle class were there still conflicts about certain kinds of employment, such as medicine, but the reasons for exclusion of women were groundless. In literature, there were outstanding women writers in all nations (pp. 64, 76, 87–9).

Another erroneous view was that the sexual instinct was more powerful and more important for men and that it must be satisfied. It was quite untrue that chastity harmed a person physically and spiritually. Like other instincts this one should be placed under the control of reason; the more powerful the instinct, the more it must be mastered (pp. 90–1).

EQUALITY FOR WOMEN

For Masaryk, 'the inequality of women and men was not natural; it was not derived from the nature of things, but developed historically. Just as many, often fateful, mistakes had been made in history, so the suppression of women was a mistake – and a very big one (p. 63). 'Emancipation' did not mean that the modern woman should conduct herself like a man and do what a man did. Imitating men, for example, in smoking and drinking, was nothing but reactionary (p. 67). It did mean, however, that, if they *were* equal, 'man and woman should and can have completely equal employment as long as women are not directed to certain special employment by virtue of their sexual functions – that is, absolute economic equality, or better said, absolute equality of work' (pp. 87, 77).

This required equality in other spheres, too. For example in education women should have equal schooling, including admission to university, and should be able to study in all disciplines, including, for instance, medicine (p. ll5). Improved education would make women more independent and less likely to conclude unsuitable marriages. They would also make better mothers. Masaryk approved coeducation, which had shown itself to be effective in the philosophical faculty. Similarly, why should women not be equally active in religion and the church? (p. 89).

A most important need was equality of women in public affairs and in politics, from which they had been more or less completely excluded. If, in the name of domesticity, we keep women distant from public work, 'we lower their horizons, deaden their energy, and waste their talents' (p. 130). Absence from public life deprived a woman of ambition and public respect; participation would provide many sources of pleasure and would encourage her energy and strengthen her will. Because there were bad sides to public life, we should not distance women from it, but rather seek to reform it (p. 77).

Women had an important 'social task' to perform. 'Women must understand the public and political tasks of the time, and like a man, and with him, dedicate themselves to public affairs' (pp. 64–5). As far as political life was concerned, facts had shown that women know how to be politically effective. 'This involved much nervous energy because women, being subjected to special attention, must perform better than men in public activity. Needless to say, every woman will not be active publicly, but would it be harmful to national life or to the family if half of the deputies in Austria were women?' (pp. 75–6)

LOVE, MARRIAGE AND THE FAMILY

Not surprisingly, Masaryk's consideration of the place of women led him to draw conclusions about the more personal side of life – love, marriage, the family, and sexual morality. Although the concept of love, for Masaryk, referred to humanity in the broadest sense, he admitted that one could not love all equally.' One must select the object of love among those closest to us – mother, father, brother, sister, wife, and children. 'Closest is the wife to the husband, the husband to the wife. True love must sanctify effectively this most intimate relationship. The wife is completely equal to her husband; only physical difference should be recognized; she is weaker.'[22]

Love must not be identified with the sexual instinct. 'Real love is not a union of bodies, but of souls' – in Elizabeth Browning's words, 'a marriage of spirit' (p. 90). 'Marriage is a fusion of independent individuals, of one spirit with another – but today a slave is more pleasant for a man... 'Marriage is the beginning of common development and common work for the whole of life, for an eternity' (p. 65). 'Pure marriage is the most intimate friendship; it is the apex of association...an association of spirit. There cannot be a more intimate association than between man and woman' (p. 90).

This kind of spiritual unity formed the basis of a moral family life. Family life was a 'real school of love for those close to one'; it was a stimulus to altruism of father, mother, brother to brother, sister to sister, so that 'all would love each other equally and equally care for each other.' The family was the 'basis of character, in which the children learn and are trained'. The father embodied authority, requiring obedience by children, but 'it is on mother's love that all human society is actually based'.[23]

It followed from such a conception of marriage and the family that divorce was not to be encouraged or permitted. Although Masaryk admitted that in some cases divorce was necessary and desirable, it should not be resorted to simply because a married couple were beginning to be bored. Everything should be done so that divorce was not necessary (p. 96). Many divorces simply encouraged frivolous marriages. 'Not divorce but purity – that must be the slogan of Czech youth. ... preserve purity for marriage and you will be happy.... Many marriages are unhappy because few men lived purely before marriage.... Divorce must not become a means of general legalized prostitution.'[24]

A marriage of the kind advocated by Masaryk also involved 'strict monogamy' of both wife and husband. This meant that 'every man should have in his life only one wife and a woman only one man, of course, in a state of matrimony.' Even a second marriage was contrary to this ideal. At the present time, Masaryk argued, monogamy existed more on paper; there was much polygamy (polygyny), both after marriage in the form of prostitution, and before marriage among young people. This was 'a social evil'. Strict monogamy, he declared, must be the goal of our sexual evolution (pp. 79–80).[25]

SEXUAL IMMORALITY: PROSTITUTION, ABORTION AND ILLEGITIMACY

Masaryk was a strong foe of prostitution, as a form of polygyny, as well as adultery. In 1884, in one of his earliest writings, he rejected the idea that prostitution was a necessary evil, or that it was primarily caused by penury. The primary cause was not physical, but moral, and was the result of failures in training and education,especially of women. The whole of modern life, and the bad moral atmosphere created by novels, the theatre and ballet, and illustrated magazines, caused a precocious awakening of the sexual instinct. This was aggravated by alcoholism. Although prostitution was forbidden by law, it was a common sin in civilized society; 'impurity' weakened both the individual and the nation. Prostitution led to the degeneration of women, and after their return to normal life in society, to an infection of society as a whole. Hand in hand with prostitution went adultery, bigamy, lewdness, unmarried sexual relations and the sexual abuse of children. It was an evil which could be fought against, like other moral evils, by improvement of moral training.[26]

Twenty years later, in 1906, Masaryk was still fighting against prostitution and urging common action against 'impurity' among the intelligentsia, especially the youth. There would not be *prostitutky* (women prostitutes), he said, if there were not also men prostitutes; the man should be blamed and punished as much as the woman. The main cause of prostitution was 'the entire outdated moral opinion about women'; the only way to correct it was to recognize the equality of women.[27]

Masaryk lamented that prostitution was not much talked about, and that neither church nor state did much to fight against this evil. Doctors, he felt, neglected to clarify such sexual issues, nor did politicians pay attention to them. However, he rejected 'state prostitution,' i.e. regulation by the state, which amounted to 'state polygamy.' The solution lay in moral self-help (*svépomoc*) by the family, the school and the individual (pp. 92–3).

Masaryk was also firmly opposed to abortion except when recommended by doctors and rejected various reasons advanced for permitting it. Although forbidden by law, it was common. Quite apart from the moral aspect, it did great harm to the woman, and weakened her and society. Masaryk was said to judge the matter from a high moral standpoint according to the principle: 'Even a life scarcely begun is life, and no one is justified in destroying it.'[28]

At the same time Masaryk deplored the growing number of illegitimate births, and believed that this was a measure of the moral level of society. He thought one should speak of 'illegitimate parents' rather than children, and deplored the fact that the blame was attached only to the woman, and not to the man. He recognized the need for the care of such children by state and society and believed that illegitimate children should have equality of legal rights. He also lamented the number of abandoned children but felt that homes for them simply encouraged illegitimate births.[29]

Yet Masaryk was also opposed to the use of contraceptives, which he regarded as another sin of modern society and which he called 'married masturbation'.[30] Incidentally he was also opposed to masturbation by young men, another evil which led to premature and immoderate sexual life and to perversity.[31]

Alcoholism, in Masaryk's view, was closely associated with prostitution and was very relevant to love and marriage, and sexual immorality. It was the cause of many economic and social ills. 'Drinking and alcoholism harm the relations of man and woman, lowering and coarsening them; animality replaces humanity. Love is pure love; love with alcohol is not love.' Alcoholism harms the relationship of parents and children. It deprives children of a father, who is separated by the tavern from wife and children; the latter thus miss the happiness of childhood.' The drinker neglected his family; money needed for food and medicine was wasted on drink. Alcoholism not only affected the father physically and mentally, but also the children, who grew up in an evil atmosphere and learned to drink from their parent. 'Only abstinence could make family life what it ought to be. After the overcoming of alcoholism the relationship between husband and wife, families and children, will be different, better, purer and more spiritual.[32]

CRITICISM OF THE CATHOLIC VIEWPOINT

In defending what he called 'a modern viewpoint', Masaryk, as was his wont, subjected other viewpoints to severe criticism. One of his chief targets was the 'old view' 'that woman is for man...that woman is a comfort for man, at best for the rearing of his children' and that 'woman must be subject to the husband and the father' (p. 61). This concept was upheld principally by 'official religion' as represented by the Catholic Church and in Masaryk's view represented 'absolutism or aristocratism of the male' (p. 84). This 'Christian ascetic ideal' was based on the false idea that body and spirit were different, the former something impure, not deserving of respect (p. 90). This led to the Catholic idea of the Madonna, representing 'physical virginity'; this cultivated 'a special Jesuitical sensualism, which devalued the ideal by a coarse opinion of a woman's lower value' (p. 66). This was expressed concretely in the requirement of celibacy for priests and monks, which confirmed 'the view that woman is something lower' (p. 74).

In Masaryk's view, contemporary Catholic teachings on women were based on, and justified by, the Old Testament and carried on in the New Testament, especially in the teachings of Paul.[33] This 'patriarchal' view treated woman as virtuous above all as a worker and home provider, one who cared in all things for her husband (Proverbs 31: 10–31) (*Masaryk a ženy*, pp. 99–101). Paul's teaching, which became the official doctrine of the church, reasserted the view that women were subordinate and drew the conclusion that they should be excluded from the priesthood. The ideal of the Church became the monk or the nun, who did not marry but abandoned family life (pp. 105–6). From this developed later the rule of celibacy for priests, although this was often more honoured in the breach than in observance, and priestly failings were hidden. It also led to the doctrine that marriages were only valid if conducted by priests and the view that marriage of Christians and non-Christians was forbidden. The cult of the Virgin Mary reinforced the view that marriage was somehow 'impure' and that virtue was equated with physical inviolability. This ascetic view, for Masaryk, degraded women and marriage and ignored the fact that a man could be purer in marriage than in virginity, since marriage constituted a relationship of body and spirit. Only St Augustine recognized that in marriage both partners were 'brothers and fellow servants' and were one in spirit and body (pp. 108–9).

Masaryk discerned a significant difference of attitude between Jesus and Paul, although he admitted that there were difficulties of interpretation. Jesus also accepted to a significant degree Old Testament views, for instance on divorce, asceticism, and celibacy (pp. 80–1). Divorce was permissible only for adultery; yet he was also willing to forgive adultery. Chastity was for him the ideal, and was better than marriage. Yet in Masaryk's view, Jesus was not an ascetic; chastity involved a great but painful sacrifice for an ideal, such as religion. His disciples must be ready to abandon family for His sake. Jesus himself did not marry although it was not foreclosed that had he lived, he would have married. Yet Jesus's religion was a religion of love, whereas official religion had no understanding of the higher union of man and woman (pp. 99ff).

CRITICISM OF SOCIALIST VIEWS

Masaryk was also extremely critical of Marxist views of women. In his book, *The Social Question*, he subjected to severe criticism Engels's historical interpretation of the rise of the family and private property, not only for its historical inaccuracy but also for its exclusively economic or materialist approach.[34] Under capitalism, according to Engels, women were servants and slaves, and the man the ruler of the family. Under socialism, the woman would be liberated; mutual love would be the basis of marriage, the hegemony of man would be abolished, the indissolubility of marriage would end, and prostitution would disappear. Although Masaryk could agree with many of these objectives, he did not believe that socialism would liberate the woman merely by removing the economic conditions of monogamy.

Masaryk believed that Engels was in error in considering marriage an overwhelmingly physiological and economic institution. This led him to 'reduce family life and its social significance too much to a sexual union', whereas in fact 'family life and sexual relations gave expression to the whole morality of society and to a complete view of the world' (*Otázka sociální*, p. 93).

Engels's standpoint led to what Masaryk called 'the doctrine of free love' and the 'decadent' view that the sexual instinct was the centre of all life and was of such an absolute character that it could not be controlled. On the contrary, in Masaryk's view, as noted above, real love was 'not a union merely of bodies, but also of spirits' (ibid.). 'It was not enough to recommend free love; we must first and foremost demand a higher, nobler love' (p. 96).

Repeating a favourite theme, Masaryk stated his belief that Engels failed to grasp the fact that the women's question was also the man's question. 'It is not a question of liberating the woman, but also of liberating the man. Woman is not to be liberated from the man, nor the man from the woman; both are to be liberated, on the one side from animalism (bestiality), on the other side from decadent corruption (depravity)' (p. 93). Moreover Masaryk could not accept the view that prostitution was something necessary and inevitable; 'prostitution, adultery and sexual immorality generally are precisely forms of immorality which arise independently and develop under all conditions' (p. 96).

'Finally I do not agree with communism in general, and I reject any kind of sexual communism, in whatever form it presents itself – whether prostitution, polygyny and polyandry, remarriage, free love and so on.' Humanity was moving towards absolute monogamy but for this to be possible, it was necessary to have, besides the necessary economic reforms, moral and spiritual reforms all along the line.[35]

CRITICISM OF MODERN LITERATURE

A third target of Masaryk's was what he called the 'modern' or 'decadent' tendency, presenting itself initially on the eve of the French Revolution (Rousseau), and then in the revolutionary ideas of liberty, freedom of the family, and free love. This was expressed in manifold ways in modernist literature, especially French (Stendhal, Balzac, Zola) but also German (Goethe, Schopenhauer) and English (Byron, Shelley, Wilde). Although there were differences according to period and country, these writers expressed in common 'the ideal of modern love': free love, free union and marriage, and freedom of divorce. Liberalism also applied the slogan of political and economic liberty to the family – 'husband, wife, and children have to be free'. Socialism, too, placed the family on the basis of political and economic equality and free love. According to these views, monogamy hindered the full development of the human being, both man and woman, and must be replaced by 'a noble, higher form of polygamy' (ibid., pp. 82–5).

Masaryk expressed his views more fully in many critical reviews on literature published in his journal, *Naše doba*, from the end of the century on.[36] These reviews showed his wide knowledge of comparative literature but his sweeping generalizations were polemical, sometimes dogmatic, and often complex and obscure. One can only somewhat arbitrarily select, from among his general arguments, some of Masaryk's thoughts on love, marriage and sex as expressed in modern literature.

Alfred de Musset wrote of 'the disease of the century' which resulted from the instability and uncertainty of the transitional period following the French Revolution. Lack of belief expressed itself in scepticism, egotism and a decline in all spheres of life, and had a damaging effect on men and women and their relationship. There was a 'fatal division of love into physical love and spiritual love, into clean and unclean love'. There could be no doubt which would win out in the struggle between them. Love was reduced to sexual passion, and this led to sensual love and cruelty, licentiousness and unnatural living, faithlessness and prostitution. Love became egotistical; the prostitute, the courtesan pushed back the dreaming, romantic, gentle, sweet *grisette*. Man separated himself from woman, for he had begun to disdain her; he threw himself upon wine, and leaving the cosy fireside of love, killed himself in foul places. Love succumbed to the spirit of the times (*Modern Man*, pp. 223–4).

Strangely enough, although religion and the Church had been rejected by the new thinking, they continued to exert a profound influence on the new thinking not only in Catholic France, but also in Protestant countries, such as Germany. Hence, according to Masaryk, the views of Goethe, as a Protestant, with his doctrine of the Superman and Faust as a 'Titan', bore striking resemblance to those of the Catholic Musset. There was 'the same fight between body and soul, sensual and ideal love, the world and the spirit' (ibid., p. 257). Goethe, for instance, 'sees a woman's beauty only in her body, and love is for him nothing but a union of bodies; he has not the least idea of the betrothal and marriage of souls. He cannot conceive of an independent woman, or of love and marriage of two loving creatures, who also think and work together. 'Goethe's type of woman corresponds with the ideals of the contemporary German bourgeoisie', wrote Masaryk. 'The German woman (*Hausfrau*) can always be certain that she will get to the heart of a man most surely through his stomach. ...On the other hand, Goethe looks upon woman as ready at any moment to respond to the advances of a lover' (ibid., pp. 260–1). 'Love is reduced to sexual, sensual love. In the whole of his creative work, Goethe does not deal with children ... and yet wrote so many words about love. How is it possible to love, and yet not to love the little ones?' (ibid., p. 284).

Czech literature did not escape Masaryk's criticism, but also won praise. He wrote that it was penetrated by impurity, and by moral laxity and indifferentism. Belonging to a small nation, 'Czech writers should support the nation by their profound, ethical core, and their healthy moral balance.' (*Masaryk a ženy*, pp. 154–5). Masaryk valued highly such Czech writers as Karel Mácha, Božena Němcová, Jan Neruda, and Josef S. Machar, who did not perceive women as inferior and maintained a healthy balance in their ethical outlook on male–female relations. Masaryk spoke of these four writers as 'pathbreakers for the Czech woman, the Czech man, and for Czech love' (pp. 67–8). It was not without significance that a number of noted Czech women writers, such as Eliška Krašnohorská and Karolina Světlá, were active in the struggle for women's rights.

THE POLITICAL RIGHTS OF WOMEN

As noted above (pp. 13–14) Masaryk strongly believed in the equality of women in public affairs and politics. He was a forceful protagonist of the political emancipation of women, including the extension of the franchise to include women. By the turn of the century most Czech political parties supported the campaign for women's suffrage. Women assumed prominent roles in the Social Democratic and National Socialist parties, and in the smaller progressive parties.[37]

In his own party programmes Masaryk was at first not as forthright as might have been expected. For instance, the programme of his Realist party in 1900 advocated full cultural and political equality of both sexes but did not develop this idea. It even expressed uncertainty as to whether there were not more substantial fields for the employment of women and pressed for extension of women's opportunities in education by proposing separate technical schools and higher middle schools for women.[38] The Progressive party progamme of 1906 confined itself to a demand that women be placed on an equal level culturally, legally and politically.[39]

The 1912 programme broadened the scope of the women's issue to include matters not generally discussed, and was stronger in its demands for political reform. It condemned the medieval view of the 'woman as a lower creature, unfree, not equal in rights, and designated only for the man, family and domestic life' and declared that 'the woman should be placed on an equal level with man economically, legally, politically and culturally. There should be equal duties, but also the right to the same privileges. There should be equal pay for women's work. All existing provisions of marriage, family and inheritance law, and criminal and civil law, which deprived a woman of certain rights only because she was a woman, should be rescinded. Celibacy as a condition of any official post should be abolished. Most important, in the political sphere, there should be general, equal, direct and secret suffrage, with proportionate representation of minorities, valid for men and women equally, in all representative bodies.[40]

MASARYK AND WOMEN'S RIGHTS

One scholar has gone so far as to say that Masaryk was 'the most influential male intellectual involved with the woman's movement'.[41] In 1905 a Moravian woman activist wrote: 'The name of Masaryk has and will have in the Czech women's movement a significance rarely accorded by women to men.' A leading Czech figure, Františka Plamínková, in retrospect, reviewed his significant contributions and described him as 'the strongest support for the political consciousness of Czech women'. Many other women testified to the great influence on their thinking of Masaryk's family life and of Charlotte Masaryk's translation of Mills, *The Subjection of Women*. In *Naše doba*, there were regular columns devoted to the women's question. When the women's journal, *Ženskárevue*, was established, it took as its slogan a question from Masaryk: 'Let women be placed on a level with men culturally, legally and politically.' Certainly he gave strong support to the women's movement in many ways, corresponding with its leaders and speaking often at women's clubs.[42]

In the perspective of present-day feminism, some of Masaryk's views would be regarded as archaic, and indeed reactionary. In the context of his time, however, they were unorthodox, and even radical, and his tireless activity made a significant contribution to public understanding of 'the women's question'. In his struggle for the rights of women, and in particular in his defence of women's suffrage, Masaryk was closer to the mood of the attentive public than he was in his campaign against the Hilsner trial, which he was conducting at almost the same time. Nonetheless Masaryk had to stand up against a popular opinion which was largely indifferent and to confront prejudices and biases deeply rooted in Czech society. He raised issues which were usually cloaked in silence and was occasionally publicly pilloried for his stand. For instance, in 1884, his lectures on prostitution provoked a Czech 'patriot' to petition several ministries in Vienna and politicians that he be stripped of his academic position for alleged corruption of students. In 1892 Masaryk was prevented from speaking at a rally of working-class women by police intervention.[43] Although he did not experience the general social obloquy which he suffered in the Hilsner case, he was, as always, a rebel against conformity and a critic of existing beliefs and practices, willing to speak out courageously against what he considered a social evil.

9 Arch-Critic of Austro-Hungarian Foreign Policy

Prior to 1914 Tomáš Garrigue Masaryk was a persistent and severe critic of the foreign policy pursued by the Monarchy, and of the system for conducting it. He criticized the Austro-German alliance and the behaviour of Austria-Hungary in the Balkans.[1] He ruthlessly condemned the handling of the South Slav question by the Foreign Minister, Count Aerenthal, and severely censured the series of trials held in this connection. His duel with Aerenthal in the Reichsrat and in the Delegations made him hated by the authorities but famous throughout Europe as a man of courage and integrity, as well as wide knowledge.[2] This helped to put Bohemia on the map of Europe and to publicize the Czech question and Czech aspirations towards greater equality and autonomy. By his crusade against Vienna's international policies Masaryk unwittingly prepared the ground for his struggle for independence during the First World War.

THE INTERNATIONAL CONTEXT

In one of his earliest works (*The Czech Question*) Masaryk briefly defined 'my foreign policy', which was, he said, 'very simple but very difficult'. It was couched, in a highly utopian manner, in terms of what, following František Palacký, he called the tendency toward 'world organization'. This meant that 'nations must cooperate and that politics must become genuinely *world* politics'. Power and violence would lose their commanding position; literature and culture, and trade, would have a greater influence. Relations between nations and states were becoming so intimate and communications so easy that the state must have different objectives towards its neighbours than in the past; the seizure of foreign territory or population was no longer necessary. Foreign policy must also become more and more oriented to people (*lidovou*) and social in its content.[3]

Somewhat surprisingly, Masaryk made no systematic analysis of the real world of international politics. His views of the main European participants may be gleaned only from *ad hoc* references, sometimes vague and not always consistent, in the course of his many speeches. Although sympathetic to democratic Britain and France, he devoted scant attention to them, and focused his attention on Germany, Russia and Turkey. Toward these three his attitudes were a blend of great distrust of their autocratic systems, based on his study of their political cultures, and a realistic assessment of their policies regarding specific situations and concrete problems.

His greatest realism was evident in his criticism of Austro-Hungarian foreign policy, to be discussed in detail below. Yet his prescription for Vienna, as given in the Realist programme of 1900, was a far cry from this and expressed pious hopes rather than real expectations. Thus it expressed the wish that 'in the interests of our nation Austria would adopt a preeminent, and as far as possible a leading role, that it would conduct a really world policy'. 'In contrast to the old diplomatic tradition, it would be more economic and more popular; it would be a non-aggressive but a firm policy, a policy of peace.'[4] The programme of the Czech Progressive party in 1912 repeated these words *verbatim*, but added more specific comments on the Triple Alliance, the European powers and militarism.[5]

THE SLAVS, RUSSIA AND PAN-SLAVISM

From his early years of public activity Masaryk showed a deep interest in what he called the Slavic consciousness of the Czechs, i.e. their awareness of belonging to a Slavic community. In *The Czech Question*, in 1895, he devoted attention to the Slavic reciprocity and to the Russophilism of the 'enlighteners', Dobrovský, Šafařík, Kollár, and others, and to its impact on Czech literature and the arts. However, while recognizing some common features of the Slavic nations, especially linguistic similarity, Masaryk laid emphasis on the distinctiveness of each, including the Czechs. He lamented the general ignorance of Czechs on this subject, especially on Russia, and urged more careful studies, even setting forth nine rules for this.[6]

Masaryk shared the widespread Slavic consciousness of most Czechs and of almost all their political leaders. He had no use, however, for the radical Pan-Slav and Russophile ideas propagated by radical Czech nationalists, such as Julius Grégr and Jan Vašatý; he regarded this as an emotional and romantic approach which ignored the realities of Russian autocracy and the profound differences among the Slavic nations. He took a similar attitude towards the Neo-Slavism advocated by Karel Kramář. Although this movement pursued primarily cultural and economic aims, Masaryk believed that it embraced parties which were profoundly divergent in political outlook and ignored political realities, such as the conflict between Russians and Poles. He doubted the likelihood of its success and did not attend either of its two congresses in 1908 and 1910.[7]

In terms of practical politics, Masaryk, like Palacký, and Havlíček, and in fact almost all Czech politicians, including Kramář, tended more to Austro-Slavism, the notion that the Slavic nations of the monarchy should cooperate in pursuit of a reformed Austria-Hungary which would recognize their national equality on the basis of a federal system.[8] In practical terms this was expressed in the Slavic Club, formed in 1893, which included Czech and South Slav parliamentary deputies, and in 1897 even the Galician Poles, and was restored again, without the Poles, in 1909. Although the programmes of Masaryk's political parties, the

People's (1900) and the Progressives (1906 and 1912), did not use the term Austro-Slavism, all supported cultural and economic, and even sometimes political, reciprocity among Slavs in general and within Austria-Hungary in particular.[9]

Masaryk also believed in the desirability of closer relations with other Slav nations, such as the Ukrainians and the Poles, and especially with the South Slavs. Having met Serbs and Croatians in Vienna, he developed a strong interest in their national ideas and even learned the Serbo-Croatian language; in 1892 he made the first of his many trips to the region and became acquainted with some of its political leaders. From the beginning of his parliamentary career he dealt with South Slav questions, especially after the occupation of Bosnia-Hercegovina. His speeches in the Reichsrat in the nineties and after 1908 aroused wide European interest and generated enthusiasm among the South Slavs. Moreover several generations of Serbs and Croatians, including future leaders, such as Štěpan Radić, studied in Prague and came under the influence of Masaryk, notably his ideas of realism and nationality. At home, younger Serbs and Croatians, and also Slovenes, read his works, including *Česká otázka*, and the newspapers, *Čas* and *Naše doba*, and were led to abandon the old dogmas of historic rights and extreme nationalism and to support the idea of a common Yugoslav nation based on nationality and democracy. After 1910 a new generation, which turned toward revolution as the only effective strategy to attain independence, moved away from Masaryk's peaceful tactics. However, after the outbreak of the first Balkan war, he shared the enthusiasm among Czechs for the Slav cause and is reported to have expressed approval of a more radical course.[10]

Masaryk had a deep and abiding interest in Russia, learning Russian as a young man, visiting the country in 1887, 1888, and 1910, and studying its philosophy, culture and religion.[11] It was natural, he thought, in 1895, that small nations like the Czechs should look to other Slavic nations, especially Russia, for support.[12] In spite of his sympathy for the Russian nation, however, he rejected the idea that they should 'love every Russian government'; he totally rejected Russian autocracy, and its creed of Orthodoxy and state absolutism over society.[13] He condemned especially the notion entertained by some Czechs that they should seek a common language with the Russians and convert to Orthodoxy. Like Kramář, he remained loyal to Austria, but unlike him, did not enthuse about closer relations with Russia, or an Austro-Russian alliance to replace the Triple Alliance.[14]

In some of his parliamentary speeches, Masaryk developed his ideas further. As early as 1893 he described Russia as one of the most important problems of Europe whose great physical power cast a shadow on the continent. Austria should adopt a realistic standpoint, which recognized Russia's strength in world affairs and her special interests in Asia as well as in the Balkans, but should seek to live in peace with her. An alliance of Germany and Russia was to be warded off.[15]

In later speeches, in 1910 and after, Masaryk made quite clear his hatred of Russian tsarism, although he professed that he was not an enemy of the Russian people. He urged Russia to adopt a constitution and change its policy of repression of the non-Russian nationalities. Absolutism meant that Russia was unschooled in politics and had no clear plan of foreign policy. Although he was opposed in principle to official Russian foreign policy, it did not, he believed, wish for war in the Balkans. He also thought that the danger of Pan-Slavism was exaggerated. Russia was not 'a lamb', true, but its opposition to Austria was natural and should not be answered with insults.[16]

CRITIQUE OF AUSTRIAN DIPLOMACY

Foreign policy in the Habsburg monarchy was almost exclusively controlled by the Emperor, on the advice of the common Minister of Foreign Affairs, who was usually a member of the Austrian, Hungarian or Polish landed aristocracy. It was conducted often in considerable secrecy, with limited public discussion. The parliaments of the two halves of the Dual Monarchy had no constitutional right to intervene in this field, except through the joint Delegations of the two bodies, which could not decisively affect the policies decided from above. It was in the Delegations, to which he was elected as a representative of the Austrian Parliament, that Masaryk was able to present his views. His target was often the budget, of which he showed a detailed mastery, and against which he usually voted.

Masaryk's attitude toward the conduct of diplomacy was part and parcel of his viewpoint on politics in general. As noted above, he counterpoised an aristocratic oligarchy to real democratism, based on parliamentarism, in which decisions were made not only in accordance with the facts (*věcně*) but also from a moral point of view.[17] On many occasions he urged that the entire system of decision-making should be democratized so as to bring the people and Parliament into the making of foreign policy, and so as to assure that the interests of the Czech nation were served.

This was formulated in more specific terms in Masaryk's party programmes. For instance, the People's Party programme in 1900 stated that they wished, in the interest of the nation, a foreign policy which would assure Austria a leading role so that it could carry out a really worldwide (*světová*) policy. It should be more economic than the traditional diplomatic policy and should guarantee markets for their domestic products.[18] The Progressive Party programme of 1906 expressed the wish for a foreign policy which would correctly inform the world of their national aims and win sympathy for them. Their concern was that 'the Czech nation would have an appropriate influence on the entire foreign policy of the Monarchy.[19] In 1912, the new party programme re-stated the words of the 1900 programme and deplored that Austrian diplomacy was too aristocratic and did not meet the needs of the time. The entire foreign service should be democratized, beginning with the consulates.[20]

In a speech in the Delegations on 8 November 1910, Masaryk elaborated his views on the inadequacies of Austria's diplomatic service. 'All diplomacy – and not only Austria's – is outdated, outmoded by its aristocratism, and its secretiveness, and by diplomatic rituals and formalistic procedures. There must be democratization in this field – publicity, openness, culture, and work'.[21] Diplomacy was still conducted in the obsolete style of Metternich. 'As I look at any diplomatic mission in a foreign land, say in the East, I always have the idea that some polar explorers stand on an ice floe and swim slowly through the sea. These people are an aristocracy closed in on itself and have nothing in common with the people and with the land in which they live'.[22] Masaryk was also sharply critical of the out-of-date and harmful commercial policy followed in the Balkans which was directed against Serbia, and the fantasy of building a railway in the direction of Egypt and India.

In a speech on Balkan policy in February 1911, Masaryk again criticized Austrian diplomacy for failing to support Austria's exports against competitors. Once more he stated his conviction that 'a reform was not possible without the democratization of our foreign policy and especially of our diplomacy. For me politics and diplomacy are not merely unscrupulous intrigue and deceit (*hochstaplerěi*), but conscientious work'.[23]

The following year, in October 1912, Masaryk returned to his attack, denouncing the shocking lack of planning and of knowledge of both foreign and domestic policy. He called for 'a policy that was not merely Czech or German, but Austrian in the democratic meaning of the word'. 'If our parliament had at least some vitality, it would of necessity have to be a constitutional or so-called parliamentary government.'[24]

Touching on the sensitive question of the role of the monarch in determining foreign policy, Masaryk in October 1912 described Austria's foreign policy as 'a personal politics, based on the person of the minister or the sovereign, bringing with it the danger of 'decisions reflecting personal moods instead of the interests of the nations'.[25] In earlier speeches, in 1908, Masaryk had condemned 'absolutism in foreign policy,' 'monarchical dilettantism' and the 'antiquated Old Austrian centralism' of foreign policy.[26] While accepting the role of the dynasty as a factor in Austrian foreign policy, he denied that it had to be Byzantinism which ignored the role of other forces such as the national idea.[27] Again in January 1913, he referred to the 'special dynastic-aristocratic or...centralistic methods' of conducting policy.[28] And in May of the same year, he spoke of 'the personal manner of governing in foreign policy, a non-democratic element which we have to tolerate'.[29]

In February 1911 Masaryk condemned what he called the predominance of 'militarism' in Austrian foreign policy, a theme which had been touched on in the People's Programme of 1900.[30] This, he said, denoted 'the neglect of justified progressive and democratic demands' and 'an incorrect economic system, striving for the privileges of the old knighthood'. Masaryk excoriated the demands of the military and the navy for more funds, asked where the money would come from for these new armaments, and pointed to the resulting neglect of cultural and social needs. For a non-maritime state such as Austria, building dreadnoughts was simply a policy of prestige and competition with the other powers. He did not accept the old slogan – 'if you wish peace, prepare for war'; orderly finances and satisfied nations were the first condition of peace. He was not, he said, opposed to the military class but did not see in the army the defence of the state and nations which conservative and aristocratic circles perceived. He saw a partial solution in the introduction of two-year military service as the beginning of a militia, and a reform of the military criminal and procedural codes.

In November 1911, Masaryk voted against the proposed 1912 budget because of the one-sided favouritism shown the army and the neglect of vital measures to deal with the hunger suffered by the proletariat and even by the bureaucracy.[31] In the same year the programme of the Progressive party condemned militarism in similar terms and urged that the one-sided favouring of the army at the expense of other classes should be ended. The so-called military spirit in the army should not be sought in a caste-like discrimination from civic strata; the army should be permeated with the national, moral and social ideals of the citizenry as a whole. Democratization of the constitution and of society should correspondingly lead to a democratization of the army and its administration.[32]

In a speech on 6 January 1913, Masaryk prophetically warned of the danger of a European conflagration and condemned militarism as contributing to this by its emphasis on military strength and its yearning for war.[33]

FOREIGN POLICY AND THE TRIPLE ALLIANCE

From 1879 until 1914 the axis of Austro-Hungarian foreign policy was the Dual Alliance with Germany. At first entirely secret, it was made public in 1888. Although there were, over the years, profound differences in the interpretation of the treaty between Berlin and Vienna, and official circles in Vienna often viewed with distrust the policies of the German Reich under Bismarck and his successors, they saw no alternative to the Dual Alliance as a protection against Russia, and especially the latter's designs in the Balkans.

As early as September 1891, in a speech at Strakonice, Masaryk cited the Triple Alliance as the cardinal question of Austrian foreign policy and one to which all Czechs were unsympathetic, but he rejected the idea of replacing it with an alliance with Russia.[34] In one of his earliest speeches in the Vienna Parliament, on 18 November 1892, he characterized the alliance as a vehicle for German aggrandizement that could lead to the Germanization of Austria. He did not think that the alliance guaranteed peace, and feared that a victory for the alliance in war would be a victory for Germany. He was most concerned, however, with the impact of the Triple Alliance on domestic political developments in Austria. Citing statements by Austrian Germans and Prussian Germans, he noted the common desire to Germanize the Czechs. 'This cast doubt on the very existence of the Austrian state as it had historically developed and challenged the right to existence of the Polish and Slovenian nations, and of all Slavonic nations'. 'We Czechs stand on guard, because we know it is a matter of our very existence.'[35]

Masaryk returned to the theme in the Delegation on 14 June 1893 when he described at length the reasons for the distrust and scepticism of the Triple Alliance among the Czech people. The Alliance served the interests of Germany more than the interests of Austria. He deplored the emphasis laid in Germany on military and strategic aspects and the conclusion drawn that Austria-Hungary should increase its arms expenditures. Once again he lamented the way in which the Triple Alliance influenced the domestic politics of the monarchy. Alluding to the Austro-German demand for *Abgrenzung* (partition) of Bohemia, he declared that the Czechs would not accept the fact that an independent German province should be established in northern Bohemia. Austria, he declared, should indeed remain a great power but, as a state made up of small nations, it must be 'powerful and great in its domestic policy'; this required a harmonizing of domestic and foreign policy. The solution of the Bohemian question was therefore very much in the interest of Austrian foreign policy. Masaryk also argued that foreign policy should become 'social', for instance by entering into negotiations with other states on the eight-hour day.[36]

Many years later, in 1910, when Masaryk became engrossed in the Balkan question, he continued to express his doubts about the Triple Alliance. The Czechs were reproached with being absolutely opposed to the Triple Alliance, whereas they only wished to judge it objectively and pragmatically. 'We only demand that the Triple Alliance, first of all, should allow Austria-Hungary the necessary freedom and independence in its external relations and secondly, that foreign politics should not guide domestic policy.' He was especially disturbed by reports of a projected occupation of Bohemia and Galicia by German forces in the event of war.[37]

Early the following year, Masaryk denied that he was personally opposed in principle to the Triple Alliance or to the German people but admitted that he was not sympathetic to Prussian militarism and reaction. The Triple Alliance should be judged according to its aim and the means used to attain this end, and according to economic, not merely political, criteria. In competing with other states in this field, Austria must follow 'an independent policy, avoiding megalomania and a policy of prestige'. Being economically weaker, it could not compete with other states by dreadnoughts and armaments, but rather by a policy of cultural reciprocity. It needed peace with its neighbours, and the freedom (at home) without which this multi-national state could not survive.[38]

MASARYK AND BOSNIA-HERCEGOVINA

In 1878 Austria-Hungary, with the approval of the Great Powers at the Berlin Congress, was permitted to occupy Bosnia-Hercegovina, although these two provinces remained nominally under Turkish sovereignty. The occupation was accomplished by the use of force against armed resistance and left Vienna with the onerous task of reconciling the occupants to Austrian rule. Henceforth the question of Bosnia-Hercegovina remained a central issue of European diplomatic relations and a festering sore in the Monarchy's domestic and foreign relations. As it turned out, it was one of the crucial factors leading to the First World War.

Masaryk expressed himself on this question as early as October 1892, when, as a newly-elected parliamentary deputy, and after a study trip to the area, he spoke at length on the question in the Delegations.[39] He did not directly question the occupation, which he regarded as the result of Turkish oppression, but he lamented that the official promises to raise the level of the population had not been carried out. In the face of a thousand-year clash of two worlds in the region, the task had professedly been to overcome the division between the medieval conditions of the people in the occupied lands, and the modern conditions of a liberal state, and thus to bring culture to the East. This had not been accomplished, he believed. He did not deny that the occupation had brought technical and material improvements. But instead of seeking to moderate and reconcile the contradictions between the religions and nationalities, the regime sought to suppress them by pressure and violence.

In seeking to explain the justified dissatisfaction of the people of the provinces, Masaryk examined in detail the sources of discontent, such as the composition and the spirit of the bureaucracy, the failure to deal with the serious agrarian situation, including the burden of the tax system, and failings in the educational and judicial system. Vienna had not granted the promised autonomy nor introduced institutions which would make it possible for the people to voice their ideas and complaints. Instead it had established a powerful police system which persecuted and imprisoned critics. He himself had been constantly followed and his informants had to meet him conspiratorially. He denied the charge that it was unpatriotic to discuss these questions openly as he had done, and argued that this would in fact contribute to a greater trust in Austria throughout Europe.

In the Delegations in June 1893 Masaryk attacked even more sharply the administration of Bosnia-Hercegovina, charging that in many respects, for instance in the agrarian question, the situation was worse than under Turkish rule. The social aspects had been neglected in favour of technical and military-strategic considerations. Citing detailed case studies of injustice and repression, Masaryk declared that he would not vote for the budget.[40]

Masaryk repeated his censure of the unsatisfactory treatment of the problems of religion and nationality. Every expression of Serbian and Croatian national feeling was violently suppressed; instead, in a Magyar spirit, an abstract and fictitious state idea was imposed. 'Gentlemen, Bosnia and Hercegovina are quite simply Slavic lands and whoever wishes to administer them justly and in a modern spirit, may not inculcate into the population an Eastern or Roman state idea.' The task of the occupation was, 'step by step, through wise measures, to raise to a higher level of European civilization a people who, as a result of centuries of Turkish rule, were...so far behind'.

THE ANNEXATION OF BOSNIA-HERCEGOVINA

The sudden annexation of Bosnia and Hercegovina in October 1908 was a serious blow at the diplomatic *status quo* established by the Berlin Congress and by other treaties concluded by Austria-Hungary. Ever since the occupation in 1878 the question of the future of the two provinces had been the subject of diplomatic negotiation and agreements, in many of which the possibility of outright annexation by Austria-Hungary was discussed and sometimes conditionally approved. Although talks with Russia on this eventuality were held just prior to the actual seizure of the territories, Vienna took the action without informing Russia, or any of the other Great Powers who were concerned, and also without consulting the Delegations. The action produced an international crisis, which threatened to lead to war, and was resolved only through lengthy negotiations leading to the reluctant acceptance of the annexation by Serbia and by the European powers. The annexation met with armed resistance from the inhabitants, thus casting further doubt on its legitimacy. In Bohemia there were demonstrations in the streets against the annexation, and martial law was declared in Prague. Czech political leaders were divided. Kramář initially approved the action, but later expressed serious reservations. Masaryk, who at first simply abstained on the question, was from the first sharply critical, as was Klofáč.[41]

The Austrian Foreign Ministry embarked on a carefully-planned attempt to justify the annexation and to discredit the Serbian Kingdom and the Croatians and Serbs within the Monarchy. In a succession of three trials, it was sought to prove that an organized movement existed in Croatia which aimed at the destruction of the Monarchy. These proceedings, instead of establishing the justice of the annexation, brought Austro-Hungarian diplomacy, and in particular the Foreign Minister, Aerenthal, into disrepute throughout Europe.[42]

Masaryk, who had been re-elected to the Vienna Reichsrat in 1907, threw himself into the fray at the earliest opportunity. During 1909, 1910 and 1911, he delivered a number of highly polemical speeches in the Vienna Parliament and the Delegations in which he denounced what he believed was the falsification of evidence, which he laid at the door of the Foreign Ministry and the Minister of Foreign Affairs, Count Aerenthal. He was savagely attacked by the official Croatian press as 'a Pan-Slav *agent provocateur* in Servian sheepskin' and was denounced by one of the investigating judges as 'a blackguard, a ragamuffin, a man without honour, a nobody, the refuse of human society'.[43] Throughout Europe, however, his campaign against the trials brought him into prominence as a bold and severe critic of Austro-Hungarian foreign policy.

In major addresses in the Delegation in November 1910, and February 1911, Masaryk rejected the reasons officially given for the annexation and described it as an ignominious diplomatic fiasco.[44] He especially condemned the way in which the annexation had been carried out; it was contrary to international law to take such action without a conference of the powers which had given Austria the mandate of occupation at Berlin. It also ignored the Delegations as 'a political body' and was carried through without the approval of the Bosnian and Hercegovinian people. It had created 'mistrust, nervousness and disquiet' and had led to increased arms expenditures. He condemned the supporting role of Germany, and was critical of the attitudes taken by Britain, Italy, Russia and Turkey. He cast doubt on the idea that the action was a sign of strength, and represented a great Austria; this could be achieved only by positive support of the cultural development of all nations. The policy toward the Balkans was dictated by Budapest and did not recognize the interests of Serbia and of Serbs and Croatians. He did not deny the 'right' of Austria to annex the provinces, but condemned the form in which it had been carried out and the falsity of the attempts to justify it. The constitution which was eventually dictated to Bosnia-Hercegovina was simply a continuance of absolutism, denying freedom of the press and of assembly.

Summing up, Masaryk declared that 'Austro-Hungarian diplomacy was not able 'to understand how the national idea is spreading in the south. What has happened and is happening in Europe, is now happening in the south. The Serbo-Croatian nation, broken up into nine states and administrative entities and divided among three churches, begins to feel itself as a nation and yearns after national and cultural unity'. Our diplomacy 'did not understand the influence of ideas' or the attitudes of the new generation, and therefore constructed the notion of 'a subsidized revolutionary movement'. Masaryk concluded by demanding a diplomacy which would be 'really Austrian, and not merely dualistic, serving the interests of Germans and Magyars'.

THE ZAGREB TRIAL

In May 1909, Masaryk introduced in the Reichsrat an urgent interpellation on 'the so-called treason trial' then in progress in Zagreb. Parliament, 'in the interests of humanity, should raise a voice of warning and condemnation', and, through a committee, should examine in detail the evidence presented to prove the existence of a treasonable movement in the south and investigate the whole question of the annexation. In two speeches justifying his action, on 15 and 18 May, Masaryk described the trial as political in nature, designed to 'frighten Serbs and Croatians and divide them from each other', with 'justice serving political acts of violation'. Having spent several weeks in the South Slav region, including Zagreb and Belgrade, Masaryk exposed in great detail what he considered the falsity of the charges against the fifty-three persons accused; some of them were his former students and personal friends, for whom 'I would place my hand in the fire'. In the end the motion received a majority of votes but failed to achieve the two-thirds majority required for adoption.[45]

The trial, which lasted for over six months, has often been described.[46] For many observers it was a travesty of justice, in view of the biased behaviour of the presiding judge (whom Masaryk called an alcoholic), the unjust treatment of the defence lawyers and of the accused, the failure to call witnesses for the defence, and above all the falsity of the evidence provided by the chief prosecution witness, George Nastić. Although Masaryk, as a non-lawyer, disclaimed expertness, the trial, in his view, brought to shame Hungarian and Croatian, and also Austrian, justice (*Tak zvaný*, p. 44).

Masaryk focused his attention on the political aspects of what he called a trial staged by the government itself. He ridiculed the attempt to prove the existence of a treasonable, anti-dynastic and anti-Austrian organized movement which was said to seek a Greater Serbia and to be directly managed and financed by the Serbian dynasty. In fact such an organization did not exist, he claimed; there was no Serbian or Croatian irredentist movement in Hungary, Croatia, or in Slavonia, among the Slovenes (ibid., pp. 14, 27, 29, 44). He rejected the veracity of the chief witness, Nastić, and called him simply 'a liar'. The copy of the statutes of the Slovenski Yug, presented by Nastić to document the existence of a revolutionary organization, was not authentic (ibid., pp. 19–22). This organization had been nothing more than a democratic student organization and in fact no longer existed. The Slav parties and movements which were accused of irredentism were seeking only to bring democratic principles into validity and to end the age-old rivalry between Serbs and Croatians (ibid., pp. 31–2).

Masaryk blamed the Ban of Croatia, Baron Levin Rauch, for staging the trial, with the purpose of breaking up the Serbo-Croatian coalition government in Croatia, and for having had the treasonable documents prepared. Masaryk also censured Dr. Heinrich Friedjung, whom he recognized as a great historian, but who had, in the press, accepted the legend of the Slovenski Yug; he condemned him for using other false documents at the behest of the Ministry of Foreign Affairs, as well as for raising false charges that payments were made by Croatian authorities to the Croatian deputies (ibid., pp. 29–43).

In concluding, Masaryk declared that Vienna should not resist the movement of the over nine million Croatians and Serbs towards national unification (not necessarily in state form), which was 'inevitable and unchangeable'. Vienna would not be able to win the hearts of the Bosnians and Hercegovinians through building railways and by other technical means, while denying them freedom. As the greatest South Slav state, it must replace the Magyar policy of violence (which was applied against the Slovaks, too) with a truly 'imperial policy' which would benefit not only the Slavs but also Austria as a whole (ibid., pp. 45–7).

The conclusion and the aftermath of the Zagreb trial were revealing. On 5 October 1909, 31 of the defendants were pronounced guilty and received sentences ranging from five to 12 years. But on 1 April 1910, the Croatian court of appeal quashed the verdict on the ground that the guilt or innocence of the accused had not been clearly established.

THE FRIEDJUNG TRIAL

Two months after the closing of the Zagreb trial, on 9 December, a new trial opened in Vienna and was to last six weeks. This time it was a civil case, in which members of the Serbo-Croatian Coalition and others brought suit against

Heinrich Friedjung and the newspaper, *Reichspost*, for their press attacks on the defendants. Professor Masaryk, who had made several visits to Belgrade and Zagreb, appeared as a witness. The trial became a *cause célèbre* throughout Europe and fastened public attention on the conduct of the Austrian Foreign Ministry and on Masaryk's critique of its foreign policy.[47]

In the proceedings, Dr Friedjung produced 24 documents to prove his charges of treason against the Croatians; the *Reichspost* submitted three more. Several Croatian witnesses denied their authenticity and the existence of a revolutionary movement against the Monarchy. Dr Masaryk supported their claims and sought to prove that the documents were falsified. In the end the Austrian authorities came to the conclusion that a continuance of the trial would damage the Monarchy's reputation and agreed to a compromise. Dr Friedjung withdrew his claims and the prosecutor dropped the charges against him, thus leading to his formal acquittal.

Masaryk presented his full case against Friedjung in the Delegations, on 8 November 1910.[48] He placed the full responsibility for the preparation of the trial, which he called 'a crude swindle', on the Austrian Minister of Foreign Affairs. He also charged that the 'highest places,' namely the Emperor, the Archduke, the Foreign Minister and Baron Beck, the Austrian prime minister, were fully aware of the falsity of the documents and that Aerenthal had in fact passed them on to Friedjung and assisted in their publication. He repeated the charge that the Ambassador in Belgrade, Count Forgách, had been directly involved and must therefore be considered a forger. Face-to-face with the Minister in the Delegations, Masaryk called upon him to deny that he knew or helped in the preparation and transmission of the documents. Aerenthal, evading a direct answer, defended and praised his ambassador, and charged Masaryk with acting out of 'political passion' and with carrying out a 'witch-hunt' against the Monarchy and stirring up Serbian public opinion against the Monarchy.

On 11 November Masaryk responded to Aerenthal's personal charges which implied that he was lacking in patriotism, describing this as an insult to the Czech delegation. He was not acting as a mere 'professor', as Aerenthal had condescendingly described him, but as a parliamentary deputy, whose task it was to supervise the work of the Foreign Minister. He accused Aerenthal of being a reactionary, who was afraid of freedom, and denounced him for failing to respond to his direct questions about the role of the Foreign Ministry.[49]

THE VASIČ AFFAIR

Austrian prestige suffered further damage when the Belgrade journalist, Vladimir Vasič, publicly revealed the role of the Ambassador, Count Forgách, in the preparation of the forged documents. As a result of his confession, Vasič was tried in Belgrade, on 22 December 1910, on charges of treason and of endangering state interests, and sentenced to five years. Although the trial was held *in camera*, Masaryk was able to attend the proceedings, and pursued the attack on Aerenthal and Austrian foreign policy in the Delegations in December 1910 and February 1911, in articles in *Čas* and *Die Zeit*, and in a booklet on the Vasič case.[50]

Having observed the trial and having visited both Forgách and Vasič in Belgrade, Masaryk was able to elaborate the relationship of the two men more fully. In his December speech and in his booklet, *Vasič–Forgách–Aerenthal,* he cited the seventeen points of the indictment and the judgement of the court, which led it to conclude the involvement of 'a foreign mission' in the forgeries. He presented documents of his own, including a photograph of an original, signed by an embassy officer, as further evidence. He charged Aerenthal with dishonesty in concealing these facts and in acting in an ungentlemanly way in his replies. He denied charges that he (Masaryk) had not been acting as 'a good Austrian'; it was Aerenthal, not he, who had damaged the reputation of the Monarchy. The attempt to justify the annexation through the falsifications had demonstrably failed. Throughout the whole of Europe, 'Count Forgách had made Austrian diplomacy laughable; Count Aerenthal had made it contemptible'.[51]

In his speeches on 22 and 24 February 1911 Masaryk pursued the matter, as he had promised, *usque ad finem*, i.e. right up to Aerenthal himself.[52] In great detail he described many other cases of what he described as 'a system of falsification', for which Aerenthal was personally responsible.

As a result of the reversal of the Zagreb verdict, the enforced compromise in the Friedjung case, the outcome of the Belgrade trial, and Masaryk's persistent criticism, Austrian diplomacy suffered a complete fiasco in its attempt to justify its Balkan policy. The upshot of the controversy was the transfer of Count Forgách to another diplomatic post in April 1911, and the offer of resignation by Count Aerenthal in June (accepted only in February 1912).

An outside observer, Wickham Steed, Vienna correspondent of the London *Times*, wrote that the trials had shown that 'the Habsburg monarchy had lost whatever inner virtue it may once have possessed...and was bound hand and foot to Germany'. 'Masaryk's bold stand', on the other hand, 'marked him anew as the most public-spirited man in Austria-Hungary and increased the moral ascendancy which he had acquired throughout the Slav world by his teachings at the Czech University of Prague.' It also, he wrote, 'made the little Czech nation great and noble throughout the world'.[53]

Among Slavic nations, and especially Serbs and Croatians, Masaryk became well-known and respected, and indeed beloved, as was shown by the tributes paid to him on his sixtieth anniversary in 1910. Professor Marković, a Serbian, wrote that Masaryk showed himself to be 'an apostle of scholarship, truth and justice and had won the sympathy of the whole Serbian nation. As a man concerned only with truth, Masaryk worked tirelessly, day and night, so that truth would prevail.' A Croatian lawyer, Josef Smodlaka, wrote: 'In our nation we do not have today a man who was so much loved, respected and honoured by progressive Croatians and Serbs as Prof. Masaryk'.[54]

THE CLOSING YEARS

With the outbreak of the Balkan War, with the Slavic nations united against Turkey, the danger of Austro-Hungarian intervention against the Serbs and of a general European war became acute. The deep sympathy of the Czech people with their fellow Slavs was manifested in repeated mass meetings in their support and against Austrian war policy, including demonstrations by reservists on the departure of troops to the Balkan fronts, and the sending of medical aid to the Serbs and Bulgarians; these were interpreted by the police and by the Vienna authorities as implicitly 'anti-state' and 'anti-Austrian'. National Socialists and Social Democrats also conducted manifestations against war in general. Czech political leaders, especially Kramář, Klofáč and Masaryk, spoke openly in Parliament and the Delegations against Austria's anti-Serbian policy. All three sought to mediate between Serbia and Austria. Kramář and Masaryk, after talks in Belgrade with Serbian leaders, were rebuffed by the Austrian Foreign Minister; Klofáč was detained at the border when he sought to visit Belgrade. Nonetheless, the main parties of the United Czech Club (except for the National Socialists), voted for war credits in parliament; the parties grouped together in the Association of Independent Progressives (Moravian People's and State Right Parties, the Progressives and the Realists), expressed their discontent by obstructing war measures in Parliament.[55]

Even before the war in the Balkans Masaryk stepped up his assault on Austrian foreign policy towards the Balkans. In May 1912, in the Delegations, he used stronger language than ever before, referring to 'a criminal policy' toward the Serbs and Croatians, both within and outside the Monarchy. In Croatia the 'system of falsifications' used in the trials remained unchanged since the replacement of Baron Rauch. Terming this a 'Hungarian policy', he also attacked the severe and shameful brutality of the Magyars towards the Slovaks. Once again he lashed out against the Triple Alliance, both Germany and Italy, and the *Schlamperei* of Vienna's policy in dealing with the domestic nationality question. He condemned the 'incredible aimlessness of Austrian policy, the unbelievable waste of its national and political strength', and its stagnation and degeneration.[56]

Several months later, in October 1912, in the Reichsrat, with the first Balkan war already under way, and Count Berchtold now in the Foreign Office, Masaryk repeated his savage attacks on what he called the 'absolutely wrong Austrian foreign policy' in the Balkans, based on ignorance of the conditions there; its economic policy was 'miserable, petty and harmful'. Austria was 'not acting as a a great power but as a state of small, petty diplomats, using the methods of chicanery and falsification'. There was no endangerment of Austria's vital interests in the Balkans; it should only pursue a reasonable commercial and customs policy in the region and refrain from one based on the 'status quo' and 'divide and rule'.[57]

Although he was opposed to war, he could not deny that the Balkan war had a moral justification as a united effort by the smaller nations to liberate themselves from century-old rule by Turkey, 'a medieval barbaric theocracy', which, he believed, was doomed to collapse. It would have been better if these nations had found a peaceful way, but 'Europe' had prevented this. Russian tsarism, a system which he 'hated more than any other', bore its share of the blame, but there was 'tsarism' elsewhere in Europe. Even Britain shared responsibility because, under the influence of the stock market, it followed a pro-Turkish policy. He called upon Austria to follow the slogan 'Balkan for the Balkans nations' and to abandon its anti-Serb and anti-Slav policy.

After another trip to Belgrade to study the situation Masaryk spoke three times in the Delegations in mid-November.[58] He hated war, he declared, and wished for an eternal peace. He could not imagine that a world war could break out as a result of the Balkan situation and could also not believe that Austria was capable of waging such a war. He did not think that Serbia was a dangerous opponent of Austria and spoke in favour of a Serbian port on the Adriatic, which would not harm Austrian interests. Moreover he did not believe that Serbia was bound to Russia, as Austrian official newspapers claimed. He also spoke at length about the Albanian question and ridiculed Austria's effort, in the name of the nationality principle, to give Albania autonomy, as she would inevitably be controlled by Turkey.

Shortly after the armistice in the first Bosnian war, Masaryk, fearing the resumption of war, proceeded again to Belgrade and held talks between December 7 and 11 1912, with the Serbian Prime Minister, Pasić, and the Austrian and Russian ambassadors. He secured Pasić's approval of concessions to Austria in return for an Adriatic port. Count Berchtold rejected outright the proposed compromise and repudiated Masaryk's role as mediator.

Masaryk was becoming all the more fearful of a general European conflagration, as he warned at a meeting of the Progressive Party executive on 6 January 1913.[59] Such a war would bring huge losses of life and property, but would hardly produce a thoroughgoing rectification of the map of Europe or its definitive well-ordering. Whether Austria won or lost, he asked, would the results be favourable to Czech national demands? In a wide-ranging speech, Masaryk continued his attack on Austria's Balkan policy and in particular its witch-hunt against Serbia. In this situation he could not preach peace but backed the struggle of the Balkan Christians and Slavs against Turkey. He railed against the whole clique of power-holders in Budapest and Vienna, and especially against the militarists who wanted to go to war against Serbia and divide the country among its neighbours.

Leaving no doubt of his support for Slav unification in the Balkans, he formulated the Austrian problem as follows: 'if a German can be an Austrian, why could not a Slav, or say a Serb, also be an Austrian?'. The Czech position was different from others. 'I do not conceal the fact that I have a lively sympathy with the Balkan Slavs; their victory would strengthen us morally.'

Just prior to the outbreak of the second Balkan war among the victors, in June 1913, Masaryk, in what was to be his final speech in the Reichsrat, on 26 May, condemned, as he had done so often before, Austria's 'personal' foreign policy; it was uncertain and had no positive plan, but only a negative one against Serbia. Masaryk made a detailed critique of the draft budget, which supported 'a comic and childish policy of armaments', at the expense of pressing social needs and commercial interests abroad.[60]

Masaryk reiterated his view that 'Austria's lamentable foreign policy reflected its impossible "domestic policy". Austria was conducting an unceasing war, not outwardly, but within, against its own good peoples.' Austrian diplomacy ought to be a creative one, based on a proper financial policy, universal suffrage, and social legislation and a completely different standpoint in the national conflicts. In what were to be his last words before the Reichsrat, Masaryk expressed the hope 'that, in the interests of Austria and of its peoples, all parties would put an end to the incapacity of its domestic and foreign policy'. He urged Austria to emulate Germany's successful commercial and cultural policy in the Balkans.

With the conclusion of peace in the Balkans in August 1913, Masaryk persisted in his efforts to assure its continuance by seeking a reconciliation of Serbs and Bulgarians, and planned to go to Paris and London to win support for his plan.[61] The outbreak of war prevented him putting this plan into effect. Toward the end of the year (27 November, 1913) he made his last public speech in Austria, in the Vienna town hall, significantly at a meeting for peace of the Austrian Peace Society.[62] Not without some justification, Masaryk's name was raised as a possible nominee for the Nobel prize for peace, a possibility which aroused consternation in official Vienna.[63]

CONCLUSION

Masaryk liked to think of the Czech question as a world question and of foreign affairs as a means of promoting Czech national interests.[64] He was unusual among Czech political leaders for his deep interest in foreign affairs and for his wide knowledge of other countries, based on his command of foreign languages, thorough study, and his travels abroad. Only two others, Karel Kramář and Václav Klofáč, could rival Masaryk in their persistent criticism of Austria's foreign policy and in their extensive foreign travel, including frequent trips to the Balkans in search of a solution of the South Slav question. Like him, too, they often spoke critically in Parliament and Delegations, and through their writings in foreign journals, sought to inform public opinion abroad of the weaknesses of Austrian policy. In this they were expressing the widespread dissatisfaction of the Czech people with Austrian foreign policy and their solidarity with the

Balkan Slavs, e.g. at the time of the occupation of Bosnia and Hercegovina and in the war against Turkey.

In his early years in Vienna Masaryk had aspired to become a diplomat but was denied entry to the Oriental Institute for diplomatic study because he was not of aristocratic origin. Ironically he eventually became one of the severest critics of Austria's foreign policy and its aristocratic practitioners. There was a further delicious irony in the fact that Masaryk, a civilian of lowly origin, and of academic profession, by his bold campaign against Austria's foreign policy, struck at the very heart of the imperial system and the special personal preserve of the Emperor and his aristocratic and military advisers.

In spite of the semi-absolutist and highly bureaucratic character of the Monarchy, Masaryk was able to use the facilities of Parliament and especially of the Delegations as a platform for democratic debate on Austria's foreign policy. For over two decades he conducted an indefatigable campaign to change the direction of that policy – to lessen its reliance on the Triple Alliance and to transform its goals in the Balkans. In the end he failed to achieve either objective but he succeeded in discrediting Austrian policy at home and throughout Europe. He was prophetic in his belief that the system was heading for war but was finally unable to avert it. He was profoundly accurate in his estimate of the inner weakness of Austria-Hungary but did not predict its collapse.

Although Masaryk's views were remarkably consistent over almost a quarter of a century, his analysis was not by any means unambiguous or free of contradictions. His position was based on a curious mixture of deep knowledge and an often dogmatic and vituperative approach; it was also a blending of realism and ideology. There was a basic conflict between his theoretical concept of world politics and the real world of power politics, and between his belief in the potential strength of a small nation and its actual powerlessness.

There were other contradictions. In spite of his sharp criticism of the Triple Alliance, he professed not to be opposed to it in principle but only to its practice. In spite of his condemnation of the way the annexation was carried out, he also saw it as an opportunity to bring modern ideas to backward nations, lamenting only that the policy pursued did not achieve this objective. He was strongly opposed to war in general, yet he could not escape the belief that the Balkan wars represented a legitimate effort of the South Slavs to achieve their goals. Although he rejected Pan-Slavism or Neo-Slavism, he became a defender of the rights of the Slav nations in the monarchy and outside. In spite of his devastating criticism of Austria's foreign policy he did not give up hope that it could be improved and made more democratic.

Perhaps the contradiction in his thinking which stood out most clearly was in his attitude toward Austria-Hungary as an entity. He made no real separation between foreign and domestic policy, and linked both together in his censure of the entire imperial system. As the spokesman of a small nation, the Czechs, he condemned the Hungarian and Austro-German dominance of both foreign and domestic policy, and constantly urged – in vain – a constitutional reordering of the Monarchy, which would guarantee the Czechs their rightful place. Although he often called for political independence for the Czech nation, he did not envisage this as a goal that could be achieved outside the Empire. His long struggle for the reform of Austria's foreign policy and the avoidance of war, and his ultimate failure in both respects, prepared him for a new orientation and for the decision to strike for independence.

10 Advocate of Czech Independence

Masaryk's attitude toward Austria-Hungary, the empire of which Bohemia and Moravia formed a part, was a changing one and reflected mixed feelings. From the beginning of his political career he never ceased demanding political independence (*samostatnost* or *nezávislost*) for the Czech nation. This meant, in his mind, cultural, economic and social independence, or territorial autonomy within the framework of the Monarchy. In fact in the early years, and even later, he repeatedly asserted that complete political independence, i.e. separation from the Monarchy, was excluded by the smallness of the nation and its geographic location.

For many decades he wrestled with the problem as to how a small nation such as the Czech could attain its national goals. Contrary to most Czech political leaders, Masaryk did not see salvation in the attainment of the ancient Bohemian state right. Although he did not reject this aim entirely, he laid greater emphasis on the natural right of the nation to equality and self-government. The most important objective was the strengthening of the nation in all aspects of its life. In pursuing this aim, he eschewed extreme nationalism and acknowledged the need for reaching a *rapprochement* with the Bohemian Germans. The Empire itself must recognize the national rights of its constituent nations and abandon its antiquated centralism in favour of a federal system. For many years Masaryk believed that the Monarchy could be reformed peacefully, and professed his loyalty to such a state. As time went on, however, his hopes for a radical change waned and he became more and more alienated from, and hostile toward the entire imperial system. Although he did not openly call for secession, he was intellectually and psychologically prepared for a break, should the circumstances favour it.

THE CZECH NATION AND NATIONALITY

The consuming passion of Masaryk's life was 'the Czech question', which he defined as the analysis of the 'mysteries' involved in the search for the meaning of Czech history, namely 'how this special nation lives culturally, what we wish and hope for'. In practical terms this meant that 'the chief and foremost aim of our national and political strivings was to maintain and cultivate language and nationality'. This was based on the natural right of a nation to preserve itself, and its duty to develop its language and nationality and its political rights. It was closely linked with the concept of humanity which dictated the paramount principle of the equality of rights of all nations.[1]

The idea of nationality (*národnost*) and of the nation (*národ*) was a modern one, based on the ideas of the American and French revolutions, on the writings of Herder, and in the Czech case, on the revolution of 1848 and the thinking of the enlighteners, Jan Kollár, Josef Šafařík, Karel Havlíček and František Palacký. National consciousness was still in its beginning and was not fully developed among Czechs; the nation was still bound by state ties. The need was to 'think Czech, to feel Czech'; 'Czechness means to work for the Czech nation, i.e. to love it effectively'.[2]

As noted in Chapter 1, the two seemingly contradictory concepts of nationality (*národnost*) and humanity (*humanita*); were in Masaryk's view intertwined. For instance, in *The Ideals of Humanity* (1901) he wrote: 'The idea of humanity (*idea humanítní*) is not opposed to that of nationality (*idea národnostní*); nationality, like the individual man, ought to be and can be human, humanitarian'. The idea of humanity, he wrote in 1912, was 'purely the state of being a human being (*člověckost*); it was mankind (*člověčenství*) organized as a moral and social whole. From humanity is derived the right of nationality (*národnost*) along side of, and against, the state and church. Mankind is an organization of nations, not of states; nationality comes into validity as a part of mankind.'[3]

Masaryk's thoughts on nationality were expressed in innumerable writings and speeches;[4] his leading ideas may be summarized as follows.

(a) The idea of nationalism was by then a powerful social force. In Austria the national movement had not yet reached its peak but would be intensified, especially with the introduction of universal suffrage. The national conflict could not be abolished but only dammed and moderated. Its solution was a great task which required great policies and great statesmen. It could not be solved on the basis of nationalism, which was often mere prejudice and fanaticism, but only on the basis of humanism and the recognition of common interests.[5]

(b) The nation was more important than the state – the former was a natural and cultural formation; the latter was artificial and historical and constituted only a small part of the life of society.[6] Even an independent Czech state would not be sufficient to assure the nation's best interests. The Austrian state, as it stood, denied the Czechs their natural rights. The nation was a 'state-forming' (*státotvorný*) force, so that every nation rightly sought its own state. Yet this did not exclude the possibility of a Bohemian state which included German citizens, nor of an Austrian state based on the equality of all its nations.

(c) The nation was primarily determined by language, but this was but one of many factors – economic and social, political, moral and religious, scientific, philosophical and cultural – each of which was in turn influenced by nationality. Racial explanations, such as the notion of pure blood, were not correct. A nation was not, however, a permanent and uniform entity. It depended on the conscious will of the individual to accept a given language and the values of a nation. Language was 'the consciousness of being a nation', and a powerful bond linking the members together. It was not itself the goal but was a means of pursuing spiritual and moral aims.[7] In the political sphere a principal objective was to secure equality of languages, in offices and schools. But it was not just a question of language, but of developing all sides of the nation's life.[8]

(d) Nationality was not limited to one or other class, but should be truly populist (*lidový*), embracing all members of the nation, including the working people, and democratic, linked historically with the struggle against absolutism. This naturally moved from political democracy to national, economic and social democracy. The nation could be defended only by democratic means, not by force but by the ballot. Freedom and nationality were therefore inextricably linked; a nationality without political freedom was impossible, and freedom without nationality was incomplete.[9]

(e) Love of one's nation or country (*vlast*) was true patriotism (*vlastenectví*). Boastful jingoism (*vlastenčení*) was harmful to the nation's real interests.[10] Genuine patriotism did not involve hatred of other nations, i.e. flag-waving zealotry or chauvinism, but on the contrary required tolerance and understanding. The virtues of other nations should be acknowledged and organically linked with one's own. No nation was a chosen nation; each had its virtues and its faults. Patriotism did not exclude criticism of one's own faults but indeed demanded it, in order to cultivate and raise the level of the nation. Critics should not be treated as traitors, as had happened so often in Czech history.

(f) As for the Germans, the Czechs had long had a close relationship with them and had been influenced by them in philosophy (e.g. Herder and Marx), in science, and literature, and in the ideas of liberalism and socialism. Czech history, however, had not been one of continual struggle against the Germans, as Palacký had argued; this had played an important but not the main role. It was necessary to resist the German domineering tendency (*panováčnost*), their defence of their privileged position in Austria, and their lack of understanding of Czech cultural achievements, rights and interests. But it was urgent to reach an agreement with the Germans, and this could be achieved on the basis *not* of nationality, but of humanity, which involved freedom and social justice. The German language was known by most educated Czechs, and they needed it. He welcomed a tendency among Germans to learn Czech. In future, with the further development of the nation, not every one would have to know German. But to forsake German would lower the level of culture.[11]

(g) A genuine nationalism, based on humanity, was not contradictory to internationalism; the cooperation of nations was necessary in the modern age. Foreign languages, including not only German, but also English, French and Russian, were absolutely necessary. Social democrats should not be condemned and excluded from the nation because they held strong international views. Other groups, including capitalists, journalists, lawyers and the Church, were also international in outlook. Moreover, the Social Democrats themselves had come to recognize the virtue of nationalism.[12]

Nourished by these beliefs, Masaryk devoted all his conscious activity to the elevation of the nation and the advancement of its interests. Condemning German national hegemony in the Monarchy and defending the equality of rights of all the non-German nations, he sought in particular to develop a Czech national programme, based in part on Palacký and Havlíček, but appropriately amended to meet the needs of the time. He condemned what he called the ignoring and suppression of Czech national rights and called for the recognition and support of Czech cultural and scholarly, economic and social needs. In the Vienna Parliament he often invoked the names of great national leaders of the past, such as Jan Hus, Amos Komenský, Palacký and Havlíček and defended the achievements of Czech culture; he described the Czech tradition as 'socialist', anti-clerical and democratic. Yet he was not afraid to admit and condemn the weaknesses of the Czech nation, both the people and their leaders, and was equally adamant in seeking out the possibilities of a compromise between Czechs and Germans. As a result he was often condemned as being unpatriotic, even a traitor to the nation. Yet he was not daunted by such labelling, and pursued his own individual course without regard for the cost.

For a quarter of a century, in countless speeches and articles, and in party programmes, he demanded equality of rights for the Czech nation and set forth what he considered its essential needs, including in his purview Moravia and Silesia as well as Bohemia. First and foremost was the necessity of improving the educational system by expanding the network of public schools, raising the level of instruction, and placing them under greater national control through special sections in the Ministry of Education and in provincial organs. He urged the improvement of the facilities of the Prague university, and the use of the Czech language in lectures, and repeatedly called for the establishment of a second university in Moravia. No less important was the guarantee of equality of the Czech language in courts and public offices throughout the Bohemian lands, a topic to be discussed separately later. He urged the support of Czech economic interests, in agriculture, trade and industry, and finance, increased Czech representation in elected bodies and in the civil service and all public institutions, and care for the interests of the poorer classes of the nation. He devoted much attention to the rights of Czech national minorities in the mixed districts of the Bohemian lands, but also in Vienna and Lower Austria, and strongly urged the establishment of minority schools in these areas.[13]

THE PROBLEM OF A SMALL NATION

Throughout his life Masaryk was absorbed by what he called 'the problem of a small nation'. In *The Czech Question*, he made only brief references to it and gave a fuller treatment of this theme only in 1905 in a lecture in which he sought to define in theoretical terms the concepts of nation and state and their mutual relationship.[14] Measured by territory and population, he said, the Czechs were indeed a small nation, although not by any means the smallest in Europe. Limited in size and numbers, and lacking economic independence, the Czech nation had had to struggle for a thousand years with a mightier neighbour for the defence and preservation of its very being.

The key question was 'how should a small nation maintain itself?' In 1895, in the introduction to *The Czech Question*, Masaryk thought that the smallness of the nation was derived, not from its numbers, but from its own 'inadequacies', and would cease when these were recognized and removed. As a small nation, the Czechs suffered from many serious disadvantages, including a 'smallness' of outlook and weaknesses of economic and cultural development. Centuries of foreign rule had created the habit of dependence and made it unaccustomed to self-rule.[15] A small nation could maintain itself only by the removal of these defects which required hard 'inner work' and 'non-political politics'. The goal could be accomplished, as he put it in an oft-quoted sentence: 'not by violence, but peacefully, not by the sword but by the plough, not by blood but by work, not by death, but by a will to live'. 'In the past the Czechs were victorious only by a predominance of spirit, rather than of physical power, and failed only as a result of the lack of spiritual activity, moral courage and bravery. The nation could claim its place in the ranks of the nations not by our numbers or by our material strength, but only by our spiritual power and our moral courage.'[16]

POLITICAL INDEPENDENCE

In *The Czech Question* Masaryk openly raised the question of 'political independence'. In his view, every non-independent nation has to strive for independence. There was no power in the world which could prevent this if the nation were in fact (nationally) conscious. The only question was by what means a nation could achieve its independence in the face of 'global centralization', as Palacký called it. For this we needed, he argued, political consciousness and political cultivation (*vzdělanost*), not force (*železo*). He made quite clear that he was thinking, as Palacký had done, of independence within the framework of Austria-Hungary, to be attained through the attainment of autonomy in the sense of the widest possible self-government (the English word was used); each nation would thus decide its own domestic politics by itself.[17]

He warned, however, that political independence alone would not save or protect the nation; it had lost its independence once because it had ceased to behave morally. Even if the nation were politically independent, this independence could only be maintained by morality and cultivation if it were not to be used as a mere political tool by a more powerful neighbour. Because of global centralization, we were forced to associate with other states and nations, and could only maintain ourselves by tireless cultural work. We would not achieve mastery of our own fate even by complete independence; we would have 'to use it in the interest of our spiritual independence'. Masaryk also recognized the tremendous difficulty of attaining the political independence of the Czech lands in view of their geographical location and their special ethnic relations. He also raised the question as to the degree of independence possible, saying, for instance, that he was unable to put into a political programme something (such as the personal union advocated by some progressives) which he did not believe he would live to see.[18]

In articles on Palacký, published in 1898, Masaryk reiterated the gist of these arguments. He noted that Palacký had recognized that the Czech nation could not be politically independent, and had placed emphasis on developing the nation's education and culture, and in particular on understanding and using the fruits of modern science. The nation must be oriented to the spirit of the new age, wrote Palacký, and seek to reach the level of other nations in industry and commerce, in all spheres of life, and in all professions. This task was all the more difficult and urgent in the present situation, observed Masaryk, in view of the progress made by the larger nations and the more intense competition in industry, education and intellectual life generally.[19]

In his study of Havlíček Masaryk cited his advocacy of complete independence, but quoted with approval Palacký's statement that absolute independence was a 'deceptive dream', and Havlíček's that it would be 'a pure misfortune', and added that, like Poland or Serbia, the Czechs would be a plaything in the hands of their neighbours, the Germans.[20]

Nonetheless, in his 1905 lecture on the problem of a small nation, Masaryk restated his belief that even a small nation *could* be politically independent – there were even smaller nations that were independent. But each small nation must solve its problem by its own special methods and not by following those used by others, for instance, violence. A small nation must gather up all its forces, great and small (including, he noted, the two million Slovaks), educate itself, develop its culture and work more intensively. Openness, not intrigue, and standing for the truth, were the means of 'convincing the world that what we wish is to its own advantage. The Czech question is a question of the whole world, not only of ourselves.'[21]

Masaryk continued to wrestle with the question of the degree of independence which could be achieved. In a later essay on the student and politics, written in 1909, Masaryk recognized that absolute political sovereignty, even for great states, and still more for small nations, 'mere shuttlecocks in the politics of the powerful', was no longer possible; the 'ever increasing reciprocity of states and nations' made it more and more relative. The increasing organization of greater entities, such as Europe, for instance, guaranteed the small states only 'a relative independence', but it did assure, not only centralization, but also autonomy or federalization.[22] Yet in the same year he wrote of the need to struggle for 'complete independence in all respects, for which we have both historic and natural right', and in union with Slovaks, but this could not be attained all at once, but only by gradually transforming the Austrian state.[23]

Masaryk's party programmes dealt with the question of political independence in similar fashion. As noted above, the People's party programme of 1900, in language similar to the arguments cited above, recognized that complete independence of the Czech lands was impossible and that even the freedom of independent states was relatively limited. The Progressive party programme of 1905 made only a single reference to political independence within the framework of a free and progressive Austria. Although the revised programme of 1912 repeated this, it recalled Palacký's statement that 'we were before Austria and we shall exist also after Austria'. While recognizing the advantages of association with other lands, it also argued for the greatest degree of self-government.[24]

Apart from the 1900 programme just cited, Masaryk usually spoke of the independence of the Czech *nation* but, as we shall see subsequently, he sometimes equated this with the independence of the Bohemian *state* (including the Germans) and did not clearly distinguish the two concepts.

STATE RIGHT OR NATURAL RIGHT

For over fifty years the concept of Bohemian state right (*České státní právo*) had occupied a central place in Czech politics.[25] It was under the banner of state right that the Czech National Party and the landed aristocracy had conducted their policy of abstinence from the Austrian Parliament after 1861. After their return to Vienna in 1879, they declared that this did not mean that they had abandoned Bohemian state right and had recognized the validity of the Austrian constitution of 1867. The Young Czechs criticized the Old Czechs for failing to act in accord with this and later similar declarations, but they themselves became the subject of criticism for doing the same when they became the dominant party. For the next forty years the state-right doctrine was included in almost all party programmes, including not only those of the Old and Young Czechs, and the nobility, but also of new parties such as the Progressive, Catholic and Agrarian parties, and was the theme of countless speeches, articles and books.[26]

The concept is not easy to define briefly in view of its inner ambiguity and its diverse interpretations at different times and by different persons. Its essence (after 1627) was defined by one of its fervent supporters, Karel Kramář, in the following words: 'The lands of the Bohemian crown (Bohemia, Moravia and Silesia), formed an undivided and indivisible whole, completely independent and autonomous (*unabhängig* und *selbständig*) *vis-à-vis* the other lands of their King (i.e. the Austrian monarch).' Many legal measures, dating as far back as 1526, had established the fact that the Bohemian King was elected by the Diets and that the latter enjoyed unlimited competence in legislation in the three lands. The constitutional acts of 1867 which had established the Dualist system and a centralized Austrian system and had *de facto* limited the powers of the Diets were 'legally invalid'; they had created 'a law (*Gesetz*) but not a right (*Recht*)' and had not affected the continuing validity of Bohemian state right.[27]

This legal fiction became a central issue dividing the Czech political parties and indicating different attitudes towards Bohemia's relationship with Austria. Right down to 1914 state-right declarations were made by the deputies of almost every party; sometimes in joint statements, sometimes separately with varying content. But as time went on, the parties often paid only lip-service to state right, and watered it down in practice to more modest immediate aims. Leading political figures, such as Kaizl, in 1895, and even Kramář, in 1906, admitted that state right could not be achieved at an early date but only by a slow policy of step-by-step advance.[28] Although state right was still often declared to be the existing legal status of the Czech nation, it came more and more to be defined as a mere practical proposal for the decentralization of the Monarchy, for autonomy or federation.

The newer parties adopted different standpoints toward Bohemian state right, criticizing the older parties either for pursuing verbally what they called an unattainable utopian objective or for abandoning state right in favour of an opportunist or pro-Austrian position. The original Progressive movement was divided on the relative importance of state and natural right, and eventually split into separate parties which placed the emphasis on one or other of the two. The People's party placed the emphasis on natural right, but did not totally abandon historic right and sought to achieve it gradually within the Empire. The Progressive party at first, in 1905, made little reference to state right and pressed for the democratization of Austria as a whole. In 1912, it placed somewhat more emphasis on state right but like its predecessor, the People's party focused on the natural right of the nation. The Moravian People's Progressive party opted for state right on the basis of both historic and natural rights. The National Socialists upheld state right and condemned the Social Democrats for abandoning it; in 1911 they reaffirmed the doctrine and used it to justify Bohemian independence. More militant parties, the State Right Radicals, and later the State Right Progressives, advocated the early establishment of state right in the form of complete independence for Bohemia, either within the Empire, or if necessary outside.[29] At the other extreme the Social Democrats stood almost alone in openly denouncing the Bohemian state-right strategy of the other parties and pressing for a reorganization of the entire Monarchy on national lines.[30]

MASARYK AND STATE RIGHT

Masaryk's attitude to state right changed over time and was not by any means clear and consistent. In one of his early speeches in the Reichsrat, in 1892, he declared firmly that he was in favour of Bohemian state right, which he equated with independence and a Czech state.[31] In another speech shortly thereafter, in 1893, he defended at some length 'the *de jure* existing state right', the demand for which 'culminated in the natural struggle for political independence'. 'This was not merely the demand of one party; their struggle against centralism was based on the state-right conviction of all parties, of the entire nation.'[32] Yet five years later Masaryk had shifted his ground so far as to give qualified approval to the Social Democratic anti-state-right declaration.[33]

In his theoretical writings Masaryk did not systematically formulate his views on state and natural rights although he made many scattered references to these concepts. In *The Czech Question* he approved without reservation Palacký's programme of historic state right and again equated this with independence, but within an Austrian framework.[34] As for natural right, Masaryk, following Palacký and Havlíček, conceived natural right as derived from the concept of humanity and considered it important in justifying the rights of nations and the freedom and equality of nations.[35]

In later works, such as his brochure on Palacký and his book on Havlíček, Masaryk reiterated his approval of Palacký's concept of historic right but described him also as a believer in natural right and noted that he had wavered as between the two concepts. For instance, he had moved from advocacy of natural right in 1848 to state right in 1865, and back to a more national position in 1872. Havlíček, although more strongly favourable to natural right, had also oscillated between the two. In the 1904 edition of his book on Havlíček, Masaryk discussed the relationship of natural and state right more fully and clearly subordinated the latter to the former.[36]

When it came to formulating the question in a party programme in 1900, Masaryk hewed to the same line, but argued that Bohemian state right or independence could only be attained with the approval of the Bohemian Germans, and this meant accepting their proposals for the national demarcation of local government regions. The programme warned that the attainment of a Czech state, with 'several million convinced and capable traitors', was impossible.[37]

In a highly polemical defence of this programme, Masaryk claimed its virtue in 'recognizing the actual position of state right, namely that our state right has been broken not only by the Crown but also by the legal representatives of the nation; the state-right continuity hitherto defended by our constitutional, legal and political theoreticians and politicians does not now exist'. He challenged the dogmatic view which ignored the fact that law develops and rejected 'any fixed and petrified concept of our state right'. He ridiculed the effort by Kramář and others to assert the primacy of 'rights' over 'facts' as scholasticism. Have not the old laws lost their validity? Were the new laws 'formally illegal'? 'The needs of our present life and the now valid positive law were more decisive than a law valid several centuries ago.' In the modern era, as Palacký realized, he asserted, nationality, not historical right, was the moving political force. There was a need, he wrote, for a more detailed clarification of the ideas of natural and state rights, but he did not himself offer it.[38]

In an article in the German periodical *Die Zeit*, in the same year, Masaryk gave a more systematic analysis of the 'contradictions between state-right historicism and modern nationalism' and described the ever-changing standpoints of the Young Czechs, in particular the two Grégrs and Karel Kramář. He reiterated his belief that historical continuity had been irretrievably broken, and that the national idea, based on a democratic standpoint, was now primary. He condemned the ultra-nationalism of the Radical State Right and Radical Progressive parties, both of which ignored or rejected the natural rights which the Bohemian Germans also enjoyed. The People's party placed national equality in the foreground, but presupposed an agreement of Germans and Czechs based on the natural rights of both.[39]

In a speech some nine years later to the Progressive party, Masaryk returned to the crucial question of the role of the Bohemian Germans in the attainment of state right. Once again he rejected state-right utopianism, now adopted, he said, by a dozen parties, this time on the ground that it downplayed national and language rights and separated off the Czechs and Germans. If it were to be carried out, he warned once again, 'we would have among the ten million people of the Czech lands four million culturally and economically capable German traitors, behind whom stands the powerful German Reich... We can attain our independence either with the Germans or without them. We cannot force the Germans to live with us in a single state and we must therefore seek a settlement with them, based on tolerable language rights. No help could be expected from foreign complications, still less from aid from Russia. Czech policy must be directed inwardly towards the greatest possible development of national rights.[40]

AUTONOMY AND FEDERATION

The question of federation (as well as state right) can only be understood in the context of the character of the Austrian political system established by the Constitution of 1867. While granting Hungary a position of virtual independence, this fundamental law established in the Austrian half of the Monarchy, so-called Cisleithania, what an eminent French historian, Louis Eisenmann, called 'masked absolutism', in which the Emperor was the core of a centralized bureaucratic system. Edvard Beneš, then a young historian studying in France, described Austria as 'une mélange de fédéralisme timide et du centralisme dynastique et absolutiste'.

Although the constitution was in principle federalist, the legislative power was assigned in large measure to the Austrian central government, leaving to the seventeen Crownlands, including Bohemia and Moravia, extremely limited residual powers, including, for instance, agriculture and, within the framework of federal laws, education and local government. The executive power was almost completely centralized in the hands of the Monarch, his subordinate ministers and the state bureaucracy. In most of the Crownlands it was exercised by a Lieutenant Governor (*místodržitel* or *Statthalter*) and his administrative office, and to a lesser degree, by a Provincial Committee, neither of which was responsible to the Diet. As in the case of the organs of local government, the *obec* (commune) and *okres* (district), this 'double' or dualist system left the autonomous or self-governing organs of the *země* (province or land) in a completely subordinated position. This made a mockery of the federalist principle and left centralism virtually unchallenged.[41]

As we have seen above, the ideas of decentralization, broadened autonomy or federation, based usually on the Bohemian state-right doctrine, were for many decades the common currency of all Czech politicians but seldom were these given any concrete substance. The many state-right declarations issued by Czech parties, usually contained an incantation of the ancient right of the Bohemian lands to unity and statehood and an attack on the centralization of the Austrian half of the Monarchy. The terms autonomy or federation were used to justify the legislative and administrative independence of the kingdoms and lands, and concretely to demand an expansion of the rights of the Diets.[42] Only the Social Democrats, as we have seen, stood against state right and pressed for a federation which would unite Czechs and Slovaks.

Czech political leaders were not usually very informative about the form or degree of the autonomy or decentralization desired. For example, Karel Kramář, in his book on Bohemian state right in 1896, without using the term federalism, wrote of the independence of the Bohemian lands and a real union with the non-Hungarian land; certain common affairs would be handled by a common parliament, and administration would be assigned to the Bohemian lands, with a minister responsible for the Bohemian lands.[43] However, two other Young Czechs, Josef Fořt and Josef Herold, advanced somewhat more detailed reforms of the provincial constitution.

According to the Fořt plan, in 1902, specific legislative competence would be assigned to the Reichsrat, which would deal with foreign policy, the military, finances and commercial affairs, and eventually civil and criminal law. Everything which was not expressly reserved to the former would fall within the sphere of the provincial Diets. The Diets would also share the power of custom duties and taxation, and would be completely independent in administering these rights. Administration would also be divided between imperial ministries, responsible to Parliament, and provincial governors responsible to the Diets.[44]

Josef Herold, in an article published in 1907–8, outlined numerous previous plans which would have broadened the competence of the Bohemian Diet and provided for independent provincial administration. He himself proposed the legislative enactment of the fundamental rights and the indivisibility of the Bohemian Kingdom (not of the Bohemian lands, be it noted) which would assign extensive legislative powers to the Diet. State administration would be conducted by the Lieutenant Governor and an advisory council, both responsible to the Diet. Autonomous administration would be conducted by a Provincial Committee, as an executive organ, elected by the Diet and responsible to it.[45]

MASARYK AND FEDERATION

Masaryk, in his earlier writings, had argued that independence, i.e. the state right or natural right, of the Czech nation could most effectively be achieved in Austria through a federation, although this could be a union of nations or of the historic Crownlands. He advanced this idea in the context of a discussion of the conflicting processes of centralization and autonomization in society. He used the latter term to refer to the tendency of the individual, the social group and class, the church, the local commune (*obec*), district and 'land' (*země*), or the nation to assert its individuality against centralist power. Autonomy in the last sense was more or less equivalent to self-government (*samospráva*) or federation.[46]

In none of his writings, however, did Masaryk develop a concrete programme for the federalization of Austria. In his book on Havlíček, he recapitulated the views of Palacký and Havlíček, but without indicating his own preference. He gave an extensive review of the changing views of Palacký on federation and summarized his 1848 programme according to which seven national groups or provinces (*země*), two of which would be (Austrian) German and Czechoslav (including the Slovaks and Czechs), would share the powers of government with the imperial authority. Administration would also be shared by the imperial and provincial governments. There would be an Imperial Council (*Reichsrat*) made up of delegates of the Diets and having only advisory powers. In other proposals in 1848 and 1849 Palacký had wavered between a federation of nations and of the historical lands, and in 1865, had abandoned the former in favour of the latter.[47]

Havlíček had not presented a detailed plan of federation and had used terms which revealed his vacillation between the two alternative bases of a federal system. Although he expressed himself strongly in favour of Austria and the dynasty, he insisted that the Czech Crown should have full administrative independence, with its own constitution and its own Diet. In no way did they wish to be a mere Austrian province; Austria should be 'a federation or union (*spolek*) of independent lands and nations'. Yet he sometimes referred to 'a federation of nations', sometimes to a union of the 'Czechoslav nation' and sometimes to one of the Bohemian lands; he spoke alternatively of three provincial Diets (*sněmy*) or a general Diet (*sněm*) for all three.[48]

Even the programmes of Masaryk's parties presented no outline of a federal reform of the Austrian system. The 1900 People's programme referred only to Palacký's proposal of federation as a basis for the independence of the Czech lands, and to 'the greatest degree of autonomy of the lands based on history and on natural factors (geographic, ethnographic, economic and cultural)'. The autonomy of the lands should be assured by making the Lieutenant-Governor responsible to the Diets.[49]

The Progressive programme of 1905 did not even use the word federation and spoke only of political independence within a free, progressive Austria; it condemned the centralism of the constitution and called for constitutional reform, namely reform of the state, provincial, and public administration in general.[50] The 1912 programme demanded political independence within a federal Austria-Hungary. It did not oppose the central and united system but argued, however, for 'the autonomy of the lands endowed by history and nature (geographical, ethnographic, economic and cultural)'. This meant the greatest self-government, including the responsibility of the provincial Governors to the Diets.[51]

ALOIS HAJN'S PLAN OF FEDERALISM

Only Alois Hajn, Masaryk's collaborator in forming the Progressive party, in his draft programme of 1905, set forth a concrete proposal for a federalist revision of the constitution. Although it did not become part of the party's programme of 1906 and was not discussed by Masaryk, this radical plan deserves to be discussed at length as the only such programme advanced by a Progressive and indeed as the fullest scheme based on the national principle. Hajn approved, as a minimal programme, the draft revision of the constitution proposed by the Young Czech deputy, Josef Fořt, discussed above, but offered his own more radical solution which combined Fořt's historical or territorial principle with the nationality principle.[52]

According to his plan, Austria would be divided into large, autonomous territories according to nationality, where possible; these independent state entities would be linked together in a common federal state. These would include the lands of the Bohemian Crown (Bohemia, Moravia and Silesia, without the Polish population), the German lands (not including, however, the German parts of the Bohemian lands), and an Italian–Slovenian–Serbian–Croatian territory. This would be combined with regions (*kraje*), as far as possible nationally homogeneous (in the Bohemian lands, 12 Czech, 7 German). The competence of the Diets would include middle schools, specialized and higher schools, trade, industry and commerce, railways and posts, provincial insurance and finance, public security, the judicial system, and a provincial military. The Reichsrat, consisting of two chambers, one for Cisleithania and one for Hungary, would have power over the common affairs of the whole Monarchy, including foreign policy, commercial treaties, the common army, imperial communications, finances, custom duties, and other common matters such as monopolies, currency, weights and measures, banks of issue, and the determination of contributions to common affairs. Although Hajn's proposal accepted Dualism for the time being, it foresaw the eventual victory of the nationality principle in Hungary and the federalization of the entire Monarchy. The rights of the 'outdated' lands would thus be replaced by the modern right of nations, which justified the incorporation of the Hungarian Slovaks into the Czech kingdom.[53]

THE CZECH–GERMAN LANGUAGE CONFLICT

The conflict over the use of the two languages in the Bohemian lands was the cardinal issue of Czech–German relations.[54] The positions taken by the two nations reflected their more fundamental attitudes toward the Bohemian Kingdom and the Austrian Monarchy. The Czechs insisted on a language settlement which would preserve the unity of Bohemia and its distinctive character; the Germans demanded a settlement which would guarantee the German character of Austria as a whole, and would divide Bohemia into German and Czech areas through administrative reorganization.

The Czech standpoint, more or less unchanged for 35 years, favoured a *bilingual* solution, which would guarantee Czech, as the *landesübliche* (customary) language, complete equality in state and autonomous offices and courts in the whole of the Bohemian lands. This solution meant in their view the right of Czech to be used not only in the outer dealings with individual parties, but also in the internal business of the offices and courts; it also meant that all officials and judges must be bilingual.

The Germans, on the other hand, preferred a *unilingual* solution according to which the German language should be legislatively declared the state language and should be the exclusive language of the inner procedures of all state institutions. This should be coupled with a general partitioning (*Abgrenzung* or *rozdělení*) of the local government areas along national lines, and also a national sectionalization of provincial institutions such as the Supreme Court, the Lord Lieutenancy, the Provincial Committee and Diet, and the Agricultural and School Councils. Judges and officials should not be required to know both languages throughout the Kingdom, but only in the specific situations where both languages were needed.

As part of a unilingual solution, the Germans were ready to accept the predominant use of Czech in the outer relations, and to a limited degree in the internal service, in nationally homogeneous districts and regions (where in their view Czech alone was *landesübliche*); in mixed areas both languages would be used. The Czechs were at certain times ready to accept this unilingual solution, provided Czech was the exclusive official language in purely Czech areas and had equal rights in mixed districts, and that Czech would be used in the outer service of German districts. National delimitation was also acceptable, provided it did not create a 'closed German' area or divide the Bohemian lands or its institutions.

Although he was an ardent advocate of Czech national interests, Masaryk, by virtue of his upbringing and his years in Vienna, and wide study of German literature, keenly appreciated German scholarship and culture. He advocated a positive approach which would recognize legitimate German interests but also the common interests of Czechs and Germans – an attitude which earned him the epithet of Germanophile in some quarters. Moreover, as we have seen, he was not a fervent advocate of Bohemian state right and repeatedly stressed that this could not be achieved without the agreement of the Bohemian Germans. Yet his position was ambiguous, in as much as he never completely gave up the Bohemian state-right position and made it the underlying basis of his proposals for the use of language.[55]

Masaryk approached the language question pragmatically and sought to reach a middle ground between the sharply opposed views of Czech and German parties. Due to the ethnic and economic complexities of the situation, there was no single formula for the solution of the question in all three of the Bohemian lands and for all areas within them. Moreover, since demographic and economic conditions were constantly changing, any settlement must be provisional and flexible. Although he was ready to accept the German idea of demarcation of the districts and regions into Czech, German and mixed, he stressed that it was not easy to apply in Bohemia, still less in Moravia, and should not be carried out one-sidedly or mechanically but should take account of the economic wishes and needs of the population and of the particular character of each area. He saw the need for a much more adequate statistical calculation of mother tongues and of the ethnic composition of local areas and suggested that a Language Office might be set up to publish statistics and act as an arbitral court. Furthermore such a national separation was but part of a more general administrative problem, namely the establishment of a democratic system of self-administration and local autonomy, based on universal suffrage. A durable agreement among Czechs and Germans was not possible without a constitutional revision, an adjustment (*upravení*) of the state-right relations of the Czech Crown and the Empire. He considered the German proposal of homogeneous regions (*kraje*) desirable, provided their representative bodies were genuinely parliamentary in form.

As for a concrete settlement of the language question, Masaryk believed that the Austrian Parliament should enact a legal framework and leave it to the Diets to apply this in legislation concretely adapted to their own special conditions. His own proposals were set forth in the two party programmes of 1900 and 1912, which differed somewhat from each other but represented a kind of compromise between multilingualism and unilingualism. Czech and German were both '*landesübliche* languages' and should have complete equality as official languages throughout the Bohemian lands (as well as Polish in Silesia). The two programmes enunciated the general principles of the multilingualism of all offices and courts, but accepted the unilingualism of officials, depending on the situation and the need.[56]

The citizen had the right, everywhere in Bohemian lands, to use his or her language in relations with the authorities, both lower and higher, and the case should also be dealt with internally in this same language. In mixed districts (which would include Prague, Brno and Opava), and in Bohemia as a whole, both languages should therefore be used both externally and internally. In nationally homogeneous districts, either Czech or German would be used, not only externally and internally for a particular case, but also as the innermost language of the offices. The central ministries in Vienna should also deal with Czech cases and correspond with lower Czech offices in Czech. Wherever necessary, national sections would be set up in provincial and central institutions, and even in regional judicial districts. In Vienna and parts of Lower Austria generally, where many Czechs had settled, they should have the right to use Czech in relations with the official organs as well as to have schools in their own language. In the German areas of Bohemia, where there were substantial Czech minorities, they should be able to use Czech in official dealings as well as to have separate minority schools using their own language. In the whole of Bohemia, public announcements should be given in one or both languages depending on the ethnic character of the districts. There should be an authentic Czech text of all laws and ordinances.

As for officials and judges, bilingualism was the ideal, but would depend on the circumstances and the quantity and type of service to be performed in each case. In practice, therefore, officials in lower offices could be bilingual or unilingual, depending on the circumstances. Those who could use both languages would receive special recompense. There should everywhere be sufficient qualified bilingual officers to meet the needs of Czech parties. In the higher provincial organs officials should be bilingual, but the agenda would be divided, where necessary, according to language, and handled by appropriate language-sections, using one language.

For 35 years Czechs and Germans sought in vain to achieve a compromise of their conflicting standpoints. In 1890, under the regime of Count Taaffe, a partial agreement between the more moderate Czechs and Germans was reached on the use of languages and on partition, but broke down due to the government's failure to implement it and the strenuous opposition of the Young Czechs. Thereafter, new efforts were made by successive Austrian prime ministers, ranging from the bilingual solution, favourable to the Czechs, decreed by Count Badeni in 1897 but reversed by Baron Gautsch in the following year, to the more unilingual proposals for a legislative settlement advanced from 1900 on, by successive prime ministers. Piecemeal government concessions to Czechs or Germans produced only parliamentary obstruction and street demonstrations. In 1905 an agreement *was* reached in Moravia, where conditions were very different, but in Bohemia the conflict remained intractable.[57] The situation worsened in 1913 when the government dissolved the Bohemian Diet, which had been financially crippled by German obstruction, and replaced it with an administrative commission, thus ending all Czech hopes of broadened autonomy. In 1914, under Count Stürgkh, a new round of talks, which for the first time included provincial reform as well as the perennial language question, produced no agreement and was brought to an end by the outbreak of war.[58] Although Masaryk took part in these negotiations, he was not able to bridge the gap between the warring national representatives and could not therefore avert the final breakdown.

AUSTRIA-HUNGARY – CONTINGENT LOYALTY

As we have seen, for almost fifty years Masaryk recognized that complete political independence for the Czechs or for Bohemia was impossible and indeed dangerous. The reverse side of the coin was a positive attitude to Austria-Hungary and a belief that the Monarchy was a necessity, especially in view of the danger which threatened the small Czech nation from Germany and Russia. Like Palacký and Havlíček, he believed that the *raison d'être* of Austria was to serve as a union of free and equal nations. In a sense, then, his loyalty was conditional on a fundamental reform of the empire and, as his hope for such a transformation waned, so did his faith in it as a viable and desirable political community.[59]

Early in his career, in 1891, while still a Young Czech deputy, Masaryk gave a speech in Strakonice which earned him the pejorative charge of 'Austrianism' (*rakušanství*). This was based mainly on a brief passage in which he cited Palacký to the effect that 'we sincerely want Austria', and avowed his intention to act accordingly. In a postscript he declared that, in the spirit of the views of Havlíček and Palacký, the Czech nation, in its own interest, needed Austria, but must strive for a federation of all Austrian peoples as the only way that Austria could continue to exist. 'If, however, contrary to our desire, Austria could not continue, 'we must be prepared, for the future, and as Palacký had indicated, for a great new test of fire'.[60]

In other speeches in Parliament during the nineties Masaryk often stated, as we have noted above, his belief in Bohemian independence as an expression of historic state right, and counterposed this to the official 'idea of the Austrian state'. On 25 January 1892, for instance, he argued that the state idea should be based not on the dominance of one nationality and on uniformity, but rather on community and work for the state structure in its entirety. In the Bohemian Diet, in April 1892, he declared: 'Compromise in Bohemia is the salvation of Austria. Without it Austria is weak – in fact almost nothing'. Over and over he hammered at the need for Austria to be truly a state of small nations. Without this, he declared on 6 July 1892, calm and order could not prevail.[61]

In a powerful speech on 18 November of that year, which earned him the opprobrium of 'traitor' from a German deputy, he declared: 'We want a living state, based, not on language, but on law (*Recht*) and justice'. 'We want independence and the right of self-determination, a Czech state right.... We desire bread and you give us stones. Due to your fault, the best intentions and the most idealistic forces of the Czech nation have involuntarily got into a position of apparent opposition to the state. And thus it comes about that the Austrian state is unable to recognize its own advantages; instead of using Czech energies, it suppresses them, unnaturally and futilely.'[62]

Again, on 20 March 1893, Masaryk forcefully reiterated his demands for state right and an independent state, and declared that this did not mean that they wished to destroy the Austrian state. 'The Czech question, the most important problem demanding solution in Austria, could be simply defined. A nation of six million economically powerful, diligent, talented and developing people, conscious of its strength and of its value for the empire, will not tolerate being placed under guardianship.' 'The Czech nation will not and cannot stop as long as it is unable to make itself felt as a political nation. Within an association of Austrian nations, we wish, not only to be heard; we wish to have equal political rights in every respect.'[63]

On 14 June 1893, in a speech devoted to foreign policy, he declared: 'In the interest of our nation, we want a policy of peace, both at home and abroad.' 'We want Austria to remain a great power, but we also wish that Austria should be great and powerful inwardly.' At the conclusion he demanded justice and equality of right and stated his conviction that a just Austria had nothing to fear.[64]

In his more theoretical works, *The Czech Question* and *Our Present Political Crisis*, published in 1895, Masaryk vigorously rejected the charge of *rakušanství*, and used the term Austro-Slavism to describe Palacký's advocacy of a federation. He acknowledged a strong interest in the fate of Austria and cited Palacký's often-quoted phrase that if Austria had not existed, it would have been necessary to create it. His was not, however, a passive loyalty to Austria, and certainly not the old Austrian patriotism; he sought, he said, to elevate Austria by reform. Austria was justified only if it recognized the idea of the equality of the nations and lands. After 1873, he noted regretfully, Palacký had confessed to having lost hope in Austria, and cited his other famous phrase that 'we were before Austria, and we shall also be after her'. He warned that if it came to a cataclysm in Europe, Bohemia would go to Germany, not Russia. But he did not expect such a catastrophe and realistically reckoned with Austria's continued existence.[65]

AUSTRIA-HUNGARY – GROWING ALIENATION

At the turn of the century Masaryk became more severe in his criticism of Austria-Hungary and more demanding in his claims for reform. The programme of the People's party in 1900 struck a somewhat new note by calling for Austria to become 'a modern, progressive, democratic and populist state'. This alone would assure it a leading role in world competition. The old unconscious Austrian loyalty was not adequate at a time when the whole social organization was being subjected to criticism and 'reasons were being demanded for all political and social institutions'. The nations of Austria must have reasons for their patriotism; nationality conflicts must be removed and the strength of the various nations unleashed if Austria were to take part in world politics in a grand style.[66]

Masaryk's position was more sharply stated in his first major speech as party leader in Velím in June 1901. Warning of the danger of a more militant and nationalistic Germany and its growing influence on Austrian policy, and the parallel development of extreme Austro-German nationalism, Masaryk pleaded for 'an Austrian idea'. 'What reasons do we and the Austrian Germans have or can we have to stand firmly with Austria?' He lamented the decline of the Austrian parliament and blamed it on 'the old Austrian lack of energy, and the lack of a positive political programme, in short, of a political idea'. The constitution was stifled by absolutism, by its aristocratic, hierarchical spirit. The solution of the Czech question required 'a foresighted and penetrating revision of the constitution and administrative reform'. In the face of this situation Czech politics needed to be democratic and progressive; the Czech people must be 'faithful to the great ideas of our great predecessors and be confident in the ultimate victory of its right and truth.[67]

The programme adopted at the founding congress of the Progressive party in 1906 placed great emphasis on civic and political freedom, and universal suffrage, and spoke of attaining 'complete political independence within a free and progressive Austria'.[68] Alois Hajn, in a draft prepared beforehand but not endorsed by the congress, was somewhat more positive toward Austria, formulating the idea of a progressive Austro-Slavism based on two principles: national freedom and equality and civic freedom and equality.[69]

In July 1907 Masaryk re-entered Parliament with somewhat greater confidence in the possibility of reform, as he indicated in his lectures in America during the summer after the opening of Parliament. He was encouraged by the introduction of universal suffrage in that year, but this was limited to the central Parliament, and Austria was still not a really parliamentary state. He did not expect much new, as some did, from the future Emperor.[70] That he still entertained serious doubts was indicated, at home, in an article published anonymously, in which he wrote; 'Anyone who expects freedom, popularism and political progress from Austria, is a political child.'[71]

In the budget debate in July 1907, he welcomed the broadening of suffrage under Baron Beck, the prime minister, and his lip-service to national equality, but found it necessary to abstain on the final vote. Masaryk placed still greater emphasis on national, democratic and social aspects of policy. Austria, he declared, was in a sense an artificial state; the driving forces had always been the nations, not the state. The central government must have a positive national policy; it must treat, with the same love, respect, and justice, and with the same understanding, not just German culture, but also Czech, Polish and Ruthenian. There must also be democratization of the Parliament and of all public institutions and an extension of the suffrage so as to include the Diets and local governments.[72]

In subsequent sessions in 1907 and 1908 Masaryk broadened his attack, censuring Hungarian policy toward the Slovaks, defending the cause of freedom of scholarship and religion against clerical assaults, and lamenting the government's lack of a creative and democratic programme. On 9 December 1908, he roundly condemned absolutism in foreign policy, and demanded the democratic reformation of the Bohemian lands and the whole of Austria. 'We do not want the old Austrianism any more; we no longer have any feeling for what you call Austrian, i.e. in the sense of stupid and antiquated centralism' (Zopf).[73]

The chief cause of Masaryk's stiffening attitude was Austria's aggressive foreign policy and, in particular, the annexation of Bosnia and Hercegovina in October 1908. In ensuing years Masaryk engaged in a strenuous campaign against this policy in the course of which he became ever more critical of Austria's domestic as well as its foreign policy. In speech after speech, he decried the failure of Austria to reform itself inwardly, especially in its relationship with the non-German nations.[74]

The first salvo was delivered on 17 December 1908, when he again called for a transformation of Austria. He reckoned with the dynasty as one of the forces involved, but urged it, in its own interest, to engage in the process of change. Masaryk strongly condemned the Dualist system, and cast doubts on a trialism which would include the Czech lands but exclude the South Slavs from consideration. 'The state must not suppress the nations, but it must utilize the force of the national idea in the interest of the nations and of the whole state'. The national problem was not just a language problem, but an economic and social one, which required agreement between the two nations.[75]

Masaryk returned to the attack in May 1909, with two major speeches on the Balkan question. Austria had become the largest South Slav state by the annexation and must find the correct relationship of state and nation; it must become an empire and pursue – not a policy of Germans, nor of Magyars, nor of Czechs, but an 'imperial policy'. 'This would make something organic of the Empire as a whole'. Closing, he declared: 'We wish to have a strong Austria but it should be conscious of its real strength, the strength of its nations.[76]

The following year (1910), in November, in the Delegations, Masaryk undertook a severe criticism of Austrian foreign policy and its aristocratic diplomacy, and warned of the danger threatening the Czechs from Germany. In closing, he declared: 'We are not against becoming Greater Austrians. Yes, let there be a Greater Austria, but this could be created not out of fantasies but only by gathering together and uniting all the forces of all the nations in one great whole. A Greater Austria must positively support its nations, culturally and economically.'[77]

In several subsequent meetings of the Delegations Masaryk concentrated his attacks on the person of the foreign minister, Count Aerenthal; he indignantly charged that the latter had impugned his patriotism by arguing that he had collected information on the South Slav trials outside Austria. 'For every decent Austrian, it goes without saying that he is a patriot.' A few days later he noted that he was charged at home for being 'too Austrian'; now the foreign minister charged him with not being 'a good Austrian (rakušan)'. He confessed that he did not know what a good Austrian was and that distinguishing between a good and a bad Austrian only worsened the actual differences among nations.[78]

In February 1911, Masaryk criticized the reliance of Austrian foreign policy on military strength. A policy of peace could be based, not on dreadnoughts, but on a positive regard for all the cultural demands of the individual Austrian nations. Neither as Slavs, nor as Austrian citizens, could they be satisfied with a dualist national policy according to which one nation was master there, and another nation here. He quoted a Russian newspaper to the effect that he, Masaryk, 'a tried and true servant of the Monarchy', had been shaken to the core by the errors of Austro-Hungarian diplomacy.[79]

AUSTRIA-HUNGARY – DECLINE OF FAITH

Returning to Vienna after re-election in 1911, Masaryk became still more severe in his denunciation of Austria's foreign and domestic policies. Criticizing the government for its neglect of the social problem and its preference for the military, he declared that 'the entire system must be reformed from top to bottom'. The state administration was 'antiquated and does not respond to the new economic, social and cultural conditions'. The Czech nation had developed so much, in population, economically and culturally, that they felt the dependence on Vienna all the more keenly. There could be no question of any inequality; Czechs must be dealt with as equals in any negotiations. He rejected a *rakušanství* which consisted of 'the treasury clipping off with its claws a piece here or there of the living organism, without plan, without system, and then daubing over the wounds with a gold and yellow tincture'. The positive element in Austria was the nations and their organizations; the negative aspect was the so-called Austrian state idea.[80]

Masaryk used even stronger words in a speech in May 1912 in the Delegations in which he condemned the criminal Balkan policies of the government, and also the treatment of the Slovaks by Hungary. 'Austria was nothing more than official and unofficial *Schlamperei* (sloppiness); policy was characterized by incredible aimlessness, an unbelievable dissipation of national and political strengths, and political and administrative degeneration'.[81] In the Reichsrat in October Masaryk denounced the helplessness and ignorance in both foreign and domestic affairs. What was needed was an Austrian policy in the democratic sense, one which would make Austria a modern, economically and culturally powerful state.[82]

At the beginning of the year a revised programme of the Progressive party had spoken unequivocally of 'the Czech and the Austrian ideas opposing each other in the sharpest possible manner'. It demanded complete political independence within the Austrian framework and professed an interest in Austria, but it cited the Palacký phrase that 'we shall exist after Austria'. It recognized the advantages of associating with other lands in a greater entity and did not even oppose 'the necessity of a central and unified organization which would enhance and assure the power position of Austria'. This would not, however, be 'the thoughtless loyalty' of old Austrian *rakušanství*; it would strive for a constitutional and general reform of the empire in a democratic spirit. It repeated verbatim the 1900 formula that the old Austrian loyalism was not sufficient for the present time, and that there was a need for removing national conflicts in the interests of Austria's place in the world.[83]

Masaryk's dilemma was expressed in a speech on 6 January 1913 to the Progressive party executive in Prague. 'We all want equality and equal rights, we all want freedom in Austria; then we would have no reason in the foreseeable future to get out of Austria. But if there was no freedom in Austria (as the most Austrian of people say in Parliament), the greater freedom abroad will exert greater attraction.' The Czech situation was difficult since, unlike the Serbs, Germans and Rumanians, Czechs did not have an independent state. 'We cannot follow the Serbian example but we must learn from the Serbs that to be faithful to the national idea leads to victory. But with all our love and sympathy for the victors, we cannot forget practical conditions.'[84]

In his final speech in the Reichsrat before the outbreak of war, on 26 May 1913, Masaryk condemned Austria's foreign and domestic policy but openly admitted that he could not indulge in dreams of the collapse of Austria; good or bad, Austria would continue. For this reason he was seriously concerned 'to make something out of Austria'. 'Our state right and administrative plans are not designed to weaken the others but to strengthen the whole. We know well that if the whole is no good, we, alas, must share in it.' 'The sad position of Austria in the world was based on its inner policy; it was conducting a war against its own good nations.' Masaryk compared the typical Austrian statesman to a poor Viennese, 'a good Austrian', who had swallowed an umbrella and who was afraid it might open at any moment. As a result he could not move. He had a good brain, good eyes and ears, but he could not see what others saw, did not hear what others heard, and could not think what all other Austrians of different languages thought. His life was without content. Following this metaphor, Masaryk uttered what were to be his final words in the Austrian Parliament. 'He wished that all parties in Parliament would finally see that it was in their interest and in the interest of our nations to put an end to the incapacity of our domestic and foreign policy.'[85]

CONCLUSIONS

Masaryk retrospectively avowed that before the war he had wavered between loyalty and rebellion *(odboj)* against Austria-Hungary; from 1907, he said, he had been driven into opposition by his realization of the moral and physical degeneration of the dynasty and of Austria.[86] The dualism of his attitude was reflected in the fact that he was called an Austrophile by some of his Czech contemporaries and a traitor by some of his German opponents. In fact, as Roland Hoffmann has written, he was both; the development from one to the other was a gradual one, and in some degree logical.[87] It is generally agreed by later scholars that in the early part of his career Masaryk did not desire the breakup of Austria but in fact wished to preserve it by reforming it.[88] Indeed he had a positive attitude to Vienna, where he had studied and taught, and was not at first hostile to the Monarchy. But his was not an old-fashioned concept of Austria, right or wrong, but a more modern expression of loyalty based on the hope and, at this time no doubt the belief, that Austria could fulfil these requirements.

But, as we have seen above, Masaryk did move gradually from an avowed loyalty to the Monarchy toward alienation and embryonic disloyalty. During the early years of the twentieth century, although Masaryk still professed loyalty and hope for reform, his statements contained an undertone of increasing distrust and doubt as to the future of Austria and a questioning of its legitimacy, and these were nourished by his profound discontent with Austria's foreign policy. As others have noted, the break was not sudden and he did not abandon his earlier principles. What Masaryk had always sought was a just and a democratic state, and this seemed increasingly to be in contradiction with everything which Austria stood for.[89]

It is difficult to know at what point he came to the conclusion that outright political independence was the only solution of the Czech question and that violence was justified for this purpose. Some believed that he had lost faith in the monarchy by 1900, others by 1908 or 1909.[90] At his birthday party in 1910, he was reported to have said that Austria did not merit anything else than a charge of dynamite which would blow it to smithereens.[91]

Certainly Masaryk was not imbued with love or sympathy for Austria and, as we have seen, was critical of almost every aspect of its organization and its policy. Not once during his second term in Parliament, it has been noted, did he vote for the government budget. Masaryk recognized, too, the sources of Austria's strength; the dynasty (which he regarded as the main evil), the aristocracy, the Catholic Church, the army, and above all the dominant role of the Magyars and the Germans, as well as the strong German minority within Bohemia and Moravia. Faced with this overwhelming array of power, what could a small nation such as the Czechs do to achieve its national aims? Moreover there appeared to be no chance of a European conflagration which would cause the collapse of Austria and offer the Czechs an escape. Was there any alternative but to remain in Austria and, against all odds, to fight for reform?[92]

Masaryk was by no means alone in professing loyalty to the Monarchy. Other Czech politicians, with rare exceptions, held similar attitudes. Like Masaryk, most of them struggled for the reform of Austria, and in particular for its transformation into a federation, a demand which implicitly accepted the continued existence of Austria and Austria-Hungary. Some, notably Old Czechs such as Rieger, proclaimed their devotion in the most fervent terms. In his final speech, in 6 March 1900, in the House of Lords, Rieger declared that he spoke from 'an

Austrian and frankly dynastic standpoint' and that the future of the Czech nation lay assured only in the Empire.[93]

At the other end of the political spectrum, the more radical Social Democrats, in accordance with their international outlook, considered the Monarchy the most suitable framework for social reform and sought to transform it into a federation which would break up Bohemia and unite Czechs and Slovaks. In December 1913, their leader, Bohumír Šmeral, warned that, if, as a result of international conditions, the Czechs were to secure independence, it would be the worst of all possibilities and would mark the beginning of a new thirty years war. The more reformist wing, as represented by F. Modráček, was closer to Masaryk in opposing Austro-Hungarian centralism as incapable of understanding the interests of a small nation such as the Czechs.[94]

Young Czechs such as Kaizl and Kramář also pledged their allegiance to Austria as the necessary framework of Czech politics. Kaizl, for instance, in 1899, wrote: 'The only correct policy for us Czechs is a genuinely Austrian policy, based on the conviction that the safest refuge for us is in a powerful and just Austria'.[95] In 1906 he declared that 'the preservation of Austria, of course, an Austria inwardly different and better, was the most serious interest of the Czech nation'. Yet he added that this admittedly 'Austrian (*rakušánská*) policy', should be 'an honest policy of equal rights of all nations'. If Austria were to remain unfriendly to its individual nations, he warned, then 'its future was problematic in spite of the interest so many of us have in preserving it'. Not only Germans, but also the Slavs, would then 'have no interest in it and would necessarily be forced to seek a better future outside Austria'. In 1913 Kramář made the case that in a state such as Austria-Hungary, where the monarchy played such a large role, the Czechs, if they were not to threaten their whole policy, had to vote for things which the dynasty regard as necessary for the great-power position of the Empire.[96]

Yet in a speech on foreign policy given in February 1912 Kramář expressed scepticism that Austria was capable of conducting a domestic policy based on all its nations, not just two; this alone would make it possible to pursue a foreign policy of peace and of economic and political expansion. He warned of the danger of a catastrophic war which would decide the fate of the Czech nation and urged that they must become inwardly strong and ready for such a possibility.

In May 1914, in an introduction to a new edition of his book on Czech state right, Kramář admitted that he had no confidence that the Monarchy could correct the century-old sins against its own vital interests.[97] Convinced that war could not be averted, and that Austria would fall, Kramář embarked on anti-Austrian conspiratorial activities for this eventuality. In June 1914 he transmitted a secret plan directly to the Tsar's government in Moscow. This proposed, in the event of victory in war, the establishment of a Slavonic Empire, in which the Russian Tsar would be Czech and Polish king, and the Czech kingdom would include Slovakia in an extended form; the empire would also include Bulgaria, Serbia and Montenegro.[98]

On the nationalist extreme, some had given up hope of reform even earlier, and had come to believe in the necessity of complete independence outside Austria. Censorship made it difficult, if not impossible, to express such views publicly. But in 1912 the National Socialist programme openly called for an independent and sovereign Czech state (no reference was made to Austria-Hungary) and strongly opposed Austrian militarism. In January 1914, its leader, Václav Klofáč, engaged in discussions in Petrograd with the Russian Foreign Minister, Count Sazonov, and with the Chief of the General Staff; he later submitted a secret plan for Czech assistance to an invading Russian army, in the event of war. He proposed that, in the event of a Russian victory in war, an independent Czech state, including the Slovaks, should be established.[99]

Even more extreme was the State Right party. One of its most radical members, Lev Borský, in several articles in 1908 and 1909, which remained unpublished, argued that the Czechs *could* have their own independent state and would achieve that goal in the event of a European catastrophe. He urged the European powers to recognize the necessity of the fall of the Monarchy and the establishment of a Czech state. Viktor Dyk, in articles which were confiscated, also advocated independence. In its programme of 1912, the party refused to recognize the legality of the Austrian constitution or Parliament, and demanded complete Czech independence; the Czech question had become an international question. In May 1914 it openly declared that the nation must have its own state and that the Czech question must be placed before an international forum. They should not fear war, which, if it were to come, would not solve the Czech question less justly than it had hitherto been solved by peace. In July 1914, Borský held discussions with a Czech from Russia about the formation of a revolutionary movement in the Czechoslovak lands in the event of war.[100]

Masaryk did not adopt an intransigent stance of this kind and took no steps to engage in conspiratorial activity. Although his hopes for fundamental reform of Austria-Hungary had been sapped, he continued to strive for it up to the outbreak of war, and even in the first months of war he sounded out future possibilities. Only when he concluded that all chance of change had disappeared and that war would bring the collapse of the Empire, did he reach the fateful decision to go abroad to work for its destruction.[101]

Conclusions

In drawing conclusions from the foregoing studies of Masaryk one must be fully conscious of the immensity of the task and approach it with appropriate humility. For at least one hundred years this great personality in Czech history has been the subject of countless efforts at re-appraisal and of conflicting judgements, some entirely negative, others largely positive, if not eulogistic, and still others more balanced. In the period on which this study has focused, prior to 1914, he was a controversial figure among his contemporaries and often condemned as well as praised. After his triumphant return in 1918 and his election as President, he became the subject of a kind of personality cult but remained the target of continuing criticism by political and scholarly opponents. During the Nazi period he was expunged from history and only revived in some measure in the three years of freedom after 1945. Under the communists, his place in history was judged very differently in successive periods. For a year or two he was treated with respect for his prewar activities, and for his role in liberation; then during the fifties he was made the victim of a vicious and orchestrated campaign; during the sixties, and especially in 1968, he was at least partially restored to his earlier greatness. The negative campaign was resumed after 1968 and continued unabated down to the liberation of 1989 when he was once again treated in positive terms. But below the surface, independent writers had continued to study and critically reassess him.[1]

The approach to a conclusion is complicated not only by the diversity of these historical phases but also by the contrasting judgements of individual scholars and commentators. These were reflected in three major attempts to revive and reassess the significance of Masaryk – in the large *samizdat* collection of essays of 1980, in an exile symposium in 1981, and in the papers given at the conference on Masaryk in 1986 at the School of Slavonic and East European Studies in the University of London, later published in three volumes. The first two publications, already referred to in the Introduction, brought out the extraordinarily wide spectrum of opinions about Masaryk among persons who were, however, agreed on his greatness.[2] The London compilation reflected a similarly broad range of critical and positive assessments. Even the three editors, in their introductions, manifested strikingly different judgements. One of them, a severe critic, acknowledged that he was a great man, if only because he was considered such at home and abroad. A second, an admirer of Masaryk, citing Erazim Kohák, admitted that before the war he had only 'moments of greatness'. The third called him a hero, although still controversial.[3]

A further impediment to evaluation lies in the vastness of Masaryk's interests in the scholarly field and in politics. The critic is daunted by the need to evaluate his theoretical writings in fields as distinct as philosophy, religion and history, as well as his practical work in politics, and in specific areas such as the Slovak question, women's rights and anti-Semitism. The symposia had the advantage of gathering together specialists in many disciplines. A few authors, such as this one, have attempted the almost impossible task of reviewing Masaryk's prewar life and work in its entirety, in theory and in practice. The task is not rendered easier by the complexity and frequent paradoxes and ambiguities of Masaryk's thought and behaviour, as well, of course, as changes in their character at distinct periods and under varied conditions.[4] Moreover, Stanislav Polák has observed, the difficulty is enhanced by the inner contradictions of Masaryk's personality and character: for instance, the conflict between reason and feeling, faith and scepticism, realism and idealism.[5]

There are special problems in fulfilling my self-assigned task of trying to appraise the Masaryk of the period before 1914 and avoiding what Winters has called the hazards of preconceptions imposed by later times. Petr Pithart, for instance, argues that the legend of Masaryk's victory in the First World War tends to obscure the fact that before the war he had in fact been isolated from the majority of his fellow-countrymen, who simply did not understand him. When he went into exile in 1914, he was an ageing professor, who had not been successful in politics; he was isolated, almost without friends and with only a handful of followers. According to Pithart, Masaryk's greatness emerged only after victory in the war and the attainment of independence, which created the illusion that these triumphs were the products of his prewar activity.[6]

Yet on the sixtieth anniversary of his birthday, in 1910, his achievements were celebrated by many of his contemporaries, including foreign admirers, in not one but two major Festschrifts, in which the contributors paid tribute to him, often in panegyric terms, as a man of great stature, both as a scholar and as a practical politician. One contributor (Beneš) asserted that 'his influence fills our entire public life'; another (Hláváč) that 'his views dominate in all our political parties other than the state righters and radicals'; a third (Veselý) that 'the results of Masaryk's works are perceptible in our whole national life, for his thoughts penetrate into ever broader circles and become more and more the spiritual property of our people.'[7]

This book, it is hoped, has brought out the counterpoints and paradoxes of Masaryk's prewar career. He was a philosopher and scholar, but like Karl Marx, he was also a man of action who believed that the purpose of thought was to bring about a change in the real world. His standpoint, which he defined at successive times as Populist, Realist or Progressive, was a curious combination of these somewhat opposing concepts. Realism, he once wrote, was based on recognizing the facts, understanding 'the core of things', but this did not exclude 'development'.[8] But it was clear, he wrote a little later, that things were not justified and right simply because they exist or once existed; progress was in fact a protest against the logic of facts.[9] Moreover, although Masaryk constantly inveighed against opportunism, radicalism, and still more against revolution, his Realist approach was often radical in penetrating to the root of things and revolutionary in demanding fundamental transformations in thinking, behaviour and institutions.

From the outset Realism also stressed the need for criticism and debate, and Masaryk was ready to admit errors, but he was often dogmatic and polemical in defending the rightness of his views and setting forth his prescriptions for action. He strongly condemned in literature and in human affairs what he called 'titanism', i.e. an individual's claim to be equal to God and to arrogate to himself a kind of supernatural ability to govern; yet there were traces of this fault in Masaryk's own presumption that he possessed the truth and that he was acting in accord with the will of Providence, always tempered, however, by his recognition of the limits set by morality, religion and humanism.[10]

Each chapter of this book has illustrated the contrariety of this remarkable man. As a scholar his breadth of knowledge was extraordinary but his credentials, for instance, as a philosopher or historian, were sometimes questioned. Moreover everything which he wrote in the scholarly sphere, whether in philosophy or history, or even literary criticism, was designed to be instrumental in affecting Czech practical behaviour in politics and life in general.[11] Nonetheless he helped to liberate Czech society from its provincialism and narrow nationalism and opened up windows to new ideas and to European thought. As a teacher he was inspiring to his students, but he gained opponents as well as admirers among them and his colleagues. He looked on young people with great affection and concern, but he laid down strict and Puritanical recipes for their lives.

As a firm believer in democracy, Masaryk held strong convictions on the virtues of individual freedom, pluralism, autonomy and on the indispensability of human rights, both political and economic. He assigned a large role in politics to science but he did not fully resolve the contradictions between expertise and popular participation. Nor did he reconcile the conflicting imperatives of the moral and the pragmatic approaches to politics. He was a strong advocate of social reform through legislation, but at the same time he assigned high priority to the moral regeneration of the individual. A fervent believer in non-violence, he was not an integral pacifist and did not fully escape from the dilemma as to when violence or revolution, or even war, was justified.

As a political activist Masaryk recognized the need for a multi-party system but he was a severe critic of all other parties, and was unable to achieve lasting cooperation with any of them. On the political spectrum he stood somewhat to the left of centre, sympathetic to the social democrats and other progressive tendencies, but severely critical of liberalism and Marxism, and even more so, of clericalism and conservatism. His own party was moderate and progressive and repudiated radicalism and extreme nationalism. It was never able to achieve widespread support and remained somewhat on the fringe of the political scene.

Masaryk was, by virtue of his upbringing and cosmopolitan training, an outsider in the Czech community, but he established deep national roots and became a fervent defender of the nation's interests. He eschewed empty or radical nationalism and chauvinism and espoused internationalism and humanism. He believed that the Czech nation had a mission, derived from its religious past, but he was searching in his criticism of its weaknesses. As a result he was singled out as anti-national, even as a traitor to the nation, but stood his ground in his struggle to win over an unresponsive nation to his views.

Masaryk had great affection for the Slovaks and counted himself as one of them. He believed strongly that Czechs and Slovaks constituted a single nation, based on history and culture, but recognized the justification of a separate Slovak language. His pro-Slovak orientation was not shared by most Czechs but he won the devotion of many younger Slovaks and the hostility of the more conservative Slovak nationalists. Prior to 1914, although he advocated cooperation of Czechs and Slovaks, he did not actively challenge the Dualist system, or seek the establishment of a Czech–Slovak state.

Masaryk strongly opposed racialism and was ready to endure abuse in his struggle against anti-Semitism. Yet he was not entirely free of prejudice and, while praising Jewish virtues, was critical of their supposed weaknesses. He considered the Jews a separate nation and was opposed to their assimilation into the Czech nation. He admired Zionism for its belief in a distinct Jewish nation and the need for its reform, but he did not consider emigration to Palestine a desirable solution.

Although Masaryk was devoutly religious, he was not a churchgoer; his faith was a highly personal one and had a deep ethical content. He believed in God and in the divine workings of Providence in human affairs. Yet this did not prevent him from also believing in the responsibility of the individual to influence his fate and the course of history. He was hostile to institutionalized religion in any form, and strongly critical of the Catholic Church, but he remained in many ways Catholic in spirit. Although he admired the Bohemian Brethren and adhered nominally to a Protestant church, he was critical of Protestantism, too. He saw no contradiction between science and genuine religion and was a strong advocate of freedom of scholarship and education, which led him to battle against clerical attempts to control these spheres.

Masaryk condemned prejudices about the inequality of men and women and advocated their equality in all spheres of life, private, social and public, including politics. He regarded the so-called 'women's question' as but part of the national and social questions, and of the general question of humanity. He was a supporter of the feminist movement of his time, but his views, unorthodox as they then were, would now be considered archaic. He had an exalted view of the sanctity of marriage and the virtues of family life, but it is not certain how far his principles were applied in his own family. He was straitlaced in his views on sex, and opposed extra-marital sexual relations, divorce, remarriage, contraception and abortion, and prostitution, as well as smoking and drinking alcohol.

Masaryk believed that the Czech question was a world question and its solution required international understanding and support. He was unusually well-informed about world affairs but was at one and the same time utopian and realistic. He had no use for *Realpolitik* and naively believed that power politics could be replaced by friendship and cultural relations. He cogently criticized the dominant role of the Monarch and the aristocracy in the conduct of Austro-Hungarian diplomacy and the militarist spirit which pervaded it, and urged that diplomacy should be subject to democratic control and given a popular content. He was realistic in his critique of Austria's foreign policy, especially the alliance with Germany and its aggressive actions in the Balkans, and rightly believed that this threatened to bring about a European war. Never a friend of Pan-Slavism, he was not sanguine about the possibility of support from an autocratic Russia which moreover represented the antithesis to all Czech traditional values. Although he was influential in discrediting the Monarchy's diplomacy, his hope of effecting a basic change either in its conduct or its content proved to be illusory.

Masaryk strongly believed in the right and the capacity of a small nation, such as the Czechs, to be independent, and based his claim on the natural right of every nation to be free. He combined this, somewhat ambiguously, with the historic state right of the Bohemian kingdom as a whole, which presupposed, he acknowledged, an agreement with the Germans of Bohemia and Moravia. He therefore made detailed proposals for the solution of the Czech–German national conflict, but based them on the continued unity of the Bohemian lands. At the same time, he acknowledged that full political independence was not the be-all and end-all of national life and, under existing circumstances, could be attained only within the framework of the Monarchy. This required the fullest development of Czech national strength and self-confidence and pressure on the Austrian authorities for the implementation of national equality and a decentralization of authority. The optimal solution was the federalization of Austria, or of the Monarchy as a whole, but he did not advance any concrete proposals in this regard.

Masaryk was unable to achieve a harmonious synthesis of these conflicting tendencies of thinking and acting. The positions which he adopted were often ambiguous and reflected the complicated nature of the problems which he faced and his own honest uncertainty as to the solution. Yet he was not satisfied with a comfortable middle way or an opportunistic compromise. Although he was realistic in his diagnosis of existing ills, his prescriptions for cure were sometimes utopian. He was a radical and consistent nonconformist and was courageously prepared to endure the consequences. Hence he was isolated from the mainstream of Czech and Austrian politics, but brought this fate upon himself not only by his unorthodox ideas but also by his own personality and behaviour.

On the crucial question of the future of Austria-Hungary, Masaryk was not as loyal an Austrian as often depicted, nor was he its inveterate enemy, as alleged by defenders of the status quo. There can be no doubt of his deep hostility to the Monarchy in its existing form but he admitted that it was a reality and saw no alternative to it in the existing constellation of European power. He was realistic in comprehending the strong forces which held the Monarchy together, but he was over-optimistic in expecting fundamental change in the system. Although he still hoped against hope for reform of the Monarchy, and henceforth its preservation, he experienced a gradual estrangement and a decline of faith in this possibility.

Hence Masaryk was more realistic than more romantic Czech political leaders who pressed for early independence and envisaged support from Russia. Although he was well aware of the danger of war he was not ready to gamble on this contingency, and did not resort, as others did, to treasonable actions prior to its outbreak. A keen advocate of peace, he exerted every possible effort to achieve a compromise of conflicting views but failed to avert the ultimate tragedy. He embarked on his course of destroying Austria only when he had satisfied himself that the Empire was indeed unreformable and was not likely to survive a world conflagration. As things turned out, he was correct in foreseeing that the odds were against Austria, that Russia was not to be relied upon, and that the best hope lay in siding with the Western powers, which stood moreover for the democratic values in which he profoundly believed. His actions in 1914 seemed quixotic at the time, even to most of his fellow Czechs, but in the end it was shown that he had chosen the realistic course.

Although Masaryk later interpreted the victory of democracy over autocracy in the war and the creation of an independent Czechoslovakia as acts of Providence, these were in fact based rather on his correct estimate of the balance of forces and of his courageous act of will in striking out for independence. His years of nonconformity culminated in this supreme act of defiance. His strength of character, often tested before the war, successfully met the even harsher test of the lonely struggle for independence. After victory his belief in democratic values and procedures provided a basis for the creation of a democratic state on the ruins of the Empire.

Many have written that Masaryk left a rich legacy for present and future generations of Czechs and Slovaks. It has been claimed that the traditions of Masaryk have been a source of strength and inspiration in troubled times and remain so in the more favourable but difficult conditions of the present and immediate future. Some have argued that they have already had an impact, not only on the First Republic, but on the Prague Spring in 1968, on the dissident movement in the late seventies and eighties, and on the democratic revolution in 1989.[12] Although it can hardly be claimed that Masaryk's ideas played the decisive role in any of these happenings (except the first), they did affect the thinking of some of the participants, and were themselves brought into greater prominence by these events. To that extent they represented perhaps a subconscious thread of continuity beneath the surface of a discontinuity of political culture.

Certainly some of Masaryk's principles and values are ubiquitous and timeless in their validity – democracy, pluralism, freedom of expression and of inquiry, a nationalism free of chauvinism and international in perspective, the evil of racialism and anti-Semitism, religious tolerance, equality of men and women, the right of small nations to their own existence, detestation of war and his striving for a pacific settlement of disputes based on compromise and justice. Even his conception of Czech independence remains relevant in the conditions of the revival of a Czech state, shorn, however, of the unity with the Slovaks which he cherished and an association with Bohemian Germans which he had hoped for.[13]

Some of his admirers, who have also been his harshest critics, have seen the most lasting and valuable bequest in his moral character and the ethical nature of his ideas and actions, and above all in his doctrine of 'living in the truth'. Václav Černý stated the case most succinctly when he wrote of Masaryk as a moral figure whose 'extraordinary integrity' was 'immensely relevant to the nation and humanity in general'.[14] It was the seeking for truth which gave unique meaning to Masaryk's humanism and to European humanism in general, wrote Erazim Kohák.[15] He strove for 'a state which was just to all its citizens'.[16] In Patočka's view, democracy, for Masaryk, was not only a state form but a 'metaphysics which conceived of man as a moral being'.[17] The Pithart team referred to Masaryk's challenge to ethical rightness, a challenge to every individual to achieve moral self-preservation through small-scale work.[18]

It would be absurd to consider Masaryk a ready-made model for today, or to treat his ideas as trusty guides in the vastly different condition of the immediate future. He himself did not always live up to all of his principles, and some of them have been outdated by later events. Nonetheless Masaryk's towering personality, his belief in truth, his remarkable courage, and his moral approach to politics, seem highly relevant to a world, and to two nations, Slovak as well as Czech, in which political partisanship, party polemics, national egoism, ideological intolerance, and narrowness of vision seem often to dominate the scene.

Notes

INTRODUCTION: RE-ASSESSING MASARYK

1. For the above and the following, and for the sources of books and articles mentioned, see my article, 'The Rediscovery of Masaryk', *Cross Currents* (Ann Arbor, 1983), pp. 87–114. The symposia were as follows: *T. G. Masaryk a naše současnost (1980)* (Masaryk and the Contemporary World), *Masarykův sborník*, VII, edited by Milan Machovec, Petr Pithart and Josef Dubský *pseudo*. (Prague, 1980 *samizdat*), later published under the same title (Prague, 1992), eds Machovec, Pithart and Milan Pojar; Milič Čapek and Karel Hrubý (eds), *T. G. Masaryk in Perspective, Comments and Criticism* (SVU Press, n. p. 1981).
2. Jan Patočka, 'The Attempt at a Czech National Philosophy and Its Failure', *Dvě studie o Masarykovi* (*samizdat*, Prague, 1977); partly translated in *Masaryk in Perspective*, pp.12, 21 (this is my own translation).
3. See *T. G. Masaryk, Bibliografie k životu a dílu*. I,. co-sponsored by the Narodní knihovna and the Filozofické Ústav. ČASV (Prague, 1992).
4. See *T. G. Masaryk and Slovensko* (Prague, 1992); *Masaryk a myšlenka evropské jednoty* (Prague, 1992); *Masarykova idea československé státnosti ve světle kritiky dějin* (Prague, 1993); *Masaryk sborník*, VIII (1993), pp. 203–5.
5. *Ústav T. G. Masaryka* (Prague, September 1991); *T. G. Masaryk Institute* (Prague, February 1993); *Masarykův sborník*, VIII (1993), pp. 197–9, 200–1.
6. Ernest Denis, in a Masaryk *Festschrift* published in 1910, reprinted in Vasil K. Škrach (ed.), *Masarykův sborník*, IV, 1930, p. 12.

Epigraph quotations are taken from *Masarykův sborník*, IV, p. 12 (Denis); Patočka, *Dvě studie*, p. 41 (Rádl) (*Masaryk in Perspective*, p. 12); Patočka, ibid., p. 72, (*Masaryk in Perspective*, p. 21).

1 ACADEMIC ICONOCLAST

1. Jan Herben, *Deset let proti proudu (1886–1896)* (Prague, 1898), p. 3, republished in somewhat revised form in Herben, *Kniha vzpomínek* (Prague, 1935); Zdeněk Nejedlý, *T. G. Masaryk* (4 vols., Prague, 1935), III, pp. 3–7, 20.
2. On his appointment, see Jaroslav Opat, *Filozof a politik. Tomáš G. Masaryk, 1882–1893* (Prague, 1937); also Karel Čapek, *Hovory s T. G. Masarykem* (Prague, 1937), pp. 47–52.
3. On Masaryk's first years at the university, see Jaromír Doležal, *Masarykova cesta životem* (Brno, 1920), Part I, pp. 33–53; Simon R. Green, *Thomas Garrigue Masaryk: Educator of a Nation*, PhD thesis, University of California, 1976.
4. *Hovory*, pp. 93–4.
5. For an excellent analysis of the atmosphere at the university see Milan Machovec, *Tomáš G. Masaryk* (Prague, 1968), chap. 4; for a detailed description of the university and the professors, see Nejedlý, *Masaryk*, III, chaps. 1–6, and IV, chaps. 1 and 2. Eva Schmidt-Hartmann warns against exaggerating the role of Masaryk in the development of Czech scholarship, arguing that the scholarly level of the new

university was high, but acknowledges his contribution as the chief spokesman of an increasingly critical tendency among Czech scholars. See her chapter on the philosophical faculty after 1882 in Ferdinand Seibt (ed.), *Die Teilung der Prager Universität 1882 und die intellektuelle Desintegration in den böhmischen Ländern* (Munich, 1984), espec. pp. 96–7, 107–10.

6. Opat, *Masaryk*, p. 48.
7. *Albín Bráf, Život a dílo*, ed. by Josef Gruber and Cyril Horáček (Prague, 1922–24), I, pp. 15–27.
8. Nejedlý, *Masaryk*, III, pp. 40ff.
9. Opat, pp. 182, 206–9.
10. Machovec, *Masaryk*, pp. 98, 106.; Nejedlý, *Masaryk*, III, p. 159. For a critical review of Masaryk's scholarship and its inadequacies, see Kamil Krofta, *Masaryk a jeho dílo vědecké* (Prague, 1930). For a collection of critical reviews of many of Masaryk's writings, see Jan Patočka, *Masaryk, Soubor statí, přednášek a poznámek* (*samizdat*, Prague, 1979); *Tři studie, o Masarykovi* (Prague, 1991). On Masaryk's later scholarly work, see below, Skilling, chap. III.
11. Hoffmann, *T. G. Masaryk und die tschechische Frage* (Munich, 1988), pp. 75–8; Nejedlý, *Masaryk*, IV, pp. 101–11
12. Ibid., IV, p. 60 and chap. 3 and 4 for full discussion of the *Athenaeum* and its contents; for the other projects, ibid., pp. 116–29. For a detailed analysis of the encyclopedia project, see Stanley B. Winters, 'Jan Otto, T. G. Masaryk, and the Czech National Encyclopedia,' *Jahrbücher für Geschichte Osteuropas*, 31 (1893), pp. 516–42.
13. For full summaries of Masaryk's early work, see Nejedlý, IV, chaps. VII, VIII, IX and X; see also Opat, chap. II. For a detailed critical analysis of these works, including his articles in the *Athenaeum*, see Green, *Masaryk*, passim.
14. For example, a laudatory review of his work which termed him 'one of the greatest figures of our literary history' (Josef Mrávacký, *pseud.*, 'Masaryk a literatura', published in the *samizdat* work, Petr Pithart, Milan Machevec, and Josef Dubsky (eds.), *T.G.M. a součásnost (1980)*, *Masarykův sborník* VII, later published under the same title, ed. by Machovec, Pithart and Miloš Pojar (Prague, 1992), pp. 72–117. Other scholars who meted out sharp criticism of Masaryk's literary theory were Karel Brušák, in 'Masaryk and Belles-Lettres', in *T. G. Masaryk (1850–1937)*, Vol. 2, *Thinker and Critic*, ed. by Robert B. Pynsent (London, 1989), chap. 10, and Robert B. Pynsent, 'Masaryk and Decadence', ibid., I, *Thinker and Politician*, ed. by Stanley B. Winters (London, 1990), chap. 3. See also Peter Drews, 'Masaryk and Machar's Literary Criticism in '*Naše doba*' ibid., 2, chap. 1. For praise of Masaryk's work in linguistics, see Roman Jakobson, 'Problem of Language in Masaryk's Writings', in M. Čapek and K. Hrubý, (eds.), *Masaryk in Perspective* (n. p. 1981).
15. *Přednašky o praktické filosofie*, 1884; summarized in full by Nejedlý, III, XI, XII and XIII, also in Opat, *Masaryk*, pp. 84–113.
16. Nejedlý, III, pp. 196, 216–17, 240, 309, 313–14; Hoffmann, *Masaryk*, p. 79.
17. Hoffmann, p. 81; Opat pp. 170, 217. On the manuscript struggle see Hoffmann, pp. 79–93; Opat, chap. III; Josef Hanuš, 'Masaryk a boj o rukopisy', V. Škrach, (ed.), *Masarykův sborník*, V, pp. 227–37, espec. 231; Zika, 'Masaryk a literatura', pp. 79–86. On the role of Gebauer, see Theodore Syllaba, *Jan Gebauer* (Prague, 1986), pp. 64–76, 126–34.
18. *Athenaeum*, III, p. 168, cited by Opat, p. 163; the entire article is given in Herben, *Kniha vzpomínek*, pp. 226–32. The latter book gives a detailed description of the entire controversy in the eyes of a contemporary participant. On truth and the moral aspects of the controversy, see Machovec, *Masaryk*, espec. pp. 104–5, 113; on Gebauer, Hostinsky and Goll, Opat, pp. 214–15.

19. For a detailed report of this and later controversies, see Herben, *Proti proudu*, pp. 63ff., *Kniha vzpomínek*, pp. 247ff.; Opat, pp. 185–203; Green, *Masaryk*, pp. 388–9.

20. Hoffmann, *Masaryk*, p. 85; Hanuš, 'Masaryk a boj', pp. 234–5; Doležal, *Masarykova cesta*, pp. 47–54.

21. *Česká otázka*; *Naše nynější krise*, 6th edn. (Prague, 1948), pp. 158–60; Hoffmann, p. 83; Machovec, p. 104; Syllaba, *Gebauer*, p. 77.

22. Opat, *Masaryk*, p. 209; Milan Otáhal, 'Vyznám bojů o Rukopisy', *T. G. Masaryk and naše současnost*, pp. 40–71, citation at p. 69.

23. Important were his studies of *The Czech Question* (1895), cited above, *Jan Hus* (1896), *Havlíček and Palacký* (1898), and *The Social Question* (1899), all cited below. For a full discussion of the idea of humanity see Hoffmann, *Masaryk*, chap. 8; van den Beld, *Humanity*, chap. 2; on national identity, Hoffmann, op. cit., chap. 9; van den Beld, op. cit., chap. 3; Vasil Škrach, 'Masaryková myšlenka humanity', *Masarykův sborník*, V, pp. 161–76; Škrach, in *Masaryk myslitel* (Prague, 1938); on humanity, democracy and the Czech question, Otto Urban, 'Masarykovo pojetí české otázky', *Československý časopis historický*, 17 (1969), pp. 525–52; on the development of the Czech national programme, Roman Szporluk, *The Political Thought of Thomas G. Masaryk*, chap. IV; on humanity, pp. 88–91. For critical analysis of Masaryk's theory of Czech history, see two essays originally published in *samizdat*, in Václav Černý, *Dvě studie Masarykovské* (1977), and Jan Patočka, *Dvě studie o Masarykovi* (1977), the latter also in Patočka, *Masaryk*, which were later published in English: Patočka, *An Attempt at a Czech National Philosophy and Its Failure*', and Černý, '*The Essence of Masaryk's Personality and What TGM Means to Us Today*', in Čapek and Hrubý (eds.), *T. G. Masaryk*. For problems of translating the words *humanita* and *národnost*, see van den Beld, *Humanita*, p. 40, n.11, p. 48, n.1.

24. *Česká otázka/N.n.k.*, p. 226, also 208.

25. Masaryk, *Jan Hus, Naše obrození a naše reformace*, first published in 1896 (Prague, 1923), p. 9. See also Palacký's religious interpretation of Czech nationality and humanism as set forth by Masaryk, *Palackého idea národa českého* (first published in 1898 (3rd edn., Prague, 1926), chaps 2, 7, espec. pp. 177–8.

26. See below, Chapters 7, pp. 10–12, and 10, pp. 2–8.

27. *Ideály humanitní* (Prague, 1968), chap. I, IX on the ethics of humanity (*Ideals of Humanity* (London, 1938), pp. 18, 201–22, 91); Masaryk, *Karel Havlíček* (Prague, 1896), chap. IX, XIV, espec. p. 242. Noting that Marx and Engels did not entirely reject the idea of humanity, Masaryk criticized their lack of understanding of nationality, their failure to link humanity with religion and with love, and their acceptance of the necessity of revolution and violence. However, he praised socialism for its rejection of extreme nationalism and its international approach: Masaryk, *Otázka sociální* (Prague, 1948), I, p. 263, II, pp. 159–65, 217–18, 230, 297 (*Masaryk on Marx* (Lewisburg, 1972), I, p. 185, II, pp. 288–95, 313–14, 324, 342–3. For more on Marxism and the use of violence, see Chapter 2 below.

28. Hoffmann, *Masaryk*, chap. 9, espec. pp. 167, 183–6; Herben, *Masaryk*, I, pp. 422–70. See Masaryk, *Havlíček*, p. 237; Denis, 'Dopis', *Masarykův sborník*, IV, p. 11; Pekař, 'Masaryková česká filosofie', *Český časopis historický*, XVIII (1912), pp. 12, 34, 44.

29. Josef Kaizl, *České myšlenky* (2nd. edn., Prague, 1896), espec. chap 1; on the state, chap. 4. Antonín Hajn agreed with Kaizl on the role of Western enlightenment in the thinking of the awakeners. See his review, *Rozhledy*, V, no. 4 (1896), given in Hajn, *Výbor práci 1889–1909* (Prague 1912), pp. 429–39. For a full analysis of the controversy, see Karel Kučera, 'Masaryk and Pekař: Their Conflicts over the Meaning of Czech History and its Metamorphoses', in *T. G. Masaryk*, I (Winters), chap. 4. See also Milan Hauner, 'The Meaning of Czech History: Masaryk and

Pekař', ibid., Vol. 3. *Statesman and Cultural Force* (London, 1990), ed. by Harry Hanak, chap. 2. For a detailed account which favours Pekař, see Karel Brušak,' The Meaning of Czech History: Pekař versus Masaryk', in Laszlo Peter and Robert B. Pynsent, *Intellectuals and the Future in the Habsburg Monarchy 1890–1914* (London). For a severe criticism of Masaryk's viewpoint, see Eva Schmidt-Hartmann, 'The Fallacy of Realism', in *T. G. Masaryk* (Winters), chap. 6, espec. pp. 135ff. For a searching critique of her views as expressed in her book, *Thomas G. Masaryk's Realism, Origins of a Czech Political Concept* (Munich, 1984), see Jaroslav Opat, 'Nad jednou knihu o realismu T. G. Masaryka (*Obsah, samizdat*, February 1986); for her reply, ibid., September 1986. For criticism of the more political aspects of Masaryk's position by Kaizl and Hajn, see Chapter 3 below.

30. Beneš, 'Několik slov o Masarykové vlivu na mládež', *Česká mysl*, XI, nos. 2 and 3, pp. 211–50. Another essay, entitled 'Masarykův vliv na naši mladou generaci', slightly different in content, was published in another Festschrift in 1910, reprinted in *Masarykův sborník*, IV, pp. 243–50. On Masaryk's lectures, with special emphasis on their 'criticalness' (*kritičnost*) see also Nejedlý, *Masaryk*, III, pp. 140–51.

31. Emanuel Rádl, 'Masaryk universitní pedagog', *Masarykův sborník*, V, Part 1, p. 432.

32. Herben, *Proti proudu*, p. 24; *Festschrift, 1930, Masarykův sborník*, IV, pp. 131–2, 337–8, 384–5, also 402–3, 410–11.

33. F. Plamínková, ed., *Masaryk a ženy* (Prague, 1930), pp. 195–7, 242–4, 278–9, 286, 301, 303, 328.

34. For the above, Herben, *Proti proudu*, pp. 24, 33–5; Nejedlý, IV, pp. 151–9, 353; Zdeněk Franta, *Masarykův sborník*, IV, pp. 411–13.

35. Beneš, 'Několik slov', pp. 213–17; 'Masarykův vliv', pp. 243–9.

36. Nejedlý, III, 234–40; T. G. Masaryk and B. Odstrčil, *Přechod ze střední na školu vysokou* (Prague, 1913), pp. 13–15. Masaryk himself gave up drinking as a result of reading articles by Dr G. z Bunge, of the University of Basel. See his introduction to Bunge, *K otázcealkoholu*, a lecture given in 1886 (Prague, 1906) He is reported to have rejected his physician's advice to drink a glass of beer daily (Josef J. Filipi, *S Masarykovými, Hrst vzpomínek* (Prague, 1947) p. 102). For Masaryk's analysis of the causes and the dangers of alcoholism, see his speech at the Vienna congress in 1901, part of which is given in *Masaryk osvoboditel, Sborník*, (Prague, 1920), pp. 317–22; a speech in 1905, ibid., pp. 322–5; and his essays on alcoholism written in 1905 and 1912 which were published separately. For citations above, see Nejedly, III, pp. 221–4, 234–40; see also Chapter 8 below, p. 123.

37. 'O úkolech Českého studentstva', *Časopis českého studentstva*, 1 June 1889, republished in *Česká otázka*, pp. 401–23.

38. *Přechod*, pp. 15–17.

39. Masaryk, 'Hus českému studentstvu', lecture on 29 June 1899, given in Masaryk, *Jan Hus*.

40. First published as a book in Czech, *Jak pracovat* (Prague, 1926). The above is based mainly on the English translation published in *The Ideals of Humanity and How To Work* (London, 1938), pp. 150–64, 177–8, but also uses material from his 1912 lecture, *Přechod*. Masaryk was reported by a close friend to have known Polish, Russian, Serbian, German, French and English well enough to read literature written in those languages. (Filipi, *S Masarykovými*, p. 46).

41. *Česká otázka / N.n.k.*, pp. 401–13.

42. Ibid., pp. 413–23, also pp. 181–5.

43. *Ramcový program český strany lidové (realistické)* (Prague, 1900), pp. 89–90.

44. *Student a politika*, 2nd edn (Prague, 1923).

45. *Demokratism v politice*, 2nd edn (Prague, 1912), (first published in *Studentská revue*, VI, 1912), p. 105. Text given in Masaryk, *Ideály Humanitní*. See also Chapter 4 below.
46. *Demokratism*, ibid., pp. 110, 109, 113.
47. Herben, *Kniha vzpomínek*, pp. 352–3; Nejedlý, *Masaryk, III*, pp. 128–33;
48. For the above, and the following, see R. Wolf, *České studentstvo v době prvního třícetiletí české university (1882–1912)*, (Prague, 1912); Karen J. Freeze, *The Young Progressives: The Czech Student Movement, 1887–1897* (PhD thesis, Columbia University, 1974); Bruce M. Garver, *The Young Czech Party, 1874–1901 and the Emergence of a Multi-Party System* (New Haven, 1978), pp. 143–6, 168–89, 447, n. 56; Zdeněk Tobolka, *Politické dějiny Československého národa od r. 1848 až do dnešní doby* (Prague, 1936), III, 2, pp. 47–59; Antonín Hajn, *Výbor prací*, Pt. I, III; Alois Hajn, *Zivot novinářův, 1894–1930 (Prague, 1930)*, I,.pp. 42–70. Of some use is the poorly organized book by Václav Gutwirth, *Masaryk a studentstvo* (Prague, 1924). The most detailed studies are those by Jan Havránek, 'Počátky a kořeny pokrokového hnutí studentského na počátku devadesátých let 19. století,' *Acta Universitatis Carolinae Pragensis, Historia Universitatis, Carolinae Pragensis*, 2, no. 1 (1961), pp. 5–33'; Die Studenten an der Schwelle des Modernen Tchechischen Politischen Lebens', *Acta Universitatis Carolinae, Philosophica et Historica*, no. 4 (1969), pp. 29–52.
49. Freeze, *The Young Progressives*, pp. 112–29.
50. For the trial, ibid., chap. 6. For the student demonstrations, see Havránek, 'Protirakouské hnutí dělnické mládeže a studentů a události roku 1893,' *Acta Universitatis Carolinae – Historia Universitatis*, 2, no. 2 (1961), 21–85.
51. *Česká otázka/N.n.k.*, pp. 309, 344, 363,
52. Freeze, *The Young Progressives*, pp. 290–6.
53. See *Česká otázka; Naše nynejší krise*, cited earlier, pp. 320–1, 327–40, 341, 352, 365.
54. See Antonín Hajn, *Výbor prací*, Part I, pp. 391–421.
55. *Česká otázka/N.n.k.*, pp. 181–5, 288–97.
56. Wolf, *České studentstva*, p. 111, and the whole of Part II. A detailed study of the conflicting tendencies among the students, and a critical analysis of Masaryk's relations with each, is given by František Červenka, *Boje a směry českého studentstva na sklonku minulého a na počátku našeho století* (Prague, 1962). See especially chap. 1 and passim, as indicated by the index.
57. See random quotations in Gutwirth, *Masaryk a studentstvo*, pp. 8, 13, 55–7.
58. See Chapter 6 below, pp. 85.
59. Gutwirth, pp. 49–50, 68–70.
60. Gutwirth, pp. 66–8; Wolf, p. 14.
61. *Stenographisches Protokoll, Haus der Abgeordneten*, XI session, 30 October 1891, pp. 2826–37; 'Hospodářský a sociální význam vzdělání,' article published in 1900, *Masarykův sborník* I, 361–7; 'O škole a vědě,' lecture in January 1908, ibid. I, pp. 379–81. For earlier parliamentary speeches on education, 6 and 30 June, 1891, see Jiří Kovtun, *Slovo má poslanec Masaryk* (Munich, 1985), pp. 33–6, 42–7.
62. *Český učitel* (1899–1900), full text not available, extensive citations given in J. B. Kozák ed., *Masaryková práce* (Prague, 1930), in chapter entitled 'Masaryk pedagog', pp. 251–86.
63. On workers' education, *Masarykův sborník*, I, pp. 352–60,; on training of teachers, ibid, I, pp. 368–81; on women's education, *Abgeordnetenhaus*, 30 October, 1891. See also Masaryk, *How to Work*, pp. 137–44, 165–78.
64. See 'Program kulturní a školský', in *Ramcový program*, pp. 42–69 and *Program české strany pokrokové* (Prague, 1912), pp. 72–135.

184   *Notes*

65. A detailed exposé of reforms of legal education was given in Masaryk's parliamentary speech, *Haus der Abgeordneten*, IX, 25 January 1892, pp. 14 714–24. See also Anna M. Drábek, 'Masaryk in the Austrian Parliament on a Reform Bill of Legal Studies', in *T. G. Masaryk*, 2 (Pynsent), pp. 10–18.
66. *Haus der Abgeordneten*, XVIII, 9 December 1908, pp. 7842–3.
67. For this, see *Reč profesora T. G. Masaryka*, 7 March 1910 (Prague, 1935). Cf. his postwar comment that he had not wanted to become a professor (*Světová revoluce*, Prague, 1925, pp. 390–1.
68. Green, 'Masaryk', p. 111.
69. Hoffmann, *Masaryk*, p. 86.
70. E. Rádl, *T. G. Masaryk*, lecture given 13 December 1918 (Prague, 1919), p. 11.
71. *Haus der Abgeordneten*, 30 October 1891, p. 2837.

2   CHAMPION OF DEMOCRACY

1. See especially Masaryk, 'Politika vědou a uměním', introduction, Z. V. Tobolka, (ed.), *Česká politika* (5 vols, Prague, 1906–13), I, pp. 1–31; Masaryk, *Potřeba pokrokové politiky* (Melník, 1908), also in *Masarykův sborník*, ed. V. K. Škrach, I (5 vols, Prague, 1925–30), pp. 183–95; Masaryk, *Student a politika* (Prague, 1909); Masaryk, *Demokratism v politice* (2nd. edn., Prague, 1912); also published in *Ideální humanitní* (1901) (Prague, 1968); Masaryk, *Nesnáze demokracie* (Prague, 1913), the two latter given in French translation in Masaryk, *Les Problèmes de la démocratie* (Paris, 1924), chaps II, III. Masaryk, in his *Karel Havlíček: Snahy a tužby politického probuzení* (Prague, 1896), presented mainly Havlíček's views and his own largely by implication. For detailed analysis of Masaryk's political ideas, see Roman Szporluk, *The Political Thought of Thomas G. Masaryk* (New York, 1981); Antonie van den Beld, *Humanity – The Political and Social Philosophy of Thomas G. Masaryk* (The Hague, 1975), chaps 4, 5, 6; Roland J. Hoffmann, *T. G. Masaryk und die tschechische Frage* (Munich, 1988), Part I, chaps 14, 15, Part II, chap. l; Josef Král, *Masaryk, filosof humanità a demokracie* (Prague, 1947); Milan Machovec, *Tomáš G. Masaryk* (Prague, 1968); Miloslav Trapl, *Vědecké základy Masarykovy politiky* (Brno, 1946); Trapl, *Masarykův program, Demokracie-socialismus–česká otázka* (Brno, 1948); Kamil Krofta, *Masaryková politická demokracie* (Prague, 1935); Eva Schmidt-Hartmann, *Thomas G. Masaryk's Realism; Origins of a Czech Political Concept* (Munich, 1984); Otto Urban, 'Masarykovo pojetí české otázky', *Československý časopis historický*, 17 (1969), pp. 525–52; *Masaryk a myslitel* (Prague, 1938).
2. See Chapters 3 and 4 below.
3. Masaryk, *Česká otázka/Naše nynější krise* (Prague, 1948), pp. 111–18, 274; Masaryk, *Havlíček*, pp. 86–8; Hoffmann, *Masaryk*, pp. 274–7; Schmidt-Hartmann, *Masaryk's Realism*, p. 127.
4. Masaryk sometimes used the word *lid* as equivalent to the nation, sometimes as referring to the working people. See Trapl, *Masarykovy politiky*, p. 100.
5. *Otázka sociální* (Prague, 1948) I, XI; II, p. 349. Cf. the abridged edition in English, Erazim Kohák (ed.), *Masaryk on Marx* (Lewisburg: Bucknell University Press, 1972).
6. Kovtun, *Slovo ma poslancé Masaryk* (Munich, 1985), p. 114.
7. *Potřeba*, pp. 5–9.
8. *Program české strany pokrokové* (Prague, 1912), pp. 11–12.

9. *Demokratism v politice*, passim.This is well analyzed by the Slovak historian Dušan Kováč in his 'Masaryková koncepce demokracie a realita prvej republiky', in *Slovensko v politickom systéme Československa* (Bratislava, 1992), pp. 21–3.

10. This is also the view of Hoffmann, *Masaryk*, pp. 278–80, 313–14 and Trapl, *Masarykův program*, pp. 53–5. Eva Schmidt-Hartmann, in 'T. G. Masaryk und die Volksdemokratie', *Bohemia*, 23, no. 2 (1983), pp. 370–87, advances the rather far-fetched argument that Masaryk's concept of *lidovost* tended away from liberal democracy toward the idea of people's democracy (*Volksdemokratie*) employed in Czechoslovakia after 1945. See below, in the conclusion of this chapter.

11. See n. 1, above, and in particular van den Beld, *Humanity*, chap. 5, espec. pp. 104ff.; *Potřeba*, pp. 5 ff.; *Nesnáze*, pp.9,15; *Student a politika*, pp. 11–2; *Demokratism*, pp. 3–4. See also Chapter 1 above, pp. 11–12.

12. Ibid., pp. 4–7; *Nesnáze*, pp. 4–5.

13. *Potřeba*, pp. 10–11.

14. *Nesnáze*, pp. 9, 13; Vývoj evropské společnosti v devatenáctém století', *Masarykův sborník*, II (1927), p. 127. *Rusko a evropa* (cited fully below, n. 19), II, pp. 640–1, 643, Eng. pp. 52, 515.

15. *Potřeba*, p. 11; *Jak pracovat?* (Prague, 1926; 2nd edn, 1946), p. 18 of the latter.

16. Ibid., in English How to Work, published with *The Ideals of Humanity* (London, 1938), pp. 178–83. See also below in this chapter, p. 23.

17. *Ideální humanitní*, pp. 23–3.

18. Masaryk, *Rusko a evropa* (cited fully below, n.19) II, pp. 510–11, 520, 530–1, and passim. In 1906 he had expressed somewhat similar views and concluded that, in politics, individualism meant the recognition of individual and subjective rights ('Politika vědou a uměmí', pp. 11–12). Miroslav Trapl, in a chapter on the 'The Idea of Freedom and Liberalism', significantly placed within part II, devoted to demo-cracy, gives a useful analysis of Masaryk and individualism (Trapl, *Masarykův program*, pp. 101–7).

19. Masaryk, *Rusko a evropa* (Prague, 1921), 2 vols; English trans. by Eden and Cedar Paul, *The Spirit of Russia* (London, 1961). A third volume was published in English, ed. G. Gibian, *The Spirit of Russia* (London, 1967). See also Hoffmann, *Masaryk*, p. 273; Szporluk, *Masaryk*, p. 66; van den Beld, *Humanity*, pp. 116–22.

20. *Student a politika*, pp. 11–12, 15–16; *Demokratism*, p. 9; *Nesnáze*, pp. 6–12.

21. Masaryk, II, *Rusko*, chap. XXIV, pp. 633–58 (*The Spirit of Russia*, chap. 24); also Hoffmann, *Masaryk*, pp. 280–6; Szporluk, *Masaryk*, pp. 66–70. See Chapter 7 below.

22. During the First World War Masaryk interpreted the war as a conflict between theocracy (including Germany) and democracy (including France but excepting Russia). See T. G. Masaryk, *The Making of a State* (London, 1927), pp. 305, 323, 325.

23. *How to Work*, pp. 108–9, 128–31. See also *Otázka sociální*, II, 304–5; *Potřeba* (1908), pp. 8–9.

24. *Demokratism*, p. 9, also available in *Ideály humanitní* (in English, *The Ideals of Humanity*); *Rusko a evropa*, II, pp. 635–6. In his study of Marxism, Masaryk paid tribute to Marx for discovering the world of small-scale work, work by the sweat of the brow, but faulted him for minimizing the value of spiritual work (*Otázka sociální*, pp. 358–64, 406–7).

25. Later, in his book on the First World War, Masaryk wrote: 'The state, even the democratic state, is not the godlike omniscient and omnipotent institution which Hegel thought it to be; it is a human institution, very human with all the weaknesses but also the perfections of those people who organized and who lead it' (Masaryk, *Světová revoluce, Za války a ve válce* (Prague, 1925), pp. 567–8).

26. For this and the following, see *Česká otázka/N.n.k.*, pp. 263–6, 377. For earlier treatment of state and society in his university lectures, see Zdeněk Nejedlý, *T. G. Masaryk* (Prague, 1930), III, chap.13. See Trapl, *Masarykovy politiky* (Pt II) for an extensive discussion of Masaryk's view of the state; this suffers, however, from his tendency to merge together his prewar and postwar views.

27. *Pol. vedou a uměním*, pp. 3–4.

28. Thus the power of local government was a little wider than under the highly centralized French system but much more limited than the British system where local government was entirely in the hands of elected local bodies. For contemporary discussion of the issues, see Tobolka, *Česká politika, 2*, no. 2, espec. contributions by Dobroslav Krejčí and Albín Bráf, pp. 1–4, 255–345, resp.

29. *Ramcový program české strany lidové (realistické)* (Prague, 1900), pp. 9–10, 122).

30. *Program pokrokové*, pp. 136–43.

31. Theorie a praxis', *Moravská orlice*, Brno, V(XIV), 23, 27 April, 5, 7, 12, 16, 19 May, 4, 13 June, 1876, reproduced in Jaromír Doležal, *Masarykova cesta životem*, 2 vols. (Brno, 1920–21) II, pp. 181–97.

32. *Politika vedou a umění*, pp. 9–10,12–14,17–19; Masaryk, *Havlíček*, chaps X, XI. See also van den Beld, *Humanity*, pp. 116f.

33. *Vývoj*, pp. 116–18, 121–2.

34. *Otázka sociální*, pp. 340–2.

35. *Nesnáze*, pp. 9–11. *Democratism*, pp. 9–12.

36. *Rusko a evropa*, II, pp. 637–42, 643–6 *(The Spirit of Russia*, pp. 510–17). For a fuller study of Masaryk's views on the conflict of Church science and Church religion, and socialism and religion, see Chapter 7 below.

37. Masaryk, *Politika vědou a uměním*, pp. 3, 8.

38. Masaryk, *Havlíček*, chap. XII, espec. pp. 281–3.

39. *Student a politika*, pp. 12–13.

40. Ibid., p. 9; Masaryk, *Americké přednašky* (Prague, 1929), pp. 95–6.

41. D. B. Shillinglaw, The *Lectures of Professor T. G. Masaryk at the University of Chicago, 1902* (Lewiston 1978), pp. 121–3.

42. *Nesnáze*, pp. 3, 6, 12–13. In *Otázka sociální* (introduction, p. XII), Masaryk wrote of the dangers of parliamentarism becoming 'a bureaucracy of deputies', as demonstrated especially by Russia. See also ibid., II, pp. 339, 345ff.

43. Masaryk, *Havlíček*, pp. 286–96.

44. Ibid., pp. 296ff.

45. Masaryk, 'Aforismy o politických stranách', *Čas*, III, 9 and 10 (1889), reprinted in *Masaryková práce*, ed. J. B. Kozák, pp. 74–9. Cf. a similar positive attitude in a series of lectures given in 1908, published as '*Politické strany a nové formace'*. *Čas*, no. 83–4, 24–5 March 1908. See also *Nesnáze*, p. 6; *Otázka sociální*, II, p. 343. A good discussion of political parties is given by Trapl, *Masarykův program*, pp. 85–91; *Masarykovy politiky*, pp. 139–43.

46. Masaryk, *Otázka sociální, Základy marxismu filosofické a sociologické* (Prague, 1898; in German translation, *Die philosophischen und sociologischen Grundlagen des Marxismus. Studien zur socialen Frage* (Vienna, 1899). The book was published in German in 1899 and in Russian in 1906, and in an abridged edition in English, in Kohák, *Masaryk on Marx*, cited above, n. 5. References are to 7th edn (Prague, 1948) (reference above, I, pp. 3–4) and to the English edition.

47. Text in Z. V. Tobolka, *JUDr; Jos. Kaizl z mého života* (Prague, 1908–14), II, pp. 607–13.

48. 26 June 1891, given in Kovtun, *Slovo má Masaryk*, pp. 37–41. In other speeches, especially that of 25 January 1892, Masaryk urged that law, legislation and legal studies must become more social in character. See Anna M. Drabek, 'Masaryk in

the Austrian Parliament on a Reform Bill of Legal Studies, in *T. G. Masaryk (1850–1937)*, 2, *Thinker and Critic* (London, 1989), ed. Robert B. Pynsent, chap. 1.

49. *Česká otázka*, pp. 163, 218–24.

50. For this and the following, see Jaroslav Opát, *Filozof a politik,T. G. Masaryk, 1882–1893* (Prague, 1987), pp. 316–28, 399–404; van den Beld, *Humanity*, chap. 4, espec. pp. 69–79; Hoffman, *Masaryk*, pp. 143–52; František Soukup, *T. G. Masaryk jako politický průkopník, sociální reformátor a President statu* (Prague, 1930), pp. 36–45, 127–49. See also Jacques Rupnik, 'Masaryk and Czech Socialism', *T. G. Masaryk*, 2 (Pynsent), chap. 9. For retrospective evaluation of Masaryk's views on socialism, and on Masaryk as a socialist, see F. Modráček, 'Masaryk und der Sozialismus', and J. Vozka, 'Masaryk, die Arbeiterschaft und der Sozialismus', both in *Festschrift: Th. G. Masaryk zum 80. Geburtstage* (Bonn, 1930), II, pp. 291–8; 299–312, and more briefly in J. Vozka, 'Masaryková cesta k socialismu', *Masarykův sborník*, IV, pp. 81–5; Karel Dědic, F Modráček and A. Sašek, ibid., V (1930–31), Pt 2, pp. 304–12. See also Evzen Stern, *Le socialisme de Masaryk* (Brussels, 1926).

51. Masaryk, *How to Work*, pp. 165–77; Masaryk, *Osm hodin práce* (Prague, 1901 and 1905);.van den Beld, *Humanity*, p. 77.

52. Masaryk, *O klerikalismu a socialismu* (Valašské meziříčí, 1907), pp. 17–23. See also Chapter 4 below, p. 55.

53. *O klerikalismu*; Charlotte Masaryk shared his view on socialism but in 1905 went so far as to join the Social Democratic Party. See also Chapter 7 below, pp. 109–10.

54. *Ramcový program*, pp. 29–41.

55. *Program pokrokové*, pp. 44–71.

56. *Otázka sociální*, preface to second Czech edition, 1906, I, p. XIII, also pp. 6–7; II, p. 357.

57. Milan Machovec, Petr Pithart and Miloš Pojar, (eds.), *T. G. Masaryk a současnost, Masarykův sborník*, VII (Prague, 1992) (originally in *samizdat* under the same title, Prague, 1980), pp. 347–78, espec. 350–1, 357. Machovec noted that Masaryk's criticisms were often well-grounded and his fears concerning Marxist beliefs were confirmed by the experience of postwar communism (p. 358). According to Machovec, this chapter had to be omitted from his biography of Masaryk published in 1968 (Machovec, *Masaryk*).

58. See, for instance, van den Beld, *Humanity*, chap. IV; Miroslav Novák, 'Some Thoughts on Masaryk's Critique of Marxism', Milič Čapek and Karel Hrubý (eds.), *T. G. Masaryk in Perspective* (n.p., 1981), pp. 240–55; Jan Milič Lochman, 'Masaryk's Quarrel with Marxism', in *Masaryk*, 2 (Pynsent), pp. 120–33; also in German, Josef Novák, (ed.), *On Masaryk* (Amsterdam, 1988), pp. 229–45. Miloslav Trapl, in his *Masarykův program*, while recognizing the wide gap between Marxism and Masaryk's 'humanist socialism', argues that Masaryk's sharp criticism of Marxism tends to obscure a considerable agreement between Marx and Masaryk on issues such as social justice and the role of revolution in history (pp. 127, 138–40).

59. Kohák, *Masaryk on Marx*, pp. 317, 324 ff.

60. *Rusko a evropa*, II, p. 644 (*The Spirit of Russia*, pp. 515–16). In this book, Masaryk restated his analysis of the crisis of Western European Marxism and the similar crisis of Russian Marxism. The book includes a detailed presentation of the development of Marxism in Russia, both in its orthodox and revisionist forms (chap. XIX) and of other movements based on Marxism, such as anarchism (chaps. XIV, XV, XX). For a searching analysis of the similarities and differences between socialism and anarchism, see especially, *R.e.*, II, pp. 39–50, 516–27; *Otázka sociální*, II, pp. 319–24. See also Masaryk, *Ideály humanitní*, chap. 3, where he described anarchism as extreme individualism and linked it with nihilism and terror. As for the Czechs,

anarchism was 'un-Czech' (*nečeský*) (p. 32). As early as *The Czech Question*, Masaryk made it quite clear that he was against anarchist theories as well as 'anarchism of the deed' (*Č. o./N.n.k.* pp. 271, 339, 364–6).

61. Masaryk's own treatment was given in *The Czech Question, Karel Havlíček, The Social Question* and *Russia and Europe*, to be cited below. See van den Beld, *Humanity*, chap. 6; Král, *Masaryk filosof*, pp. 102–26; Hoffmann, *T. G. Masaryk*, pp. 152–7, 287–94; Trapl, *Masarykův program*, pp. 39, 42–9, 92–100, 124–31; Antonín Obrdlík, 'Masaryk a problém revoluce', *Masarykův sborník*, VI, no. 2, pp. 70–9; Jaroslav Werstadt, *Od 'český otázky' k 'nové Evropě', Linie politického vývoje Masaryka* (Prague, 1920), pp. 14–19, 31–46. See also Chapter 3 below.

62. Citations given by Zdeněk Franta (ed.), *Mrávní názory* (2nd. edn., Prague, 1925), pp. 43–61, cited by van den Beld, *Humanity*, p. 130, n.14.

63. *Česka otázka/N.n.k.*, pp. 130, 145.

64. Ibid., pp. 273–4, 309, 327–52. In a correction to the 1908 edition, Masaryk stated that 'a "reform revolution" was justified; without revolution all that good progress would not have happened. I was writing against playing with evolution'(p. 274). He also omitted the polemic with Hajn from that edition. See also Chapter 1 above, pp. 13–14.

65. According to Havlíček, the revolutions in France and those in Bohemia in 1620 and 1848 demonstrated the ineffectiveness of violence, and the revolutions in England and North America the value of the peaceful approach. At the same time Havlíček accepted the need for a defensive struggle, but only in the most extreme case of self-defence. Such a defensive revolution, however, must seek real freedom and must be conducted with reason and morality. Revolution would not bring benefit to the Czechs in view of the smallness of the nation and the likelihood of outside intervention (Masaryk, *Havlíček*, chap.V, and chap.VII, pp. 185–200).

66. *Otázka sociální*, I, pp. 329–31, II, pp. 269–72, 299–307 (in English, Kohák, *Masaryk on Marx*, pp. 337–53).

67. Ibid., I, 58; II, pp. 272–9 (Kohák, *op. cit.*, pp. 51, 344–51, 353). See also van den Beld, *Humanity*, p. 134, n. 33.

68. *Rusko a evropa*, II, chaps XIX, XXVI, the latter entitled 'Democracy and Revolution'. See also Chapter 1 above.

69. Ibid., II, pp. 658ff, 444ff. (English, pp. 528ff., 338–44).

70. Ibid., II, pp. 665–71 (English, pp. 535–41).

71. In 1912 Masaryk declared even more emphatically that the right to revolution was indisputable, but the revolution needed to be not only physical but also moral. Although many said that evolution was replacing revolution and that progress by small steps was possible, political revolutions were not excluded. No one could guarantee that there would not be revolution, and a great revolution at that (*Demokratism v politice*, pp. 14–15). See Chapter 1 above, p. 12.

72. Gibian, *The Spirit of Russia*, chap. 13. pp. 177–9, 183–9. On Tolstoi, see also *Rusko a evropa*, II, p. 667 (English, p. 585).

73. In an earlier work, Masaryk had evaluated the French Revolution positively for overthrowing an absolutism which showed itself incapable of reform. He noted, however, that France had gone through a dozen or so revolutions, including some that were reactionary. (*Nová doba* (Pilsen), 16 January 1907, XII, no. 4, p. 1; ibid., 23 January 1907. XII, no. 6, p. 1.). Cf. Masaryk's ambivalence on the French Revolution as embodying the ideas of liberty, equality and fraternity, but as not being democratic. See above, in this chapter, p. 23.

74. Gibian, *The Spirit of Russia*, III, p. 185. According to Trapl (*Masarykův program*, p. 94) Masaryk treated war in the same way as revolution, condemning it as an evil, but justifying it in self-defence. However, apart from this one reference in the

unpublished volume written in 1912, he seems to have done this only after the war and not, as Masaryk himself later claimed, prior to the war (Masaryk, *Svetová revoluce*, p. 75). Note also his condemnation of Dostojevsky for defending war (*Rusko a evropa*, I, pp. 133–4). See Chapter 9 below for Masaryk's condemnation of militarism and of Austria's warlike Balkan policy. Although he hated war, he said, he saw the moral justification of the effort of the Slavic peoples to free themselves from Turkey by war (pp. 143, 145).

75. *Hovory s T. G. Masarykem* (Prague, 1969), p. 102.
76. *Havlíček*, chap. XVIII, espec. pp. 429, 438, 447. Havlíček derived this idea from the Polish philosopher, Trentowski, who, in similar circumstances of political repression, urged the establishment of a 'moral government', in which intellectuals would exercise leadership.
77. *Otázka sociální*, II, pp. 345–9. Masaryk himself once said that he was a parliamentary deputy out of a conviction that politics was important, but it was not everything, as he showed by retiring in 1893. To be a deputy should not be the ideal of a young man. (Masaryk, *O pokrokovém postavení slovenské mládeže*, speech in Hodonín, 15 August 1911 (Uherské hradiště, 1935), pp. 7–8.
78. Szporluk, *Masaryk*, chaps 2, 3, espec. pp. 45–7, 65–6, 71–2, 75–7.
79. Schmidt-Hartmann, 'Masaryk und die Volksdemokratie', pp. 371–7 (n.10, above).
80. *Masaryk's Realism*, pp. 13–85. See Chapter 3 below.
81. *Česká otázka/N.n.k.*, pp. 272–3, 362, 394, 408.
82. *Nesnáze*, pp. 14–15.

POLITICAL DISSENTER

1. For historical reviews of Masaryk's political programme, see Kamil Krofta, 'Masaryk und unser Politisches Programm', *T. G. Masaryk, Staatsmann und Denker* (Prague, 1930), pp. 25–50; Zdeněk Šolle, 'O smyslu novodobého českého politického programu', *Československý časopis historicky*, XVIII, no. 1 (1970), pp. 1–22.
2. H. Gordon Skilling, 'The Politics of the Czech Eighties', in Peter Brock and H. Gordon Skilling (eds.), *The Czech Renascence of the Nineteenth Century* (Toronto, 1970), pp. 275–8.
3. Otakar Odložilík, 'Enter Masaryk: A Prelude to his Political Career', *Journal of Central European Affairs*, 10, no. 1 (April 1950), pp. 32–6; Odložilík, 'T. G. Masaryk and the Czech "Nineties"', *The Spirit of Czechoslovakia*, VI, no. 1 (London, 1945), pp. 10–12, 21; Odložilík, 'Na předělu dob', *Zítřek*, 1943, no. 2 pp. 30–68, citation at p. 46. For Czech politics in general, see Bruce M. Garver, *The Young Czech Party 1874–1901 and the Emergence of a Multi-Party System* (New Haven, 1978); Otto Urban, *Česká společnost 1848–1918* (Prague, 1982); Urban, *České a slovenské dějiny do roku 1918* (Prague, 1991), pp. 196–222; Zdeněk Tobolka, *Politické dějiny. československého národa od r. 1848 až do dnešní doby* (Prague, 1894), III.
4. Zdeněk Nejedlý, *T. G. Masaryk* (Prague, 1931–35), I, p. 165; II pp. 177–89; Masaryk, 'Můj poměr k Jul. Grégrovi', in Jan Herben, 'Dvácet pět let *Času*', *Čas*, no. 347, 16 December 1911, supplement, Part III, pp. 3–6; Masaryk, 'Theorie a praxis', *Moravská Orlice*, V (XIV), 93, 23 April 1876, republished in J. Doležal, *Masarykova cesta životem*, 2 vols (Brno, 1920–21) II, pp. 181–97.
5. For a full study of Realism see Václav Vaníček, 'V počátcích realismu', in five parts, in V. Škrach (ed.), *Masarykův sborník* (1926–30), II and III, espec. part IV pp. 210–22; V, pp. 303–29. See also Jurij Křížek, *T. G. Masaryk a česká politika*

(Prague, 1959); Jan Herben, *Kniha vzpomínek* (Prague, 1935), Part II, Proti proudu, pp. 328–450; Herben, *T. G. Masaryk, 3 vols* (2nd. edn., Prague, 1926) I, pp. 79–109; *Paměti dra. Karla Kramáře*, ed. Karel Hoch (Prague, n.d.), pp. 79–109; Z. V. Tobolka (ed.), *Josef Kaizl; Z mého života* (Prague, 1908–14) II, III, nos 1 and. 2; Roland J. Hoffmann, *T. G. Masaryk und die tschechische Frage* (Munich, 1988), chaps 5, 6, 7; Eva Schmidt-Hartmann, *Thomas G. Masaryk's Realism* (Munich, 1984).

6. Masaryk, 'Můj poměr, p. 4.

7. For a full analysis of the content and purposes of *Čas* during its first years by its editor, see Herben, *Kniha*, pp. 319–73. See also Herben, 'Z historie Času', in 'Dvácet pět let', parts I–V.

8. Tobolka, *Politické dějiny*, III 1, p. 275. For an excellent comparison of the three Realist leaders, ibid., pp. 276ff.; for an exposition of Realist ideas, ibid., pp. 282–8. See also Tobolka, *Kaizl*, II, pp. 428ff.; Vaníček, *Mas. sborník*, IV, pp. 215–22; Křížek, *Masaryk*, chaps. 1, 2. The name "Realist" was pinned on them by the Old Czech newspaper editor, F. Pazdírek, but was accepted by them as appropriate

9. Vaníček, *Mas. sborník*, V, pp. 306–17; Tobolka, *Pol. dějiny*, III, 1, pp. 283–4.

10. For the text, *Čas*, IV, no. 44, November 1890; given in Tobolka, *Kaizl*, II, pp. 607–13; Herben, *Kniha*, pp. 436–43. The draft was prepared by all three of the Realists. See a critique of the programme by Schmidt-Hartmann, *Masaryk's Realism*, pp. 102–5.

11. Masaryk, 'Aforismy o politických stranách', *Čas*, III, 9 and 10 (1889), reprinted in *Masaryková práce*, ed. J. B. Kozák, pp. 74–9. For a fuller summary, see Chapter 2 above, pp. 28–9.

12. Tobolka, *Kaizl*, II, p. 470.

13. For the most detailed reporting of the conversations and the text of Realist proposals, see Herben, *Kniha*, pp. 380–95, 434–6; a different version was given by Albín Bráf, *Život a dílo*, 1, 'Mé styky s T. G. Masarykem', 21–7. See also Hugo Traub, 'F. L. Rieger a T. G. Masaryk', *Masarykův sborník*, III, pp. 97–108; Vaníček, ibid., V, pp. 317–22; Křížek, *Masaryk*, chap. 3; Tobolka, *Pol. dějiny*, III, no. 1, pp. 289–95; Tobolka, *Kaizl*, II, pp. 439–45; Kramář, *Paměti*, pp. 115–221.

14. In spite of mutual distrust and recriminations over tactics, Young Czechs and Realists had established contacts as early as 1885, and had even held talks parallel with the conversations with the Old Czechs. There had also been some secret discussions on the forming of a new party which would include Realists, some Old Czechs opposed to the Compromise, and moderate Young Czechs. See Křížek, *Masaryk*, pp. 125–32, 152; Tobolka, *Pol dějiny*, III, 1, pp. 302–3; Kramář, *Paměti*, pp. 202ff.

15. For these talks, see Vaníček, *Mas. sborník*, IV, pp. 215–16, V, 323–4, 324–9; Křížek, *Masaryk*, chap. 1, pp. 116–54; Garver, *Young Czech Party*, pp. 151–2, 433, n. 64; Tobolka, *Pol. dějiny*, III, 1, pp. 295–303; Tobolka, *Kaizl*, II, pp. 445–56; Herben, *Kniha*, pp. 443–4; Kramář, *Paměti*, pp. 212–63; Kramář, 'Vstup realistů do strany mladočeské', in *Půl století 'Národních Listů'* (Prague, 1911), pp. 49–53; J. Chlubna, 'Vstup realistů do mladočeské strany,' *Národní myšlenka*, XIII (1935–36), pp. 76–84; Jozef Folprecht, 'Z doby předmladočeské', *Sborník Karela Kramáře* (Prague, 1930), pp. 239–42. The role of Kramář in the negotiations leading to the agreement was stressed in most of the sources cited, especially those by or about Kramář, but was challenged by Jan Herben. See Herben, 'Z Historie Času', II, p. 1.

16. For this period, see Stanley B. Winters, 'Kramář, Kaizl, and the Hegemony of the Young Czech Party, 1891–1901', in Brock and Skilling, *The Czech Renascence*,

espec. pp. 282–91; Garver, *The Young Czech Party*, pp. 159–62; Kramář, *Paměti*, pp. 264ff; Herben, *Masaryk* (1946), pp. 109–42; Křížek, *Masaryk*, chaps V and VI.

17. For many of his speeches, see George Kovtun, *Slovo má poslanec Masaryk* (Munich, 1985); Ernst Rychnovsky, *Masaryk* (Prague, 1930); Herben, *Masaryk, I*, pp. 109–16ff.; Schmidt-Hartmann, *Masaryk's Realism*, pp. 106–16; on foreign policy, and see Chapter 9 below.

18. Urban, *Česká společnost*, pp. 426–30.

19. For Masaryk's conflict with Grégr, see Herben, 'Dvácet pět let', Pt III, pp. 2–4; for his own account, Masaryk, 'Muj poměr', pp. 4–6; for differences among the Realists, see Kramář, *Paměti*, pp. 270, 296–300, etc.; Tobolka, *Kaizl*, III, 1, pp. 44–9. Many years later, in a controversy with Karel Kramář in 1906, Masaryk insisted that his early relations with Grégr had been good, and that his disillusionment with the party was due to its failure to carry through its own reform as he had hoped. See Chapter 4 below, p. 56.

20. Kramář, *Paměti*, ibid., pp. 214, 216–17, 229.

21. *Čas*, V (1891), no. 39, pp. 622–4. Text is also given in full in Kozák, *Masaryková práce*, pp. 80–85.

22. For the affair, see Herben, *Masaryk*, I, 137–42; Josef Holeček, *Tragedie J. Grégra* (Prague, 1914), pp. 428–61; Kramář, *Paměti*, pp. 380–7; Tobolka, *Kaizl*, III, 1, pp. 252–62; Masaryk, 'Můj poměr', pp. 5–6; Křížek, *Masaryk*, p. 321, n. 154. According to Křížek, Masaryk sought a Young Czech candidacy in late 1893 and again in 1896, and tried to reach agreement with the Young Czechs as late as 1901 (ibid., pp. 45, 50, 75).

23. Text was published ten years later in *Čas*, XVI, no. 6, 7 February 1903, pp. 81–3; also given by Bedřich Hlaváč, 'Masaryk and Rakousko', in *Masarykův sborník*, VI, no. 2, pp. 115–21; Hlaváč, *František Josef I* (Prague, 1933), pp. 644–52.

24. Kramář, *Paměti*, pp. 343, 377–88; Hugo Traub, 'Kaizl a Masaryk', *Masarykův sborník*, III, pp. 293–98; Masaryk, 'Můj poměr', pp. 5–6.

25. Odložilík, 'Na předělu dob', pp. 58–61. The historical and theoretical aspects of these writings have been examined fully in other chapters of this book (2, 7). For a detailed critical analysis, see Schmidt-Hartmann, *Masaryk's Realism*, chaps 6, 7; Hoffmann, *Masaryk*, chaps 8, 9. See also Herben, *Masaryk* (1946), I, pp. 142–70; Garver, *The Young Czech Party*, pp. 206–16, 465, n. 64.

26. These two books appeared in 1895 and were later published together as *Česká otázka, Snahy a tužby národního obrození/Naše nynější krise, Pad strany staročeské a počátkové směrů nových* (Prague, 1948), henceforth cited as Č. o. and NNK respectively.

27. Č. o., p. 225; NNK, pp. 233, 302.

28. Č. o., pp. 114–16, 185–7, NNK. pp. 235–40, 302. Although Masaryk acknowledged that clericalism was better than liberalism in its recognition of the social question, it was anti-national in denying the idea of the national awakening and in supporting anti-Semitism (ibid., pp. 224, 259). For a full treatment of Masaryk's condemnation of clericalism, see Chapter 7 below.

29. Č. o. pp. 116–19, 179–80, 228; NNK, pp. 251–4, 286, 395. Masaryk referred to liberalism in disparaging terms as an 'alien ideological influence' which tended to weaken the idea of our revival by describing it as derived from Western European humanism. Liberalism in essence was 'a philosophical rationalism' which rejected religious and ethical meaning of life and culture; socially it was an aristo-plutocratic philosophy'. For this see Roman Szporluk, *The Political Thought of Thomas G. Masaryk* (Boulder, 1981), p. 92, 197, nn. 42–4. The sources cited were not found in *Česká otázka*. Masaryk's fullest exposition of European and Russian liberalism

was given in *Rusko a evropa* (Prague, 1921), II, chap. XXI. He there praised the original ideas of liberalism – liberty, equality and fraternity – but believed that in more recent times it had abandoned these values and was everywhere in decline. See also Chapter 7 below, p. 99.

30. Č. o. pp. 180–5, 249–51, 256–59, NKK, pp. 288–326, 390–7; on the lack of philosophy, pp. 394, 306–8, 320, 326, 390–7. See also Chapter 1 above, pp. 13–15, n. 29.
31. NNK, pp. 296–8, 327–423, espec. 388–9. See also Chapter 2 above, p. 33.
32. *Otázka sociální*, first published in 1898 (2 vols, Prague, 1948); also Masaryk, *Ideály humanitní* (Prague, 1968), pp. 13–22. See Chapter 4 below, pp. 59–60.
33. Č. o., pp. 221–3, 268–70, 319, 345, 383. See also *Otázka sociální*, II, pp. 148–54, 163–4ff; on Russian social democracy and Marxism, see Masaryk, *Rusko a evropa* (Prague, 1921), II, chap. XIX.
34. J. Kaizl, *České myšlenky* (2nd edn., Prague, 1896), chaps 2 and 3, espec. pp. 14, 85; chap. 4, pp. 132ff. See also Schmidt-Hartmann, *Masaryk's Realism*, pp. 145–8.
35. Antonín Hajn 'Realism', *Rozhledy*, IV, 1895, nos 4–7, in Hajn, *Výbor prací 1889–1909* (Prague, 1912), I, pp. 391–429, espec. 396–401, 423–6; on Kaizl, ibid., pp. 429–39, espec. 408–10, 419–21.
36. Č. o., 150–1, 155. On historicism, see pp. 104–5, 114, 148–51, 155, 161–2, 241, 355. For criticism of political realism, see Hoffmann, *Masaryk*, pp. 180–1, 188; Schmidt-Hartmann, *Masaryk's Realism*, chap. 8, pp. 139–40; Schmidt-Hartmann, 'The Fallacy of Realism: Some Problems of Masaryk's Approach to Czech National Aspirations', in *T. G. Masaryk (1850–1937)*, (London, 1990) I, *Thinker and Politician*, ed. Stanley B. Winters, chap. 6. Note the severe criticism of her interpretation by Jaroslav Opat, 'Nad jednou knihu o realismu T. G. Masaryka', *Obsah* (*samizdat*), February 1986, and her reply, ibid., September 1986. See Chapter 2 above, pp. 36, 185 n. 10.
37. Č. o., pp. 155, 161–3, 396–7; on realism and the old parties, pp. 164–6, 254–6, 390; on historicism, *Otázka sociální*, I., pp. 101–3, 177.

4   LEADER OF AN INDEPENDENT PARTY

1. Roland J. Hoffmann, *T. G. Masaryk und die tschechische Frage* (Munich, 1988), pp. 129–34, 167, 171, 210–26; Zdeněk Tobolka, *Politické dějiny československého národa od r. 1848 až do dnešní, doby* (Prague, 1936) III, pp. 2, 282–90; Eva Schmidt-Hartmann, *Thomas G. Masaryk's Realism* (Munich, 1984). For the text, *Ramcový program české strany lidové (realistické)* (Prague, 1900) which also contains Masaryk's speeches at the conference (pp. 113–24, 174–90). For Czech politics in general, see sources listed above, 'Political Dissenter', n. 1.
2. *Ramcový program*, pp. 70–95, Masaryk, pp. 174–9.
3. For details on the Realist crisis, see Hoffmann, *Masaryk*, pp. 295–300. See also E. Chalupný *Vznik české strany pokrokové* (Tabor, 1911), for a vitriolic attack on Herben and on Masaryk, whom he accused of being the chief culprit and whom he described as 'a smug demon who is madly driven on by ambition and for whom all people are but instruments' (p. 56).
4. For the earlier progressive movement and Masaryk's relationship with it, see above, Chapter 1. For details of the emergence of the Progressive party and its programmes, see Bruce Garver, 'Masaryk and Czech Politics, 1906–1914', in *T. G. Masaryk (1850–1937)*, I, *Thinker and Politician*, edited by Stanley B. Winters (London, 1990), pp. 225–57; Garver, *The Young Czech Party 1874–1901 and the*

Emergence of a Multi-party System (New Haven, 1978), pp. 231–3, 299–308; Hoffmann, *Masaryk*, pp. 300–14; Alois Hajn, *Život novinářův, 1894–1930* (Prague, 1930), pp. 121–59, 164–99; Antonín Hajn, *Výbor prací*, I, pp. 441–65 (Prague, 1912); E. K. Rosol, *Česká strana pokroková* (n. d., 1906) in *Politické čtení*, no. 4, 1909. For the programme and speech by Alois Hajn, see *Program a úkoly strany radikálně pokrokové* (Prague, 1897); Adolf Srb, *Politické dějiny národa českého od počátku doby konstituční* (Prague, 1926), II, pp. 199–202, 462–4.

5. See *Česká strana pokroková a její ustavující sjezd den 21. ledna 1906* (Pardubice, 1906) and *Program a organisační statut české strany pokrokové* (Prague, n. d.). The programme was much weaker than the fuller draft prepared by Alois Hajn, *K programu pokrokové strany českoslovanské* (Pardubice, 1905), which had clearly opted for natural right as a basis for historic state right and had used the phrase 'attainment of political power in Austria', a term not previously used in Masaryk's writings. Note that the 1906 programme abandoned the term 'Czechoslav' in the title which had been used in the Hajn draft. For a fuller exposition of the aims of the Progressive party, see Masaryk's speech in Písek on 30 September 1906, given in *Čas*, nos. 270–2, 1, 2 and 3 October 1906, published separately as *Program a úkoly české strany pokrokové* (Písek, 1906).

6. *Program české strany pokrokové* (Prague, 1912), p. 15 ff. For a full discussion, see Garver, 'Czech Politics', pp. 235–40. Garver quotes at length the sentences concerning independence and state right (p. 238), as though they were new, but both are to be found in the *Ramcový program* (pp. 1–2). The programme referred to a second conference in 1908 about which the author has no information. See also Chapter 10 below, pp. 154, 171.

7. For the 1899 programme and the 1908 declaration see Srb, *Pol. dějiny*, II, 517–18, and *Státotvorně a pokrokově, Epištoly*, no. 2 (Prague, 1913). See also Tobolka, *Pol. dějiny*, III, 2, pp. 458–9. Alois Hajn denounced his brother's party as little more than a worse form of Young Czechism, which represented an inhuman and un-cultured nationalism. See Hajn, *Politické strany u nás* (Pardubice, 1903), pp. 38–50.

8. For this, and the following, see Garver, *The Young Czech Party*, passim, especially pp. 298–9; and for detail, Richard Fischer, *Pokroková Morava, 1893–1918* (Prague, 1937), which gives the 1893 programme (I, pp. 25–6).

9. *Čas*, VII, no. 11, pp. 162–4, given in J. Kozák, (ed.), *Masaryková práce* (Prague, 1930), pp. 100–5. See also Masaryk's earlier speeches in 1888 and 1892, in which he had called for a programme and for better organization, better leaders and better newspapers in Moravia. 'The Czech question was the Moravian question; the Moravian question was the Czech question', he said (*Čas*, II, no. 2, pp. 17–23 and VI, no. 24, p. 370, both given in Kozák, *Masaryková práce*, pp. 65–7, 96–100).

10. See Fischer, *Pokroková Morava*, for Young Moravia, I, p. 49 passim, and for the Political Association for Northern Moravia and the Progressive Political Association for Moravia, I, p. 33 passim, and 141 passim.

11. Fischer, ibid, II, pp. 243–4, 263 ff; programme at pp. 285–9.

12. Ibid., pp. 391–4.

13. For the last comment, see Jan Herben, *T. G. Masaryk*, 3 vols. (Prague, 1926), I, pp. 310, 326–8. During the first phase (1900–1907) Masaryk continued his scholarly output, re-issuing, sometimes in several languages, important studies written earlier – *The Social Question* (German, 1899, Russian, 1900 and 1906); *Havlíček* (1904, 1906), and *Suicide* (1904). He also published new studies on European society (1899), marriage (1899), the women's question (1899, 1900, 1902), Jan Hus (1899, 1903), the Hilsner case (1899, 1902), the eight-hour day (1900, 1905), historical and natural right (1900), the ideals of humanity (1901, 1902), his American lectures (1902), religion (1904) and the modern philosophy of nationalism (1905). Other

shorter works included his important essays on political parties (1899) and political science (1900), and speeches and short articles on alcoholism (1902, 1906, 1908), religion and clericalism (1904, 1906, 1907), students (1905), Havlíček (1906), freedom of conscience (1908), and contemporary politics (the political situation, 1901 and 1906, the Young Czech Party, 1903, students and politics, 1905 and Progressive politics, 1906).

In the second phase, after 1907, in addition to his parliamentary activity, Masaryk found time to prepare his speeches for Chicago (1907), and to produce long articles on clericalism and socialism (1907), religion and clericalism (1907, 1908), and Jan Hus (1910), as well as lectures on alcoholism (1909, 1912), Progressive politics (1908), students and politics (1909), the political situation (1911) and democracy (1912, 1913).

In the final stage, after 1911, in the midst of a very busy parliamentary life, Masaryk produced, as well as his major book on Russia, articles on alcoholism (1912), democracy (1912, 1913), and education (1913). The two Festschrifts were 'Prof. Dru. T. G. Masarykovi k šedesátým narozeninám věnováno, 1850–1910', published in a special number of *Česká mysl*, XI (1910), pp. 6–228; *T. G. Masarykovi k šedesátým narozeninám*, ed. Edvard Beneš and others (first edition, Prague, 1910; second edition in *Masarykův sborník*, ed. V. K. Škrach, (4 vols., Prague, 1930), IV, 435 pp.

14. The fullest source on the election is Stanislav Jandík, *Masaryk na Valašsku; jeho boj o poslanecký mandát* (2nd, edn., Prague, 1936), which contains the text of his electoral speech and of clerical campaign documents. See also B. Kučera, 'O spojenectví sociální demokracie s Masarykem při říšských volbách v roce 1907', *Časopis Matice moravské*, LXXIII (1955), pp. 166–73. Less useful are *Hrst vzpomínek, Na dobu poslanecke činnosti T. G. Masaryka na Valašsku*, no editor given (Valašské Meziříčí, 1935); V. Dědina, 'Jak jsme volili Profesora T. G. Masaryka poslancem za valašská mesta', *Masarykův sborník*, III, pp. 193–9. See also Garver, 'Masaryk and Czech Politics', pp. 242–3; *Paul Selver* (London, 1940) pp. 202–7; Herben, *Masaryk*, I, pp. 275–89; Fischer, *Pokroková Morava*, pp. 240–3, 318. See also Chapter 7 below.

15. Herben, *Masaryk*, I, pp. 311–13.

16. For praise by Jaromír Doležal, see Selver, *Masaryk*, pp. 241–2. For his speeches in 1891–93 and for sources, see Chapter 3 above, p. 191, n. 17; for his speeches after 1907 see Chapter 9 below.

17. The most authoritative accounts of the Young Czech party are by Bruce Garver, *The Young Czech Party*, and by Stanley B. Winters, 'The Young Czech Party (1874–1914): An Appraisal', *Slavic Review*, 28, no. 3 (September 1969), pp. 426–44; 'Kramář, Kaizl and the Hegemony of the Young Czech Party, 1891–1901', in Peter Brock and H. Gordon Skilling, *The Czech Renascence of the Nineteenth Century* (Toronto, 1970), pp. 239–53; 'T. G. Masaryk and Karel Kramář, Long Years of Friendship and Rivalry', in Winter, (ed.), *T. G. Masaryk*, I, pp. 153–90. See also Hoffmann, *Masaryk*, pp. 355–9. For Masaryk on the Young Czechs see Chapter 3 above, pp. 44–5.

18. This was published as *Desorganisace mladočeské strany* (Prague, n. d). See a similar analysis of the party's decay, which he blamed not only on its lack of an independent policy, but on the electorate and its lack of self-confidence (Masaryk, 'O politické situace', *Čas*, XVI, no. 14, 4 April 1903); also ibid., no. 18, 2 May 1903; no. 37, 12 September 1903. For Masaryk's critique of liberalism, see Chapter 3 above, p. 45.

19. Kramář, *Poznámky o České politice* (Prague, 1906); also in German, *Anmerkungen zur böhmischen Politik* (Vienna, 1906).

20. See his lectures published as a brochure, *Politická situace, Poznámky. k poznámkám* (Prague, 1906). Once again he denied any personal antipathy between himself and Julius Grégr in 1891. See Chapter 3 above, p. 44 n. 19, 22.

21. Scholarly accounts of the National Socialist Party are given by Detlef Brandes, 'Die tschechoslowakischen National-Sozialisten', in *Die Erste Tschechoslowakische Republik als multinationaler Parteienstaat*, ed. Karl Bosl (Munich, 1979), pp. 101–53 and, on its pre-1897 origins, H.Traub, *Jak se připravoval a rodil český národní socialismus* (Brno, n.d.). Adulatory but informative are the works by Bohuslav Šantrůček, *Václav Klofáč, 1868–1928* (Prague, 1928); 'Sedmnáctiletá' in his *Buřicia tvůrci; vzpomínky, úvahy, kus historie, životopisy, 1897–1947* (Prague, 1947), pp. 103–61; *Českoslovenští národní socialiste včera a dnes* (Prague, 1946); and, above all, his massive study, *Masaryk a Klofáč, Srovnávácí studie* (Prague, 1938). See also J. Klofáč, 'Dvácet pět let bojů a práce', in *25 let práce Československé strany socialistické, 1897–1922* (Prague, 1922). For briefer accounts, see Garver, *The Young Czech Party*, pp. 295–8; Tobolka, *Pol. dějiny*, III, 2, pp. 127–31. For communist interpretations, see Josef Harna, *Kritika ideologie a programu českého národního socialismu* (Prague, 1978), pp. 12–32; Josef Šafařík, in *O úloze bývalé nár. soc. strany* (Prague, 1959), pp. 29–43; Ctíbor Nečas, *Balkán a česká politika* (Brno, 1972), pp. 81–100.

22. For the 1897 statement and the 1898 programme, see Srb, *Pol. dějiny*, II, pp. 217–18, 464–7; for a completer version of the latter (partially censored), see Klofáč, *Program a zásady národně-sociální strany* (Prague, 1901). The 1902 and 1911 programmes were published under the same title, *Program české národní sociální 1902 and 1911*). The 1902 programme was not available to the author but is summarized briefly in Garver, *The Young Czech Party*, pp. 296–7. For a bitter critique of the National Socialists, see Hajn, *Politické strany*, pp. 69–78.

23. Brandes, 'National-Sozialisten', pp. 105–7; the declaration is given by Šantrůček, *Masaryk a Klofáč*, pp. 273–4.

24. Ibid., pp. 30–75 (on Havlíček), 231–2, 246–52, 297, 362ff; Brandes, op. cit., pp. 103, 109–11.

25. Nečas, *Balkán*, pp. 72–3, 92–3, 100, 133.

26. Klofáč was elected to the Delegations in 1906 as the spokesman of the State Right Concentration, which included the National Socialists, the State Right Progressives and the Radical Progressives (ibid., p. 87).

27. Šantrůček, *Masaryk a Klofáč*, pp. 208–9, 221, 332–62. The most radical anti-military movement was conducted by the National Socialist youth movement, under Emil Špatný. See his *Český militarismus: kus historie a trochu vzpomínek* (Prague, 1922). See also Jan Beránek, *Rakouský militarismus a boj proti němu v Čechách* (Prague, 1955), which, in Stalinist spirit, praises the anti-militarist actions of the masses in 1908–9 and 1912 but criticizes both the National Socialists for their anarchic and petty-bourgeois nationalism, and the Social Democrats for their opportunist efforts to dampen the movement. For Masaryk's criticism of militarism, see Chapter 9 below, pp. 133–4. Most Czech parties were critical of specific features of the army but sometimes, unlike Masaryk, they voted for military credits (Tobolka, *Pol. děj.* III, 2, pp. 618–19, 628).

28. Šantrůček, *Masaryk a Klofáč*, pp. 384–6, 388–9, 391–9. See Chapter 10 below.

29. Nothing is known of the content of these negotiations. For this and the Šviha case, see Šantrůček, *Masaryk a Klofáč*, pp. 405–14; Šantrůček, *Klofáč*, pp. 141–5; Santrůček, 'Sedmnáctiletá', pp. 140–6; Herben, *T. G. Masaryk*, I, pp. 319–22, and especially Winters, 'T. G. Masaryk and Karel Kramář: Long Years of Friendship and Rivalry', in Winters, *T. G. Masaryk*, I, pp. 175–9; and Bruce Garver, 'Masaryk and Czech Politics, 1906–1914', ibid.; I, pp. 241–2. The trial proceedings were published as *Zrádce dr. Karel Šviha před porotou* (Prague, 1914); Masaryk's

testimony at pp. 46–9. For Masaryk's postwar comments, see Karel Čapek, *Hovory s T. G. Masarykem* (*Prague, 1937*), p. 136; Masaryk, *Světová revoluce* (Prague, 1925), p.12.

30.   Karel Pichlík, *Zahraniční odboj 1914–1918 bez legend* (Prague 1968), pp. 34–5.

31.   See Chapter 1, p. 14; Chapter 3, pp. 59–60; Chapter 7, pp. 109–10; and above in this chapter, pp. 54–5, 60–2. On Masaryk and Social Democracy, see *inter alia*, Hans Mommsen, *Die Sozialdemokratie und die Nationalitätenfrage im habsburgischen Vielvölkerstaat* (Vienna, 1963), I, espec. pp. 260–70; Jacques Rupnik, *Histoire du Parti communiste tschécoslovaque* (Paris, 1981), pp. 29–36; Garver, *The Young Czech Party*, pp. 163–8, 171–82, 241–3, 282–3. Of the countless articles and books devoted to the Czech workers' movement published during the communist period, Jan Galandauer, *Od Hainfeldu ke vzniku KSC* (Prague, 1986), pp. 115–42, stands out, but barely mentions Masaryk. Other Marxists caricature Masaryk as a spokesman of the bourgeois class and an enemy of the working class, who had indoctrinated the workers with nationalist and opportunist ideas, e.g. Jurij Křížek, *T. G. Masaryk a naše dělnická třída* (Praha, 1955); Z. Šolle, 'Vliv masarykismu na české dělnické hnutí konce minulého století', *Nová mysl*, no. 3, March 1954, pp. 286–302. See a similar Soviet interpretation by M. Silin, *A Critique of Masarykism* (Moscow, 1975). Contrast the more positive Marxist interpretation given by Zdeněk Nejedlý, *T. G. Masaryk ve vývoji české společnosti a Čs. staťu* (Prague, 1950).

32.   Masaryk had suggested to them a more moderate version, which rejected the primacy of state right and subordinated it to natural right. See František Soukup, *Revoluce práce* (Prague, 1938), I, pp. 48, 613–23; Šantrůček, *Masaryk and Klofáč*, pp. 212–13.

33.   For good discussion of the dialectic of nationalism and socialism within Czech Social Democracy, see Jacques Rupnik, 'The Czech Socialists and the Nation (1848–1918)', in Eric Cahm and Vladimir Fišera, (eds.), *Socialism and Nationalism in Contemporary Europe (1848–1945)*, 2, pp. 115–32; Rupnik, 'Masaryk and Czech Socialism', in *T. G. Masaryk (1850–1937) 2, Thinker and Critic*, ed. Robert B. Pynsent, (London, 1989), pp. 137–48. Somewhat strangely, Masaryk did not address himself to the theories of Karl Renner and Otto Bauer on the national question in Austria-Hungary which in some respects approached his own idea of territorial and personal autonomy. For Masaryk, however, this was designed to protect national minorities, both Czech and German, and not to replace the historic entity of the Bohemian lands. Austro-Marxism was approved by Šmeral, but rejected by the more nationalist members of Czech social democracy (František Modráček *et al.*) who were closer to Masaryk. See Hoffmann, *Masaryk*, Part III, chap.4.

34.   For these events and Masaryk's analysis, see *Čas*, XVIII, nos. 46 and 47, November 11 and 18, 1905; see also S. (T.G.M), 'Na přechod k demokracii', *Naše doba*, 14 (1906–7), pp. 1–2. For Stalinist interpretations of the influence of the Russian revolution on Czech politics, see Jiří Doležal and Jan Beránek, *Ohlas první Ruské revoluce v českých zemí* (Prague, 1955), and the collections of documents, ed. O. Kodedová, *Rok 1905* (Prague, 1959) and *Léta 1906–1907* (Prague, 1962).

35.   For these speeches, Hoffmann, *Masaryk*, pp. 320–2, 325–39; *Čas*, 2, 5 September 1905, no. 265, pp. 1–2; ibid., 3 October 1906, no. 272, p. 1.

36.   These lectures, given in Pilsen, and published in the local Social Democratic organ, (*Nová doba*, 12 (1907), nos 4, 6, 8, 10, 11, 12), presented a wide-ranging historical survey of socialism in various countries, in which he distinguished French socialism as revolutionary, British as reform-oriented state socialism, German as scientific and philosophical, based on Marxism, and Russian as revolutionary and anarchistic.

In his final lecture on socialism and democracy, he rejected anarchism and communism, and argued that social democracy had overcome its revolutionary phase; reform could now be attained without revolution.

37. Pichlík, *Zahraníční odboj*, pp. 24–7. See also Chapter 10 below, p. 170. In his Písek speech (1906), cited in n. 35, Masaryk again stressed the national character of his party, which cared first and foremost for nationality and its furtherance.

38. Tobolka, *Pol. děj.* I, 2, pp. 457–8, 487–8, 515, 571–3. For general discussion of Czech political parties, see Otto Urban, *Česká společnost, 1848–1918* (Prague, 1982), pp. 473–80, 531 passim; Urban, *České a slovenske dějiny do roku 1918* (Prague, 1991), pp. 211–22; Garver, *The Young Czech Party*, passim; Garver, 'Czech Politics', pp. 238ff.

39. Masaryk, 'O t.zv. koncentraci stran', *Čas*, XIX, no. 36, 7 September 1906.

40. The following is based on Masaryk, 'Politické strany a nové formace', *Čas*, nos. 83–4, 24–5 March 1908; Hoffmann, *Masaryk*, pp. 315–24, 331–9, 349–54. Masaryk did not give up hope of cooperation with the Young Czechs, seeking a common front with them and the Agrarians during the Bohemian Diet elections in 1908; however, he failed to be elected. In 1909 the Realists joined the Czech parliamentary club (ibid., pp. 393–4, 441). For briefer comments on the Czech parties see the Realist 1900 programme (ibid., 3–4) and Masaryk, *Potřeba pokrokové politiky* (Mělník, 1908), pp. 14–16.

41. For his earlier discussion of political parties in general, see Chapter 2 above, pp. 28–9.

42. These were the parties of the Conservative Large Property owners, which went back to 1860, and were organized at different times in one or two parties.

43. These were the Christian Social parties, formed in Bohemia and Moravia in the mid-nineties and reorganized as a national party in 1904. It, too, had a more progressive wing; in 1911 it broke into three parts, the Conservative People's, the Christian Social and the Catholic National parties.

44. In fact the Agrarian party, at first strongly conservative, had gone through successive reorganizations and by 1905 had moved toward a more liberal and democratic position, hostile to clericalism and favourable to universal suffrage. See Garver, *The Young Czech Party*, pp. 288–95; Tobolka, *Pol. Děj*, III, no. 2, pp. 269–81, 448–51.

45. See the anonymous pamphlet, *Oko za oko neboli Politická komedie s Wolfem* (Prague, 1908), on Masaryk's support of the proposal of the German deputy, Wolf, for a separate German Academy in Prague, in the hope that this would lead to an independent Czech Academy.

46. Garver, *The Young Czech Party*, pp. 297, 304, 308; Garver, 'Czech Politics', pp. 240–1; Winter, 'Masaryk and Kramár', p. 173; Hoffman, *Masaryk*, pp. 317–39, 393–4;Tobolka, Pol. děj. III, 2, 457–8, 487–9, 496–7; Pichlík, *Zahraniční odboj*, pp. 24, 34–5; Nečas, *Balkán*, passim.

47. No mention has been made of Jaroslav Hašek's Party of Moderate Progress Within the Framework of the Law, whose only candidate, Hašek, received 36 votes in the 1911 elections. Although this was not a serious party, Hašek's writings were not entirely off the mark when he lampooned all the existing parties for their hypocrisy and opportunism, and some for their extreme nationalism. Among the few references to Masaryk and the Realists, he wrote that it was painful to say that the Realists had the truth; in fact it always evaded them. He cynically argued that the success of the parties depended on the quality of beer served at their meetings and that the failure of the Realists was due to the fact that they served only soda-water. See Hašek, *Politické a sociální dějiny strany mírného pokroku v mezích zákona*, written in 1912, but first published in full in 1963. See the edition published in

Výbor z díla Jaroslava Haška (Prague, 1982), pp. 64–6, 364; for other references to Masaryk and the Realists, pp. 15, 48, 64, 213, 355–7, 363–4. See also Hašek, *Z doby 'Strany mírného pokroku v mezích zákona'* (Prague, 1956).

5 FRIEND OF THE SLOVAKS

1. The most important sources on Masaryk and the Slovaks used for this essay were Thomas D. Marzik, 'T. G. Masaryk and the Slovaks, 1882–1914', in A. W. Cordier, (ed.), *The Dean's Papers: Columbia Essays in International Affairs, 1965* (New York, 1966), pp. 155–74; Antonín Štefánek, *Masaryk a Slovensko* (Bratislava, 1920); Štefanek, 'Masaryk a Slovensko', in M. Weingart, (ed.) *Sborník přednasek o T. G. Masarykovi* (Prague, 1931), pp. 205–58; Štefánek, 'Masaryk a Slovensko' in J. B. Kozák et al., *Masaryková práce* (Prague, 1930), pp. 241–50; Albert Pražák, *Masaryk a Slovensko* (Prague, 1937) (a revision of 'Pražák, 'Masaryk a Slovaci,' in *Masarykův sborník*, (5 vols. 1925–31) ed. V. Škrach, V, no. 2, pp. 198–259); Ludwig von Gogolák, 'T. G. Masaryks Slowakische und Ungarlandische Politik', *Bohemia, Jahrbuch*, 4 (1963), pp. 174–227. See also the 1910 essay by Vavro Šrobár, 'Vliv Masarykov na Slovakov', republished in *Masarykův sborník* III, pp. 251–63. Much of this essay was repeated in Šrobár, 'T. G. Masaryk a Slováci', in Jozef Rudinský, (ed.), *Slovensko Masarykovi* (Prague, 1931). This volume consists for the most part of laudatory memoirs, as does Št. Krčméry, 'T. G. Masaryk a Slováci', *Slovenské Pohl'ady*, XLVI (1930), pp. 175–86. See also Jan Juríček, *Vajanský, Portrét odvážneho* (Bratislava, 1988), on Masaryk, pp. 121–8.

2. On this question, the fullest study is that by Thomas D. Marzik, 'Masaryk's National Background', in Peter Brock and H. Gordon Skilling, *The Czech Renascence of the Nineteenth Century* (Toronto, 1970), chap. 15. Important sources on his childhood and youth and on his national feelings are Paul Selver, *Masaryk: A Biography* (London, 1940), espec. pp. 16–17, 33, 50–1; Karel Čapek, *Masaryk on Thought and Life: Conversations with Karel Čapek* (London, 1938) pp. 34, 97, 190, 220; and in great detail, Zdeněk Nejedlý, *T. G. Masaryk* (Prague, 1931–37), I, Pt 1, pp. 79–87, 102; Pt 2, pp. 199–206. See also Masaryk, 'Slovenské vzpomienky' (1917), in Jaromír Doležal, *Masarykova cesta životem* (Brno, 1921), pp. 19–25; Masaryk, *O pokrokovém postavení slovenské mládeže* (speech on 15 August 1911) (Uh. Hradiště, 1935), p. 2; T. G. Masaryk, *The Making of a State* (London, 1927), pp. 41, 209. Reports that Masaryk was of Jewish origin, the illegitimate son of a Jewish father in Vienna, were not supported by any evidence (Gogolák, 'Masaryks Politik', pp. 186–7; Marzik, 'Masaryk's Background', p. 242, n. 9).

3. For the above see L'udovít Holotík, 'Die Slowaken', in A. Wandruszka and P. Urbanitsch (eds), *Die Habsburgermonarchie, 1848–1918* (Vienna, 1973), III, no. 2, chap. X.

4. For this, see Peter Brock, *The Slovak National Awakening* (Toronto, 1976).

5. Zdeněk Tobolka, *Politické dějiny Československého národa od r. 1848 až do dnešní doby* (Prague, 1936), III, Pt 2, pp. 356–74, 595–610; Jozef Lettrich, *History of Modern Slovakia* (New York, 1955), pp. 37–8.

6. For a detailed analysis of Slovak politics between 1880 and 1909 see Gogolák, in *Beiträge zur Geschichte des slowakischen Volkes* (Munich, 1972), III, pp. 93–4; *Dějiny Slovenska* IV, ed. Samuel Cambel, (Bratislava, 1986), chaps IV, V and VI; Pavla Vošahlíková, *Slovenské politické směry v období přechodu k imperialismu* (Prague, 1979); František Bokes, *Dějiny Slovenska a Slovákov od najstarších čias po oslobodenie* (Bratislava, 1946), chap. XVIII; František Votruba, 'Slovensko v

politickej aktivite; *Milan Hodža a Slovenské politické prebudenje'*, in *Milan Hodža, publicista, politik, vedecký pracovník*, edited by A. Stefánek, F. Votruba, and F. Šěda (Prague, 1930); Edita Bosák, 'The Slovak National Movement, 1848–1914', in S. J. Kirschbaum and A. C. R. Roman, *Reflections on Slovak History* (Toronto, 1987), chap. V. See also Jozef Jablonický, 'Prispevok k česko-slovenským vzt'ahom od konca 19 stor. do roku 1914', *Historické studie*, IV, 1958, pp. 5–54; Gogolák, *Masaryks Politik*, pp. 177–89, espec. p. 209, and Šrobár, 'Vliv', pp. 251–62, pp. 253, 262 for the citations below. More recent studies include Otto Urban, *České a slovenské dějiny do roku 1918* (Prague, 1991), pp. 206–11, 222–8; Edita Bosák, 'T. G. Masaryk and the Emergence of the Hlasist Movement, 1898–1914', paper given at the conference of the Czechoslovak Society for art and scholarship, Prague, June 1992 (unpublished); Milan Podrimavský, 'Slovenská politika v uhorsku', in *Slovensko v politickom systéme Československa*, ed. V. Bystrický (Slovak Historical Institute, Bratislava, 1992), pp. 29–35.

7. P. Hapák and J. Butvín, in *Dejiny Slovenska* (Cambel), IV, p. 270.

8. Hapák, M. Danilák and M. Podrimavsky, ibid. pp. 309–10.

9. Šrobar, 'Vliv', pp. 252, 262.

10. For a full exposition of Hlasist thinking, see Jan Bodnár, 'The Ideological Foundations of Hlasism', in Elena Várossová, ed., *Prehl'ad dejín slovenskej filozodfie* (Bratislava, 1965), espec. pp. 317, 328–34. Bodnár, himself a Marxist, rejected dogmatic Marxist interpretations of Hlasism and assessed it in essentially positive terms.

11. The fullest discussion of *Jednota* and other pro-Slovak tendencies among Czechs is found in Jablonický, 'Prispevok', espec. pp. 10ff. Other authors barely mention, or entirely ignore *Jednota*, e.g. Marzik, 'Masaryk and Slovaks', p. 171, n. 39. An early attempt to substitute Ceskoslovenská (Czechoslovak) for Českoslovanská (Czechoslav) in the title failed. The term *Jednota* had the double meaning of association and unity. In the early years Vajanský was associated with *Jednota* and with the Luhačovice meetings. See Bokes, *Dejiny Slovenska*, pp. 325–8; Hapák *et al.*, in *Dejiny Slovenska* (Cambel) IV, pp. 274–9, 280–7, 301-3.

12. Jablonický, 'Prispevok', pp. 29–34, 34–48; Bruce M. Garver, *The Young Czech Party 1874–1901 and the Emergence of a Multi-party System* (New Haven, 1978), pp. 266–8; L. Holotík, ed., *O vzájomných vzt'ahoch Čechov a Slovákov*. (Bratislava 1956), Pt II, espec. Zdeněk Urban, 'Česko-slovenská vzájemnost před první světovou válkou'. The Holotík essays are written from a narrow Marxist approach, depicting Masaryk as an exponent of the class interests of the Czech and Slovak bourgeoisie. Several contributors deal with the relations of Czechs and Slovaks within the social democratic movement. On the agrarian movement, see Hapák and Butvín, in *Dejiny Slovenska* (Cambel), IV, pp. 282–5.

13. Jablonický, 'Prispevok', pp. 8, 9; Gogolák, 'Masaryks Politik', pp. 183, 195–7, 207. Yet the veteran Old Czech, Karel Mattuš, in his memoirs, spoke strongly of uniting with 'our brothers under the Tatras' as a nation of ten millions, as a hard core of the Danubian Reich and as a bridge between Slavs, South, North, West and East (*Paměti*, Prague, 1921, pp. 219–22).

14. *Ramcový program české strany lidové (realistické)* (Prague, 1900), espec. pp. 14, 71, 194. According to Jan Herben, the letter came from V. Šrobár (Jan Herben, *T. G. Masaryk*, Prague, 1926, I, pp. 238–9). On state and natural right, see the programme, pp. 4–7, 71 passim, 114–16, 128. In Štefánek's view the young Slovaks interpreted Masaryk's accent on natural rights in favour of the Czechoslovak idea (Weingart, *Sborník*, pp. 237–8).

15. *Program a organisační statut české strany pokrokové* (Prague, 1900), p. 8; *Česká strana pokroková* (Pardubice, 1906), p. 32.

16. *Program české strany pokrokové* (Prague, 1912), pp. 29, 30; on historical and natural rights, pp. 9–10, 17–19.
17. T. G. Masaryk, *Česká otázka* (Prague, 1895), 6th edn, with *Naše nynější krise* (Prague, 1948), pp. 60–3, 66. For a full scholarly analysis of Masaryk and Kollár, see Pražák, *Masaryk a Slovensko*, pp. 14–35.
18. Masaryk, *Karel Havlíček* (Prague, 1896), pp. 391–7.
19. Ibid., pp. 114–18, 357–60. Masaryk, in referring to Palacký's ethnic proposal in other writings, was equally brief and non-committal. See *Česká otázka* (1948), pp. 97–9, 106–7; Masaryk, *Palackého idea národa českého* (5th edn, Prague, 1947), p. 29.
20. See Masaryk, *Právo přirozené a historické* (Prague, 1900). In 1917 and 1918 Masaryk stated that he had linked historical and natural rights in the interests of defending the Slovaks ('Slovenske vzpomienky', Doležal, *Masarykova Cesta*, p. 23; Pražák, *Masaryk a Slovensko*, p. 103). See above, note 14 and Chapter 10 below, p. 158.
21. *Problém malého národa* (Kroměříž, 1905), p. 28. See Chapter 10 below, p. 152.
22. See Chapter 9 below. For the Budapest speech, Štefánek, *Masaryková práce*, pp. 246–9; Pražák, *Masaryk a Slovensko*, pp. 104–5.
23. Marzik, 'Masaryk and the Slovaks', pp. 165–6; Jablonický, 'Prispevok', pp. 24–6; Gogolák, 'Masaryks politik', pp. 207–9; P. Hapák and J. Butvín, in *Dejiny* (Cambel) IV, p. 220; Pražák, *Masaryk a Slovensko*, pp. 39–40.
24. For the above, see especially Edita Bosák, 'Czech–Slovak Relations and the Student Organisation Detvan, 1882–1914' in Stanislav J. Kirschbaum, (ed.), *Slovak Politics* (Cleveland, 1983), chap. 1; also Jablonický, 'Prispevok', pp. 27–8. See also Bosák, 'Masaryk and the Hlasist Movement'.
25. Štefánek describes his experiences in Prague in his lecture on Masaryk's eightieth birthday, in 1930, 'Masaryk a Slovensko', Weingart, *Sborník*, pp. 219–27. See also Štefánek, *Masaryk a Slovensko* (1920); Štefánek, *Masaryková práce*, pp. 241–50. For his son's evaluation of his views, see Branislav Štefánek, 'Masaryk and Slovakia', in Milič Čapek and Karel Hrubý, (eds), *T. G. Masaryk in Perspective* (n.p., 1981), pp. 202–17.
26. Bosák, in Kirschbaum, *Slovak Politics*, pp. 27–34; Jan Mlynárik, 'Milan Rastislav Štefánek v Masarykovej korešpondencii', in Milan Machovec, Petr Pithart and Miloš Pojar, (eds), *T. G. Masaryk a naše současnost* (Prague, 1992) (originally published in *samizdat* under the same title, 4 vols., Prague, 1980), pp. 42–70.
27. Gogolák, *Beiträge*, pp. 111, 125–30, 139–43; Gogolák, 'Masaryks Politik', pp. 211, 214–16; Tobolka, *Pol. dějiny*, III, 2, pp. 362–8; Hapák *et al.*, in *Dejiny* (Cambel), IV, pp. 296–7; Susan Mikula, 'Milan Hodža and the Politics of Power, 1907–1914', in Kirschbaum, *Slovak Politics*, chap. 2; Milan Štefánek, 'Hodža; Osobnošt a práca', in Stefánek *et al.*, *Milan Hodža*, pp. 62–118.
28. Gogolák, *Beiträge*, pp. 130–9; Tobolka, *Pol. dějiny*, III, 2, pp. 369–70; Jablonický, 'Prispevok', pp. 29–32.
29. Štefánek, in Weingart, *Sborník*, pp. 213–14, 214–15, 246–9, 251–6; V. Fajnor, 'Masaryk a Slovenské študentsvo v Pešti začiatkom rokov devät'desiatych', in Rudinský, *Slovensko*. pp. 81–4; Jablonický, 'Prispevok', pp. 40–1.
30. Herben, *Masaryk*, I, 184–6.
31. The text of the programme was given by Šrobár, 'Vliv', pp. 251–63; also in Šrobár, 'T. G. Masaryk', in Rudinský, *Slovensko*, pp. 87–96.
32. The justification of anti-Semitism for economic reasons in Slovakia was an exception to Masaryk's strong condemnation of anti-Semitism in general. See Chapter 6 below. Vajanský, on the other hand, roundly condemned the Jews, referring to them on one occasion as 'a physically obscene race, capable of the

greatest crimes and living in negation of patriotism and nationality' (Pražák, *Masaryk a Slovensko*, p. 50).

33. For Masaryk's retrospective view of Bystřička in connection with the language question, see above, pp. 79–80.
34. For the above and the following, see especially Marzik, 'Masaryk and Slovaks', p. 168; Štefánek, in Weingart, *Sborník*, pp. 231–6. See also Gogolák, 'Masaryks Politik', pp. 213–14; A Pražák, 'Vliv T. G. Masaryka na Slovenské Hlasisty', in Rudinský, *Slovensko*, pp. 97–104.
35. Štefánek, Weingart, *Sborník*, pp. 232–4; Jablonický, 'Prispevok', p. 23. Similarly, *Hlas*, in 1902, wrote of two nations who should cultivate the greatest reciprocity; to talk of a single literary and written language was harmful (Hapák and Butvín, Dejiny [Cambel], IV, p. 222; Štefánek, *Masaryk a Slovensko*, p. 19). The columns of *Hlas* contained writings of Masaryk, e.g. *Jak pracovat*?, and a speech on Hus, and articles by Šrobár criticizing the Martin leadership and Slovak Catholics. (See Gogolák, 'Masaryks Politik', pp. 222–3.)
36. Pražák, *Masaryk a Slovensko*, 1937, pp. 99–102.
37. For the attacks on Masaryk, see Marzik, 'Masaryk and Slovaks', pp. 172–4; Gogolák, 'Masaryks Politik', pp. 191–3, 201–7; Štefánek, in Weingart, *Sborník*, pp. 242–4; Jablonický, 'Prispevok', pp. 14–15, 33–4; Štefánek, in *Masaryková Práce*, p. 249. For Vajanský's campaign against Masaryk, see Pražák, *Masaryk a Slovensko*, pp. 46–57, 75–99, citation at p. 76; for official Hungarian views, ibid., pp. 95–6. While condemning Vajanský's general attitude, Pražák acknowledged that some of his views were correct (pp. 97–9).
38. Štefánik bitterly condemned Czambel's brochure (Jabonický, 'Prispevok', p. l5). So did Šrobár (Hapák and Butvín, in *Dejiny* (Cambel) IV, p. 221).
39. Pražák, *Masaryk a Slovensko*, pp. 90–3.
40. For the above, Gogolák, 'Masaryks politik', pp. 193–5, 202–3; Jablonický, 'Prispevok', p. 26. The pamphlet has been ascribed to various Slovak writers, and even to Masaryk, although it expressed a view different from Masaryk's on the language question. Its author was presumed to be the Evangelical pastor, L. Novomeský.
41. *Naše doba*, IX, 1901, pp. 66–9; XI, 1904, pp. 1–2. For a report on other articles, see Gogolák, 'Masaryks Politik', pp. 225–7.
42. *Naše doba*, VIII, nos 1–5; see also Štefánek, in Weingart, *Sborník*, pp. 238–45. For Kálal's collaboration with Masaryk, see Thomas D. Marzik, 'The Slovakophile Relationship of T. G. Masaryk and Karel Kálal prior to 1914', in Winter (ed.), *T. G. Masaryk (1850–1937)*, I, chap. 8.
43. Urban, in Holotík, *O vzájomných vzt'ahoch*, pp. 245–6.
44. *Naše doba*, XIV, 1907, p. 470; Jablonický, 'Prispevok', pp. 49–50.
45. Bokes, *Dejiny Slovenska*, p. 335. See also Miroslav Pekník, 'Slovenská politika v Uhorsku a kryštalizácia jej politických koncepcií pred vznikom I. svetovej voyny', in Bystrický, *Slovensko*, p. 44. See also an undated article by Rudolf Pilat on the need for Czech–Slovak cooperation and for a federalization of the Monarchy (Votruba, 'Slovenko v politickej aktivite', in Štefánek, *Hodža*, pp. 465–6, 468, 469. In 1914 the Czech journal *Přehled* carried an article by J. Gallas and V. Hauner which urged the end of dualism and close cooperation of the nine million Czechs and Slovaks in a single empire (Pekník, *Slovensko*, p. 45).
46. Pekník, *Slovensko*, p. 43.
47. Pražák, *Masaryk a Slovensko*, p. 105. Štefánek, in his reply, regretted that Slovakia was *terra incognita* for Czech politicians and urged that they become better acquainted by personal visits (Pekník, *Slovensko*, p. 44).

48. Jablonický, 'Prispevok', p. 50; a slightly different version is given by Urban, in Holotik, *O vzájomných vzťahoch*, p. 244. See also Pekník, *Slovensko*, p. 44.
49. Stefánek, in *Sborník přednašek*, p. 253. See articles by Hodža on 29 July 1912 and on 26 September 1913 (the latter entitled 'The Living Corpse'), in which he invoked Palacký and Havlíček in favour of a transformed Monarchy in which all nations would have self-governnment (Votruba, in Štefánek, *Hodža*, p. 465 n.).
50. Štefánek, *Sborník*, pp. 253–4; Jablonický, 'Prispevok', p. 50.
51. Jablonický, 'Prispevok', pp. 50–1. Cf. Bokes, *Dejiny Slovenska*, pp. 336–7; *Dejiny Slovenska* (Cambel), IV, p. 308.
52. Gogolák, *Beiträge*, p. 142. This important meeting was not mentioned by Bokes or other authors. According to Pekník, Štefánek considered the meeting very successful; even Karel Kramář was brought closer to the Slovaks (*Slovensko*, p. 45).
53. Gogolák, 'Die historische Entwicklung des slowakischen Nationalbewusstseins', in *Die Slowakei als Mitteleuropäisches Problem* in *Geschichte und Gegenwart* (Munich, 1965), pp. 74, 77, 98. For the citation of Vajanský, see Joseph A. Mikus, *Slovakia, A Political History: 1918–1950* (Milwaukee, 1963), p. xxxii.
54. Masaryk, 'Slovenské vzpomnienky', in Doležal, *Masarykova cesta*, pp. 23–4. It seems quite inaccurate to describe Masaryk and the Hlasists as 'Czechoslavists' who were bent on wiping out Slovak national identity and replacing the Slovak language by Czech, as was argued by Michal Gávrik, 'Hlazismu alebo scestnosť' jedného apriorizmu', *Tvorba*, XI, 1, March 1991, pp. 23–5. The only evidence offered was his comment in a letter to Karel Kramář of 29 January 1889, that 'Slovak is nothing other than Czech and who wishes to make something else out of it, cannot manage it; ergo Russianism'. Masaryk's many later statements contrary to this earlier view are not noted.
55. Kálal, *Masarykův sborník*, IV, 1930, pp. 378–89; Šrobár, ibid., III, pp. 262–3.
56. Šrobar, 'Vliv', p. 263. See also Štefánek, in *Masaryková práce*, p. 241; Štefánek, in Weingart, *Sborník přednašěk*, p. 208.

6 FOE OF ANTI-SEMITISM

1. His alleged crime was justified in anti-Semitic circles as a 'ritual murder', according to the myth that Jews killed Christians and used their blood for ritual purposes.
2. Roland J. Hoffmann, *T. G. Masaryk und die tschechische Frage* (Munich, 1988), chap. 10, p. 198.
3. Stefan Schwarz, *Thomas G. Masaryk* (Nürnberg, 1949?), p. 15.
4. Important earlier sources include the following: Ernst Rychnovsky, *Masaryk und das Judentum* (Prague, 1931); in English, *Thomas G. Masaryk and the Jews*, tr. Benjamin R. Epstein (New York, 1941), in particular the contributions of Jan Herben, 'Thomas G. Masaryk, Jews and anti-Semitism', and Ernst Rychnovsky, 'The Struggle Against the Ritual Murder Superstition'; Jan Herben, *T. G. Masaryk* (Prague, 2nd edn, 1928–30; 5th edn, Prague, 1946), chap. 5; Ernst Rychnovsky, *Masaryk* (Prague 1930), pp. 91–103. Later scholarly studies, included in addition to Hoffmann cited above, František Červinka, 'The Hilsner Affair', *Yearbook XIII*, Leo Baeck Institute (London, 1968), pp. 142–67; Christopher Stölzl, 'Die "Burg" und Die Juden', in Karl Sosl, ed., *Die "Burg," Einflussreiche politische Kräfte um Masaryk und Beneš* (Munich and Vienna, 1974), 2, pp. 79–110; Jan Patočka, *Masaryk v boji proti antisemitismu* (published in *samizdat*, without title, or date). The latter, probably written in the fifties, was based on the archives of the Masaryk Institute where Patočka was engaged in the editing of Masaryk's works and is a

mine of bibliographic information (Patočka, pp. 20, 92). See also a popular book of reportage by the historian, Bohumil Cerný, *Vražda v Polné* (Prague 1968), 215 pp., and the anti-Semitic tract by Jan Rys (pseudo. for Jan Rozsévači), *Hilsneriáda a TGM* (Prague, March 1939), 293 pp. The latter was published on the eve of the Nazi occupation by the Czech fascist *Vlajka* for the fortieth anniversary of the Hilsner trial and called Nazi policy toward the Jews 'the common interest of all European nations' (Rys, p. 5).

A more recent source is Steven Beller, 'The Hilsner Affair, Nationalism, Anti-Semitism and the Individual in the Habsburg Monarchy at the Turn of the Century', in *T. G. Masaryk (1850–1937)* (London, 1989), II, ed. Robert B. Pynsent, chap. 4. See also Zdeněk Šolle, 'Malá česká dreyfusiáda', *Dějiny a součastnost*, X, 5, pp. 20–3.

5. On this report, see Roman Szporluk, *The Political Thought of Thomas G. Masaryk* (Boulder and New York, 1981), pp. 203–4; Cerný, *Vražda*, pp. 213–14; Červinka, 'Hilsner Affair', p. 156; Wilma Iggers (ed.) *Die Juden in Böhmen und Mähren* (Munich, 1986), p. 294.

6. For the above, see Masaryk's brochures cited more fully in n. 8 below: *Nutnost*, pp. 8–9; *Význam*, pp. 73 (on Hilsner), 37, 54, 59, 64–7 on the ritual-murder myth. For a full analysis of the ritual superstition, see T. G. Masaryk, 'O pověře rituelní' (On the ritual superstition), *Naše doba*, VII, 1900, pp. 321–35, 481–91, 579–89.

7. Patočka, pp. 24, 18 resp.

8. T. G. Masaryk, *Nutnost revidovati proces Polenský* (The Necessity to Review the Polná Trial) (Prague, 1899); Masaryk, *Význam procesu polenského pro pověru rituálni* (The Significance of the Polna Trial for Ritual Superstition) (Berlin?, 1900), both also available in German translation. For Masaryk's close following of the Písek trial, see his correspondence with the defence lawyer, in *T. G. Masaryk a náse součastnost*, (Prague 1980), *samizdat*, pp. 530–8.

9. On Bulova, Patočka, pp. 63–4; Červinka, 'Hilsner Affair', p. 148; on the medical faculty opinion, Patočka, pp. 53–5; Cerný, *Vražda*, pp. 150–4. See also Masaryk's partly censored article, 'Zur Motivation des Polnaer Verbrechens', *Die Zeit* (Vienna), 17 January 1900, pp. 51–3.

10. T. G. Masaryk, 'Zweiter Bericht über die Revision des Polnaer Processes', *Die Zeit* (Vienna), 17 November 1900, pp. 99–100. It is impossible to review here the proceedings of the two trials. The stenographic record of the Kutná Hora trial in 1899 was summarized by Rychnovsky, in *Masaryk and the Jews*, pp. 151–95. For a contemporary legal analysis by a German lawyer, see Arthur Nussbaum, *Der Polnaer Ritualmordprocess: Eine kriminal-psychologische Untersuchung* (Berlin, 1906, 1st and 2nd edns). See also Nussbaum's later article, 'The "Ritual-Murder" Trial of Polna', in Guido Kisch (ed.), *Historia Judaica*, IX, no. 1, (New York, 1947) in which he cites important legal studies on both sides of the controversy and subjects them to critical evaluation. Nussbaum notes the 'sinister significance' of the Hilsner trial as 'the only one which as the result of ritual-murder agitation has led to the sentencing of an innocent Jew' (p. 73).

11. *Význam*, p. 17.

12. Herben, *Masaryk*, p. 212.

13. *Význam*, pp. 78–9; Hoffmann *Masaryk*, p. 207; *Nutnost*, p. 1.

14. Herben, *Masaryk*, p. 200; *Masaryk and the Jews*, p. 12; Patočka, p. 29 for reservations on the authenticity of this version.

15. F. Soukup, *T. G. Masaryk jako politický průkopník, sociální reformátor a president státu* (Prague, 1930), pp. 56–7.

16. *Význam*, p. 5.

17. Masaryk, *Čas*, 18 November, 1899, cited in Hoffmann, *Masaryk*, p. 201.

18. *Význam*, p. 77.

19. On Rohling, see Cerný, *Vražda*, pp. 100–1; *The Jews of Czechoslovakia* (see n. 40 below), p. 67 n. 69; Dr Rohling, the author of *Der Talmudejude* (1971), was later charged with plagiarism and falsification, and had to resign his university position.

20. *Protokolle, Haus der Abgeordneten*, Session XVIII, pp. 3043–6, 5 December 1907; also given in part in Rychnovsky, *Masaryk and the Jews*, pp. 149–51.

21. For this and the following, see Herben, *Masaryk*, pp. 212ff. Rys later charged, without offering evidence, that Masaryk was of Jewish origin, through his 'real' father. The Jews, he wrote, dominated all spheres of public life in Austria, especially the press, and Masaryk was acting purely 'in the interest of Jewry' in taking up the Hilsner case. He thus gained a false reputation at home and abroad and became a kind of hero for Jews the world over; he eventually made Czechoslovakia 'a paradise for Jews' (*Hilsneriáda*, pp. 189, 190, 229, 231).

22. On publishing difficulties and the trials, Patočka, pp. 213, 44–6, 74; on political problems, ibid., p. 77; Stölzl, 'Die "Burg"'; pp. 87, 90.

23. For papers supporting Masaryk, see Černý, *Vražda*, p. 160; for student statements, J. Rokycana, 'Friends in Need', in *Masaryk and the Jews*, pp. 237–8; Červinka, 'The Hilsner Affair', p. 153. For student and social democratic support, especially on the issue of academic freedom, see Červinka, *Boje a smery českého studentstva na sklonku minulého a na počátku našeho století* (Prague, 1962), pp. 135–41. For Progressive views, see Alois Hajn, *Osvěta lidu*, no. 47, 21 November 1899; booklet by J. J. Moural, *Studentské demonstrace proti Masarykovi* (Prague, n.d.). On the workers, Patočka, p. 33.

24. Paročka, p. 78; Masaryk, *Čas*, 4 March, 1914, given in Herben, *Masaryk and the Jews*, pp. 18–9. See also Josef Jaroslav Filipi, *S Masarykovými, Hrst vzpomínek* (Prague, 1947), pp. 108–112.

25. Patočka, pp. 41–6: Hoffmann, *Masaryk*, pp. 208–9.

26. For the following, see espec. Gary Cohen, *The Politics of Ethnic Survival: Germans in Prague, 1861–1914* (Princeton, 1981), pp. 76–83, 221–32, 238–44, 260–3; Christoph Stölzl, *Kafka's böses Böhmen, Zur Sozialegeschichte eines Prager Juden* (Munich, 1975), espec. chap. III (on the Hilsner case), pp. 67–71;) Michael Riff, 'Czech Antisemitism and the Jewish Response Before 1914', *Wiener Library Bulletin*, 29, no. 39–40, pp. 8–20. See also Stölzl, 'Die "Burg"', pp. 79–88; Hoffmann, *Masaryk*, passim; Patočka, pp. 9–12; Roman Szporluk, *Political Thought*, pp. 120–3. For a personal testimony on Czech anti-Semitism, see Viktor Vohryzek, 'Masaryk v procese Polenském' (Masaryk in the Polná trial), in V. K. Škrach, ed., *Masarykův sborník* (Prague, 1930), IV, pp. 315–20. Bruce Garver, in *The Young Czech Party, 1874–1901 and the Emergence of a Multi-party System* (New Haven, 1978), pp. 302–3; n. 104 and 111, p. 502, gives scant attention to Czech anti-Semitism and minimizes its importance.

27. Cerný, *Vražda*, pp. 72–3.

28. Ibid., p. 160; Hoffmann, *Masaryk*, p. 204. See also Skilling, 'Austrian Origins of National Socialism', *University of Toronto Quarterly*, X, no. 13, (July 1941), pp. 482–92.

29. Rokycana, *Masaryk and the Jews*, p. 243; Patočka, pp. 78–9.

30. Herben, *Masaryk and the Jews*, p. 15.

31. Schwarz, *Masaryk*, pp. 13–14; 34–6; Masaryk, 'Naš Pan Fixl', in Masaryk, *Dvé povídky* (Prague, 1930), pp. 15–20, given in part in Herben, *Masaryk and the Jews*, pp. 3–5.

32. Masaryk, *Suicide and the Meaning of Civilization* (Chicago, 1970), pp. 214–15; Herben, *Masaryk and the Jews*, pp. 5–6.

33. Szporluk, *Masaryk*, pp. 119–21, 204; Schwartz, *Masaryk*, pp. 13–14.

34. Masaryk, *Karel Havlíček* (Prague, 1896), pp. 419–25; Patočka, pp. 6–7.

35. *Otázka sociální* (5th edn, Prague, 1948), chap. 8, section 120, pp. 173–82. This section was omitted in an abridged English version, Erazim V. Kohák, (ed.), *Masaryk on Marx* (Lewisburg, 1972).

36. Rychnovsky, *Masaryk and the Jews*, pp. 77–8. The book, by B. Kronberg, was entitled *Zionisten und Christen* (Leipzig, 1900).

37. *Ramcový program české strany lidové* (realistické) (Programme Framework of the Czech People's (Realist) party) (Prague 1900), pp. 85–9. According to Patočka Masaryk almost certainly wrote this section himself (pp. 47, 58–9). In his book, *Russia and Europe* (1906), Masaryk touched on the Jewish question only in one footnote where he praised the work of the Russian Jewish philosopher, Achad Haam, and found support for his own opinions on anti-Semitism, assimilation and Zionism. See Masaryk, *Rusko a Evropa*, II (Prague, 1921), 331, n. 2. On Achad Haam, see also Masaryk's review of church and religious life in 1904, *Naše doba*, 12 (1905), 522–3. See also Friedrich Thieberger, in *Masaryk and the Jews*, pp. 58–9: Schwarz, *Masaryk*, pp. 20–2; Patočka, p. 80.

38. Masaryk's article on the language conflict and anti-Semitism, *Die Zeit*, 4 November, 1899. See Patočka, pp. 15–16; Hoffmann, *Masaryk*, pp. 204–6, espec. n. 66.

39. The fullest treatment of Czech–Jewish relations, Jewish assimilation and Zionism, and Masaryk's position, is given by Hillel J. Kieval, *The Making of Czech Jewry. National Conflict and Jewish Society in Bohemia, 1870–1918* (New York and Oxford, 1988), espec. chaps 3 and 5. Kieval notes that Masaryk's religious views were particularly appealing both to the Czech–Jewish movement (Viktor Vohryzek) and to the Prague Zionists (pp. 87–92, 107–12). Also valuable are Kieval, 'Masaryk and Czech Jewry; The Ambiguities of Friendship', in *T. G. Masaryk (1850–1937)* (London, 1990), I, ed. Stanley B. Winters, chap. 13; Michael Riff, 'The Ambiguity of Masaryk's Attitude on the "Jewish Question"', ibid, II, chap. 5, in Winters, *T. G. Masaryk*, I, chap. 13; Steven Beller (ibid, II, chap. 4). See also Patočka, pp. 80, 84–6; Schwarz, *Masaryk*, pp. 23–5; Riff, 'Czech Antisemitism', pp. 16–19; Stölzl, 'Die "Burg"', pp. 102–3.

40. For the following, see Riff, 'Antisemitism', pp. 16–19; Hans Kohn, 'Before 1918 in the Historic Lands', and Ruth Kestenberg-Gladstein, 'The Jews between Czechs and Germans in the Historic Lands, 1848–1918', in *The Jews of Czechoslovakia, Historical Studies and Surveys*, 3 vols (Philadelphia and New York, 1971), I, pp. 12–20, 21–71 resp.; Felix Welsch, 'Masaryk and Zionism', in *Masaryk and the Jews*, pp. 76–81; Szporluk, *T. G. Masaryk*, pp. 120–21.

41. For this and the following, see Rychnovsky, *Masaryk and the Jews*, pp. 79–80; Patočka, pp. 84–6.

42. Cited above, p. 84. See also Patočka, pp. 80, 83.

43. For this see I. R. Polak, 'Mendl Bejlis', *Masaryk and the Jews*, pp. 248–58; Patočka, 87–91.

44. For the above, see Welsch, 'Masaryk and Zionism', pp. 81ff.; Stölzl, '"Die Burg"', pp. 87ff.

45. On the above, see especially Hoffmann, *Masaryk*, pp. 190 passim, incl. n. 83. Stölzl used the term 'ethical catharsis' but only to deny it had occurred, and presents conclusions which are contradictory and obscure but on the whole negative.

7 RELIGIOUS HERETIC

1. R. R. Betts, 'Masaryk's Philosophy of History,' *Slavonic Review*, XXVI, no. 66 (November 1947), p. 42. For Masaryk's later exposition of his views, see Karel Čapek, *Hovory s T. G. Masarykem* (Prague, 1969), pp. 111–15, 202–43.

2. Jaroslav Opat, *Filozof a politik, Tomáš Garrigue Masaryk, 1892–1893* (Prague, 1987), p. 42.

3. For this and the following, see especially Zdeněk Nejedlý, *T. G. Masaryk* (Prague, 1931–1937), espec. I, II *passim*; for this reference, I, pt 2, p. 121.

4. Simon R. Green, *Thomas Garrigue Masaryk: Educator of a Nation*, PhD thesis, University of California, 1976, pp. 35–7, 100.

5. Čapek, *Hovory* (Prague, 1969), p. 65.

6. Ferdinand Císař, V. K. Škrach (eds.), *Masarykův sborník* (Prague 1940), IV, pp. 354–65; Nejedlý, II, 271.

7. Roland J. Hoffmann, *T. G. Masaryk und die tschechische Frage* (Munich 1988), pp. 242, 263.

8. Opat, *Masaryk*, p. 41.

9. According to his close friend, Jozef Laichter, he was interested in individual rather than collective worship. Mrs Masaryk, he reported, felt that this contradicted the fact that they were registered in the Church, and she eventually decided to leave the Church. See Jozef Laichter, *T. G. Masaryk doma i na veřejnost* (Prague, 1938), pp. 75–89, 198–202.

10. *T. G. Masaryk, Sebevražda hromadným jevem společenským* (Prague 1904) (2nd edn, 1926). The original version of his habilitation thesis, written in 1879–80, was published in German in 1881. For an English version, see Masaryk, *Suicide and the Meaning of Civilization*, trans by William B. Weist and Robert G. Batson (Chicago, 1970). See Nejedlý, *Masaryk*, chaps IV, V. For a critical analysis of this work, see Hanus J. Hajek, *T. G. Masaryk Revisited: A Critical Assessment* (Boulder Colo. 1983), chap. VI. In 1913 Masaryk expressed similar views on suicide in Russia in his *Rusko a Evropa* p. 247ff. (*The Spirit of Russia*, pp. 219–22). For fuller reference, see below, n. 45.

11. Masaryk, *Suicide*, p. 84, *Sebevražda*, p. 90 (English translation modified from the Czech version).

12. For example, his lectures on practical philosophy and his book on concrete logic. (Nejedlý, *Masaryk*, III, pp. 292–5, IV, pp. 231–45).

13. *Moderní člověk a náboženství* (Prague, 1934); *Modern Man and Religion* (London, 1938, reprinted in 1970).

14. Machovec, *Tomáš G. Masaryk* (Prague, 1968), p. 139, passim, chaps V, VI.

15. J. B. Kozák, 'Masaryk as Philosopher', *Slavonic Review*, (March 1930), p. 494. See also Masaryk, *Americké přednášky* (2nd edn, Prague, 1929), pp. 37–73, 120–55. For useful summaries of Masaryk's views on religion, see *Masaryk Osvoboditel: Sborník*, (Prague, 1920), pp. 52–9, 126–37, 333–45. For analysis, see Miloslav Trapl, *Vědecký základy Masarykovy politiky* (Brno, 1946), pp. 128–38; Antonie van den Beld, *Humanity, The Political and Social Philosophy of Thomas G. Masaryk* (The Hague, 1975), chap. l; W. Schmidt, 'Masaryk a nábožnoství, in V. K. Škrach, (ed.), *Masarykův sborník*, IV, pp. 94–105; F. Žilka, 'Masaryk a protestantism', ibid., pp. 106–19; J. L. Hromadka, 'Masaryk as European', in *La Pensée de T. G. Masaryk* (Prague, 1937); W. Preston Warren, *Masaryk's Democracy, A Philosophy of Scientific and Moral Culture* (London, 1941), chap. 9; for a Jewish view, Friedrich Thieberger, 'Masaryk's Credo and the Jewish religion', in Ernst Rychnowsky, *Masaryk and the Jews* (New York, 1941), pp. 48–72. See also *Masaryk myslitel* (Prague, 1938).

16. *V boji o náboženství* (Prague, 1904), 3rd. edn, 1947.

17. Roman Szporluk, *The Political Thought of Thomas G. Masaryk* (New York 1981), p. 8 and chaps II, IV; Hoffmann, *Masaryk*, pp. 46–55, 141–3. For a useful summary of his thought on religious aspects of Czech history, see Draga B. Shillinglaw, *The Lectures of Professor T. G. Masaryk at the University of Chicago, Summer, 1902* (Lewisburg, 1978). See Chapter I above, I, pp. 6–7 and Chapter 10 below, pp. 147–8.

18. *Česká otázka; snahy a tužby národního obrození* (Prague, 1895), published later together with *Naše nynejší krise* (Prague, 1895) under both titles (Prague, 1948), pp. 13, 208. These important works were not translated into English. For excerpts, see René Wellek (ed.), *The Meaning of Czech History by Tomáš G. Masaryk* (Chapel Hill, N. Carolina, 1974). See also above and below, Chapters 1 and 10.

19. Masaryk, *Palackého idea národa českého*, 5th edn.(Prague, 1947), pp. 8–9. 17–18, 25–6.

20. Published, with other materials, as *Jan Hus, Naše obrození a naše reformace*, 3rd edn (Prague, 1923).

21. Lecture given in 1892, on the 300th anniversary of Komenský's birth, *J. A. Komensk'y* (2nd edn, Prague, 1920), pp. 8, 15. The government had banned any celebration of Komenský in the schools. At another time (date not given) Masaryk said that Christianity was given pure and genuine expression in the work and life of Komenský. (See Rudolf J. Vonka, 'Comenius und Masaryk', *Festschrift Th. G. Masaryk zum 80. Geburtstage* (Bonn, 1930), II, pp. 144–6.

22. The 1910 speech is given in Masaryk, *Hus*, pp. 147–9, 152, 1545–9.

23. T. G. Masaryk, *O pokrokovém postavení slovenské mládeže*, lecture on 15 August 1911 (Uherské hradiště 1935).

24. The following is based in large part on the full treatment of these issues in Hoffmann, *Masaryk*, chap. 11.

25. Ibid., pp. 243, 251. See also Masaryk's speeches in this connection in *Jan Hus*, pp. 163–78.

26. Hoffmann, pp. 254–9.

27. For this and the following, ibid., pp. 245–53. See also Chapter 1 above, pp. 6–7.

28. For the following, see Hoffman ibid., chap.13. For Masaryk's views, see *Lectures of Masaryk*, chap. 17 and also *Los von Rom, An Address by Thomas Garrigue Masaryk* (Boston, 1902).

29. See Masaryk, *Česká otázka*, pp. 191–207, espec. pp. 193–4. also p. 255.

30. 30 January 1893, given in Jiří Kovtun, *Slovo má poslanec Masaryk* (Munich, 1985), pp. 77–82. Most of the political programmes of parties with which Masaryk was associated called for the removal of religious teaching from the schools. Only the Realist Programme (1900) spoke of the teaching of religion by clergymen of different denominations as a basis of moral behaviour. The laicization of schools was put most strongly in the 1912 programme of the Czech Progressive party which demanded a school free of religious influence of any confessional creed. Religious teaching should be carried out by lay teachers and would be non-confessional. See *Program česke strany pokrokové* (Prague, 1912), pp. 77–8.

31. T. G. Masaryk and V. Bouček, *O svobodě a volnosti přesvědčení* (Prague, 1904) also given as chap. 1, *V boji o náboženství*.

32. Masaryk, 'Řeč ke studentům o vědě a náboženství; náboženství ve škole', *Studentský Almanac*, 1906 (Prague, 1906); a German version in Masaryk, *Ein Katechetenspiegel* (Frankfurt am Main, 1906), with explanatory material by the anonymous translator. The booklet also included sixty-five depositions which Masaryk had collected of cases of denunciation of teachers by catechists (instructors in religion in the schools).

33. For Catholic attacks on Masaryk, see Hromadka, 'Masaryk as European', p. 17, n.42.

34. For various versions of this passage, see Paul Selver, *Masaryk, A Biography* (Prague, 1940); Jan Herben, *T. G. Masaryk* (Prague, 1926, I, p. 258;

Katechetenspiegel, pp. 5, 30. On the trial see V. Bouček, 'Profesor Masaryk v soudní síni', P. Maxa and L. Sychrava (eds), *Sborník vzpomínek na T. G. Masaryka* (Prague, 1930), pp. 94–8.

35. The text of the speeches given in *Inteligence a náboxnost* (Prague, 1907).
36. Herben, *Masaryk*, II, pp. 275–83; Selver, *Masaryk*, pp. 197–207. See Chapter 4 above pp. 54–5.
37. For speeches by Masaryk and F. Drtina on 3, 4 and 5 December 1907, *Za svědomí a učení* (Prague, 1908).
38. *Masaryk, Freie wissenschaftliche und kirchlich gebundene Weltanschauung und Lebensauffassung; Die kirchenpolitische Bedeutung der Wahrmund-Affäre* (Vienna, 1908).
39. For the text of the confiscated parts of Machar's booklet and the debate in Parliament on 17 May, see Emil Saudek (ed.), *Dichter Machar und Professor Masaryk im Kampfe gegen den Klerikalismus* (Vienna and Leipzig, 1912).
40. Originally published as *Přednášky profesora T. G. Masaryka* (Svaz svobodo-myslných, Chicago, 1907). These lectures, plus two others, were published twenty years later as *Americké přednášky*.
41. Ibid., pp. 31–5.
42. *O klerikalismu a socialismu* (30 March 1907) (Valašské mezříčí, 1907).
43. Masaryk, *Otázka sociální* (2 vols, Prague, 1948), chap. 9; abridged English translation, *Masaryk on Marx*, ed. and trans. E.V.Kozák (Lewisburg, 1972), chap. 8. See above, Chapter 4, pp. 59–60.
44. Ibid., Czech, I, pp. 188–93, II, 141–7, 194–216; English, pp. 131–40, 279–85, 296–312.
45. First published in German, it later appeared in Czech, *Rusko a Evropa, k ruské filosofii dějin a nabožensví*, (2 vols Prague, 1919, 2nd edn, 1930) and in English, *The Spirit of Russia, Studies in History, Literature and Philosophy*, trans. Eden and Cedar Paul (2 vols, London, 1919). The following is based mainly on part III, 'Democracy versus theocracy: the problem of revolution'. Citations are to the Czech edition. A third volume, discovered much later, appeared as *The Spirit of Russia*, ed. George Gibian, trans. Robert Bass (III. London, 1967).
46. Van den Beld, *Humanity*, p. 32.
47. Čapek, *Hovory*, p. 206.
48. See F. Žilka, 'Masaryk a protestantism', pp. 106–19.
49. Machovec, *Masaryk*, p. 119 and passim.
50. Warren, *Masaryk*, p. 220. See also Vonka, 'Comenius und Masaryk', II, pp. 133–52.
51. Van den Beld, *Humanity*, pp. 29–37. For quotations from his works on this theme, Z. Franta, (ed.), *T. G. Masaryk, Mrávní názory* (Prague, 1925), pp. 16–37.
52. Čapek, *Hovory*, pp. 210, 214, 235–6.
53. On theism, see ibid., pp. 202–5.
54. Schmidt, 'Masaryk a náboženství', Masarykův sborník, IV, pp. 96–125.

8 DEFENDER OF WOMEN'S RIGHTS

1. See the important article by Maria L. Neudorfl, 'Masaryk and the Woman's Question', *T. G. Masaryk (1850–1937)* (New York, 1989) I, *Thinker and Politician*, ed. Stanley B. Winters, p. 258.
2. Hajn, 'Masaryk a ženská otázka', *Osvěta lidu*, on the 70th anniversary of Masaryk's birth, published in F. F. Plamínková, *Masaryk a ženy*, (Prague, 1930), pp. 249–50.

3. Bruce N. Garver, 'Women and Czech Society, 1848–1914', paper given at the Masaryk conference, 1986, not published. See also Tereza Nováková, *Ze ženského hnutí* (Prague, n.d., circa 1912), espec. pp. 84–5, 244, 315–20.

4. On Charlotte Masaryk, see Pavel Kosatík, 'Česká z Ameriky. Charlotta Garrigue Masaryková (1850–1923)', in *Osm žen z Hradu. Manželky prezidentů*, pp. 11–70; Stanislav Polák, *Charlotte Garrigue Masaryková* (Prague, 1992). A biography by I. J. Fischerová, *Charley Garrigue-Masaryková* (Prague, 1936) is informative but eulogistic. On Charlotte Masaryk and her relations with Masaryk, see also Zdeněk Nejedlý, *T. G. Masaryk*, (5 vols, Prague, 1930–37), I, part 2, pp. 351–82; II, pp. 26–30; Vojtech Lev, *Pamatce Ch. G. Masarykové* (Prague, 1923); Jozef Laichter, *T. G. Masaryk doma i veřejnost* (Prague, 1938), II, pp. 91–129.

5. Čapek, *Hovory s T. G. Masarykem* (Prague, 1937), pp. 8, 74.

6. Hajn, *Ženská otázka*, p. 254.

7. Letter of 29 January 1910, given in *Mnohoženství a jednoženství* (Prague, 1925), pp. 6–7; also published in *Masaryk a ženy*, p. 78; also Miladá Veselá, ibid., p. 188. A close friend, Josef Jaroslav Filipi, recalled Masaryk's statement that he attached the greatest importance to what his wife said, and that he undertook nothing without her approval (Jozef J. Filipi, *S Masarykov'ymi, Hrst vzpomínek* (Prague, 1947), p. 25.

8. *Přednášky o practické filosofii*, 1884, unpublished, circulated in lithograph form, cited by Zdeněk Franta, ed., *Morální názory* (2nd. edn, Prague, 1925), pp. 136–8. For a full summary of these lectures, see Nejedlý, *T. G. Masaryk*, III, chap. 11.

9. Herben, *Masarykův rodinný život* (7th edn, Prague, 1937), pp. 23, 64.

10. Alice G. Masaryková, *Dětství a mladí* (Pittsburgh, 1960), pp. 87–97; Laichter, *Masaryk doma*, III, pp. 133–88; L. Schieszlova, in *Masaryk a ženy*, pp. 177–8.

11. Ruth Crawford Mitchell, *Alice Garrigue Masaryk* (Pittsburgh, 1980), pp. 83–4. See also Charlotte G. Masaryková, *Listy do vězení* (Prague, 1948), pp. 68–9.

12. Mitchell, *Masaryk*, p. 240; Polák, *Masaryková*, p. 30.

13. Herben, *Rodinný život*, p. 51.

14. There is no convincing evidence of the reasons for his departure. According to Marcia Davenport, the father was probably troubled by the fact that Jan abhorred study and never attended a university. She also cites the scarcely credible report, given her by Jan, that his father beat him again and again. When he decided to leave for America he is said to have reported that his father consented and gave him such money as he could. According to her, he enjoyed gambling and girls during his American sojourn. He accepted employment from Masaryk's friend, Charles Crane, and eventually married his daughter (Davenport, *Too Strong for Fantasy*, New York, 1967, pp. 317–23).

15. Talk given in Boston in October 1893, *Naše doba*, I, no. 1, pp. 46–9, given also in *Masaryk a ženy*, pp. 155–61.

16. His four major speeches, all published in *Masaryk a ženy*, were *Mnohoženství a jednoženství* (Polygyny and Monogyny), 1899 (also published separately, see above, n. 7); *Moderní názor na ženu* (A Modern Standpoint on Women), 1904; *Postavení ženy v rodině a ve veřejném životě* (The Position of The Woman in Family and in Public Life), 1907, also published in *Americké přednášky* (American Lectures) (Prague, 1929); *Ženy u Ježiše a Pavla* (Jesus and Paul on Women), 1910, published as *O ženě* (On Women), (Prague, 1929; also given in V. K. Škrach (ed.), *Masarykův sborník* (Prague, 1926–27), II, pp. 24lff.). In the following pages a composite picture of Masaryk's views as expressed in these essays is given, often in his own words, with citations to *Masaryk a ženy* in the text where appropriate.

17. 'Žensky sjezd', *Naše doba*, IV, 1897, pp. 826–9; also in *Masaryk a ženy*, pp. 159–60.

18. Ibid., p. 67; see also Masaryk, *Otázka sociální* (Prague, 1948), II, 92.

19. Franta, *Morální názory*, p. 148.
20. Hajn,*Ženská otázka*, p. 211.
21. In his earlier study of suicide Masaryk expressed different views, emphasizing the differences of the two sexes as to the motivation of suicide and stating, without offering evidence, that women suffer greater pangs of conscience, shame and jealousy, but were on the other hand more removed from the worries of politics and business. In their struggle for emancipation women were threatened more than men as they were not accustomed to the harsher competition of life. See Masaryk, *Suicide and the Meaning of Civilization* (Chicago and London, 1970), pp. 25–7. See also his lectures on practical philosophy, in which Masaryk spoke of women as having more gentle than reasoning characteristics, and being therefore more suited for work in the family or in schools or nursing. At that time he believed that women would not be successful in politics (Nejedlý, *Masaryk*, III, 227).
22. Masaryk, *Humanitní ideály*, (Prague, 1968), pp. 57–8.
23. *Přednášky*, 1884, cited by Franta, *Morální názory*, pp. 136–9.
24. *Česká otázka; Naše nynější krise* (Prague, 1948), pp. 313–14. But in his 1907 election campaign Masaryk advocated the legalization of divorce (see Chapter 4 above, p. 55).
25. In his lectures on practical philosophy Masaryk described monogamy as 'a union of two people who marry on the basis of mutual understanding and mutual recognition of one another and from a noble love, and the desire to live together, guided by the moral and reasonable rules of ethics, politics and sociology' (Nejedlý, *Masaryk*, III, p. 230). Although Masaryk used the term polygamy as well as the Czech word *mnohoženství* what he seems to have had in mind was polygyny, i.e. having sexual relations with more than one person. This applied equally to men and women – polyandry was also taboo. Although he did not refer to homosexual relations, there is no doubt that he would have condemned this, too, had it been a matter of public concern at the time.
26. *Přednášky*, cited by Franta, *Morální názory*, pp. 142–44.
27. Speech, published in *Čas*, nos. 330 and 332, 1906, cited by Franta, ibid., pp. 144–8.
28. V. Bouček, in *Masaryk a ženy*, pp. 306–7.
29. Franta, *Morální názory*, pp. 140–1.
30. Ibid., p. 142.
31. Karel Čapek, *Hovory s T. G. Masarykem*, pp. 51–2.
32. Masaryk, *O etice a alkoholismu* (Prague, 1912), pp. 18–20); the greater part of this work is also given in Franta, *Morální názory*, pp. 148–56; Masaryk, *O alkoholismu* (Prague, 1908), pp. 16–18. See also Anna Snižková, in *Masaryk a ženy*, pp. 328–9; Chapter 1 above, p. 36 and n. 9.
33. 'Žena u Ježiše a Pavla', *Masaryk a ženy*, pp. 97–111.
34. Masaryk, *Otázka sociální*, II, pp. 29–58, 82–97.
35. Ibid., p. 97. Masaryk also condemned the views of August Bebel, the German social democratic leader, for views similar to those of Engels on divorce and free love, the powerfulness of the sexual instinct, and the neglect of morality. See Masaryk, *Česká otázka*, pp. 315–9.
36. For a brief summary of some of these articles, see Kamil Harmach, 'Ženská otázka v Masarykové "Naše době"', in *Masaryk a ženy*, pp. 139–54. For a full text of the articles on Musset and Goethe, see Masaryk, *Modern Man and Religion* (London, 1938), pp. 218–55, 256–86 resp. See also B. Prokešová, 'Masaryk on Women in Society', University of London conference on Masaryk, 1986, mimeographed, not published. For a severe critique of Masaryk's interpretations see Karel Brušak, 'Masaryk and Belles-lettres', in *T. G. Masaryk, 2, Thinker and Critic*, ed. Robert B. Pynsent, 154–7.

37. Garver, 'Women in Czech Society', cited above, n. 3; also Garver, 'Masaryk and Czech Politics, 1906–1914', Winters, *T. G. Masaryk*, I, pp. 237–8.
38. *Ramcový program české strany lidové (realistické)* (Prague, 1900), pp. 11, 34, 54–5.
39. *Česká strana pokroková a jeji ustavující valný sjezd* (Pardubice, 1906), pp. 58, 62. Alois Hajn's draft programme of 1905 had declared that women must be placed on an absolutely equal level with men as to human and civic rights. One could not speak of 'a really free people if its greater half is subjugated morally, culturally, politically and economically'.
40. *Program české strany pokrokové* (Prague, 1912), pp. 70, 112–15, 154–6. The programme also included extensive proposals for equal training for women in coeducational schools at all levels, and for special institutions for needy or unmarried mothers, for abandoned and orphaned children, and for feeble-minded and needy children.
41. Neudorfl, 'Masaryk and the Women's Question', Winters, *Masaryk*, p. 258.
42. *Masaryk a ženy*, pp. 122, 125, 126, 129, 185.
43. Neudorfl, 'Masaryk and the Woman's Question', pp. 261, 272.

9 ARCH-CRITIC OF AUSTRO-HUNGARIAN FOREIGN POLICY

1. O. Butter, 'Zahraniční politika T. G. Masaryka', *Zahraniční politika*, 18, no. 4, 1939, pp. 124–42; Jaromír Doležal, 'Masarykovy boje s Aerenthalem', V. K. Škrach, (ed.), *Masarykův sborník*, V, pp. 133–63. Brief references to Masaryk's foreign policy views were given in 'T. G. Masaryk and Karel Kramář, Long Years of Friendship and Rivalry,' in *T. G. Masaryk (1850–1937)*, I, *Thinker and Politician*, ed. Stanley B. Winters (London and New York, 1990), chap. 7. On Czech foreign policy, see Zdeněk Tobolka, *Politické dějiny československého národa od r. 1848 až do dnešní doby* (Prague, 1936), III, no. 2, pp. 461–76, 611–34. For outside analysis, see Irwin Abrams, 'The Austrian Question at the Turn of the Twentieth Century', *Journal of Central European Affairs*, 2 (July 1944), pp. 186–201; A. J. P. Taylor, *The Habsburg Monarchy, 1809–1918* (London, 1948), chap. 17. For Marxist analysis, see Jiři Kořalka, 'The Czech Question in International Relations at the Beginning of the 20th Century', *Slavonic and East European Review*, 48 (1970), pp. 248–60; Jiři Křížek, 'Česká buržoasní politika a "česká otázka" v letech 1900–1914', *Československý časopis historický*, VI (1958), pp. 621–61; the former is marred by total neglect of Masaryk, the latter by an interpretation of his role exclusively as a defender of bourgeois interests.
2. The texts of Masaryk's speeches in the Austro-Hungarian Delegations and Reichsrat are given in the official parliamentary protocols, *Stenographisches Protokoll, Delegation des Reichsrathes* (cited below as DRR), and *Haus der Abgeordneten* (cited as HA). Some of these were excerpted by J. Kovtun, *Slovo má poslanec Masaryk* (Munich, 1985); some were summarized by Ernst Rychnowsky, *Masaryk* (Prague, 1930, 2nd edn). Several were published by Masaryk as booklets which sometimes differed in content from the original texts: *Tak zvaný velezrádný proces v zahřebě* (The So-called Treason Trial in Zagreb), Prague, 1909 (henceforth *Tak zvaný*), for Reichsrat speeches on 14 and 18 May 1909; *Rakouská zahraniční politika a diplomacie* (Austrian Foreign policy and Diplomacy) henceforth *Rak. pol.* (Prague 1911), for speeches of 8 and 11 November 1910. See also Masaryk's analysis of his speeches of November 1910 and February 1911, and other material, in *Vasić–Forgách–Aerenthal, Einiges Material zur Charakteristik unserer*

Diplomatie (Some Materials on the Character of Our Diplomacy) henceforth cited as *Vasić* (Prague 1911).

3. Masaryk, *Česká otázka; Naše nynější krise* (first published in 1895) (Prague, 1948, 6th edn), pp. 284–5.

4. *Rámcový program české strany lidové (realistické)*, (Prague, 1900) pp. 14–15.

5. *Program české strany pokrokové* (Prague 1912), pp. 310–32.

6. *Česká otázka*, p. 16 passim, pp. 66–8, pp. 124 passim. See Adolf Černý, *Masaryk a slovanstvo* (Prague, 1921) for a detailed outline of Masaryk's prewar and postwar views.

7. Masaryk, 'O novoslavismu', *Čas*, 13–15 January 1910. See, in particular, Paul Vyšný, *Neo-Slavism and the Czechs 1898–1914* (London, 1977). On Slavism in general, see Winters, 'Austroslavism, Panslavism, and Russophilism in Czech Political Thought, 1870–1900', in Winters and Joseph Held (eds), *Intellectual and Social Developments in the Habsburg Empire from Maria Theresa to World War 1* (New York and London, 1975), pp. 165–202. Brief references are given by Roland J. Hoffmann, *Masaryk und die tschechische Frage* (Munich, 1988), pp. 360–68; Bruce M. Garver, *The Young Czech Party 1874–1901 and the Emergence of a Multi-Party System* (New Haven, 1978), pp. 12, 273; Garver, 'Masaryk and Czech Politics, 1906–1914', in Winters, *Masaryk*, I, pp. 247–9. For Marxist accounts of Kramář and Neo-Slavism, see Karel Herman and Zdeněk Sládek, *Slovanská politika Karla Kramáře* (Prague, 1971) and more dogmatist in spirit, Vladislav Šťástný, (ed.), *Slovanství v národním životě Čechů a Slováků* ((Prague, 1968), espec. chap. IV by Karel Herman, chap. VIII by Šťastný. Of interest is the retrospective study by Edvard Beneš, *Úvahy o slovanství, Hlavní problémy slovanské politiky* (first published in 1925–6) (London, 1944) and Kramář's polemical reply, *Na obranu slovanské politiky* (Prague, 1926).

8. The most significant study of Austro-Slavism is that of Winters, 'Austroslavism'. Of less value is Hugo Hantsch, 'Pan-Slavism, Austro-Slavism, Neo-Slavism: The All Slav Congresses and the Nationality Problems of Austria-Hungary', *Austrian History Yearbook*, 1 (1965), pp. 23–37. On Kramář's Austroslavism, see Vyšný, *Neo-Slavism*, pp. 27–9, 248–9; on Masaryk, ibid., pp. 95, 186; Winters, *Masaryk*, I, pp. 170–2; Winters, 'Austroslavism', pp. 187–91.

9. Masaryk rarely used the term Austro-Slavism, except in referring to the views of others. But see Ctíbor Nečas, *Balkán a česká politika* (Brno, 1972), p.107.

10. Milada Paulová, *Tomáš G. Masaryk a jihoslované* (Prague, 1938), pp. 5–34; also in M. Weingart, (ed.), *Sborník přednášek o T. G. Masarykovi* (Prague, 1931), pp. 177–200; Irena G. Godina, 'The Influence of T. G. Masaryk on the Slovenes up to 1914', in Winters, *Masaryk*, I, chap. 9. On the last points, see Paulová, *Masaryk a jihoslované*, pp. 48, 53–4. For her study on the Balkan wars and the Czech people, see below, n. 55.

11. His ideas on Russia were embodied much later in his great study, *Russland und Europa* (2 vols. Jena, 1913). This was published in English, *The Spirit of Russia* (London, 1919); a hitherto unpublished third volume was published under this title (New York, 1967), ed. George Gibian. Critical essays on Masaryk's interpretation of Russia were published in *T. G. Masaryk (1850–1937)* (London, 1989 and 1990), vol. I, ed. S. B. Winters, chap. 12, by Hans Lemberg; vol. 2, ed. by Robert B. Pynsent, chap. 6 and 7, by Rolf H.W. Theen and James P. Scanlan; vol. 3, ed. by Harry Hanak, chap. 9 and 10, by Antonín Měšťan and Paul. I. Trensky. See also Hanus J. Hajek, ed., *T. G. Masaryk Revisited. A Critical Assessment* (Boulder, 1983), pp. 133–44.

12. *Česká otázka*, p. 22.

13. E.g in his speech at Strakonice in 1891, given in part in J. B. Kozák (ed.), *Masaryková práce* (Prague, 1930), pp. 80–5.

14. Vyšný, *Neo-Slavism*, p. 248.

15. DRR, Session XXIX, 14 June 1893, pp. 20–1; Rychnowsky, *Masaryk*, pp. 80–3.
16. DRR, 44, 8 November 1910, p.95; 11 November 1910, p. 275; 45, 22 February p. 60; DRR, XXI, 31 October 1912, pp. 5667–69; XXI, 26 May 1913, p. 7239.
17. *Democratism v politice* (Prague, 1912), also published with *Ideály humanitní*, (Prague 1968), p. 104. See Chapter 2 above, pp. 26–8.
18. *Ramcový program*, pp. 14–15.
19. *Česká strana pokroková a její ustavující valný sjezd*, 21 January 1906 (Prague 1906), p. 32.
20. *Program strany pokrokové*, p. 31.
21. Masaryk, *Rak.pol.*, pp. 14–17.
22. DRR, 44, 8 November 1910, p. 92.
23. DRR, 45, 22 February 1911, pp. 63, 59.
24. HA, XXI, 31 October 1912, p. 5670; Kovtun, *Slovo*. pp. 197–201, Kozák, *Masaryková práce*, pp. 168–73.
25. HA, 31 October 1912, p. 5665; Kozák, *Masaryková práce*, p. 170.
26. 9 December 1908, Rychnowsky, *Masaryk*, p.124.
27. Ibid., 17 December 1908, pp. 125ff.
28. 6 January 1913, Kozák, *Masaryková práce*, p. 175.
29. 26 May 1913, Kovtun, *Slovo*, p. 204.
30. 22 February 1911, in *Rak. pol.* pp. 60–4. Cf. version in DRR, 22 February 1911, pp. 58ff. On the 1900 programme, see below, n. 32.
31. DRR, XXI, 7 November 1911, pp. 1374–9; excerpts in Kovtun, *Slovo*. pp. 191–5.
32. *Program strany pokrokové*, pp. 33–4. The wording of the People's party programme of 1900 was essentially the same (*Ramcový program*, p. 15).
33. Kozák, *Masaryková práce*, pp. 173–5.
34. Cited in note 13 above; also Jan Herben, *T. G. Masaryk* (Prague, 1926), pp. 118–19. See also Butter, *Zah. pol.*,p. 133.
35. Kovtun, *Slovo*, pp. 71–6. Masaryk was not alone in his stand. His parliamentary colleagues, Karel Kramář and Gustav Eim, also condemned the Triple Alliance for similar reasons (Winters, *Masaryk*, pp. 168–70; Nečas, *Balkán*, pp. 30–4). Kramář favoured a *rapprochement* with Russia in place of the Triple Alliance.
36. DRR, XXIX, 14 June 1893, pp. 15–25; Rychnowsky, *Masaryk*, pp. 80–83.
37. DRR, 44, 8 November 1910, pp. 88–9 and 45, 22 February 1911, pp. 59–60; given in a somewhat different version in *Rak. pol.*, pp. 9–10, 65–6.
38. 22 February 1911, *Rak. pol.*, pp. 65–6; cf. version in DRR, 45, pp. 59–60. This argument was reproduced almost verbatim in the Progressive party programme of 1912 (*Program*, pp. 31–2).
39. 18 and 19 October 1892, DRR, XXXVII; excerpts in Kovtun, *Slovo*, pp. 53–6.
40. DRR, XXIX, 14 June 1893.
41. Nečas, *Balkán*, pp. 57–66, 89, 108; Vyšný, *Neo-Slavism*, p. 129 passim; Winters, *Masaryk*, I, p. 172.
42. For contemporary discussion of the trials, see Seton-Watson, *The Southern Slav Question and the Habsburg Monarchy*, first published in 1911 (New York, 1969); for a later scholarly analysis, based on archival documents, see Doležal, 'Masarykovy boje', pp. 133–63.
43. Seton-Watson, *Southern Slav Question*, pp. 192–3.
44. DRR, 44, 8 November 1910, pp. 86–97 and 11 November 1910, pp. 265–75; 45, 22 February 1911, pp. 59–73 and 24 February pp.163–4. See also *Rak. pol.* for these, and for a speech on 16 November pp. 52–6. For the following, ibid., pp. 6, 13, 18, 24–5, 38, 44–5, 55–6, 74–5.
45. Texts of both speeches given in Masaryk, *Tak zvaný*. For citations, see pp. 32, 40. Text of interpellation, p. 150. The texts differ somewhat from the excerpts given by Kovtun, *Slovo*, pp. 137–56, and Rychnowsky, *Masaryk*, pp. 132–41.

46. For a detailed contemporary study, see Seton-Watson, *The Southern Slav Question*, See also Arnold Suppan, 'Masaryk and the Trials for High Treason against South Slavs in 1909', in Winters, *T. G. Masaryk*, I, chap. 9.
47. See Seton-Watson, *South Slav Question*, chap. 10; pp. 198–207 for the Friedjung articles, and pp. 250–5 for Masaryk's evidence.
48. For the text, see DRR, 44, pp. 86–97; abridged in Kovtun, *Slovo*, pp. 157–73. Masaryk, *Rak. pol* (pp. 5–41) gives a somewhat different version and includes also excerpts from Aerenthal's responses.
49. DRR, 44, 11 November 1910, pp. 266–75; excerpts in Kovtun, *Slovo*, pp. 168–73.
50. See Masaryk, *Vasić.* For his speeches in the Delegations see *Rak. pol.*, pp. 57–93, given in part in Kovtun, *Slovo*, pp. 179–90. See also Seton-Watson, *South Slav Question*, chap. XI.
51. DRR, 45, 29 December 1910, pp. 21–32; Kovtun, *Slovo*, pp. 173–8.
52. Text in DRR, 45, pp. 59–73, and pp. l63–4; Kovtun, *Slovo*, pp. 178–90; a somewhat different version is given in *Rak. pol.*, pp. 60–9.
53. Henry Wickham Steed, *Through Thirty Years, 1892–1922, A Personal Narrative* (New York, 1924), p. 313.
54. See *Masarykův sborník*, IV, espec. 24–30. Slovene students of his also bore witness to the influence of his ideas (pp. 42–50). See n. 10 above.
55. For this see well-documented Marxist accounts by Milada Paulová, *Balkánské války 1912–1913 a česka lid'*, Rozpravy Československé Akademie věd, no. 73, 1963 (Prague, 1963); Nečas, *Balkán a české politika*, on war credits, pp. 72–3.
56. 2 May 1912, Rychnowsky, *Masaryk*, pp. 165–8. Nečas charges that the main Czech political leaders supported Austria-Hungarian imperialism in the Balkans and opposed German imperialism in the interests of the Czech bourgeoisie.
57. HA, XXI, 31 October 1912, pp. 5662–71; detailed excerpts given in Kozák, *Masaryková práce*, pp. 168–73; also in Kovtun, *Slovo*, pp. 196–202. Earlier, in November 1910, Masaryk had dealt at length with Turkish backwardness. Although he sympathized with the Young Czech objectives, he doubted that they could change ancient customs and abolish absolutism. (DRR, 44, 8 November 1910, p. 96).
58. 16, 19, and 20 November 1912, summarized briefly by Rychnowsky, *Masaryk*, pp. 170–3.
59. Čas, XXVII, no. 8, 9 January 1913, given in part in Kozák, *Masaryková. práce*, pp.173–7.
60. HA, XXI, 26 May 1913, pp. 7237–44; excerpts in Rychnowsky, *Masaryk*, pp.173–7; Kovtun, *Slovo*, pp. 204–9.
61. Kovtun, *Slovo*, p. 209.
62. Rychnowsky, *Masaryk*, p. 177, n. 1. Text was not found.
63. Roman Szporluk, *The Political Thought of Thomas G. Masaryk* (Boulder and New York, 1981), pp. 123–4.
64. See Chapter 10 below, p. 152; and n. 21.

10   ADVOCATE OF CZECH INDEPENDENCE

1. Introduction to the first edition, 1894, *Česká otázka*, published with *Naše nynější krise (NNK)* (6th edn, Prague, 1948) p. 3 and pp. 12, 22, 90–2. Other references to the Czech question, the nation and nationality are too numerous to cite and may be located in the index. See also Masaryk, *Palackého idea národa českého* (Prague, 1947), pp. 39–40.

2. 'Vývoj evropské společnosti' (cited in note 4), p. 131. Masaryk's terms *českost* and *češství* may be translated as 'Czechness' or 'Czechism'. Masaryk occasionally used the term 'nečeský' (non-Czech), *Česká otázka/NNK*, pp. 172, 228, 244, 249.

3. *Ideály humanitní* (Prague, 1968), p. 11; *The Ideals of Humanity* (London, 1938), p. 17; *Demokratism*, p. 2. In his postwar *Making of a State* (London, 1927) Masaryk wrote: 'the more national we are, the more human we shall be, the more human, the more national' (p. 409) (in Czech, *Světová revoluce*, p. 559). See Chapter 1 above, pp. 6–7.

4. These include Masaryk, *Karel Havlíček* (Prague, 1896), chaps XIV, XVII, XVIII, pp. 460–80; *Otázka sociální* (7th edn, Prague, 1948), II, chap. 8; *Rusko a evropa* (Prague, 1919), I, p. 333–46; 'Zur deutsch-böhmischen Ausgleichsfrage', *Die Zeit* (Vienna), IV, 25 April 1896, also in Czech, 'Dohodnutí Čechů s Němci', in *Anketa Rozhledů*, V, 1896, pp. 418–25; the latter reproduced in J. B. Kozák (ed.), *Masaryková práce* (Prague, 1930), pp. 114–21; 'Humanity and Nationality', *Naše doba*, IV (1897), pp. 193–205, plus an editorial note also probably written by Masaryk, ibid., pp. 256–9; *Beseda* (discussion) with others, on nationality, internationalism and humanity, *Čas*, XI, no, 7 (30 January 1897), 72–6; *Řeč posl. T. G. Masaryka v debatě o zatímním rozpočtu, dne 20 července 1907* (Prague, 1907); letter to *Neue Freie Presse*, 24 December 1907, published in A. von Czedik, *Zur Geschichte der k. k. oesterreichischen Ministerien, 1861–1920* (Teschen, Vienna and Leipzig, 1917–1920), IV, pp. 226–34, also published in *Čas*, 24 December 1907; 'State and Nationality', ibid., XXIII, no. 101 (11 April 1908), pp. 1–2; 'Vývoj evropské společnosti v devatenáctém století' (1899) in V. K. Škrach, (ed.) *Masarykův sborník*, II (1926–7), pp. 127–32; *Národní filosofie doby novější* (Jičín, 1905); *Problém malého národa*. (Kroměříž, 1905), 4th edn, published with *Ideály humanitní* (Prague, 1968), pp. 66–95. See also Miroslav Trapl, *Vědecké základy Masarykovy politiky* (Brno, 1946), chaps. 5, 6, 7; Roman Szporluk, *The Political Thought of Thomas G. Masaryk* (Boulder and New York, 1981), chap. V; Roland J. Hoffmann, *T. G. Masaryk und die tschechische Frage* (Munich, 1988), pp. 21–2, 449–61; František Kaufman, 'T. G. Masaryk and the Problem of National Identity', *Kosmas*, IV, 2 (Winter, 1985), pp. 71–81; in Czech, in *Masaryk a soucašnost*, ed. Milan Machovec, Petr Pithart and Miloš Pojar (Prague, 1992) (originally published in *samizdat*, 1980), pp. 118–27; Zdeněk Suda,' The Theories of Nation in the Work of T. G. Masaryk and Emanuel Rádl', in Josef Novák, ed., *On Masaryk, Texts in English and German* (Amsterdam, 1988), pp. 317–32.

5. Letter to *Neue Freie Presse*, 24 December 1907.

6. 'State and Nationality', *Čas*, 1909, p. 1.

7. On the constituent elements of nationality, see ibid, pp. 1–2; *Problém*, pp. 67–8; *Narodní filosofie*, pp. 14–18; on language, ibid., pp. 10–14.

8. Ibid., p. 32.

9. Masaryk, *Havlíček*, pp. 327, 330; *Česká otázka/NNK*, pp. 189, 263–4; The Development of the Modern Science of Socialism', *Nová doba* (Pilsen), XII, no. 12, 12 February 1907, pp. 1–2.

10. 'Humanity a Nationality', pp. 202–4; *vlastenčení* and traitor-mongering (*zradcování*) were even more sharply condemned in the editorial note, ibid., pp. 256–9.

11. *Česká otázka/NNK*, pp. 163, 165, 172, 186, 374; on the German language, ibid. pp. 402–6. See also Masaryk, 'Dohodnutí'. On Czech–German relations, see Szporluk, *Masaryk*, pp. 101–11 and Hoffman, *T. G. Masaryk*, pp. 160–2, 389–448. See below, in this chapter, pp. 160–2.

12. *Otázka sociální*, II, pp. 148–9, 164–5.

13. Among notable parliamentary speeches were those of March 1893 and 7 July 1907 – partial texts in Jiří Kovtun, *Slovo má poslanec Masaryk* (Munich, 1985), pp. 83ff.

and 111ff. An English translation of the latter is given in George J. Kovtun, *The Spirit of Thomas G. Masaryk, 1850–1937: An Anthology* (London, 1990), pp. 53–60.

14. *Problém*, pp. 65–95. For similar views see Masaryk, *Palackého idea*. pp. 19–21, 43–9. See also Masaryk's lecture in London in 1915, *The Problem of Small Nations in the European Crisis* (London, 1916).

15. *Česká otázka/NNK*, pp. 121, 209–17, 363, 419–20.

16. Ibid., pp. 4, 144–7.

17. Ibid., pp. 362, 163. See also Masaryk's speech in the Bohemian Diet, 7 April 1892, Kozák, *Masaryková práce*, p. 92; 'Dohodnutí', ibid., p. 119.

18. *Ceská otázka/NNK*, pp.123–4, 188, 247, 377–8.

19. Masaryk, *Palackého idea*, pp. 35–6, 43–9.

20. Masaryk, *Havlíček*, pp. 111, 333–6, 352–4. See also Masaryk, *Havlíček* (2nd edn, 1904), p. 142.

21. *Problém* (1905), pp. 22–9. This final statement has been termed a significant feature of Masaryk's effort to give 'a world orientation' to the Czech national programme and thus to secure suport for Czech national aims in the world at large. The idea of humanity and the national idea were fused together as one (ibid., p. 12). See Butter, 'Zahraniční politika T. G. Masaryka', *Zahraniční politika*, 18, no. 14 (1939), pp. 124–5, 132.

22. *Student a politika* (Prague, 1923), pp. 14–16.

23. *Čas*, 18 May 1900, cited in Evžen Štern, *Názory T. G. Masaryka* (Prague, 1910), p. 49.

24. See above, chap. 4, pp. 49–50, 51–2.

25. For brief summaries of state right in Czech politics, see Skilling, 'The Politics of the Czech Eighties', in Skilling and Peter Brock, *The Czech Renascence of the Nineteenth Century* (Toronto, 1970), pp. 259–62; Bruce M. Garver, *The Young Czech Party 1874–1901 and the Emergence of a Multi-party System* (New Haven, 1978), pp. 49–59, 71, passim; Hoffmann, *T. G. Masaryk*, pp. 157–9, and the whole of Part III; Szporluk, *Masaryk*, pp. 101ff.

26. See Jaroslav Houser, 'Státoprávní program na přelomu století', *Právně historické studie*, 15 (Prague, 1971), pp. 45–62.

27. Karel Kramář, *České státní právo* (Prague, 1896); *Das böhmische Staatsrecht* (Vienna, 1896), pp. 10, 20, 34 and passim. For other expositions of state right, see Alois Rašín, *České státní právo* (Prague, 1891) (Progressive); B. Pacák and J. Kaizl, *O státoprávní programu české* (Prague, 1896) and Josef Herold, *O státoprávní programu českém* (Prague, 1896) (both Young Czech); Józa Skalák, *Přirozená práva národů* (Prague, 1897) (Social Democrat); Václav Choc, *České státní právo* (Olomouc, 1900) (National Socialist); Antonín Hajn, 'Státoprávní politika v přitomnosti i budoucnosti', in Lad. Macháč *et al.*, *Státoprávní politika* (Prague, 1903) (State Right Progressive); Antonín Hajn, *Výbor prací 1889–1909*, (Prague, 1913), III, pp. 49–69 (State Right Progressive); Josef Fořt, *O českém problému státoprávním* (1913) (Young Czech).

28. Kaizl, speech in Parliament, 13 December 1895, in Zdeněk V. Tobolka, *JUDr Jos. Kaizl: Z mého života* (Prague, n. d.), I, Pt. 1, pp. 457–69; Kramář, *Poznámky o české politice* (Prague, 1906); see above, Chapter 4, p. 56. A somewhat similar view was expressed by Kramář in 1903 when he is reported to have said that, in order to achieve state right, Austria must first be made better, through a positive policy (Kamil Krofta, *Politická postava Karla Kramáře*, edited by Karel Hoch (Prague, 1936), pp. 22–3).

29. For the programmes of these parties, see above, p. 154 and Houser, cited in n. 26. Garver incorrectly states that the National Socialists gave up state right in 1911 (*The Young Czech Party*, p. 297).

30. For text of the the Social Democratic declaration in 1897, see ibid., p. 24. For their later position see Zdeněk Šolle and Alena Gajanová, *Po stopě dějin, Češí a Slováci v letech 1848–1938* (Prague, 1969), pp. 117–22.

31. According to Szporluk, Masaryk referred, in a speech in 1892, to a 'Bohemian nation of Czech and German nationality', and to 'Bohemians of both nationalities'. I have not been able to confirm this formulation which seems to be unique in Masaryk's writings.

32. 18 November 1892 and 20 March 1893, Kovtun, *Slovo má poslanec Masaryk*, pp. 65, 70–1, 76, 83–94.

33. See Chapter 4 above, p. 59.

34. *Česká otázka/NNK*, pp. 163, 188, 283.

35. Ibid., pp. 90–2, 98, 107–12, 208.

36. Masaryk, *Palackého idea*, pp. 31–2, 35; *Havlíček*, pp. 124, 275–7, 325, 352–60; *Havlíček*, 2nd edn, 1904, pp. 137–45.

37. *Ramcový program české strany lidové (realistické)* (Prague, 1900), pp. 7, 12–13. This formulation was repeated in the 1912 Progressive party programme (*Program české strany pokrokové* (Prague, 1912), p. 18.

38. Masaryk, *Pravo přirozené a historické* (Prague, 1900). See also Masaryk's criticism of the inconsistency of the Young Czechs on state and natural right in *Desorganisace mladočeské strany* (1903), pp. 19–30.

39. 'Die staatsrechtliche Stellung der czechischen Parteien', *Die Zeit*, 1, 8, and 15 September 1900.

40. 'Our State Right Programme', *Čas*, XXIII, no. 89 (30 March 1909). See also Hoffmann, *T. G. Masaryk*, pp. 442–8.

41. Edvard Beneš, *Le problème autrichien et la question tchèque* (Paris, 1908), p. 229; Louis Eisenmann, *Le Compromis Austro-Hongrois de 1867; Étude sur le dualisme* (Paris, 1904), p. 668. See also Josef Redlich, *Oesterreichische Regierung und Verwaltung im Weltkrieg* (Vienna, 1916), espec. pp. 25–30, 34–5. For contemporary Czech constitutional analysis, see articles by Dobroslav Krejčí and F. Vavrínek, in Zdeněk Tobolka, (ed.), *Česká politika* (Prague, 1906–1913), II, 2, pp. 1–14, 77ff, 451ff, 723ff. For a more recent analysis, see Robert A. Kann, *The Multinational Empire; Nationalism and National Reform in the Habsburg Monarchy, 1848–1918* (New York, 1950), 2 vols.

42. For instance, that of 12 February 1898 (drafted by Kramář, in Adolf Srb, *Politické dějiny národa českého od počatku doby konstitučni* (Prague, 1926), vol. 2, pp. 382–5; that of 22 June 1907, Zdeněk Tobolka, *Politické dějiný československého národa od r. 1848 až do dnešní doby* (Prague, 1936), III, 2, pp. 488–9.

43. Kramář, *Böhmische Staatsrecht*, parts IV and V.

44. Fořt's plan in 1902 was not available; a summary was given by Alois Hajn (see below, n. 52). Fořt advanced a similar proposal in September 1910 (Tobolka, *Pol. dějiny*, III, 2, 504–5).

45. Herold, 'Reform of the Provincial Constitution', *Česká revue* (1907–8), 7, pp. 256–62, 339–45, 428–32, 468–73. For an extended listing of provincial powers, see his lecture, Herold, *Reforma zemského zřízení král. českého* (Prague, 1908) pp. 15–16.

46. E.g. *Česká otázka*, pp. 106–7, 115, 163; *Palackého idea*, pp. 131, 137, 144; *Otázka sociální*, II, pp. 162, 198, 339; *Havlíček*, pp. 362–5; 'Dohodnutí', p. 118. See also M. Trapl, *Vědecké základy*, pp. 75–6, and above in this chapter, pp. 156–7.

47. *Havlíček*, pp. 109ff. The term *země* (land) has usually been translated here as province, but occasionally as land.

48. Ibid., pp. 243, 285, 333–6, 343–4, 355ff. He sometimes used the term *sněm* (diet or assembly) to refer to a parliament in general (p. 289).

49. *Ramcový program*, p. 7.
50. *Česká strana pokroková a její ustavující valný sjezd* (Pardubice, 1906), p. 31.
51. *Program české strany pokrokové*, pp. 15, 19–22.
52. Hajn, *Ku programu pokrokové strany českoslovanské* (Pardubice, 1905), pp.40–59.
53. In sharp contrast, Antonín Hajn, in 1902, rejected both autonomy and federalism as mere reforms of the existing constitution and called for 'state independence appropriate to ethnographic, cultural and economic conditions and their development. See Hajn, Macháček, *Státoprávní politika*, pp. 127ff., 171–2.
54. Among the host of books dealing with the language question, see, for a good brief summary, Robert A. Kann, *The Multinational Empire, Nationalism and National Reform in the Habsburg Monarchy 1848–1918* (2 vols, New York, 1950, reprinted in 1964 and 1970) I, 191–215. See also Heinrich Münch, *Böhmische Tragödie; das Schicksal Mitteleuropas im Lichte des tschechishche Frage* (Brunswick, 1949), pp. 700–26; Hoffman, *T. G. Masaryk*, the whole of Part III and passim.
55. For the above and the following, see Masaryk's important article, 'Ausgleichsfrage', 1896, ('Dohodnutí') and his letter to the *Neue Freie Presse*, 24 December 1907. For strong pleas for a compromise with the Germans, see also 'O politické situaci', *Čas*, XVI, no. 114, 4 April 1903; speeches in 1908, Hoffman *T. G. Masaryk*, pp. 417–18, 438–40. On state right, ibid., pp. 414–15, 434, 443–4. See also Szporluk, *Masaryk*, pp. 105–10.
56. *Ramcový program*, pp. 19–28; *Program*, 1912, pp. 35–43. The 1906 Progressive party programme did not contain detailed language provisions. *(Česká strana pokroková*, p. 32). Hajn, in his draft programme, did give details, but he argued that the language question could not be settled for the time being; the Czech nation must first strengthen itself economically and culturally (Hajn, *Ku programu*, pp. 19–31).
57. The Moravian compromise was highly original in its provisions for national curiae for the election of the Diet, national representation on the Provincial Committee and the national partition of the School Council, as well as a more democratic electoral law. But its language provisions dealt only with the autonomous and not with the state organs. The ethnic heterogeneity of Moravia ruled out any thought of a national demarcation of districts or regions, or the sectionization of the Supreme Court. See Tobolka, *Pol. dějiny*, III, 2, pp. 394–415. Masaryk considered the Moravian pact a progressive step, but an imperfect solution.
58. Ibid., pp. 580–6.
59. This evolution has been well described by Miroslav Trapl, *Vědecké základy*, pp. 114–18; Trapl, *Masarykův program. Demokracie-Socialismus-Česká otázka* (Brno, 1948), pp. 167–77; George J. Kovtun, 'Thomas G. Masaryk's Road to Revolution', in Miloš Čapek and Karel Hrubý (eds), *T. G. Masaryk in Perspective. Comments and Criticism* (n.p., 1981), pp. 139–69; Erazím Kohák, 'Masaryk und die Monarchie; Versuch einer Demythisierung', in Novák, *On Masaryk*, pp. 363–90; Jaroslav Werstadt, *Od 'české otázky' k 'nové evropě', Linie politického vývoje Masaryka* (Prague, 1920), pp. 19–29. See also Bedřich Hlaváč, 'Masaryk and Austria', in *Masarykův sborník*, V, 2, pp. 120–32, also in Hlaváč, *František Josef I* (Prague, 1933), chap. 28. Zdeněk Šolle, 'Masaryková cesta k Nové Evropě, in *Masaryk a myšlenka evropské jednoty* (Prague, 1992), pp. 40–59.
60. For the full text, *Čas*, 26 September 1891, V, no. 39, 622; long excerpts are given in Jan Herben, *T. G. Masaryk* (Prague, 1926), I, pp. 116–23 and Kozák (ed.), *Masaryková práce*, pp.80–5. The postscript was cited, without source, by Karel Krofta, 'Masaryk a naše politický program', in *Masarykův sborník*, V, no. 2, p. 99, and was quoted by Kovtun, 'Road to Revolution' (p. 145) and Trapl, *Masarykův program*, pp. 169–70, also without source.

61. Extracts of parliamentary speeches are given in Czech by Kovtun, *Slovo*, and in German by Ernst Rychnowsky, *Masaryk* (2nd edn, Prague, 1930). Citations of several important passages are also given by Kohák, 'Masaryk und Versuch', pp. 369–79; Kovtun, 'Masaryk's Road to Revolution', pp. 145–7. For the Bohemian Diet speech, see Kozák, *Masaryková prace*, p. 91.

62. Kovtun, *Slovo*, pp. 62–76; Rychnowsky, *Masaryk*, pp. 69–71.

63. Kovtun, pp. 83–94, Rychnowsky, pp. 76–7.

64. Kovtun, pp. 95–103, Rychnowsky, pp. 80–2.

65. *Česká otázka*, pp. 97–9, 100, 106, 125–8, 164; *NNK*. pp. 283–4, 374-6. Cf. Masaryk, *Palackého idea*, p. 31.

66. *Ramcový program*, pp. 15–16.

67. *Naše politická situace* (Prague, 1901). On the Velím speech, see Hoffmann, Masaryk, chap. 12; Trapl, *Masarykův program*, pp. 174–5; Garver, *The Young Czech Party*, pp. 271–6. Masaryk had already privately expressed more radical views in letters to Karel Kramář. In January 1898, he wrote that Kramář had acquired a trust in Austria (even a love of it) which he did not share. In January 1899, he wrote: 'The main thing is that you worry about Austria! I don't. Palacký said we were before Austria and we will be after it. But while for him this was but a phrase – I want it to become a fact. (Such facts do happen, too)' (Herben, *Masaryk*, I, pp. 228–9). The latter is also cited by J. Doležal, *Masarykova cesta životem* (2 vols, Brno, 1920–21), I, p. 51. In 1903 Masaryk wrote that they wanted a strong Austria, but this would be, not centralist, but progressive and popularist. The interests of the dynasty of a multi-national state were identical with the interests of all the nations.('O politické situace', XVI, no. 14, 4 April 1903). Cf. an editorial note in *Čas* (XVIII, 96, 1904) under the title, 'Interest in Austria', which stated that Masaryk disagreed with Palacký as to the necessity of Austria and that Czech policy must be very different if we were to attain our independence (Trapl, *Masarykův program*, p. 174).

68. *Česká strana pokroková*, p. 31.

69. Hajn, *Ku programu*, pp. 39, 42.

70. Masaryk, *Americké přednášky* (Prague, 1929), pp. 90–2.

71. 'Universal suffrage and Czech democracy', *Naše doba*, 14, no. 3 (20 December 1906), pp. 161–2. In a series of public lectures in Písek the preceding autumn Masaryk acknowledged his interest in Austria, but 'we want to transform the old Austria in our interest'. In response to the charge that he was an Austrian (*rakušan*), he admitted that 'the old Austria stifled him, and that he wanted to make Austria modern.' (*Čas*, 1, 2 and 3 October 1906, quotation from part 2).

72. 20 July 1907, Kovtun, *Slovo*, pp. 111–19. At the outset of his speech he spoke at length on the need to include in the parliamentary records speeches given in non-German languages.

73. 31 October and 3 December 1907, 4 June and 9 December 1908, Rychnowsky, *Masaryk*, pp. 113–24, quotation at p. 124.

74. See Chapter 9 above. For these speeches see Kovtun, *Slovo*, and Rychnowsky, *Masaryk*. See also Kovtun, 'Road to Revolution', pp. 150–1; Kohák, *Masaryk*, pp. 381–7.

75. 17 December 1908, Rychnowsky, *Masaryk*, pp. 125–8. See also a speech by Masaryk on 26 November 1908, in which he said that the Austrian state idea must offer something to both Germans and Czechs so that the latter could remain in Austria. There would be no peace in Austria until the Czechs and Germans, for the sake of economic considerations, reached agreement (cited by Münch, *Böhmische Tragödie*, pp. 534–5).

76. 14 and 18 May 1909, Kovtun, *Slovo*, pp. 139–56; Rychnowsky, *Masaryk*, pp. 132–41. In an article of April 1909, Masaryk had written that Austria could

'politically and morally continue only as long as it positively benefits its peoples in their development and as long as it benefits *all* its peoples' ('State and nationality', *Čas*, 4 April 1909).

77. 11 November 1910, Kovtun, pp. 168–73; Rychnowsky, pp. 143–7.
78. 9 November 1910, Rychnowsky, pp. 148–55; 29 December 1910, Kovtun, pp. 177–8.
79. Speeches of 22 and 24 February 1911, in Kovtun, pp. 179–90; Rychnowsky, pp. 155–60. The last sentence, from the speech of 22 February, was given in Masaryk, *Rakouská zahraniční politika a diplomacie* (Prague, 1911), p. 75
80. 7 November 1911, Kovtun, pp. 191–5; Rychnowsky, pp. 161–5.
81. 2 May 1912, Rychnowsky, pp. 165–8.
82. 31 October 1912, Kovtun, pp. 196–202.
83. *Program* (1912), pp. 8, 19–23. See also Chapter 4 above, p. 52.
84. *Čas*, XXVI, no. 8 (9 January 1913) given in part in Kozák, *Mas. práce*, pp. 173–7; also in Herben, *Masaryk*, I, pp. 316–17 This speech was dated 25 February 1914 by Doležal, *Masaryka česta*, II, 88.
85. 26 May 1913, Kovtun, pp. 203–9; Rychnowsky, pp. 173–7. Earlier in the speech, according to Rychnowsky (p. 173), Masaryk recalled Palacký's statement that if Austria did not exist, it would have to be created. This statement now had to be reformulated, he said; something must be made of Austria by remodelling it as a constitutional monarchy and, like Britain, with a parliamentary system and a legitimate opposition. This statement was not included in the Reichsrat record nor in the Kovtun text.
86. Masaryk, *Světová revoluce* (Prague, 1925), p. 40; *The Making of a State, Memories and Observations, 1914–1918* (London, 1927), pp. 46–7. During the war, he had privately admitted that for a long time he had striven to modernize Austria and change it according to the Czech democratic programme, but 'the better I came to know it, and the greater experience I had with it, the more I distrusted Vienna and the dynasty, and the more radical I became toward Austria'. See Werstadt, *Od 'české otázky' k'nové Europě*, p. 27.
87. Hoffmann, *Masaryk*, pp. 455–6.
88. Kovtun, 'Road to Revolution', p. 139; Kohák, 'Masaryk und die Monarchie', pp. 364–5, 370, 373; Trapl, *Masarykův program*, pp. 168, 177. See also Hlaváč, 'Masaryk and Austria', pp. 110–14, 123–8; Hlaváč, *František Josef I*, chap. 28.
89. Trapl, *Masarykův program*, p. 177; Kovtun, 'Road to Revolution', p. 143; Kohák, 'Masaryk und die Monarchie', pp. 370, 375, 386–8; Krofta, 'Program', pp. 108–9; Hlaváč, 'Masaryk and Austria', pp. 125, 129, 132.
90. Kovtun (pp. 150–1) suggests the date 1908; Hoffmann, 1909 (p. 447). According to Szporluk Masaryk had concluded by 1900 that the most desirable goal was a self-governing state (*Masaryk*, pp. 124–5, n. 69).
91. Henry Wickham Steed and Jan Herben, as cited by Kovtun, 'Road to Revolution', p.152.
92. Hlaváč, 'Masaryk and Austria', pp. 122–7. In the winter of 1913, in Munich, Masaryk is reported to have given a relatively moderate speech in which he called for an Austrian idea which gathered together and organically developed the rich forces of the different nations (Münch, *Tragödie*, pp. 639–40). Münch cites this and other speeches by Masaryk as evidence of his loyal Austrian attitude. At another point he wrote that Masaryk had the greatest understanding of the Austrian state idea (ibid., pp. 693–4). See also his positive appraisal of Masaryk in general, ibid., pp. 557–71. See also Kann, *The Multinational Empire*, I, 209–15. 'A basically pro-Austrian Czech national policy, as long as there was any reason to believe in an organic, peaceful reorganization of Austria, was logically not at variance with a

revolutionary policy after any reasonable hopes for the preservation and reorganization of Austria had disappeared' (p. 209).

93. Gustav Kolmer, *Parlament und Verfassung in Oesterreich* (Vienna, 1908–10), Vol. 8, pp. 25–6. See also Münch, *Böhmische Tragödie*, pp. 683–99.
94. Šolle and Gajanová, *Po stopě dějin*, pp. 116–20; Karel Pichlík, *Zahraniční odboj 1914–1918 bez legend* (Prague, 1968), pp. 26, 36–8.
95. Tobolka, *Pol. dějiny*, III, no 2, p. 200; see other letters in this vein, Tobolka, *Kaizl*, III, 2, pp. 865, 903.
96. Kramář, *Poznámky*, pp. 52, 55, 5; *Problémy české politiky* (Prague, 1913), p. 35. See Chapter 4 above, p. 56. Other 'Austrian' speeches by Kramář are cited by Münch, *Tragödie*, pp. 528–9, 577–8 and by Nečas, *Balkán*, pp. 69ff., espec. 73, 78–9. Even in speeches in which he passionately defended Neo-Slavism and the common interests of Slavs (13 July 1908 and 1 January 1913). Kramář argued that this was in no way directed against Austria-Hungary or its interests (German text given by Münch, op. cit., pp. 593, 598–9).
97. *České státní právo* (Prague, 1914), pp. 4–5; Kamil Krofta, *Politická postava Karla Kramáře* (Prague, 1930), pp. 422–4.
98. Tobolka, *Pol. děj.*, III, 2, pp. 633–4; Pichlík, *Odboj*, pp. 30–31.
99. See Chapter 4 above, p. 58; B. Šantrůček, *Masaryk a Klofáč* (Prague, 1938), pp. 389–97; Pichlík, *Odboj*, pp. 28–9; Tobolka, *Pol. děj.*, III, 2, p. 633.
100. Nečas, *Balkán*, pp. 125–9; Tobolka, *Pol. děj.*, III, 2, pp. 459, 634; Pichlík, *Odboj*, pp. 17–19, 29–30.
101. Hlaváč, 'Masaryk and Austria', pp. 127–31.

CONCLUSIONS

1. For the above, cf. Jaroslav Opat, 'T, G. Masaryk and Czech Society', in Opat, M. Tomčík and Z. Urban, *T. G. Masaryk a Slovensko (soubor statí)* (Prague, 1992). This booklet contains an excellent study by Tomčík of Masaryk's prewar relations with the Slovaks, including Vajanský, which was not available at the time of writing Chapter 5.
2. For citations to the symposia, see above, Introduction, n. 1. These works, and biographies of Masaryk by Roman Szporluk, Milan Machovec and others, were the subject of a detailed review by this author in 'The Rediscovery of Masaryk', *Cross Currents* (Ann Arbor, 1983), pp. 87–114.
3. *T. G. Masaryk (1850–1937)* (London, 1989–1990), 1, edited by Stanley B. Winters, 2, by Robert B. Pynsent, and 3 by Harry Hanak.
4. On the problems of distinguishing facts and values, and emotional and rational features, in Masaryk's writings, see Hana Voisine-Jechová, 'Masaryk's Style in the Framework of Czech Realist Tendencies', ibid. (Pynsent), 2, chap. 12. On the difficulty of understanding created by the 'inwardness' of Masaryk's thinking, see Petr Pithart, 'Prophet', cited in note 6.
5. Stanislav Polák, 'The Personality of T. G. Masaryk, Thoughts on the Methodology of Biography', *Český časopis historický*, 89, no. 5–6, pp. 761–76.
6. 'Recognition of a Prophet in Bohemia', *Masarykův sborník*, VII, *T .G. M. a naše současnost* (1980), originally in *samizdat* (Prague, 1992), pp. 218ff. cit. at p. 224. Cf. Winters, *T. G. Masaryk*, I, pp. 17–18. The theme of Masaryk's isolation in prewar Czech society and politics is developed further in a critical interpretation of Czech history and politics presented in a book which was prepared over many years but published only after the democratic revolution in 1989: *Podiven* (pseudonym for

a collective of three authors, Milan Otáhal, Petr Pithart and Petr Přihoda), *Češí v dějinách nové doby (Czechs in Contemporary History)* (Prague, 1992), on pre-1914 Czech politics, pp. 212–40, 251–70; on Masaryk, pp. 183ff., 192–6, 241–2, passim. For other comments on this theme, see Skilling, 'Rediscovery', pp. 103–4.

7.   Edvard Beneš, 'A Few Words on Masaryk's Influence on the Youth', in a special issue of *Česká Mysl*, ed. by F. Čáda and F. Krejčí, XI (1910), p. 213; Bedřich Hlaváč, 'The Structure of Ideas of Masaryk's Politics', *T. G. Masarykovi k šedesátým narozeninám*, (Prague, 1910), ed. by Edvard Beneš *et al.*, published in V. K. Škřach, ed., *Masarykův sborník* (Prague, 1930), IV, p. 287; František Veselý, ibid., p. 303.

8.   *Ceská otázka* (Prague, 1948), p.150; see also p. 597.

9.   *Otázka sociální* (Prague, 1948), I, p. 181.

10. On titanism in Masaryk's thought, see Milan Machovec, *Tomáš G. Masaryk* (Prague, 1968), pp. 153–4; Frederick M. Barnard, 'Humanism and Titanism: Masaryk and Herder', in *T. G. Masaryk*, I (Winters), pp. 24–6. See also Polák, 'Personality of Masaryk', p. 775.

11. For comments on this by a number of persons, see Skilling, 'Rediscovery', pp. 97, 106.

12. Ibid., pp. 104-5.

13. For similar views see Jaroslav Opat, *Filozof a politik, Tomáš Garrigue Masaryk, 1882–1893* (Prague, 1987), p. 469; new edn. (Prague, 1992), p. 402.

14. Černý, 'The Essence of Masaryk's Personality and What TGM Continues to Be For Us', Černý, *Dvě studie Masarykovské (samizdat,* 1977) p. 49, republished in English translation in Milič Čapek and Karel Hrubý (eds), *T. G. Masaryk in Perspective, Comments and Criticism* (n. p., 1981), pp. 107, 114–17, cit. at 115–16. For fuller discussion of this and the following, see Skilling, 'Rediscovery', pp. 95–6, 99, 104–6.

15. Kohák, 'Life in the Truth', in Pithart *et al.*, *Masaryk a současnost*, pp. 379–406, cit. at pp. 381–2, republished in English in Čapek, *Masaryk in Perspective*, espec. pp. 38–43, 59, 60, cit. at p. 39.

16. See Kohák's contribution to Josef Novák, ed., *On Masaryk* (Amsterdam, 1988), pp. 389–90.

17. Patočka, *Dvě studie o Masarykovi (samizdat,* 1977), pp. 27–8, republished in English in Čapek, *Masaryk in Perspective*, pp. 3–13, cit. at p. 8.

18. Otáhal, Pithart and Přihoda, *Češí* , pp. 183, 242.

Index